THE MIRACULOUS CONFORMIST

Frontispiece: Portrait of Valentine Greatrakes, Wellcome Library, London (oil painting on wood, date and artist unknown; after engraving by W. Faithorne, 1666, 37 x 33 cm) Location: 45644i.

The Miraculous Conformist

Valentine Greatrakes, the Body Politic,
and the Politics of Healing
in Restoration Britain

PETER ELMER

OXFORD
UNIVERSITY PRESS

OXFORD

UNIVERSITY PRESS

Great Clarendon Street, Oxford, OX2 6DP,
United Kingdom

Oxford University Press is a department of the University of Oxford.
It furthers the University's objective of excellence in research, scholarship,
and education by publishing worldwide. Oxford is a registered trade mark of
Oxford University Press in the UK and in certain other countries

First Edition published in 2013

Impression: 1

British Library Cataloguing in Publication Data

Data available

ISBN 978–0–19–966396–5

Printed in Great Britain by
MPG Books Group, Bodmin and King's Lynn

Acknowledgements

This book has been an intolerably long time in the making. It was originally conceived as a simple case study of one man and his attempt to convince the world of his gift of healing. In time, I became convinced that in order to explain his actions, I needed to understand a great deal more about many other facets of early modern life that had, to that point, passed me by. As a second generation Irish Protestant settler, it was essential to know more about Greatrakes' Irish roots, which in turn demanded immersion in Irish archives. At the same time, it was imperative that I knew more about the wider context in which Greatrakes was operating, and how factors other than the purely medical helped to shape reaction to him among patients, supporters, and detractors. Very soon I became aware that Greatrakes' story and his appearance on the historical scene represented more than just a marginal footnote to Restoration history. Instead, his story seemed to offer a unique vantage point from which to observe contemporaries struggling to make sense of a world that had been thoroughly turned upside down by decades of civil war and religious and political strife. The early years of the Restoration were indeed a watershed moment in the religious, political, and intellectual life of Britain—a fact now widely recognized by a generation of historians who have immersed themselves in the rich archives of this period. As a historian of medicine and witchcraft, I owe a great debt to all my colleagues who work in this field, especially to those who have sought to break down the traditional barriers between social and intellectual history in an attempt to recover the early modern world in all its messy, but endlessly fascinating, detail.

Among many debts, I would particularly like to thank the organizers of various conferences and seminars who were kind enough to offer me a platform upon which to expatiate about my miracle healer. Audiences at All Souls' College, Oxford, Essex, Belfast, and the Institute of Historical Research provided much valuable feedback, for which I am extremely grateful. I also owe a great debt of gratitude to Toby Barnard, Michael Hunter, Jonathan Barry, and Stuart Clark, who were kind enough to read and comment on early drafts of the book. I am particularly grateful to Michael for our frequent conversations on Greatrakes and related topics, which has helped, I hope, to steer me away from too many egregious errors, particularly in relation to Greatrakes' extensive Boyle connections. Above all, however, I wish to register my thanks to Stuart Clark who first stimulated my interest in early modern history in the 1970s and has remained a constant source of intellectual stimulation ever since. I would also like to thank Willie Fraher, Julian Walton, Stephen Brogan, Louis Caron, and Wanda Henry for sharing their knowledge of the period and issues germane to Greatrakes' life and career. Many friends have also provided invaluable help and encouragement in bringing this book to fruition. In particular, I would like to express my deepest thanks to Mark Roper and Jane Keen in Ireland, not only for providing wonderful hospitality on my frequent visits to Munster, but also for their unparalleled knowledge of local sources and hostelries. One day, perhaps, we might yet launch 'Greatrakes Tours' on the Blackwater. On the other side of the Irish Sea, I am deeply indebted to Mark Jones for his unfailing encouragement and support and for making the ultimate sacrifice in reading the whole book in draft. I'm sure it reads better as a result.

This book could not have been written without the comfort of an institutional home. For the last seventeen years, the Open University has provided that base, and I would like to record my gratitude to the Dean and Faculty of Arts for financing short periods of study leave for writing and research. It is my good fortune to have encountered and worked with some inspiring colleagues at the OU, but none has made a more profound impact on my work and career than Anne Laurence, without whom this book would never have been written. I wish her and all my former colleagues best wishes in the future as I prepare for pastures new. Finally, I would like to pay tribute to my wife Vicky, boys Richard and Tom, and the rest of my family and friends, who have displayed exemplary patience and understanding, as well as encouragement and support, for more years than I (or they) care to remember. Sadly, four of the most important are no longer with us to share in the moment. I therefore dedicate this book to the memory of my dad, Gus, in-laws Eileen and David, and dear friend Ros, without whom my life would have been very different and greatly impoverished.

St Valentine's Day (14 February 2012)

Contents

List of Illustrations

List of Abbreviations

Besse	J. Besse, *A Collection of the Sufferings of the People Called Quakers…from 1650, to…1689*, 2 vols (London, 1753).
BL	British Library, London.
Bloom and James	J. H. Bloom and R. R. James, *Medical Practitioners in the Diocese of London…1529–1725* (Cambridge, 1935).
Bodl.	Bodleian Library, Oxford.
Boyle, *Correspondence*	*The Correspondence of Robert Boyle*, eds M. Hunter, A. Clericuzio and L. M. Principe, 6 vols (London, 2001).
Cal. Rev.	*Calamy Revised: Being a Revision of Edmund Calamy's Account of the Ministers and Others Ejected And Silenced, 1660–2*, ed. A. G. Matthews (Oxford, 1934; reissued 1988).
CH	Chatsworth House, Derbyshire.
Conway Letters	*Conway Letters: The Correspondence of Anne, Viscountess Conway, Henry More, and Their Friends, 1642–1684*, ed. M. H. Nicholson (New Haven, 1930; revised ed., S. Hutton, Oxford, 1992.
CSPD	*Calendar of State Papers, Domestic.*
CSP Ireland	*Calendar of State Papers, Ireland.*
CUL	Cambridge University Library.
D'Arcy Power, Diary	Wellcome Library, London, D'Arcy Power, 'Transcript of the Diary of John Ward, 1648–1679', 5 vols [formerly in library of the Medical Society of London].
DCNQ	*Devon and Cornwall Notes and Queries.*
DRO	Devon Record Office, Exeter.
ESxRO	East Sussex Record Office, Lewes.
Firth & Rait	C. H. Firth and R. S. Rait (eds), *Acts and Ordinances of the Interregnum, 1642–1660*, 3 vols (London, 1911).
Foster	J. Foster (ed.), *Alumni Oxonienses: The Members of the University of Oxford, 1500–1714*, 3 vols (Oxford and London, 1891–2).
Greatrakes, *Brief Account*	Valentine Greatrakes, *A Brief Account of Mr. Valentine Greatrak's, and Divers of the Strange Cures by Him Lately Performed. Written by Himself in a Letter Addressed to the Honourable Robert Boyle Esq.* (London, 1666).

Green, *CPCC*	M. A. E. Green (ed.), *Calendar of the Proceedings of the Committee for Compounding, &c, 1643–1660*, 5 vols (London, 1889–92).
GRO	Gloucestershire Record Office, Gloucester.
Grosart	Rev. A. B. Grosart (ed.), The Lismore Papers, 1st series, 5 vols (1886).
Henning	B. Henning (ed.), *The History of Parliament: The House of Commons 1660–1690*, 3 vols (London, 1983).
HMC	*Historical Manuscripts Commission Reports.*
JCHAS	*Journal of the Cork Historical and Archaeological Society.*
JRL	John Rylands Library, Manchester.
LMA	London Metropolitan Archives, London.
LPL	Lambeth Palace Library, London.
Munk	W. Munk, *The Roll of the Royal College of Physicians of London, 1518–1800*, 3 vols (London, 1878).
NAI	National Archives of Ireland, Dublin.
NLI	National Library of Ireland, Dublin.
Oldenburg, *Correspondence*	*The Correspondence of Henry Oldenburg*, eds A. R. and M. B. Hall, 13 vols (Madison, Milwaukee, London & Philadelphia, 1965–86).
ODNB	*Oxford Dictionary of National Biography*, 60 vols (Oxford, 2004).
RCBL	Representative Church Body Library, Dublin.
RCPL, Annals	Annals, Royal College of Physicians, London, 3 vols
RS	Royal Society, London.
SARS	Somerset Archive and Record Service, Taunton.
SHC	Surrey History Centre, Woking.
SUL, HP	Sheffield University Library, Hartlib Papers.
TCD	Trinity College, Dublin.
TDA	*Transactions of the Devonshire Association.*
Thurloe, *State Papers*	*A Collection of the State Papers of John Thurloe, Esq.*, ed. T. Birch, 7 vols (London, 1742).
TNA	The National Archives, Kew, London (formerly the Public Record Office).

VCH	*Victoria County History.*
Venn	J. Venn and J. A. Venn (eds), *Alumni Cantabrigienses ... from the Earliest Times to 1751*, 4 vols (Cambridge, 1922).
Wal. Rev.	*Walker Revised Being a Revision of John Walker's* Sufferings of the Clergy during the Grand Rebellion 1642–60, ed. A. G. Matthews (Oxford, 1948).
WCSL	West Country Studies Library, Exeter.
Worthington, *Diary*	*The Diary and Correspondence of Dr John Worthington*, ed. J. Crossley, 3 vols (Chetham Soc., Manchester, vols 13, 36, 114, 1847–86).
WRO	Worcestershire Record Office, Worcester.
WSA	Wiltshire and Swindon Archives, Chippenham.
WSxRO	West Sussex Record Office, Chichester.

1

Introduction

It may be concluded no less necessary to dissect and make inspection into the defects of a dead king, or ruins of a tattered state, then for a physician to anatomize a body whose life was through evill and extravagant courses forfeited to the Law: by both honest men may be cured and commonwealths better governed.

Francis Osborne, *Traditionall Memoires of the Reigns of Queen Elizabeth & King James* (London, 1658), Pt 2, sigs A4v-A5.

Sometime in January 1666, an Irish gentleman named Valentine Greatrakes made the short but dangerous voyage across the Irish Sea to mainland Britain, where, amid widespread excitement at his coming, he made his way to the ancestral home of the Conway family at Ragley Hall in Warwickshire. There, the man at the centre of our story, attempted to heal the lady of the house, Anne, Viscountess Conway, who suffered from debilitating headaches or migraine, by stroking the affected parts of her head with his hands. On this occasion, his gift deserted him, but public confidence in his ability to heal a vast range of diseases remained high. Nicknamed the 'stroker', Greatrakes had in fact been practising the gift of healing in his native Ireland for some three to four years prior to his visit to England. Initially, his practice was restricted to his local neighbourhood, but by the summer of 1665, his fame had spread to the rest of Ireland as well as across the Irish Sea, so much so that according to various reports in the popular press of the day, thousands were flocking to him for cure from all parts of the British Isles. Failure to cure Lady Conway, moreover, did not lead to any lessening of interest in Greatrakes. If anything, his reputation grew as he proceeded to offer relief to hundreds of sufferers within the vicinity of Ragley Hall and at the nearby city of Worcester. Within weeks he had decamped to London where he was asked to demonstrate his 'miraculous' cures before an impressive cross-section of the nation's elite, including the recently restored king, Charles II, and members of his court and government. 'Greatrakes mania' subsequently reached its peak in the spring of 1666. Thousands more flocked to London to receive relief from the charismatic healer before he returned home to Ireland at the end of May, having left instructions for the publication of a brief autobiographical pamphlet in which he sought to authenticate his claims to heal the sick by, among other things, appending the testimonials of various witnesses, including contemporary 'celebrities' such as the scientist Robert Boyle and the poet Andrew Marvell. Thereafter, Greatrakes returned to his life as an obscure country gentleman leaving others in England to dispute the veracity of his claims and to mull over the possible motives that may have led him to pursue a career as a charismatic healer.

The remarkable story of Greatrakes' mission to heal the sick is one that has been told before, though it rarely features in general histories of the period. On the whole, curiosity surrounding Greatrakes has tended to focus on attempts to explain the apparent success of his unorthodox methods or, alternatively, to dismiss them altogether as the product of a superstitious, pre-modern world. In more recent times, interest in Greatrakes has shifted somewhat. Today, if discussed at all, Greatrakes is largely of interest to historians of science who have eagerly latched on to the controversy engendered by his cures for evidence of the continuing uncertainty and debate in early modern scientific circles as to where the boundary between natural and supernatural phenomena might lie in an age of growing scientific enlightenment. Either way, discussion of Greatrakes has largely led to his marginalization in the historical record. In what follows, I hope to show that there is much more to be learned from a detailed study of Greatrakes' life and career as a so-called miracle healer. In particular, I argue here, on the basis of close examination of a large range of surviving sources, that the controversy surrounding Greatrakes provides important insights into a crucial period in the history of a nation that was struggling to recover from the recent trauma of civil war, regicide, and political, religious, and social upheaval. The Restoration of Charles II in 1660 was, by and large, a hugely popular event. However, efforts to restore harmony and heal old wounds within the wider body politic after two decades of internecine conflict proved taxing and controversial. By 1665, religious and political divisions were once again threatening the peace of the three kingdoms of Charles II, a situation that was exacerbated by the outbreak of war with the Dutch as well as the onset of one of the most virulent strains of bubonic plague in European history. Greatrakes' appearance on the scene was not, I believe, unconnected to these wider events. Through close study of his own background as well as that of his most fervent supporters, we can begin to see how a growing body of opinion in Restoration Britain was beginning to articulate its concerns and fears for the wider health of the political nation in a way that conventional political histories of the period have overlooked.[1] In short, I argue here that Greatrakes was offering more than simply a panacea for the cure of sick individuals. While stroking thousands of patients, the

---

[1] The interpretative model that helps to frame this study derives from what the cultural anthropologist Clifford Geertz has termed 'thick description'. In essence, it aims to provide insights into alien or unfamiliar cultures, including those of our own past, through micro-historical examination of a single event. In the words of Kevin Sharpe and Stephen Zwicker, it allows 'the explication of one incident as a point of entry into a broader system of values and beliefs'. Understanding is thus attained through a full and fine contextualisation of all the available evidence where stress is placed upon the crucial interplay between structure and process, or ideas and events; C. Geertz, 'Thick Description: Towards an Interpretative Theory of Culture', in Geertz, *The Interpretation of Cultures* (New York, 1973), 3–30; K. Sharpe and S. Zwicker, 'Introduction', in Sharpe and Zwicker (eds), *Refiguring Revolutions: Aesthetics and Politics from the English Revolution to the Romantic Revolution* (Berkeley, 1998), 2. For a good example of the application of such an approach to an understanding of the ideological origins of the English Civil War, see J. Walter, *Understanding Popular Violence in the English Revolution: The Colchester Plunderers* (Cambridge, 1999).

charismatic Irish healer was both imitating and upstaging the restored monarch, whose powers of healing were thought to extend to the cure of those suffering from the king's evil or scrofula. In the process, through his exemplary actions and carefully cultivated self-image, which stood in stark contrast to that of the bawdy and promiscuous Charles II, Greatrakes provided an alternative blueprint for restoring the health of the nation *en masse* or, to use a contemporary term with particular resonance, the body politic.

In the first three chapters, I attempt to reconstruct the life and career of the Irish gentleman, Valentine Greatrakes, as a case study in the reactions and responses of one individual to the vicissitudes of life in the British Isles in the middle decades of the seventeenth century. In the process, I seek to establish how the events of Greatrakes' life helped to shape his personal response to the dramatic events unfolding on a national stage as well as inform his later career as a self-confessed miracle healer. In particular, I focus in Chapter 2 on Greatrakes' troubled upbringing as the child of a second-generation planter family in Munster in southern Ireland, where issues of identity come to the fore. This was especially apparent following the outbreak of a large-scale Catholic revolt against Protestant English rule in Ireland in October 1641, when the adolescent Greatrakes, along with his mother, siblings, and others of his class, fled to mainland Britain and the relative security of ancestral connections in Devon. Greatrakes subsequently spent much of the 1640s in England, where his education proceeded against the background of civil war and social turmoil. These formative years, combined with the loss of his patrimonial estates in Ireland, were to profoundly shape the outlook of the future miracle healer and remind us today of the extent to which Ireland's history in this period was firmly wedded to, and shaped by, developments in other parts of the British Isles.[2]

In Chapter 3, I continue to trace Greatrakes' life and career as a propertied gentleman in southern Ireland within the context of the return of the monarchy and restoration of episcopal government to England and Ireland after 1660. The Restoration itself has recently become the subject of intense debate in historical circles. While most now agree that Charles' reign was a failure in that it was unable to prevent the re-emergence of deep-seated divisions within the realm, there is little consensus as to why this was the case and at what point it can be said to have failed. The merry monarch's reign had begun promisingly with the King's pledge at Breda to use 'gentle, restorative medicines' in order to abolish 'all notes of discord, separation and difference of parties' in his three kingdoms.[3] But concord soon gave way to discord when Charles' first parliament, nicknamed the Cavalier Parliament, began to enact a series of repressive laws aimed at punishing and neutering all those

[2] Much recent writing on the English Civil War has stressed the British or three-kingdom context in which those dramatic events were played out. At the same, a number of historians of early modern Ireland have sought to emphasize the extent to which the island of Ireland was tied to the mainland through a range of social, economic, familial, cultural, and political connections. For a wide-ranging discussion of the issues, see for example B. Bradshaw and J. Morrill (eds), *The British Problem, c.1534–1707: State Formation in the Atlantic Archipelago* (Basingstoke, 1996).
[3] J. P. Kenyon, *The Stuart Constitution 1603–1688* (Cambridge, 1966), 357–8.

suspected of engaging in rebellious activity in the two decades prior to 1660. Traditional accounts of this period have tended to promote an overly simplistic approach to such divisions in which it has often been assumed that contemporary participants in these events and debates fell into one of two well-defined categories, namely 'royalists' and 'Anglicans' on the one hand, who supported the Restoration, and Cromwellians, rebels and 'puritans' on the other, who rejected the new order. While this is no longer the case, and historians are now much more deft at detecting a subtle range of responses to religious and political issues in this period, it nonetheless remains the case that too little emphasis has been placed on that large and often silent majority that occupied the middle ground between diehard extremists on both sides of the divide. Greatrakes, I argue in Chapter 3, is interesting in this respect as he, like many of his neighbours in Ireland, fell into this ill-defined middle group that was seeking to steer the political and religious settlement of the country toward a more consensual and accommodating conclusion. Greatrakes' aims in this respect, as I make clear, were not simply motivated by what on the surface may look like an ideological aversion to intolerance and conflict. They were also clearly informed by a degree of pragmatism borne out of the fact that he, like others of his class, had fought for Cromwell in Ireland, prospered as a result, and now, in the aftermath of the Restoration, wished to retain his ill-gotten gains.

The Restoration in Ireland held some features in common with that process in England, but also differed significantly in crucial respects. This was most obviously evident after 1660 in the threat posed by a major redistribution of land to those Catholics and royalists (often one and the same) from whom it had been seized by soldiers, adventurers and settlers in the wake of the Cromwellian conquest in the previous decade. For propertied men like Greatrakes, the Restoration in Ireland thus represented a potential disaster. In the event that much land would now return to its original Catholic owners, men like Greatrakes, who had invested vast sums speculating in estates expropriated from Catholic 'rebels' in the 1650s, stared bankruptcy in the face. It was against this background that Greatrakes discovered his gift of healing and chose to reveal it to the world. In the process, I suggest that Greatrakes the man embodied the hopes and aspirations of a large section of Irish Protestant society, and that his mission to heal the sick helped to forge a sense of unity and solidarity among this important group in the face of a resurgent Catholic majority.

The answer to Ireland's problems, or at least those of Greatrakes and his class, did not however lie exclusively in Ireland. The fate of that country's Protestant minority was essentially dependent on decisions made in England, at court and in Parliament, and it was no coincidence that Greatrakes' healing mission to England in 1666 was punctuated by an attempt to lobby the government over his own claims to retain lands appropriated from neighbouring Catholics in the 1650s. In order to achieve these ends, Greatrakes self-consciously projected an image of himself as the archetypal Protestant gentleman—loyal, morally upstanding, and moderate—and it was one that clearly struck a chord with admirers on the English side of the Irish Sea. In Chapter 4, I examine more closely this process of 'self-fashioning' on Greatrakes' part, and the extent to which those values which he now sought to project were shared by others, both in England and Ireland, who rallied to his cause. In particular, I analyse in some detail the religious and political backgrounds of those men and women who clamoured to authenticate his therapeutic claims. Based largely on a series of testimonials that Greatrakes appended to his published 'autobiography' of 1666, and supplemented by other sources, I suggest here that support for Greatrakes was to a large extent motivated by a complex web of factors shaped by events prior to 1660 which included deep-seated anxieties for the health of the restored body politic. Critically, such fears were shared by some within the re-established Church and state as well as those who faced exclusion from religious and political power as a result of their former allegiances. One of the most notable features of Greatrakes' following, for example, consists in the degree to which he attracted the support of nascent 'latitudinarians' or moderates from within the restored Anglican Church who sought common ground with those now excluded from it following the mass ejection of nonconformist clergy in 1662. Many of the former had themselves, for various reasons, chosen the path of rapprochement and reconciliation in the 1650s when they opted for ordination in Cromwell's church. In the process they forged strong links with their ousted 'puritan' colleagues, often cemented through ties of kinship and education, and now in the altered circumstances of the early 1660s sought to repay former obligations through various means, including the promotion of schemes designed to achieve a more 'comprehensive' or inclusive religious settlement. Such sentiments were likewise shared by others outside the Church, many of whom had collaborated with Cromwell's governments of the 1650s while holding on to office after 1660. The tumultuous events of the middle decades of the seventeenth century undoubtedly created strange bedfellows in the early years of the Restoration. That so many were attracted to the Irish stroker, however, should come as little surprise. His exemplary moderation and moral integrity, so often commented upon by his admirers, stood in stark contrast to the bitter recrimination, intolerance, and debauchery associated with those at the centre of government. In short, he embodied those virtues which a sizable number on both sides of the new political divide now saw as the answer to a growing crisis in the state.

Under such circumstances, it is unsurprising that Greatrakes, man and healer, should engender controversy and debate. In Chapter 4, I look in more detail at this debate, focusing on the brief pamphlet war that broke out in 1666 in which his claims to heal the sick were subjected to close scrutiny. Whereas some eulogized his god-given talents, others saw him as a fraud, or worse, as an agent of the devil. Such responses, I suggest, were largely conditioned by political allegiance and partisanship. Ultimately, Greatrakes withdrew from the fray and returned to his native Ireland, though not, as has often been assumed, to a state of retirement. Greatrakes, in fact, continued to exercise his gift of stroking, while at the same time retaining close contact with a number of his English supporters. At his death in 1683, however, he was a largely forgotten figure on both sides of the Irish Sea. The murder of his close friend Sir Edmund Berry Godfrey in 1678 was to spark yet another political crisis which this time proved beyond the restorative medicines of the King. The ensuing Exclusion Crisis saw the revival of deep-seated partisan

divisions which, unresolved, were to lay the basis for the emergence of a new kind
of politics based on party allegiance. At the same time, religious differences became
set in stone as those on both sides of the divide increasingly accepted the fact that
religious unity in a single ecclesiastical polity, the Church of England, was no
longer feasible. By the end of the century, Britain was well on the way to becoming
one of the first genuinely plural societies in the world. Widely applauded today,
most contemporaries, Greatrakes included, would almost certainly have seen such
an outcome as a general cause for regret.

At the heart of the contemporary debate over Greatrakes and his cures, and
indeed a central element of historical enquiry since, lies the paradoxical nature of
his status as a 'miraculous conformist'. In coining the phrase, the physician Henry
Stubbe was deliberately seeking to stir controversy on numerous fronts. In 1666,
there was only one individual in Britain who merited the title, namely the ruling
monarch. As head of the Anglican Church, Charles II inherited at his coronation
certain divinely ordained attributes that included the gift of healing. By virtue of
his restored royal office then, the King was *the* miraculous conformist. In depicting
Greatrakes as a rival, Stubbe, a man with his own chequered past, was thus engaging in mischievous muck-raking, something at which he was particularly adept.
On another level, however, there is little doubt that Stubbe, in coining such a
phrase, hoped to expose more profound inconsistencies in contemporary religious
and political debate. Since the re-foundation of the Anglican Church in the early
years of the reign of Queen Elizabeth, the official line of English Protestantism was
to downgrade and underplay the role of the miraculous in everyday life. From the
1560s onwards, Anglican apologists as well as spokesmen from other mainstream
Protestant churches had consistently argued that the age of miracles had long since
ceased, terminating with the establishment of the first Christian churches in the
Mediterranean in the fourth century BCE. Continued faith in miracles in this view
was thus construed as the special preserve of those dual enemies of Christ, the
church of Rome and the radical sects, who, it was widely feared, were co-conspir-
ators in an attempt to subvert true religion and godliness. Protestantism, by this
argument, did not require divine intervention in the form of miracles to prove the
validity of its dispensation. The Bible alone provided sufficient grounds to defend
its authority. In describing anyone other than the King as a 'miraculous conformist' then was to invoke and contest a fundamental tenet of Protestant thinking, and
to cast those Anglican supporters of Greatrakes in a most difficult light. In order to
understand how the latter were able to square this particular circle, we need to
understand more fully the wider context in which discussion of the miraculous
took place in this period.

In Chapter 5, I thus seek to situate the debate over Greatrakes within the context of contemporary attitudes to the supernatural in general in an era in which it
was widely feared that growing disbelief in the existence of a spiritual realm would
lead to the erosion of all forms of religious belief and morality. Interest in these
issues, as we shall see, was not confined to learned specialists such as divines, physicians, or natural philosophers, though they clearly occupied a prominent place in
the ensuing public debate. On the contrary, these were issues that engaged, agi-

tated, and obsessed men and women of all backgrounds, informing as they did some of the most fundamental beliefs of our early modern forbears.

The period of the 1660s, in which Greatrakes came to the fore, has often been seen as a watershed in terms of the decline of a range of traditional beliefs related to the idea of God as a providential deity who intermittently cast aside the regular laws of nature in order to intercede in the affairs of humankind. The growing acceptance in academic circles of a new form of science based on the dualist materialism of the French natural philosopher Réné Descartes (1596–1650) opened the way to radical new theories relating to the role of God and spirit in the natural world. In England, the foundation of the Royal Society of London in 1662 provided an important new venue for the discussion and promotion of such views. It has long been assumed that one of the by-products of such activity was a lessening of belief in society in general of a range of ideas and practices, including magic, astrology, and witchcraft, that were predicated on the interconnectedness of the material and spiritual realms. This process, it has also been argued, left its imprint upon contemporary politics. The execution of Charles I in 1649 dealt a blow not just to the Stuart dynasty but to the whole edifice of mystical political thinking upon which early modern notions of divine right monarchy were constructed. Despite the 'miracle' of the Restoration and the attempt to resurrect the quasi-magical attributes of Stuart kingship, such as the ritual of the royal touch, politics in England had been irrevocably transformed by the events of the 1640s, culminating in the regicide. And along with such outmoded beliefs, so too, it has been argued, did the period after 1660 witness the demise of related forms of political thinking in which it was widely assumed that the body of the monarch was inviolable, invested as it was with elements of the divine. The demystification or 'desacralization' of politics, as exemplified in the famous image of the new, artificial body politic of Thomas Hobbes' *Leviathan*, now ushered in a new form of political thinking based upon precepts congenial to the mechanical philosophy of Descartes. At the same time, it has been widely assumed that more traditional notions of the body politic, in which orderly government was thought to reflect the hierarchical organization of the human body, as created by God, were now a dead letter. In the age of Descartes and Hobbes, God no longer spoke to believers immediately through their bodies or natural calamities, but was absent from the material world. Greatrakes, by this reckoning, represented what Peter Laslett evocatively referred to as 'the world we have lost' and as such, was more easily confined to the dustbin of history along with other representatives of that superstitious and mystical pre-modern age.

As many familiar with recent writing in the history of science will appreciate, this story of what some have referred to as the 'disenchantment of the world' is no longer universally accepted. In particular, it is now widely agreed that the transition from a cosmology in which the presence of spirit was commonplace to one devoid of supernatural influence was a much more problematic and convoluted process. Late seventeenth-century Britons, including men of the stature of Robert Boyle, one of Greatrakes' admirers, proved remarkably obdurate in their desire to retain a place for a providential and active deity in their evolving worldview. The impact of the scientific revolution of the late seventeenth century, a complex and multifaceted process, was neither sudden nor wholly rational by modern-day standards. It alone was not responsible for the 'disenchantment of the world'. At the same time, it is equally apparent that the period after 1660 witnessed a sustained attempt to preserve a range of phenomena and beliefs that underpinned the idea of a universe governed by a purposeful, omnipotent, and ubiquitous deity. In Chapter 5, I discuss the enduring appeal of these ideas in providing a broader context in which to understand the Greatrakes affair, placing particular emphasis on the way in which Greatrakes' contemporaries viewed the human body as a potential conduit for the divine. Integral to this discussion is the concept of the body politic, a commonplace of early modern political thought, which, I argue here, maintained its widespread appeal and continued to shape political discourse after 1660. Much has been written in recent years about the body as a resource for understanding and interpreting the social, cultural, and political conventions that governed the lives of our early modern forbears. Literary scholars in particular have been quick to co-opt the body in order to deconstruct meaning from literary texts.[4] Oddly, however, political historians have been slow to follow suit, with the result that we still lack a comprehensive and overarching account of the role played by seminal concepts such as the body politic in early modern Britain. Those, moreover, who do treat the subject have tended to assume that any attempt to draw understanding other than metaphorical meaning from the concept died with the executed king in 1649.[5] In opposition to such claims, I argue here that ideas about the body in general, and the notion of the body politic in particular, continued to exert a strong fascination and unifying influence on men and women from across the religious and political spectrum in the early years of the Restoration. The broad-based support for Greatrakes' mission to heal the sick is otherwise inexplicable.

This becomes even more evident when I turn to discuss Greatrakes' own attempt to explain the origin and nature of his stroking as a form of exorcism. Here, I suggest that Greatrakes' thaumaturgical approach to patients echoed a wider concern in Restoration society for a general dispossession of the body politic in the wake of the upheavals of the preceding two decades. Typically, such concerns permeated the sermon literature of the early 1660s in which the body politic was widely construed as sick, possessed, and in dire need of cure. Greatrakes himself was something of an expert in the field of demonology, having taken part in one of the few

---

[4] The new historicist fascination with the corporeal, spawned by the seminal work of the literary scholar Stephen Greenblatt, has given rise to a vast literature on the early modern body. For a good introduction to the subject, which typically emphasizes the inherently unstable and malleable nature of the body politic analogy in early modern thought, see M. Schoenfeldt, 'Reading Bodies', in K. Sharpe and S. N. Zwicker (eds), *Reading, Society and Politics in Early Modern England* (Cambridge, 2003), 215–43.

[5] The chief advocate of this view, which continues to inform much thinking on the subject, was Michael Walzer, who argued that traditional ideas of order and cosmic correspondences, implicit in notions of the body politic, were effectively argued out of existence by puritan revolutionaries in the civil wars of the 1640s; M. Walzer, *The Revolution of the Saints: A Study in the Origins of Radical Politics* (London, 1966).

well-documented witchcraft trials in Ireland in 1661. It was a passion he shared with many of his closest admirers. At first glace, this appears counter-intuitive. How could a man who posed as a healer of the nation's ills, and exemplified moderation in the face of religious hatred, condone the persecution of innocent women for witches? And why should those drawn to him share such beliefs? The answer, I suggest, lies in the particular way in which a deep-seated attachment to ideas like witchcraft commonly functioned in this period as a vehicle for the promotion of religious reconciliation and political unity in a body politic facing permanent dismemberment. Greatrakes was certainly not alone in taking this approach. Many of his most ardent supporters from among the latitudinarian wing of the Anglican Church were equally obsessed with demonological and related issues, which in turn provided a point of mutual contact with those dissenters excluded from office and power. In the face of growing scepticism in certain circles, belief in spirits, demons, and witches thus offered a platform upon which moderate clergy on both sides of the divide might build a new, consensual, middle ground in religion.[6]

Witch-hunting for men like Greatrakes then was itself a form of healing, integral to his self-image as a charismatic and exemplary Christian. Averse to the doctrinal squabbling that threatened to destroy Protestant unity in Britain, through his mission to heal and dispossess the sick, he offered a new vision of a regenerate society in which the true enemies of the godly state such as witches were prosecuted in place of those 'surrogate witches' or nonconformists who now faced the full rigour of the Clarendon Code.[7] Such views, moreover, would appear to have attracted wide support in the early years of the Restoration. They permeated both the judiciary and the church and were warmly received by an important cross-section of society. For many, the prospect of continuing religious division, persecution, and hostile debate was altogether repugnant. By focusing on those enemies of the state, such as witches, who lay outside the boundaries of the established social order, Greatrakes and his supporters thus sought to build bridges among old enemies and heal the wounds of a body politic that many saw as desperate though not terminal.

As it happens, such thinking turned out to be wishful. One of the reasons why Greatrakes has been so readily overlooked by historians relates to the fact that he was on the losing side, the proponent of a world view that was in terminal decline by the time of his death in 1683. In the last years of his life, Greatrakes was witness to the onset of renewed religious and political conflict that threatened once again

---

[6] For an earlier attempt to place such developments within the broader context of witchcraft as a 'political' crime, see my 'Towards a Politics of Witchcraft in Early Modern England', in S. Clark (ed.), *Languages of Witchcraft: Narrative, Ideology and Meaning in Early Modern Culture* (Basingstoke, 2001), 101–18.

[7] For the use of the term 'surrogate witches' to discuss the way in which various governments from the 1640s onwards sought to stigmatize and eradicate those who opposed them, see my '"Saints or Sorcerers": Quakerism, Demonology and the Decline of Witchcraft in Seventeenth-Century England', in J. Barry, M. Hester and G. Roberts (eds), *Witchcraft in Early Modern Europe: Studies in Culture and Belief* (Cambridge, 1996), 145–79.

to tear the country apart in a new civil war. Rebels, not witches, were now top of the magistracy's agenda, and a new miracle worker, in the form of James, duke of Monmouth, pretender to the throne, emerged to replace Greatrakes in the affections of some of his former supporters. The fate of the latter, briefly described in Chapter 6, illustrates neatly the final demise of the eirenic aspirations of the Irish stroker and his closest followers. In brief, they were hopelessly divided, some opting to support the Whig cause, while others threw their weight behind the Tory reaction. Greatrakes' moment had come and gone, but we need to remember that the outcome was not clear at the time. The decade of the 1660s—a key moment in British history—offered a range of potential outcomes, including Greatrakes' own vision of a divinely ordained, regenerate, and godly state in which Protestants of various denominations might coexist, and external threats to the peace of the same, such as that posed by malevolent witches, were subjected to the full rigour of scripture and law. Ultimately unsuccessful, Greatrakes was soon forgotten. His story, however, is worthy of our consideration for it illustrates neatly the real dilemma which he and his contemporaries faced in their attempt to make sense of a world on the cusp of radical change, the outcome of which remained uncertain and open to debate.

2

The Making of an Early Modern Miracle Healer: Valentine Greatrakes, 1629–1660

'Tis not lawful for ordinary persons to assume so great a power, their skill in healing is not the Gift of God, as appeareth by the quality of the persons, who are generally ignorant, and prophane; for which very cause, God will not reveal his Counsels to them.

T. A., *XEIPEΞOKH*. *The Excellency or Handy-Work of the Royal Hand* (London, 1665), 5.

GREATRAKES AND THE VERDICT OF HISTORY

It is probably fair to say that the figure of the Irish gentleman and self-proclaimed miracle healer Valentine Greatrakes does not figure prominently on the radar of most students of early modern Britain. Indeed, it is quite possible that his name, if known at all, is more familiar to readers of historical novels in the period.[1] Despite the fact that his appearance in England in 1666 briefly raised him to celebrity status in a society threatened by the ravages of plague, few, if any, histories of this period have barely

---

[1] In recent years, Greatrakes has appeared as a charlatan and a quack in novels set in seventeenth-, eighteenth- and nineteenth-century England; see I. Pears, *An Instance of the Fingerpost* (London, 1997); M. Lovric, *The Remedy: A Novel of London and Venice* (London, 2006); S. Clarke, *Jonathan Strange and Mr Norrell* (London, 2004). His life and tortured psyche has also been subjected to poetic and dramatic exploration at the hands of modern Irish writers; T. McCarthy, 'Greatrakes, the Healer', in *The First Convention* (Dublin, 1978), 42; J. Nolan, *Blackwater Angel* (Oldcastle, Meath, 2001). In an earlier attempt to fictionalize the life of Greatrakes, the Irish author William Carleton (1794–1869) portrayed him as an upright magistrate imbued with the power to relieve those suffering from the malevolent effects of the evil eye; W. Carleton, *The Evil Eye; or, The Black Spectre: A Romance* (Dublin, 1860). Greatrakes' name was also included in a long list of absurd and outlandish Irish 'heroes' in James Joyce's *Ulysses* (1st edn, Paris, 1922; Harmondsworth, 1969), 295. I am indebted to Mark Roper for alerting me to this and other literary references and for suggesting that Joyce's intention in this passage was to parody old Irish tales of ancient heroes. Greatrakes' name appears alongside those of Dolly Mount, Sidney Parade and Ben Howth, all places in and around Dublin! Finally, it should be noted that in 2006 there appeared a popular account of Greatrakes' life, written in the form of a travelogue-cum-voyage of self-exploration, by an American enthusiast Leonard Pitt. Unfortunately, however, it adds little new to our picture of the historical Greatrakes; see L. Pitt, *A Small Moment of Great Illumination: Searching for Valentine Greatrakes, the Master Healer* (Emeryville, CA, 2006).

acknowledged his existence, even with a footnote.[2] One explanation for this lack of scholarly interest in the Greatrakes affair almost certainly relates to the fact that most historians of the Restoration have failed to detect any profound significance in his mission to heal the sick. As a result, academic curiosity surrounding Greatrakes has largely been confined to historians of early modern medicine and science who have sought to locate the controversy generated by his cures within a wider debate concerned with the place of miracles in seventeenth-century natural philosophy.

Before examining more closely the issues raised by this debate in academic circles, it is worth pointing out that those writing in the period immediately after Greatrakes' death were more appreciative of his place in the broader history of the Restoration. Early historians such as Laurence Eachard (1672–1730), John Oldmixon (d.1742), and Thomas Salmon (1679–1767), who between them represented a broad swathe of political opinion in early Hanoverian England, all made a point of commenting upon Greatrakes' stroking in their highly popular accounts of the period. While the non-partisan Eachard and Tory Salmon were largely even-handed in their assessment of the attributes and abilities of the charismatic healer, Oldmixon, a Whig, left his readers in no doubt as to how the past should judge Greatrakes, considering him 'a notorious Cheat [who] sneak'd off as soon as his Credit began to sink'.[3] Other allusions to Greatrakes in the first half of the eighteenth century suggest that he had become something of a political football whose controversial methods provided useful capital in the partisan political disputes of the first age of party. Medicine, as I argue elsewhere, had become deeply politicized by this period, a trend illustrated by the reactions of two surgeons, hailing from different sides of the party divide, to the legacy of Greatrakes. Thus, in 1722 the Whig William Beckett (1684–1738) felt little compunction in evoking the memory of Greatrakes' successes, which he ascribed to various natural explanations, in order to undermine the grandiose claims made by the Jacobites on behalf of the Old Pretender.[4] The Tory John Atkins (1685–1757) took a very different tack in 1742, when he engaged in a vicious campaign of character assassination aimed at the 'Miracle-monger' Greatrakes

---

[2] The Greatrakes affair, for example, is absent from the major reassessments of the Restoration undertaken by Ronald Hutton, Nigel Keeble, Tim Harris and Gary de Krey; R. Hutton, *The Restoration: A Political and Religious History of England and Wales 1658–1667* (Oxford, 1985); N. H. Keeble, *The Restoration: England in the 1660s* (Oxford, 2002); T. Harris, *Restoration: Charles II and His Kingdoms, 1660–1685* (London, 2005); G. S. De Krey, *Restoration and Revolution in Britain: A Political History of the Era of Charles II and the Glorious Revolution* (Basingstoke, 2007). To this list, we can now add J. Uglow, *A Gambling Man: Charles II and the Restoration* (London, 2009).

[3] L. Eachard, *The History of England … Vol. 3 From the Restoration of King Charles the Second, to the Conclusion of the Reign of King James the Second* (London, 1718), 152–3; J. Oldmixon, *The History of England During the Reigns of the Royal House of Stuart, wherein the Late Errors of Late Histories are Discover'd and Corrected* (London, 1730), 526; T. Salmon, *Modern History: or the Present State of All Nations*, 31 vols (London, 1724–38), xxii, 295. The careers of all three men are recounted in the *ODNB*.

[4] W. Beckett, *A Free and Impartial Enquiry into the Antiquity and Efficacy of Touching for the Cure of the King's Evil* (London, 1722), 30–1. In dismissing the claims made on behalf of the Stuarts, Beckett argued that their power to heal was of very recent provenance and as such could be as easily explained by the power of the over-excited imagination of the patient as attributed to any inherent power in the body of the king.

and his followers. Greatrakes, according to Atkins, was simply a dupe of the Whigs, his supporters being drawn from the ranks of 'Low-Churchmen' and 'Anti-Courtiers' who promoted his cures in order to detract from those performed by Charles II. The ruse had failed, however, and Atkins betrayed his true political colours by inferring from Greatrakes' false cures 'the Reality of the Kings; which though obscured a Time by bungling Imitation and Politicks, does for that reason, at length to all unprejudiced People, shine with so much the clearer Truth'.[5]

There is no evidence to suggest, however, that the reaction to Greatrakes in the immediate aftermath of his death followed strict party lines as is evident from the criticisms levelled against him by Whig propagandists such as John Oldmixon. A further complicating factor here was undoubtedly the attempt by some, evident from the moment Greatrakes appeared on the national stage in 1665–6, to equate his cures with those of Christ. The furore created by the likes of Henry Stubbe in 1666 (discussed more fully in Chapter 4) continued into the eighteenth century when radical critics of the Church such as the deists Thomas Woolston (1668–1733) and Arthur Ashley Sykes (c.1684–1756) revived the memories of Greatrakes' cures in order to cast doubt on some of the most fundamental tenets of revealed religion and the Christian faith.[6] Under such circumstances, middle-of-the-road Whig clergymen such as Richard Smalbroke (1672–1749) and later John Douglas (1721–1807) showed little compunction in discrediting the 'miraculous' status of the Irishman's cures. The former, for example, echoing the approach of the celebrated natural philosopher Robert Boyle, who had witnessed at first hand Greatrakes' ministrations, argued that they might as easily proceed from natural causes such as the physical effects of friction 'in a Mechanical Manner'.[7]

---

[5] J. Atkins, *The Naval Surgeon; or, Practical System of Surgery* (London, 1742), 34–5. For continuing support for the royal touch in Jacobite circles in the century after the deposition of James II, see especially P. K. Monod, *Jacobitism and the English People, 1688–1788* (Cambridge, 1989), 127–32.

[6] The freethinker Woolston proposed that Greatrakes' cures, alongside those of Apollonius Thyanaeus and Vespasian, were on a par with those of Christ; T. Woolston, *A Discourse on the Miracles of Our Saviour, in View of the Present Controversy Between Infidels and Apostates* (London, 1727), 11. Sykes, a noted religious controversialist who stopped short of describing Greatrakes' successes as miraculous, was nonetheless almost certainly seeking to invoke Greatrakes as part of a wider campaign of deist subversion. In the same work and elsewhere, he downplayed the significance of the miracles of Moses and Christ, poured scorn on the idea of the reality of witchcraft, and argued that it was more appropriate to envisage the New Testament demoniacs as insane rather than possessed. Isaac Newton, in fact, had argued much the same with respect to the latter. It is tempting to speculate that Sykes' deism was heavily influenced by Newton. Not only was the great scientist a member of Sykes' London congregation, but the latter was approached soon after Newton's death in order to see whether he would help with the publication of some of his theological writings; A. A. Sykes, *A Brief Discourse Concerning the Credibility of Miracles and Revelation* (London, 1742), 24–6, 141–2; *ODNB*.

[7] R. Smalbroke, *A Vindication of the Miracles of our Blessed Saviour: In which Mr Woolston's Discourses on Them are Particularly Examin'd*, 2 vols (London, 1728), i, 25–8; J. Douglas, *The Criterion or Miracles Examined with a View to Expose the Pretensions of Pagans and Papists* (London, 1757), 205–13. For Smalbroke and Douglas, who were both rewarded with bishoprics for their loyalty to the Whig establishment, see their respective entries in *ODNB*. It seems highly likely that the republication of Greatrakes' *Brief Account* (London, 1723) was meant as a contribution to this debate. An anonymous advertisement appended to this edition states that Greatrakes' cures 'appear to be clear Evidences of a supernatural Operation, which is the great Motive of the Publication thereof at this Time, when almost everything of that kind is called into Question, and by many, who know no better, made the Subject of Ridicule'; A2r.

By the end of the eighteenth century, interest in Greatrakes had dwindled and was largely confined to 'enlightened' critics like Richard Walker, who wished to equate the charlatans of his own age, in particular the mesmerists, with men like the Irish stroker, 'that crafty and audacious Magnetiser of our grand-fathers'.[8] Within a matter of decades, interest in the stroker had effectively evaporated. It was not until the curiosity of one of his ancestors was stimulated in the mid-nineteenth century, that he resurfaced, this time as the subject of genealogical and antiquarian enquiry in a period in which the study of history was undergoing radical transformation. In the mid-1860s, Samuel Hayman (1818–1886), an Anglican minister who held a number of livings in county Cork in southern Ireland, published two articles in *The Reliquary*, which have formed the basis of serious study of Greatrakes and his antecedents to the present day.[9] New evidence of the stroker's activities appeared thereafter in occasional contributions to journals such as *Notes and Queries*, but it was not until the 1950s that Greatrakes' reputation as a healer was once again subjected to serious scrutiny.[10] At first, much of the interest in him consisted of attempts to subject his cures to the scrutiny of modern medical and psycho-pathological thinking.[11] By the 1970s, however, stimulated by the work of historians such as Keith Thomas, there emerged renewed interest in Greatrakes as a representative figure of his age rather than an eccentric pandering

[8] R. Walker, *Memoirs of Medicine: Including a Sketch of Medical History, from the Earliest Accounts to the Eighteenth Century* (London, 1799). Walker described himself as apothecary to the Prince of Wales. He was not alone in construing Greatrakes as an early mesmerist. As ambassador to France in 1784, Benjamin Franklin, with a group of leading French scientists and physicians, included Greatrakes in a list of early proponents of 'animal magnetism' or mesmerism; *Report of Dr Benjamin Franklin, and Other Commissioners, Charged by the King of France, with the Examination of the Animal Magnetism, as Now Practised at Paris … Translated from the French* (London, 1785), 12–13. He was still being described as a mesmerist in 1847 when the celebrated Irish physician Richard Madden (1798–1886) wrote a brief synopsis of his career; R. R. Madden, 'Some Notices of the Irish Mesmerists of the Seventeenth Century: Greatrakes, Cooke and Finaghty', *Dublin Quarterly Journal of Medical Science*, 4 (1847), 254–72. More recently, the Canadian psychologist A. Bryan Laver has situated Greatrakes' approach within this tradition of healing, albeit one reduced to a psychosomatic explanatory method; 'Miracles No Wonder! The Mesmeric Phenomena and Organic Cures of Valentine Greatrakes', *Journal of the History of Medicine and Allied Sciences*, 33 (1978), 35–46.
[9] Rev. S. Hayman, 'Notes on the Family of Greatrakes', *The Reliquary. Quarterly Archaeological Journal and Review*, 4 (1863–4), 81–96, 220–36; *idem*, 'Notes on the Family of Greatrakes: Addenda and Corrigenda', *The Reliquary. Quarterly Archaeological Journal and Review*, 5 (1864–5), 94–104. Hayman was related to Valentine Greatrakes through the marriage of the latter's daughter, Mary, to Major Edmund Browning whose only surviving son, also called Valentine, married Jane Hayman. As well as providing a detailed, if flawed, genealogy of the stroker, Hayman claimed to possess many of the family's papers, including the original manuscript of Greatrakes' *Brief Account* with the author's signature; Hayman, 'Notes on the Family of Greatrakes', 87.
[10] Of these, the most intriguing is a description of Greatrakes' cures dating from about 1680 transcribed by a local Manchester historian, John Eglington Bailey (1840–1888), and published in *Notes and Queries*, 9 (1884), 61–3. According to Bailey, they were taken from 'Mr Gratrix's volume of tracts' lent to him by a 'good neighbour', one Samuel Gratrix of West Point. Unfortunately, I have not been able to locate the missing manuscripts, which may well survive unnoticed among family papers.
[11] Examples include R. A. Hunter and I. Macalpine, 'Valentine Greatrakes and "Divers of the Strange Cures by Him Lately Performed" on Patients from St Bartholomew's Hospital in 1666', *St Bartholomew's Hospital Journal*, 60 (1956), 361–8; O. B. Appleyard, 'A Seventeenth-Century Healer, Valentine Greatrakes, 1628–1683', *Practitioner*, 182 (1959), 342–6; D. Wilson, 'Valentine Greatrakes—Ophthalmologist', *Transactions of the Ophthalmological Societies of the United Kingdom*, 87 (1967), 893–6.

to the superstitions of the ignorant masses.[12] In particular, historians of science were attracted to the Greatrakes episode for the light which they hoped it might help to shed on a critical debate in historical circles, namely that surrounding the religious and ideological origins of the scientific revolution in late seventeenth-century Europe.

Concern with the potential significance of Greatrakes and his cures in this debate was largely initiated by the work of J. R. Jacob. In a series of books and articles on Robert Boyle and his circle, he attempted to analyse their response to Greatrakes' miraculous claims within the wider context of the religious and political allegiances which he saw as underpinning the emergence of the 'new philosophy' in the second half of the seventeenth century.[13] Jacob, in particular, argued that the principal support for scientific innovation, as epitomized by the guarded response of figures like Boyle to Greatrakes, emanated from moderate or 'latitudinarian' circles within the restored Anglican Church. Others however, most notably Eamon Duffy and Nicholas Steneck, have challenged this view on the grounds that it is impossible to discern any clear link between science and ideology in an age in which well-defined scientific, religious, and political identities were largely non-existent.[14] On balance, it is probably fair to conclude that Steneck's more nuanced and careful reading of the evidence has been vindicated by subsequent commentators on the ideological origins of the new science and the role played by institutions such as the Royal Society in promoting change. Consensus now suggests that the Greatrakes affair did represent an important opportunity for those engaged in natural philosophical speculation to investigate the extent to which God was still active in his creation, and thus establish more firmly the boundary between the natural and supernatural worlds.[15] And while few agree as to the extent to which,

[12] K. V. Thomas, *Religion and the Decline of Magic: Studies in Popular Beliefs in Sixteenth- and Seventeenth-Century England* (London, 1971), 203–4. Thomas' approach, based on the methods pioneered by anthropologists in the study of non-western cultures, created a renewed respect in academic circles for the role of magical and related beliefs in early modern Europe. Its influence is evident, for example, in the reappraisal of the Greatrakes affair by the Irish historian Lawrence Arnold, who in 1976 argued that it would be a mistake to 'dismiss it as an isolated and farcical episode inspired by an outlandish eccentric and rooted in mass hysteria'. On the contrary, he claimed that the career of the Irish stroker shed important light on society in general, and science in particular, in a 'twilight' stage in Europe's past when there existed no clear distinction between the natural and supernatural realms; L. J. Arnold, 'Valentine Greatrakes, A Seventeenth-Century "Touch-Doctor"', *Eire-Ireland*, 11 (1976), 3–12.

[13] See especially J. R. Jacob, *Robert Boyle and the English Revolution* (New York, 1977), 164–76; idem, *Henry Stubbe, Radical Protestantism and the Early Enlightenment* (Cambridge, 1983), 50–63.

[14] E. Duffy, 'Valentine Greatrakes, the Irish Stroker: Miracle, Science and Orthodoxy in Restoration England', in K. Robbins (ed.), *Religion and Humanism* (Oxford, 1981), 251–73; N. H. Steneck, 'Greatrakes the Stroker: The Interpretations of Historians', *Isis*, 73 (1982), 161–77. The latter appeared alongside a short article emphasizing the extent to which Greatrakes' cures were amenable to a range of contemporary medical and scientific explanations, both old and new; see B. B. Kaplan, 'Greatrakes the Stroker: The Interpretations of His Contemporaries', *Isis*, 73 (1982), 178–85. For Jacob's reply to Steneck's criticisms of his interpretation of Stubbe's role in the Greatrakes affair, see Jacob, *Henry Stubbe*, 164–74.

[15] For a good example of this approach, see S. Schaffer, 'Regeneration: The Body of Natural Philosophers in Restoration England', in C. Lawrence and S. Shapin (eds), *Science Incarnate: Historical Embodiments of Natural Knowledge* (Chicago, 1998), 106–16.

if at all, these positions became fixed in this period, there is now general agreement that the resort to overarching categorizations such as 'liberal Anglican', 'latitudinarian', and 'corpuscularian' has proved inadequate as a means of explaining the wider ideological roots of science in Restoration Britain.

The work of later commentators on Greatrakes has largely echoed this approach. In particular, Michael Hunter has consistently urged caution in the use of over-simplistic categories to describe scientific affiliations in this period, preferring instead to locate the religious, political, and scientific attitudes of scholars and thinkers in a complex web or matrix of beliefs ranging across the spectrum.[16] In discussing Robert Boyle's reaction to the Greatrakes affair, he thus describes his 'convoluted' response to the stroker as 'in many ways the most striking feature of the episode'. Elsewhere, he characterizes Boyle's attitude to the Irish healer and his much-vaunted miracle cures as 'non-committal', and thus indicative of the natural philosopher's innate reluctance to commit to any public profession of partisanship in a dispute that, as we shall see, threatened to divide onlookers on religious and political grounds.[17] For Hunter then, Boyle was largely reticent to subscribe, in public at least, to the idea that Greatrakes' cures were true miracles, though he was unwilling to rule out the possibility that they might proceed from the immediate hand of God. Conventional wisdom suggests that Boyle was out of step here with contemporary sensibilities, particularly given his social status as an 'orthodox' Anglican and highly educated son of an Irish, Protestant peer. Belief in miracles, or so we have been led to believe, was restricted to Roman Catholics, radical Protestants, and the uneducated masses, and had ceased to form part of elite discourse in post-Reformation Britain. Two recent studies, however, which both invoke the debate surrounding Greatrakes in the 1660s, strongly suggest that Protestant attitudes to miracles in this period were not set in stone and that faith in their possibility continued to permeate belief at all levels of society throughout the seventeenth century.[18]

Robert Boyle's cautious reaction to Greatrakes and his ambivalent stance on miracles was entirely in keeping with the general tenor of scientific discussion in this period. It also reflects a growing appreciation among historians of science that it is largely futile to seek a clear-cut correlation between specific scientific theories

[16] M. Hunter, *Science and the Shape of Orthodoxy: Intellectual Change in Late Seventeenth-Century Britain* (Woodbridge, 1995), 11–18.

[17] M. Hunter, 'The Conscience of Robert Boyle: Functionalism, "Dysfunctionalism" and the Task of Historical Understanding', in *idem, Robert Boyle (1627–1691). Scrupulosity and Science* (Woodbridge, 2000), 64; *idem, Boyle: Between God and Science* (New Haven, 2009), 151. Hunter's approach echoes that of Caoimhghin Breathnach, who suggests that Boyle was reluctant to see Greatrakes' cures as true miracles, arguing instead that they were the natural product of corpuscularian processes of fermentation in the body; C. S. Breathnach, 'Robert Boyle's Approach to the Ministrations of Valentine Greatrakes', *History of Psychiatry*, 10 (1999), 87–109. Elsewhere Breathnach, a professor of human anatomy and physiology in Dublin, focuses on modern-day medical explanations of the stroker's methods, suggesting, in line with Boyle, that his cures were to some extent indebted to psychological factors and the power of 'an exalted imagination' in his patients.

[18] R. Gillespie, *Devoted People: Belief and Religion in Early Modern Ireland* (Manchester, 1997), 120–1; J. Shaw, *Miracles in Enlightenment England* (New Haven, 2006), 74–97.

and corresponding religious and political beliefs in an age of flux. Steneck's contention, on the basis of his analysis of the Greatrakes affair, that there was no 'unity of opinion...at the heart of the English Scientific Revolution, be that unity liberal Anglican, Puritan or whatever', is now widely accepted as the default position for most scholars working in this field. There are, however, dangers in this approach. Harold Weber, for example, who commendably claims that 'the strange case' of Valentine Greatrakes 'represents more than a mere freak of Restoration history' and has highlighted its wider social and cultural significance, nonetheless concludes that political concerns were, in the final assessment, largely peripheral, 'and remain on the edge of the debate, always threatening to overwhelm the medical and scientific transactions but never quite imposing themselves'.[19] However, the inability to detect clear-cut religious or political divisions among Greatrakes' supporters and opponents does not, of necessity, argue for an absence of broader, ideological factors in shaping the ensuing debate. In opting to stress the wondrous or preternatural quality of Greatrakes' cures, and thus avoid the twin extremes of materialistic or supernatural causation, the strokers' followers were, I argue below, promoting a specific, political agenda, albeit one that defies conventional categorization. In looking afresh at the Greatrakes affair, I hope to show that the 'moderation' of the Irish healer's supporters should not be construed as a form of ideological apathy or a turning away from politics. On the contrary, the adoption of such a stance by Greatrakes himself and his followers was replete with political meaning.[20] In what follows, I seek to show that the middle way advocated by Greatrakes' diverse group of supporters represented anything but a neutral or apolitical stance, especially when seen within the context of the experiences, beliefs and relationships of those who publicly proclaimed his cures. Before examining these in detail, however, we need to know more about the man who so divided opinion in Ireland and England in the middle years of the 1660s. Who was Valentine Greatrakes, and what clues can one find in his early life in Ireland to shed light on his future career as a miracle healer?

A SETTLER FAMILY IN IRELAND, *c*.1590–*c*.1641

Valentine Greatrakes was born on the 14 February 1629, the son of William Greatrakes of New Affane, county Waterford, in the province of Munster in southern Ireland (see Fig. 1). The family home of Norris Land was situated on the west bank of the River Blackwater, its tumbledown remains still visible today standing isolated in a field just a few hundred yards from the river's edge (see Fig. 2).

---

[19] H. Weber, *Paper Bullets: Print and Kingship under Charles II* (Lexington, 1996), 67–77 [quotes at 70–1, 76].

[20] This mood is best captured, I feel, by Michael McKeon who has described the furore surrounding Greatrakes, and its prophetic significance, as 'ideologically problematic' and 'ideologically ambiguous'; M. McKeon, *Politics and Poetry in Restoration England: The Case of Dryden's* Annus Mirabilis (Cambridge, MA, 1975), 209–15.

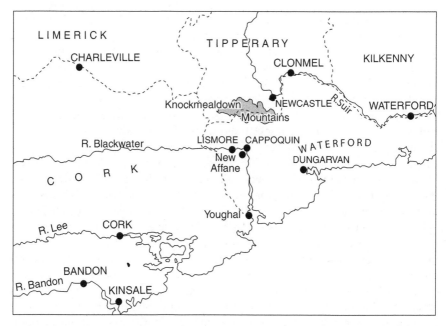

Fig. 1. Map of southern Ireland.

The settlement of Old Affane was in fact situated on the east bank of the river and within easy reach of the expanding port and commercial centre of Youghal from where merchants plied their trade with south-west England and continental Europe. Economically, the region surrounding the Greatrakes' lands at Affane was prosperous and offered real potential to speculators and investors from other parts of Britain, many of whom began to settle here from the late sixteenth century onwards. The rural economy of this part of Munster was mixed with a growing emphasis on the export of live cattle to England via ports such as nearby Youghal. In addition to the agricultural wealth of the region, the River Blackwater afforded, as it does today, excellent fishing, and on both sides of the valley the limestone hills provided the basis for a nascent iron-smelting industry, much of it controlled by the entrepreneurial Boyle family, who owned most of the kilns in the neighbourhood.[21] A few miles north of the Greatrakes' estates at Affane lay the town of Cappoquin, which controlled a strategically important bridging point across

---

[21] For the Boyles' ironworks at Lismore, Affane and Cappoquin, see T. Power, 'Richard Boyle's Ironworks in County Waterford', *Decies*, 6 (1977), 26–30; 7 (1978), 30–5. The works themselves were in severe decline by the middle of the seventeenth century. The naturalist and member of the Hartlib circle Gerard Boate concluded, on the evidence of 'knowing persons', that the Earl of Cork had made £100,000 from his ironworks; G. Boate, *Irelands Naturall History* (London, 1652), 137.

Fig. 2. Remains of Greatrakes' home at Norris Land situated on the west bank of the River Blackwater. Photograph by Paddy Dwan, with kind permission of Kristin Jameson.

the Blackwater and was destined to become an important garrison town in the 1640s.[22] It was also a thriving commercial hub in the first half of the seventeenth century, its role as a centre for the timber and iron trades augmented in this period by expansion into the cloth trade. In most of these activities, the Greatrakes family are known to have engaged or possessed an interest, as well as acting as pioneers in a specialist field of production, that of cider manufacture.[23]

The Greatrakes' connection with Ireland dated back to Valentine's grandfather, William (*c.*1568–1628), one of the original investors in the Elizabethan plantation of Munster who, according to family tradition, accompanied Sir Walter Raleigh to these parts in the late sixteenth century. The Raleigh connection was in all probability a fiction. More probably, William Greatrakes arrived in Ireland some time in the 1580s and settled in or near the new plantation of Bandon Bridge in

[22] In the summer of 1642, Roger Boyle reported to his father, the Earl of Cork, that if Cappoquin had not been garrisoned against Catholic insurgents, as Lord Inchiquin had wished, then 'it would have bin the ruin of this Country and in time the starving of Yoghill [Youghal]'; CH, Lismore Papers, vol. 23, no. 94.

[23] R. Gillespie, 'Small Towns in Early Modern Ireland', in P. Clark (ed.), *Small Towns in Early Modern Europe* (Cambridge, 1995), 159–60, 162; C. Smith, *The Antient and Present State of the County and City of Waterford* (Dublin, 1746), 60, 62. Valentine Greatrakes apparently upheld the family tradition as a specialist producer of high quality apples and cider; Boyle, *Correspondence*, iv, 432. His extensive orchards at the family home at Norris Land are fully described in a perambulation of the bounds of his estate, undertaken at the behest of his landlord, Richard Boyle, the second Earl of Cork, in 1669; NLI, MS 8143, *sub* 24 May 1669.

county Cork, a scheme undertaken by the west-country adventurer, Phane Beecher (d.1593). William, whose family were originally from Derbyshire, soon prospered, acquiring land, local office, and social status in the process.[24] In addition, and in time-honoured fashion, good marriages were arranged for the children of the founder of the Greatrakes' fortunes. In particular, his eldest son, also named William (*c*.1600–1643), forged close links with other upwardly mobile settler families of English origin, all of whom rapidly profited from the expropriation of the lands of the native Irish. The family's rise to prominence in Munster society was effectively sealed by the marriage of William Greatrakes the younger to Mary Harris, the daughter of Sir Edward Harris (1575–1636), a Devon gentleman, who served as chief justice for the province of Munster for much of the first half of the seventeenth century. It also established, or possibly reaffirmed, links between the Greatrakes' and Devon that were to prove of some significance in the unfolding life and career of William Greatrakes the younger's eldest son, Valentine, who was born in 1629.[25]

About ten miles west of Affane lay the castle and town of Lismore, seat of the Boyle family whose founder, Richard Boyle (1566–1643), was one of the leading figures in pre-Civil War Irish politics and society (Fig. 3). He was also the domi-nant figure in Munster, owning large tracts of land in the newly settled province and attracting a large group of clients and tenants in the vicinity of Lismore. Among them were Valentine's grandfather and father, both of whom seem to have served the role of loyal retainer to the Boyle family for much or most of their adult lives. References to the Greatrakes' abound in the private papers of the first Earl of Cork, and provide the most useful source for the early history of the family in Ireland. On the evidence of this rich archive, it would appear that Valentine's grandfather, William, benefited in numerous ways from the patronage of Sir Richard Boyle. He first appears as a witness to a rental payment of a fellow tenant

---

[24] G. Bennett, *The History of Bandon, and the Principal Towns in the West Riding of County Cork* (Cork, 1879), 9. In a deposition before the Council of Munster in August 1610, William Greatrakes of 'New Aughmaine, gentleman' confirmed that he had 'formerly exercised and used the severall of-fices of Clarke of the Crowne & Clerke of the peace' in Munster from 1593 to 1605 'but nowe doth not exercise eyther of them or any other'. In the same deposition, he gave his age as 'xxxxii yeares or thereabouts', thus bringing forward his date of birth from that suggested by the family's nineteenth-century historian, Samuel Hayman, by at least twenty-eight years; BL, Harleian MS 697, fos. 40r–v. Hayman mistakenly interprets this document as referring to Greatrakes' eldest son, also William, whose date of birth he gives as 1573; Hayman, 'Notes on the Family of Greatrakes', 83–4. William Greatrakes the elder would appear to have been succeeded in the post of clerk by his relation, John Greatrakes, who occupied the position from at least 1610 to 1618; BL, Harleian MS 697, fos. 78r, 78v, 79r, 80r.

[25] In all likelihood, the founder of the Irish line of the family was, like Raleigh, a native of Devon. In 1619, William Greatrakes, 'of Devon, gent.', matriculated at Exeter College, Oxford, aged 19. I think, on balance, it is a fair assumption that this is a reference to Valentine's father, William, as many of the original planters chose to leave their families in England during the early years of the Munster settlement; Foster, iv, 596; Bennett, *History of Bandon*, 9. His stay at Oxford was brief. A year later, he entered as a student at the Inner Temple in London, where he was described as the eldest son of Wil-liam Greatrakes of Aughmane (i.e. Affane) in Ireland; W. H. Cooke (ed.), *Students Admitted to the Inner Temple, 1571–1625* (London, 1868), 153.

Fig. 3. Tomb of Richard Boyle, first Earl of Cork. South transept of the Collegiate church of St Mary the Virgin, Youghal, county Cork, Ireland. Photograph by Paddy Dwan, with kind permission of Youghal Town Council. It depicts Boyle flanked by his two wives, with his eight children aligned at the base of the monument.

in 1611, and thereafter is frequently referred to as a tenant of the Boyles and loyal servant to their interests in the region.[26] In 1612, for example, William acted as a referee on behalf of Sir Richard in a local dispute over land and timber. Six years later, he faithfully pledged a gift of money to his patron, payable on the birth of Sir Richard's next son.[27] In return for his loyalty and support, William Greatrakes the elder was able to call on his patron in time of need. In 1613, for example, he wrote to Boyle requesting his help and intervention in a dispute with his in-laws over property that he had recently acquired in the vicinity of Affane. During the course of these exchanges, it is apparent that Greatrakes had also been employed as Boyle's horticultural adviser 'in respect of my oversight of your garden at Youghal', as well as supplying his ironworks with lime.[28]

It was also at about this time that William Greatrakes the elder first attempted to purchase several hundred acres of land at Affane. It is unclear from the surviving

[26] CH, Lismore Papers, vol. 3, no. 80, fo. 103. In the same year (1611), Greatrakes was referred to in Boyle's household expenses as 'your ordinarius'; ibid. vol. 3, no. 100, fo. 124v.

[27] Ibid. vol. 4, no. 8, fo. 12; vol. 8, no. 185, 12 January 1618. The gift was intended for the purchase of a horse at the birth of Sir Richard's son, Lewis. In July 1619, however, Boyle reported that the preacher, Mr Souther, to whom Greatrakes had duly given £15, 'hath not yet delivered it me'; Grosart, i, 225.

[28] CH, Lismore Papers, vol. 4, no. 68, fos 120r–v.

evidence as to whether or not he was already settled there prior to his displacement of the previous owner (or tenant), Roger Dalton. Nor is it clear as to whether he was responsible for constructing a new house on the site of the Dalton estate. Whatever the case, the family estate at New Affane was secured and held in tenancy from the Boyle's, the first lease dating, according to Sir Richard in 1638, from 23 February 1615. In that year, William Greatrakes the elder was granted a lease for a house, barn, and 500 acres of land at an annual rent of £22 13s 4d. In addition, Boyle claimed that land held by William Croker, a relative of Greatrakes the elder's first wife, Anne, in neighbouring Kilbree, had been assigned to his client, Greatrakes, at roughly the same time.[29] One year later, however, in 1616, Greatrakes was still not in full possession of his new holdings at New Affane. In April of that year he wrote to Boyle requesting his help in accommodating the demands of the outgoing tenants, the Daltons, who were seeking an alternative tenancy agreement that was equal in value to their former estates at Affane.[30] It is not clear when Greatrakes did finally enter into possession of these lands, although one incontrovertible fact does stand out from this confused situation. William Greatrakes the elder was deeply indebted to his patron, Sir Richard Boyle, for facilitating the move to Affane, which in turn laid the foundation of a long and successful, if unequal, association between the two families. From this date forward until the end of the seventeenth century, the fortunes of the Greatrakes' would remain inextricably tied to those of the Boyle family, the fate of Valentine Greatrakes as much dependent upon the next generation of the Boyle dynasty as the destiny of earlier generations of his family had been indebted to the influence of the rising figure of Sir Richard Boyle, who was created first Earl of Cork in 1620.

William Greatrakes the elder died, intestate, at Affane on 2 June 1628.[31] His heir, William, was the only child of his first marriage to Anne, the daughter of Richard Croker, of Kill, county Waterford. Despite his second marriage to Elizabeth, the daughter of John Smith of Kent, which produced four children (Allen, Richard, Susan, and Elizabeth), the more important liaison in terms of the future prospects of the family was that which tied the Greatrakes to the Crokers.[32] In all probability it was William the elder's marriage into the Croker family that brought the Greatrakes' into the social, economic, and political orbit of the Boyle dynasty. Various members of the Croker family had served the Boyle interest in the area around Lismore for many years prior to William Greatrakes the elder's purchase of

[29] CH, Cavendish MS 78, vol. 2, 292. The Boyle estates in the vicinity of Affane were originally held in fee from the bishop of Waterford. During the course of the 1630s, they became the object of a concerted effort on the part of the Earl's inveterate enemies, Sir Thomas Wentworth, Lord Deputy of Ireland, and William Laud, Archbishop of Canterbury, to see them returned to the ownership and control of the church. For a brief account of the controversy, see P. Marshall, *Mother Leakey and the Bishop: A Ghost Story* (Oxford, 2007), 71–5, 81–3.

[30] CH, Lismore Papers, vol. 7, no. 18.

[31] His funeral certificate is in BL, Add. MS 4820, 212. It states that he was buried in St John's church, Dublin.

[32] According to Hayman, the Crokers were descended from another old Devon family, the Lynehams; Hayman, 'Notes on the Family of Greatrakes', 83. For a revised family tree, based on Hayman and other sources, see Appendix 1.

the lease of New Affane. In particular, Ensign Hugh Croker, described by Great-rakes in 1613 as 'brother Croker', was a long-standing and faithful servant of the Boyle family, who is frequently mentioned in the latter's private papers and busi-ness accounts. Among other duties, he would appear to have acted as a rent collec-tor and land agent for Sir Richard, as well as transacting business on his behalf as far afield as Padstow in Cornwall.[33]

Further evidence of the close relationship between the Boyles and the Crokers is suggested by the various disputes involving one of William Greatrakes the elder's relations, whom he referred to in his correspondence with Sir Richard as 'mother Croker'. In 1613, she would appear to have become embroiled in an acrimonious disagreement over land in the parish of Lismore that was causing serious embar-rassment to William Greatrakes, as well as jeopardizing his protracted negotiations over the purchase of the lease of New Affane. In July of that year he wrote to his patron, imploring him to 'settle her once and peace, & Let her have your favour, or else give her reason for what she hath or ought to have, that she may remove from thence, because I would not have her offensive unto you'.[34] If, as seems likely, William Greatrakes the elder's marriage into the Croker clan had provided the ini-tial opportunity for social climbing via the entourage of the Boyles, it is equally apparent that by 1613 the various familial and commercial relationships between Greatrakes and his in-laws were beginning to unravel in a way that threatened to disrupt the plans of the ambitious and upwardly mobile tenant of New Affane. Despite these setbacks, however, William Greatrakes the elder continued to pros-per. At his death in 1628, he not only owned land in the neighbouring county of Tipperary, a few miles to the north of Affane, but he also possessed an interest in lands near Bandon in west Cork. In addition, in 1623 he held the lease on some common land in the town of Kinsale.[35] Clearly, Greatrakes' expanding estates

[33] CH, Lismore Papers, vol. 3, no. 29, fos 43r–v; no. 83, fo. 106; vol. 4, no. 7, fo. 11; no. 68, fos 120r–v; vol. 5, no. 34, 20 May 1614; vol. 7, no. 202, 22 December 1617; vol. 11, no. 88, 24 July 1620; vol. 16, no. 94, 31 March 1628. In later years Croker fell into debt with his patron and land-lord, though he continued to play a central role in the social and military life of the neighbourhood and was actively involved in defending the Protestant cause in the area following the outbreak of the rebellion in 1641; see note 47.

[34] Ibid. vol. 4, no. 68, fos 120r–v. It is difficult to determine from the extant correspondence the identity of 'mother Croker'. It is highly unlikely that she was either Greatrakes' mother-in-law or mother, both of whom were probably dead by the date of these exchanges. In all probability, she was the wife of the man referred to in the same business as 'my uncle Croker, by whom I am so eagerly importuned & threatned with forfeiture of my land'. The cause of this protracted dispute was a parcel of land at Ballyanchora in the parish of Lismore which Greatrakes had recently purchased. Greatrakes was of the view that the estate, part of the old Anchorists' lands, included the rights of the parsonage. Before sealing the deal, however, the Crokers sought legal advice in England in order to clarify the details of the lease and the property that was to be assigned to them by Greatrakes in return for their support in the purchase of the Dalton estate at Affane. Though a deal was finally concluded, Sir Richard Boyle failed (not for the first time) to uphold Greatrakes' request to issue a new lease clarifying full entitlement to the lands of Ballyanchora, and certain rights were ceded to the local parson. In 1636, Boyle's agent Hugh Croker leased the lands of 'Ballyanker' to one Barnaby Gosse of Ballynyty; ibid. vol. 4, no. 68, fos 120r–v; vol. 18, no. 143, 7 November 1636.

[35] Hayman, 'Notes on the Family of Greatrakes: Addenda et Corrigenda', 94; *Analecta Hibernica*, 15 (1944), 167.

underpinned his growing wealth and status. In common with other large landowners in the area, however, he was not simply reliant upon agricultural profits. An
additional source of income was provided by the production of timber and lime,
which Greatrakes supplied to the large iron manufacturers such as Sir Richard
Boyle (in the latter's case at preferential rates). Eager not to place all his eggs in a
single basket, the astute scion of the Greatrakes family in Ireland also sought other
markets for the lime which he quarried in the hills around Affane. In 1613, for
example, he entered into an agreement with the corporation of Youghal to supply
'well burnt lime' to the port town for use in the building and iron-smelting indus-
tries. Eleven years later, his close relations with the town and its leading citizens
paid dividends when he was made a freeman of the borough.[36]

William Greatrakes the elder described himself variously as 'esquire' or 'gentleman', and would appear to have prospered under the protection of his landlord
and patron, Sir Richard Boyle, whose upward trajectory augured well for the future
of his client family. As we have seen, before his death in 1628, William the elder
had laid the foundations for future prosperity through the marriage of his son,
William, to Mary, the third daughter of Sir Edward Harris, whose family seat lay
at Piltown in county Waterford. Two aspects of this marriage call for comment.
Firstly, it is worth noting once again the reaffirmation of links between Munster
families who shared Devonian roots and connections. Like so many other families
who either accompanied or followed Sir Walter Raleigh to Munster in the late
sixteenth century, those of Greatrakes and Harris possessed west-country
genealogies. Valentine Greatrakes' maternal grandfather, Sir Edward, was the son
and heir of Sir Thomas Harris (d. 1610) of Cornworthy Priory in Devon, who sat
as an MP in Elizabeth I's parliaments and was a prominent member of the English
judiciary (see Fig. 4).[37] And secondly, equally worthy of note are the close bonds of
friendship which appear to have characterized relations between Sir Edward Harris
and Sir Richard Boyle for much of the early part of the seventeenth century.

As Chief Justice of Munster, Harris was in a powerful position to assist his
friend, Sir Richard, particularly in regard to the formidable, legal obstacles which
came the latter's way following his acquisition of the lands of the attainted Sir
Walter Raleigh. In 1609, for example, Harris offered friendly, off-the-record, advice
to Boyle in relation to the protracted legal wrangling over the extent of his control
of Raleigh's estates in Munster.[38] The two men were also partners in various business transactions.[39] Relations between the two families were further sealed by close
social ties and obligations. In his diary, Boyle frequently records sharing Harris'
company at the assizes and on at least one occasion he played host to Harris at

---

[36] R. Caulfield (ed.), *The Council Book of the Corporation of Youghal* (Guildford, 1878), 25–6; Grosart, ii, 372. For an example of Greatrakes supplying Sir Richard Boyle with lime, see CH, Lismore
Papers, vol. 4, no. 68, fos 120r–v.
[37] P. W. Hasler (ed.), *The History of Parliament: The House of Commons, 1558–1603*, 3 vols (London,
1981), ii, 260–3.
[38] CH, Lismore Papers, vol. 3, no. 2, fo. 2. For other letters between Harris and Boyle, see vol. 7,
no. 55; vol. 8, no. 115; vol. 11, no. 112.
[39] See, for example, Grosart, i, 264; ii, 245.

Fig. 4. Tomb of Sir Thomas Harris, the great-grandfather of Valentine Greatrakes, and scion of the Harris dynasty, Cornworthy church, Devon. Photograph by Kim Sayer. It was commissioned by his wife Elizabeth (d. 1634), who lies next to him, and depicts him in his lawyers robes.

Lismore while the latter was riding the circuit.[40] Such occasions undoubtedly provided opportunity for mixing business with pleasure. Further evidence of the cordial nature of the relationship between the two families is suggested by the fact that Sir Edward's wife, Elizabeth, served as godmother to Sir Richard's daughter, Katherine Boyle, who was born at Youghal on 22 March 1615. On a subsequent occasion, she was confident enough in her relations with Sir Richard to importune him, on her absent husband's behalf, to supply stakes and wattles that were urgently needed to repair a weir.[41] Though there is no direct evidence to support the claim, the warm relations that prevailed between the two families make it highly

---

[40] Ibid. ii, 122, 135; iii, 99; iv, 122.
[41] Ibid. ii, 109; CH, Lismore Papers, vol. 8, no. 27; vol. 8, no. 35.

likely that the match between William Greatrakes the younger and Mary Harris owed a debt of some kind to the intercession of the former's patron and landlord, Sir Richard Boyle.

In 1666, Valentine Greatrakes the stroker described his father, William, as 'a worthy Person and well esteemed in his Country a man lookt upon to be of a generous spirit, but one that had a mind above his fortune'.[42] Autobiographies are frequently unreliable guides for the historian, particularly when, as in this case, the account was for public consumption and designed to convince a wider audience of the moral integrity of the author. As we shall see, there was a manufactured quality to Greatrakes' published autobiography that was often at odds with what we now know of his upbringing and life. In this instance, however, his enigmatic comment that his father had possessed 'a mind above his fortune' was firmly based in fact, for William Greatrakes the younger was perpetually burdened with debt. Within a short time of his father's death, he was forced to sell his estates in county Tipperary and Cork and had mortgaged his farm at Affane to Sir Robert Tynte (1571–1643), whose son, also Robert (d. *c.*1645), would later marry his sister-in-law, Philippa Harris.[43] Worse was to follow. By 1638, Sir Richard Boyle, now Earl of Cork, was conspiring with Sir Hardress Waller to eject Greatrakes from Affane in order to encourage his wealthy and well-connected English friend to settle in Ireland near his own country seat at Lismore. In that year, Boyle wrote a long letter to Waller, outlining various potential locations, with Affane at the top of the list. Of William Greatrakes the younger, he confided to Waller that he 'had growne so ill a husband of his estate, and growes soe in arrears of his rents, and forfeits his leases soe to me, as I am confident when God shall send me home, it wilbe a very easy matter for me to buy him out of those two short leases'. He ended, however, on a cautionary note, for 'this is but opinion, and must be compassed by time and silence'.[44]

For reasons unknown, Sir Hardress Waller declined to take up the Earl of Cork's offer. In the mean time, William Greatrakes the younger's financial problems continued to deteriorate. By January 1640, he was a prisoner in Dublin, the house and lands of Affane having been briefly forfeited to one George Comerford of Wells in county Carlow in lieu of a debt for some three or four hundred pounds.[45] On the eve of the great rebellion of 1641, the Greatrakes' lands were thus encumbered with large debts and were under constant threat of repossession. Indeed, it is pos-

---

[42] Greatrakes, *Brief Account*, 15.

[43] Hayman, 'Notes on the Family of Greatrakes: Addenda et Corrigenda', 95. In June 1632, Boyle recorded in his diary: 'Remember to pay Sir Robert Tynt one hundred pounds sterling for the redempcon of Mr greatreaks his ffearme in Affane'; Grosart, iii, 148. Sir Robert had presumably bought out the lease and reassigned it to Greatrakes. Tynte's name appears on the rental, the property assigned to William Greatrakes, in 1637, 1641 and 1642; NLI, MSS 6239, 17; 6247, 23 April 1641; 6248, 16; 6249, 17.

[44] CH, Cavendish MS 78, vol. 2, 291–3: Waller (*c.*1604–1666) was originally from Kent, and had first come to Ireland in 1629 to marry an Irish heiress. He eventually settled in Limerick, and was to play a prominent role fighting on the side of Parliament in England during the Civil War. An Independent in religion, he supported the regicide; see *ODNB*.

[45] CH, Lismore Papers, vol. 20, no. 143. The reference to Greatrakes' imprisonment was made in the context of the failure of John Walley, steward to the Earl at Lismore, to secure a supply of fruit trees 'for the storing of your new orchard'. Clearly, the Greatrakes' were still held in high regard as experts in the cultivation of fruit trees.

sible that they may even have been alienated from the family by the time that the young Valentine Greatrakes sought refuge in England with his mother's family, some time in the early 1640s. That 'competent estate left him by his father', to which he referred in 1666, had shrunk by the early 1640s to the family farm at Affane and various holdings in neighbouring Ballygillane and Kilbree, much of which consisted of uncultivated mountain and forest.[46]

William Greatrakes the younger's embarrassing financial plight, however, would soon be overshadowed by national events triggered by the outbreak of a major uprising of the Roman Catholic population in Ireland in the autumn of 1641. In part precipitated by the growing political conflict in England, the province of Munster was about to be propelled into a period of ferocious conflict between the native Catholic population, who had long resented the economic, religious, and political ascendancy of the English 'newcomers', and those Anglo-Irish families like the Boyles and Greatrakes, whose first instinct was the preservation of their newly acquired land and political supremacy. Valentine Greatrakes, writing in 1666, has surprisingly little to say about these events. Still not yet thirteen years old when the rebellion broke out in Ireland, his memory of them may well have been vague and uncertain. Their place, however, in the broader consciousness of Irish Protestants, as well as among their co-religionists in mainland Britain, was secure, thanks in large part to the series of propagandistic images and pamphlets which issued from English presses after 1641. Refugees from Ireland, the young Valentine Greatrakes among them, flooded into England, bringing with them stories of massacres and looting as well as horrific tales of torture inflicted on the Protestant settlers by their Catholic neighbours. In Ireland itself, those Protestants who remained were only too eager to testify to Catholic atrocities, Greatrakes' father, William, among them. Some time in 1642, he deposed that on 1 April of that year three 'English Protestants' were murdered by Captain Edmond Fennell at Dungarvan. He also testified to the murder of six men and women in the garrison at Cappoquin in the following month, the culprit identified there as Captain Scurlocke or Sherlock, a relation, probably brother-in-law, of the late Earl of Barrymore.[47]

Just how much the young Valentine Greatrakes was informed of these events, and his father's part in them, is impossible to discern. What is evident, however, is that

---

[46] Greatrakes, *Brief Account*, 15. William Greatrakes the younger acquired Ballygillane and Kilbree in 1632 or 1633 on a twenty-one year lease from the Earl of Cork. In 1638, the Earl described the farm of Ballygillane, on the east bank of the river Blackwater, as 'a very good scope of very good mountayne, and some bottome lands and has iust on thother side of the water, against Kilbree'; CH, Cavendish MS 78, vol. 2, 292–3. The lot of Kilbree consisted of 40 acres. In 1642, fourteen of Greatrakes' cows were distrained in lieu of arrears of rent for Kilbree. A further distraint was carried out later in the year, with the Earl's steward reporting that it was highly unlikely that it would ever be redeemed; CH, Lismore Papers, vol. 23, nos 42, 67. By the summer of 1642, Greatrakes was not alone in defaulting on his rents. The rebellion had led to widespread economic dislocation in this part of Munster, and many of Greatrakes' sub-tenants at Ballygillane had fled across the river to seek sanctuary on their landlord's estates at Kilbree.

[47] TCD, MS 821, fo. 2r. The latter incident is described in some detail by Sir Richard Osborne in a letter to the Earl of Cork, in which it is clear that William Greatrakes' close relation, Captain Hugh Croker, was widely blamed for the embarrassing lapse in security at the garrison that enabled the Catholic rebels to enter the town and murder, unimpeded, six of its inhabitants; CH, Lismore Papers, vol. 23, no. 27.

in 1666 he made little attempt to describe his father's role in this unfolding drama, contenting himself and his readers with the sole reflection that his father died 'when I was tender in years', and was thus unable to make arrangements for his eldest son's education. The phrase itself is a curious one, suggesting as it does, within the context of early modern sensibilities with regard to age, that the author of the *Brief Account* had been orphaned as a young boy. The fact that his father was still alive in 1642, when Valentine was fast approaching adulthood, adds to the mystery surrounding William Greatrakes. Embarrassment at his father's lack of financial prudence was one thing, but it does not explain why the mature Valentine sought to expunge him so completely from his autobiographical record. The answer, in all probability, lay in the manner of his father's death. On 21 February 1643, the Earl of Cork's steward, John Walley, wrote to his master with details of local news. Among various accounts of a financial and military nature, he went on to describe how 'Lieutenant Greatrakes being in Lismore on Saturday last, and opprest with drink, in the way towards Cappoquin, accompanied with one of Captain Thornton souldurs, they differed upon words, and the Soldier ther killed him'.[48]

The unseemly nature of his father's death—drunk and murdered by one of his own confederates—must have cast a long shadow over the family honour. Valentine Greatrakes expunged the deed by simply writing his father out of the script. In his place, he chose to focus on the role played by his mother in his upbringing, a woman whom he described as 'a most indulgent and provident Parent', whose gentle status, both in birth and deed, was unimpeachable. In order to affirm his credentials as a truthful witness to his own cures in 1666, it was essential that Greatrakes, in his autobiographical account, fashioned an image of himself that accorded with contemporary expectations of a gentleman. In much the same way that Greatrakes' patron, the eminent natural philosopher Robert Boyle (1627–1691), to whom he dedicated his *Brief Account*, self-consciously constructed a public image of himself as a scientific truth-teller, so too the Irish stroker sought to manufacture as positive an image as possible of his family upbringing and gentle origins. The word of a gentleman was sacrosanct. Consequently, if Greatrakes' claims to heal the sick were to be taken seriously, it was essential that he should exclude from his public persona any hint of scandal or wrong-doing that might subvert contemporary notions of honesty and truth-telling.[49]

---

[48] Ibid. vol. 23, no. 195. That this was in fact William Greatrakes the younger, and not another member of the family, is evident from a description in the Earl of Cork's receipt book for September 1644, where it states that one John George owed £4 for half a year's rent for 140 acres of Kilbree, 'land held before by Lieutenant Greatraks'; NLI, MS 6900, 8–14 September 1644.

[49] S. Shapin, *A Social History of Truth: Civility and Science in Seventeenth-Century England* (Chicago, 1994). As we shall see, Valentine Greatrakes and Robert Boyle shared much else in common, including their Anglo-Irish roots and the fact that both were forced to live the lives of exiled orphans and refugees in the 1640s. Boyle was just two years older than Greatrakes, and his father, the first Earl of Cork, died in the same year as Valentine's father, William, in 1643. Some critics of Shapin have depicted Boyle as a less artful beneficiary of his privileged background, and have stressed the complexity of both his private and public persona. Michael Hunter, in particular, has suggested 'a more convoluted picture of the man'; see the various essays in his *Robert Boyle (1627–1691)* [quote on p. 11] as well as his recently published biography of Boyle.

THE EXPERIENCE OF EXILE, *c.*1642–*c.*1648

The early life of the stroker, overshadowed by impoverishment, bereavement, and the inscrutable vagaries of divine providence, must have left a profound imprint on the adolescent Greatrakes. It also culminated in forced exile from the land of his birth. In the wake of the outbreak of rebellion, he removed with his mother and siblings to England, where the family was afforded shelter and protection under the care of Greatrakes' elderly uncle, Edmund Harris (d. *c.*1642), who lived at Cornworthy in Devon. Of Harris virtually nothing is known apart from the brief description which Greatrakes provided in 1666. There, he alludes to the great debt he owed his uncle for instilling in him the basic principles of religion. An exemplary figure in other respects, Greatrakes records that he was 'one of so severe a pious life, that he devoted his whole time to the Service of God and the works of Charity ...[i]n brief, he was a Saint in his Life and conversation, and one whose memory I shall ever reverence and love'. The contrast with what little is known of the life and death of Valentine's own father is stark, the saintly Edmund Harris taking the place of his improvident father in the idealized account which he wrote over twenty years later. Predictably, the death of his uncle soon after his arrival in England precipitated yet another crisis for the family that was only partly mitigated by his mother's inheritance of a one-third share in the Harris estates in Devon.[50]

In addition to the acute sense of dislocation and anxiety which the family must have experienced in this period, we need also to remind ourselves that the English county in which the Greatrakes' sought refuge in the early 1640s was itself embroiled in a bitter conflict engendered by the outbreak of civil war in England in the late summer of 1642. The young Valentine's education, which had begun at the free school in Lismore (another charitable foundation of the first Earl of Cork), was once again disrupted by events in Devon and any intention on the part of his mother, Mary, to send Valentine to university was shelved. Instead, Greatrakes had to make do with private tuition at the hands of a neighbouring clergyman, John Daniel Getsius (d. 1672), Vicar of Stoke Gabriel in Devon, whom Greatrakes later described as 'an High-German minister' at whose house he was taught 'Humanity and Divinity'.[51] Just what kind of an education Greatrakes received at the hands of

---

[50] Greatrakes, *Brief Account*, 16. Again, Greatrakes would appear to be embellishing the facts as he could only have known his uncle for a very brief period. According to his aunt, Philippa, the widow of Arthur Harris (d.1640), Edmund Harris died within two years of her own husband, i.e. in about 1642; TNA, C 6/111/56. The Greatrakes' probably arrived in Devon some time in late 1641 or early 1642. By February of that year, the port of Youghal, which was full of English Protestants eagerly awaiting repatriation, was effectively cut off from all surrounding settlements, including those located further to the north on the Blackwater; J. Gibbs, *Good and Bad Newes from Ireland: In a Letter of Credit from Youghall* (London, 1642), 1, 3. The exodus was certainly in full swing by November 1641, when the mayor of Youghal reported that 'divers women both married & widdowes of good note ...are resolved to embarque them selves togither with the best part of their goods & chattels and theire children also for the Kingdom of England'; CH, Lismore Papers, vol. 22, no. 94.

[51] Getsius (alias Goetz), a native of the Palatinate, was incorporated BA at Cambridge in 1628 and served as vicar of Stoke Gabriel from 1636 until his death in 1672; Foster, ii, 559; *ODNB*. I have not been able to verify the suggestion made in the *ODNB* that Greatrakes gave a small annuity to his old mentor. This may stem from a misreading of Greatrakes' comment, following his praise of Getsius'

Getsius is impossible to say. It is clear, however, that he held his teacher, both as instructor and friend, in high esteem. Perhaps the fact that teacher and pupil shared a common background as refugees assisted in forging a lasting bond between the two men. Whatever the case, there can be little doubt that Getsius exerted an important influence upon the young Greatrakes, none more so, one might anticipate, than in helping to shape his response to the religious and political controversies of the day. Given the charge directed at Greatrakes by his detractors and repeated by some contemporary historians that his claim to heal diseases such as the king's evil was little more than 'a veiled sectarian protest against the Restoration', it is worth noting the highly orthodox and conservative nature of his mentor's religious and political leanings. Far from being a supporter of Parliament or advocate of puritanism, Getsius was a loyal defender of the religious and political status quo. In 1643, for example, he had got into trouble with the Devon Parliamentarians for preaching a loyal sermon before Prince Maurice at Dartmouth. His views, moreover, may have been shared by many of his parishioners. Stoke Gabriel has been described as one of the most loyal communities in Devon in respect of its support for the royal cause. Above all, however, the German émigré was a survivor. Throughout the many upheavals in church and state which occurred in the two decades after the outbreak of civil war in 1642, Getsius managed to hold on to his living at Stoke Gabriel.[52] Accommodating to the needs of the moment was a fact of life for refugees like Getsius, and it was a skill that he may have imparted to his young protégé who, as we shall see, was similarly adept at the art of survival in difficult times.

It is quite possible, in fact, that the young Greatrakes was sent to Getsius for instruction because of his family's deep-seated loyalty to the Stuart cause. The surviving evidence strongly suggests that this may have been the case. When he and his family left Ireland, probably in the general exodus of early 1642, they would appear to have been accompanied by their well-connected relations, the Tyntes, to whom William Greatrakes had become indebted for saving the family home in the 1630s. Three of Valentine's uncles, Robert, Henry, and William Tynte, fought among the

---

teaching, where he states: 'for which kindness I pray God to recompense him and his'; Greatrakes, *Brief Account*, 16–17. There is no mention of Greatrakes in the surviving abstract of Getsius' will; WCSL, O. M. Moger, transcripts of Devon wills, vol. 9, no. 2842. Little is known about the precise nature of the education that Greatrakes underwent at Lismore. However, if the comments of one of the Earl of Cork's correspondents are to be trusted, it was likely to have been a severe introduction to the world of learning. In 1639, Richard Goodrich, the tyrannical schoolmaster at Lismore, was the subject of a number of highly critical reports that prompted his patron and employer, the Earl, to issue a stern warning as to his future conduct. He received his last quarterly allowance in December 1641, 'the freeschoole at Lismore, being for the present dissolved'; CH, Lismore Papers, Cavendish MS 78, vol. 2, 301, 331, 336; N. Canny, *The Upstart Earl: A Study of the Social and Mental World of Richard Boyle, First Earl of Cork 1566–1643* (Cambridge, 1982), 108; NLI, MS 6,900, accounts, week ending 18 December 1641.

[52] Thomas, *Religion and the Decline of Magic*, 203–4; *Wal. Rev.*, 113; M. Stoyle, *Loyalty and Locality: Popular Allegiance in Devon During the English Civil War* (Exeter, 1994), 224. It has been suggested that Getsius owed the preservation of his living during the upheavals of the 1640s and 1650s to Arthur Upton of Lupton, an important figure in Devon county government in this period; see I. Gowers, 'Corrections and Additions to *Walker Revised* as Relevant to Devon Entries. Part 2', *DCNQ*, 37 (1993), 142. In 1658, Upton was one of the dedicatees (the others were Francis Rous and John Hale, JP) of Getsius' paean to peace and unity in the church, *Tears Shed in the Behalf of His Dear Mother the Church of England, and Her Sad Distractions* (Oxford, 1658).

armies of Charles I in the west country. Robert subsequently died in Devon in September 1645 and was buried at Cornworthy. Henry and William, unlike their father and older brother, survived the Civil War, but were forced to compound with Parliament. Like Valentine Greatrakes, both men also returned to Ireland in the late 1640s, where they subsequently enrolled to fight in the ongoing war against the 'rebels'.[53] Further evidence of the staunch loyalty of the Greatrakes' family and their closest kin can be found in a series of depositions made in the early 1650s relating to a protracted dispute in the court of Chancery over the last will and testament of Valentine's grandfather Sir Edward Harris. Details of this complex suit need not concern us here.[54] Suffice it to say that both sides in the dispute were keen to stigmatize the other with the taint of disloyalty and disaffection to those now in authority. The series of claims and counter-claims cannot disguise the fact, however, that Greatrakes' maternal family were transparently hostile to the cause of Parliament and that many of them had provided the King with both money and military service. The case of the Tyntes, whose loyalty to the royal cause was beyond doubt, we have already noted. Others, such as Valentine's cousin John Lancaster (*c*.1623–*c*.1683), who later played a prominent role in first publicizing his healing claims in 1665, was said to have been 'a continuall opposer of the Parliament in the late warres' and to have committed 'so great an offence that he dares not shew himselfe in publicke but lives very privately'.[55] Similarly, Valentine's mother, Mary, was reported to have employed

---

[53] The Tyntes were descended from a Somerset family and like the Greatrakes' were tenants and clients of the Boyle interest in Munster. Sir Robert Tynte (1571–1643), the founder of the Irish dynasty, was buried in the church of Kilcredan, alongside Sir Edward Harris, where elaborate funeral monuments to the two men survived until 1920. Sir Robert's connection with the Greatrakes' went back as far as 1613, when William Greatrakes the elder was in debt to a Captain Tynte, a rank which Sir Robert held in the early days of the plantation; *HMC Calendar of the Carew Manuscripts*, 6 vols (London, 1873), vi, 88; W. H. Welply, 'More Notes on Edmund Spenser', *Notes and Queries*, 65 (1933), 111–16; *idem*, 'Pedigree of the Tynte Family', *JCHAS*, 22 (1928), 61; CH, Lismore Papers, vol. 4, no. 68, fos 120r–v. In 1643 Sir Robert Tynte bequeathed £4,000 to the King to fight the rebels in Ireland; TNA, PROB 11/199, fos 147r–v. Five years later, John Tynte of Chelvey, Somerset, who also suffered for his royalism, claimed that his uncle, Sir Robert, had lost £60,000 in the rebellion, and that twelve of his children and grandchildren were then serving in Ireland under the command of royalist turncoat Murrough O'Brien, Lord Inchiquin (1614–1674); Green, *CPCC*, ii, 1037.

[54] The suit was brought by Philippa Harris, the widow of Arthur Harris, one of Sir Edward's three sons, who died in the autumn of 1640. She claimed that the terms of her husband's late will, dated 20 April 1638, had never been carried out by the two principal beneficiaries (his brothers, Sir Thomas and Edmund Harris, both of whom were said to have died in about 1642). As they died without issue, ownership of the Cornworthy estates was now contested by Philippa on the one hand and the other three surviving heirs, namely her sisters-in-law Mary Greatrakes and Philippa Tynte and nephew John Lancaster; TNA, C6/111/56. Greatrakes himself later repeated the claim that his mother was left a third share of Edmund Harris' estate; Greatrakes, *Brief Account*, 16.

[55] TNA, C 6/111/56. Greatrakes' cousin, John Lancaster (*c*.1623–*c*.1683), was the grandson of a former bishop of Waterford. His father, also John (d.1630), was a clergyman, who married Elizabeth Harris, daughter of Sir Edward Harris. He held numerous benefices in Munster, mainly through the patronage of the Earl of Cork, with whom he was engaged in long-running disputes over the payment of tithes. His son, John, would appear to have crossed to England with his cousins, the Greatrakes and the Tyntes, in the early 1640s and to have been provided with a safe refuge at his wife's family home at Cornworthy. He was briefly a student at Trinity College, Dublin, where he entered aged 15 in 1638, and later enrolled at Gray's Inn in February 1657; *ODNB*, Lancaster, John (d. 1619); Grosart, i, 102, 125, 129, 230; iii, 29, 243–4; CH, Lismore Papers, vol. 8, no. 166; vol. 9, no. 123; vol. 16, nos 113, 114; J. Foster (ed.), *The Register of Admissions to Grays Inn, 1521–1889* (London, 1889), 281.

Lancaster's brother-in-law Andrew Woodley, a captain in the late King's army and 'a man very powerfull and prevalent with the King's Commissioners' in Exeter, to use his influence with the royalist authorities in Devon in order to overturn the claims of her adversary Philippa Harris.[56]

The proceedings in Chancery seem to have rumbled on for many more years, the suit seemingly decided in favour of the three defendants. Leastwise, some time around 1656 Valentine Greatrakes would appear to have entered into his disputed inheritance at Cornworthy. Curiously, he failed to mention the loyalist credentials of his family in 1666. Eager to protest his own loyalty to the restored regime of Charles II, and to dispel any suggestion that his healing gift was in any way intended as a covert attack upon the credibility and legitimacy of the restored Stuart regime, it would have been perfectly reasonable for him to have mentioned such connections when writing his autobiographical account in 1666. One possible explanation for the omission may lie in the complex history surrounding the precarious fate of the Greatrakes' holdings in Ireland following the departure of the family to Devon and the death of Valentine's father in 1643. As late as 1642, Sir Robert Tynte's name appeared on the rental for Affane as assignee to William Greatrakes, and it may well be that the heirs of Sir Robert claimed some kind of right to the property in the confused circumstances of the late 1640s and early 1650s. When Henry Tynte, the grandson of Sir Robert, compounded in January 1647, he claimed to be heir to an estate in Ireland worth almost £4,000. Others have estimated the total losses of the family in the Irish rebellion as between thirty and sixty thousand pounds. That he intended to recover some of these losses is suggested by the fact that at the time of his composition he was serving a command in Ireland under Lord Inchiquin. If so, the Tyntes now represented a potential threat to the Greatrakes' Irish estates, the resumption of which, as we shall see, constituted one of the central aims of the young Valentine Greatrakes, who was at this time planning his own return to the country of his birth. Consequently, he may have wished to draw a discreet veil over this episode in his earlier life, an approach that, as we shall see, he adopted on more than one occasion in his *Brief Account*.[57]

RETURN FROM EXILE: GREATRAKES AND CROMWELLIAN IRELAND, *c.*1648–1660

Some time between 1647 and 1648, Valentine Greatrakes, now a young man, returned to Ireland determined to make his fortune and to alleviate the plight of his mother and younger siblings.[58] For Greatrakes, financial security almost certainly

---

[56] TNA, C 6/111/56. Andrew Woodley married John Lancaster's sister, Mary, some time before 1646. The births and deaths of their various children are noted in the parish registers for Cornworthy between 1646 and 1654. During the Civil War, Woodley served as a captain in a company that formed part of the regiment of the moderate royalist, Edward Seymour, Governor of Dartmouth, where he was captured in January 1646; DRO, MFC 46/8; MF2; H. Peters, *Mr Peters Message Delivered in Both Houses ... With the Narration of the Taking of Dartmouth* (London, 1646), 8.

[57] NLI, MS 6249, 17; Welply, 'More Notes on Edmund Spenser', 115, 116.

[58] William, Edward and Mary Greatrakes; see Appendix 1.

entailed reclaiming the lost family estates, though how this was to be achieved amid the chaos and uncertainty that characterized life in Munster in the late 1640s must have taxed the young and inexperienced Valentine to the full. Greatrakes' personal sense of shock on returning to his native land is vividly recalled in his autobiography where he summed up the situation as follows:

> [I]t was not as formerly a National Quarrel, Irish against English, and Protestants against Papists, but there were high and strange divisions throughout the kingdom, English against English, and Irish against Irish, and Protestants and Papists joining hands in one Province against the Protestants of another…which differences to me seemed so unnatural, that I resolved not to intermeddle therein, till the mist of confusion was over.[59]

In the brief outline that follows, it is not possible to do justice to the complexity of the political and religious situation prevailing in Ireland in the 1640s during Greatrakes' absence. A brief synopsis is, however, essential if we are to make sense of Greatrakes' reaction to his homecoming and his subsequent role in Munster politics at this crucial juncture in his life. Following the outbreak of the rebellion in 1641, the Catholic insurgents had rapidly established an alternative government in Ireland under the leadership of the Catholic bishops based at Kilkenny whose main demand was the restoration of land to the native population. Throughout much of Munster, including the lower Blackwater valley, these claims had already been put into effect by the *de facto* seizure of estates, accompanied, according to dispossessed Protestants like William Greatrakes the younger, by ritual acts of barbarism and slaughter. Not surprisingly, tales of putative atrocities were assiduously collected by Irish Protestants and subsequently relayed, via various channels (including lurid and crudely illustrated pamphlets), to audiences in England and beyond. Despite the undoubted sympathy of British Protestants at this time, little help was forthcoming. The outbreak of the Civil War in England in 1642, which itself had been partly ignited by events across the Irish Sea, effectively isolated Ireland from the rest of the British Isles for much of the 1640s.

Between 1642 and Greatrakes' return to Ireland sometime between 1647 and 1648, the political situation throughout the country, including Munster, can best be described as an uneasy and volatile stalemate. Under the leadership of the royalist James Butler, Duke of Ormond (1610–1688), the English government in Dublin pursued a policy of peaceful coexistence, anxiously concluding truces with the rebels against whom it was largely powerless to act. However, given the progress of the Civil War in England, this policy, and the authority of Ormond himself, was increasingly subject to opposition from the 'hotter' Protestant settlers in Munster and elsewhere whose growing alienation stemmed from their material losses as well as a growing sympathy for the Puritan and parliamentarian cause in England. Such divisions within the ranks of the Protestant establishment in Ireland undoubtedly played into the hands of the Catholic Confederation,

---

[59] Greatrakes, *Brief Account*, 17.

though it too was showing signs of internal disagreement, particularly in regard to the level of support it was willing to provide for the beleaguered Charles I. The end of the Civil War in England in 1646 brought no immediate relief to either side, as both watched anxiously to see how the peace negotiations on the mainland, particularly those surrounding the fate of the king, would ultimately impinge upon the future of Ireland. This was the political context, then, in which Greatrakes found himself embroiled on his return to Ireland and through which he would need to manoeuvre with extreme care if he was to succeed in reclaiming the family estates at Affane.

While it is impossible to ascertain with any certainty the precise nature of Greatrakes' response to the events outlined above, one thing is clear: he was not, as he strongly intimated in his later, published account, an innocent bystander in the political chicanery that characterized Munster politics at this time.[60] According to Greatrakes' version of events, he became so disillusioned by the state of his homeland on his return in the late 1640s that he opted to spend a year walled up in the garrison town of Cappoquin where, wearying of the world, he lived the contemplative life of a hermit. Only when relief finally materialized in the shape of the parliamentary forces under the command of Colonel Robert Phaire did Greatrakes, according to this later account, throw in his lot with the invading Cromwellians, thereafter assisting in the pacification of Munster under the command of Roger Boyle, Lord Broghill, son of the first Earl of Cork (see Fig. 5). This 'official' version of events does not, however, tally with evidence gleaned from other sources, most notably the papers of the Duke of Ormond. Here it is apparent that as late as September 1649 (i.e. just a few months before the successful Cromwellian subjugation of Munster) Greatrakes' faith in, and loyalty to, the royalist cause in the shape of Ormond was sufficiently strong for him to petition the Duke for the return of the family lands at Affane. The petition itself refers to the death of his father some time in the 1640s, and to his own brief possession of Affane during the time of 'the Cessacion between the right honourable the Lord Barron of Inchiquin, and the Irish Roman Catholiques'.[61] This seems unlikely, however, unless Greatrakes did not depart for Devon until after the death of his

---

[60] The complex political and military events in Munster during these years, particularly as viewed from the perspective of Greatrakes' future mentor, Roger Boyle, Lord Broghill, are fully discussed in Patrick Little, *Lord Broghill and the Cromwellian Union with Ireland and Scotland* (Woodbridge, 2004), 33–55. Greatrakes' confusion and uncertainty as to what course of action he should take, politically, in these years was mirrored by that of Broghill, who spent much of 1648 and early 1649 brooding in Somerset considering his options. These included support for the royalist cause; ibid. 51–3.

[61] Bodl., Carte MS 156, fos 15–16. Greatrakes must have arrived back in Ireland some time after 2 May 1647, when the garrison town of Cappoquin was recaptured from the rebels by the royalist Inchiquin. A contemporary account describes the town as 'an excellent Garrison both in respect of securing our own Quarters, and annoying the Rebels, for which it is most commodiously seated, having a strong Castle to countenance the Towne and Out-works, and a bridge also very well fortified with a defensible work at the further end from the Towne'; B. M., *A Letter from a Person of Quality in the Parliaments Army, in Munster, in Ireland, to an Honourable Member of the House of Commons* (London, 1647), unpaginated. Inchiquin himself deserted to the king in April 1648, Greatrakes presumably remaining loyal to his commander while holed up at Cappoquin.

Fig. 5. Portrait of Roger Boyle, Earl of Orrery. Engraving after portrait, *c.*1660.

The Bridgeman Art Library. Boyle, both before and after the Restoration, played a critical role in Greatrakes' life and career, securing his official pardon in 1661.

father in February 1643. Whatever the case, Affane soon fell into the hands of one Colonel Charles Hennessey, of whom, unfortunately, little is known.

In all probability, Hennessey was the same person as the Captain Henesy or Henesie referred to in the papers of the first Earl of Cork, who in January 1642 was commended by William St Leger, Lord President of Munster, for his 'good service' following the outbreak of the Rebellion.[62] Within a few months, however, Hennessey had changed sides. By the summer of 1642, he was commanding three regiments of rebel forces in the service of Lord Muskerry, Lord Ikeryn, and one McDonnagh. Two years later, in August 1644, Inchiquin, Broghill, and others reported to the Lord Lieutenant, Ormond, details of a conversation with one Captain Hennessey during the course of peace negotiations with the rebels in Munster. According to Broghill, he had intimated to Hennessey that peace might be possible if Poynings' Law was repealed and they, the rebels, 'would then be content to stand in the condicion wherein they were before the warres'. To which Hennessey is alleged to have replied that 'there was never an Irish gentleman in the kingdome, but

[62] CH, Lismore Papers, vol. 22, no. 122. Earlier, in August 1639, the Earl referred to the arrival in Munster of one Captain Henesie, with several other local dignitaries, from Scotland, following the cessation of hostilities in the Bishops' Wars; Grosart, v, 103.

would spend the last dropp of his blood, before they would sitt downe with satisfaction, in those particulars only'. Broghill concluded that 'it is evident to the world, that they expect seek and strive for, with all possible vehemency, and earnestness, those condicions'.[63] In all likelihood, Hennessey had come into possession of Affane some time in or after 1642, when many of the Protestants in the area, William Greatrakes included, had retreated to the safety of the nearby garrison town of Cappoquin. Following the latter's death in February 1643, Hennessey's claim to the estate was probably uncontested, a legacy of the attempt by the Duke of Ormond to preserve an uneasy peace in Munster between the Catholic insurgents and the weak and uneasy alliance of Protestant forces under the command of Inchiquin.

By September 1649, when Greatrakes petitioned Ormond, the latter's authority in Ireland, particularly in Munster, was on the wane, with many of his erstwhile allies threatening to desert to the invading Cromwellians. Cromwell's forces, led by the commander-in-chief himself, were at this time encamped in south-east Ireland, leaving men like Greatrakes with a difficult, and potentially critical, choice of allegiance. In the event, he chose to side with the usurper, Cromwell, but whether this choice was motivated by ideological commitment to the new regime in England, or political pragmatism, is a moot point. As we have seen, there was certainly little in Greatrakes' background, or that of his family, to suggest that he was by nature or upbringing inclined to support those who had opposed and overthrown the monarchy. Moreover, his appeal to the authority of Ormond as late as September 1649 also suggests that he harboured few, if any, reservations about the authority of the crown and its representatives in Ireland despite the recent execution of Charles I. Nonetheless, when he finally opted to throw in his lot with the Cromwellians, he did so with some gusto. According to depositions taken in 1655, Greatrakes played a leading role in the Cromwellian capture of the important garrison of Cappoquin on, or about, 6 November 1649. Not only was he implicated as one of the ringleaders in the plot to overthrow the royalist commander of the garrison, Governor Whitby, but also, according to several eyewitnesses, he played a key role in the formulation and execution of the planned seizure of the town which was achieved with a minimum of bloodshed.[64]

[63] CH, Lismore Papers, vol. 23, no. 45; J. Hogan (ed.), *Letters and Papers Relating to the Irish Rebellion between 1642 and 1646* (Dublin, 1936), 60; BL, Add. MS 25,287, fo. 11r. Hennessey was acting at these talks as one of the Catholic commissioners responsible for negotiating the continuation of the Cessation, a role he continued to perform in early 1645; *HMC Manuscripts of the Earl of Egmont* (London, 1905), i, 245. Many of the details of Hennessey's career highlighted here, including the claim that he was granted protection and immunity by Ormond, are confirmed in one of the articles exhibited against Inchiquin by Broghill in 1647; [R. Gething], *Articles Exhibited to the Honourable House of Commons Assembled in Parliament, Against the Lord Inchiquine Lord President of Munster ... Together with a Full and Cleare Answer* (London, 1647), 1–2, 8.

[64] Bodl., Carte MS 66, fos 249r–255r. One of the three men responsible for taking these depositions, John Denison, later converted to Muggletonianism and became a fervent supporter of Greatrakes' cures in Dublin; see pp. 158, 188.

In the light of Greatrakes' subsequent career and the suggestion that his mission to heal the king's evil and other diseases in the 1660s may have been motivated by his opposition to the restoration of the Stuarts, the evidence of Greatrakes' actions at Cappoquin in 1649, carefully excised from his 'official' autobiography, would appear, on the surface at least, to offer concrete evidence of his commitment to the new regime. But this view of Greatrakes, as I have tried to show, does not fully convince. In the first place, it is clear from the series of depositions that were taken in February 1655 that this was an exercise designed to clarify the loyalty of middle-ranking officers in the Cromwellian army to the Irish regime of the Protector. The inference behind such a review is that there may have been question marks in some minds as to the full extent of the loyalty of men like Greatrakes to Cromwellian rule in Ireland.[65] In the second, there is the evidence of Greatrakes' education and upbringing in Devon, particularly his tuition at the hands of the émigré minister Getsius, and the close ties of kinship with the royalist Tyntes, all of which contradicts the notion that Greatrakes was reared in an atmosphere unsympathetic or hostile to the government of Charles I and the Anglican Church. And in the third, and perhaps most important of all, one needs to acknowledge the strong possibility that for many land-owning Irish Protestants in late 1649, support for Cromwell represented a far sounder investment than continuing loyalty to the dwindling authority of old royalists like Ormond, particularly if one's prime concern was the repossession and future security of property and estates which had fallen into the hands of Catholic rebels.

On balance then it seems more likely that Greatrakes' momentous decision in late 1649 to throw in his lot with the invader, Cromwell, was motivated not so much by ideological enthusiasm for the commander-in-chief of the new English government, but rather, as for so many of his fellow co-religionists and countrymen, that it was prompted by fear and pragmatism. In late 1649, with the authority of Ormond waning in Munster, and that of Cromwell advancing by the hour, Greatrakes' material interests, particularly retrieval of the patrimonial lands at Affane, were more likely to be secured and better served by support for the Cromwellians. If Greatrakes had harboured strong parliamentary or republican sympathies, he was hardly likely to have petitioned the royalist Ormond for the return of Norris Land just one month before plotting the seizure of Cappoquin. These were not the actions of an ideologue. Rather, they represent the actions of a practical and penurious young man, an opportunist, whose prime motivation was the restoration of the honour, dignity, and wealth of his family.

It need not be inferred from this, however, that Greatrakes was entirely devoid of all principles or ideological fervour. Although he may have felt no particular attachment to the aims and principles of Cromwellian republicanism, Greatrakes, in common with so many of his fellow countrymen of similar social and religious

---

[65] The order to examine witnesses and collect evidence in the rendition of the various Munster garrisons so that arrears might be paid to loyal officers like Greatrakes can be found in King's Inns Library, Dublin, Prendergast Papers, vol. i, 434.

background, did fear the revival and encroachment of militant native Catholicism which was a constant source of anxiety throughout the seventeenth century. Here, in anti-Catholicism, was a unifying principle around which Irish Protestants of very different religious and political hues might coalesce, made all the more real in Greatrakes' case by the recent experiences of his own father. Consequently, if the interests and prejudices of settler families like the Greatrakes' were best served by supporting Cromwell in 1649, then at least the choice might be rationalized in such a way that appeared to remain consistent with the wider goals of the English in Ireland. In order to underline the appeal of this kind of thinking, one need look no further than the career of Roger Boyle, Lord Broghill (1621–1679), second son of the first Earl of Cork, who was destined to play a pivotal role in the pacification and government of Munster in the early 1650s (Fig. 5). Throughout the 1640s Broghill had consistently supported Parliament in the belief that military and financial support in the campaign against the forces of the Irish Confederates was more likely to come from this source. He briefly toyed with supporting the royal party in 1648–9, but any qualms that Broghill might have harboured with regard to the new republican regime in England were rapidly dispelled by his much greater fear of resurgent Catholicism in his native Ireland. Seventeenth-century Ireland, in contrast to England, was governed by a different set of principles in which the interests of a Protestant minority had to be protected at all costs from the latent hostility and opposition of the Catholic majority. What this meant in practice was that the material interests of powerful families like the Boyles, and their clients such as the Greatrakes, were always best served by supporting the government in England, regardless of its specific form or ideological stance, because to do otherwise was to jeopardize their own shaky claims to dominion in an island where they constituted a small and often beleaguered minority of the population. Like Broghill, Greatrakes opted to pledge allegiance to Cromwell in 1649 as the best guarantor of the Protestant ascendancy in Ireland, a pragmatic decision that may also have owed a debt to familial ties and ancient loyalties.[66]

To what extent Broghill's defection to Cromwell in 1649 helped to influence Greatrakes' own decision to abandon Inchiquin and Ormond is impossible to determine with any confidence. What remains beyond doubt, however, is the important role played by the Boyle family in Munster after 1649 which almost certainly encouraged young officers like Greatrakes to fall under the spell of Broghill in the 1650s. For approximately six years, from 1650 to 1656, Greatrakes served as lieutenant in Broghill's regiment of horse, and their acquaintance continued into the 1660s when the former was frequently a visitor to Broghill (now Earl of Orrery) at his new house at Charleville in county Cork. Moreover, Broghill's patronage paid real dividends when in April 1661 he secured a royal pardon for Greatrakes and

---

[66] The chief source here is Little's recent account of Broghill (note 60 above) in which he argues persuasively for a view of the Irish aristocrat as a consistent and principled advocate of the interest of the New English in Ireland that was to a large part based on a strident anti-Catholicism and Calvinist belief in providence. Broghill's debt to providentialist ways of thinking, and that of the rest of his family, is discussed more fully in Chapter 5 below.

many of his former army colleagues and associates.[67] There can be little doubt that one of the key factors in Greatrakes' successful rehabilitation at the Restoration of Charles II was the continuing support of Broghill (Orrery) whose influence among ex-Cromwellians in Munster was, as we shall see, vital to a regime that was faced with the constant fear of further uprisings and rebellions among both disaffected Protestants and Catholics in the province.

As for Greatrakes' active service on behalf of the Cromwellian regime in Ireland in the 1650s, details are scant, but it is nonetheless possible both in the brief sketch he provided in 1666 and from other sources to gain some idea of the extent of Greatrakes' commitment to the new government. In 1656, following the disbandment of the army in Ireland, Greatrakes finally returned to civilian life and, in his own words, resumed residence at Affane, 'the habitation of my ancestors, where I have continued ever since'.[68] In the same year, he was made Clerk of the Peace for county Cork and served in his home county, Waterford, as a Justice of the Peace. In addition, he also acquired the important office of registrar for the transplantation of Irish Catholics to Connaught, an ambitious and radical plan on the part of the Cromwellian regime in Ireland to resolve the land question once and for all by banishing the majority of the native Catholic population to the remote and barren lands of the west coast. In their place, Protestant settlers from England were encouraged to emigrate to Ireland, a policy that was particularly attractive to the Government in London since it provided a means by which all those who had bought debentures in Irish land in the 1640s to finance the war against the Catholic rebels might secure compensation. Moreover, the adoption of this programme of land annexation and redistribution also provided the Government with a cheap and easy solution to another pressing financial problem; namely, the payment of arrears to those soldiers who had served in Ireland since 1649. During the 1650s, many of these men (especially the officer class), who had followed Cromwell across the Irish Sea to 'pacify' Ireland, now decided to accept land in lieu of arrears. The result was the creation of another tier of Protestant settlement in Ireland much of which, not surprisingly, was extremely hostile to the lingering claims of the dispossessed Catholic majority.

Given Greatrakes' office as one of the registrars for the transplantation of recalcitrant Irish Catholics, we should not be surprised to learn that he was to take a keen interest and play an active role in the purchase and re-sale of these land holdings. As we shall see when I come to discuss his role as a property speculator in the 1650s, Greatrakes' financial interests were closely tied to those of the many soldiers who decided to remain in Ireland, as well as private and corporate investors in England who had taken advantage of the booming market in Irish land. Before we look at these transactions in detail, however, and discuss their potential significance for our understanding of Greatrakes the miracle healer, we ought briefly to ponder his own comments on this critical phase in his life and career. Not surpris-

---

[67] *CSP Ireland, 1660–1662*, 316–19.
[68] Greatrakes, *Brief Account*, 19.

ingly, perhaps, he went out of his way in 1666 to stress his own honesty and personal integrity in the day-to-day administration of the office of registrar. No bribes or rewards ever crossed his desk, he affirmed, despite the fact that he 'had many and great ones offered to me'. What seems odd here, however (and at first sight, not a little unlikely), is Greatrakes' persistent claim to have shown unwavering moderation in the pursuit of his official duties, particularly with respect to those who held religious beliefs in conflict with his own. Given the eirenic message implicit in his healing mission of the early 1660s (see chapters 3 and 4), the expression of such sentiments is not altogether surprising. Less expected, however, is his attitude to Catholics to whom we might reasonably have expected him to show little sympathy and few favours. As a justice of the peace, he claimed in 1666 to have demonstrated extraordinary sympathy for the plight of the Catholic majority at a time when hostility to them must have been intense and often violent. Conversion, rather than repression, typified his approach, and 'though there were Orders from the Power that then was (to all Justices of the Peace for Transplanting all Papists that would not go to Church) I never molested any one that was known, or esteemed to be innocent, but suffered them to continue in the English quarters, and that without prejudice'.[69]

Is it possible to square this image of Greatrakes the conciliator with that of a man who was given responsibility for overseeing the forced removal of Catholics to Connaught in the mid 1650s? And if not, why, we might ask, ten years later did he go to such lengths to proclaim his personal innocence in this act of 'ethnic cleansing' instigated by the Cromwellian authorities in Dublin and London? The answer, I believe, lies partly in another facet of Greatrakes' life which has hitherto received little attention from historians, namely his role as a land speculator in the 1650s. Ideally placed to exploit the buoyant market in land made possible by the Cromwellian conquest of Ireland, Greatrakes missed few opportunities to profit from the sale and purchase of expropriated lands. From various sources it is clear that he retained some of the land which he purchased in this period, leasing to tenants (often former soldiers) in the time-honoured fashion. The vast majority of his transactions, however, were concerned with the purchase and rapid resale of estates in the form of lots which were allocated to debenture holders in England in the mid-1650s. With large sums of money tied up in this enterprise, the collapse of the Republic and Restoration of the monarchy, which sought to compensate loyal Catholics and royalists who had lost their estates in the 1650s, threatened financial ruin to men like Greatrakes. The latter's claim to have shown moderation to Catholics in 1666 should therefore be seen as part of a wider strategy on his part designed to protect his investments in land and to stave off financial insolvency. As we shall see, it had little to do with any profound commitment on Greatrakes' part to protecting the material, religious, and political interests of his Catholic neighbours.

---

[69] Ibid. 19–20, 21.

This process of land redistribution, which had been initiated by Parliament in the early 1640s and was only brought to fruition after 1656, is a complex affair that has been fully explained and analysed elsewhere.[70] Given its importance to our understanding of Greatrakes, we ought to consider in a little more detail the historical background to this process. During the early 1640s, the opportunity to acquire cheap entitlements to Irish land, while at the same time striking a blow for militant Protestantism, was hugely appealing to a broad spectrum of the English public. The prospect of profiteering from appropriated Irish Catholic lands was too good to be missed, and thousands, including individual small-scale investors as well as corporate bodies (guilds, borough corporations, etc.), availed themselves of the opportunity. Many, no doubt, expected a rapid return on their investments, though such hopes were soon quashed by the protracted nature of the military and political struggle in England. It was not until the final defeat of Irish Catholicism in the early 1650s that the first opportunities arose to cash in parliamentary debentures, the initial lots for Irish land being drawn in 1656. The allocation of lots provoked the creation of a vibrant market in the sale, repurchase, and subletting of land. Some, not surprisingly, decided to cash in their entitlements to remote and unknown Irish holdings, while numerous other claimants became enmeshed in a series of complex, legal suits surrounding the ownership of the original debentures (by 1656 many of the original purchasers had died, or had sold their debentures to others).

In Ireland itself, the distribution of lots was further complicated by the need for the Government to set aside newly acquired land in order to pay off disbanded soldiers. The realization that many of these lots were either worthless or at best barren and in need of much improvement almost certainly encouraged many rank-and-file soldiers to sell their interests and return to England. The major beneficiaries in this process were the army officers, many of whom were able to amass large, consolidated estates in Ireland at relatively low cost.[71] The process of land redistribution set in chain by the Cromwellian Government in England thus constituted a major enterprise involving thousands of men and women on both sides of the Irish Sea that required sophisticated administrative and governmental support on a scale hitherto unseen in Ireland. Among other things, it necessitated a major undertaking to conduct a thorough survey of Ireland (subsequently known as the Down Survey), using up-to-date methods and techniques and the labour of large numbers of men, many of whom had previously served in other capacities in the Cromwellian army. But above all, the land settlement of the 1650s combined what

---

[70] The seminal study on this subject remains K. S. Bottigheimer, *English Money and Irish Land: The Adventurers in the Cromwellian Settlement of Ireland* (Oxford, 1971).

[71] According to Bottigheimer, only a quarter of the 30,000 soldiers who fought in Ireland settled there in the 1650s. Even fewer adventurers took up their lots; only 500 had been confirmed in their estates by the mid 1660s. As a result, adventurers' and soldiers' claims to Irish land became 'a commodity in which to speculate, rather than the hoped-for mechanism to people the waste land'; K. S. Bottigheimer, 'Kingdom and Colony: Ireland in the Westward Enterprise 1536–1660', in K. R. Andrews, N. P. Canny, and P. E. H. Hair (eds), *The Westward Enterprise: English Activities in Ireland, the Atlantic, and America 1480–1650* (Liverpool, 1978), 61–2.

on the surface looked like little more than unfettered greed with a political imperative that attracted widespread support in England and the Protestant community
in Ireland, involving men who might otherwise have differed in their religious and
political outlooks. Ireland was now a land of economic opportunity, a fact clearly
recognized, among others, by a number of those reform-minded correspondents
and associates of Samuel Hartlib (*c*.1600–1662) during the 1650s. Typically, it was
envisaged as a place in which it was possible for Protestant adventurers to pursue
their material interests while at the same time reassuring themselves that their actions formed part of a larger, divine plan, in which the elimination of Irish Catholicism was seen as a necessary prelude to the final millennium.[72]

We are now in a much better position to understand how someone in Greatrakes' position was able to welcome the events of the 1650s and to pledge allegiance to the Cromwellian regime in Ireland in a way that was fully consistent with
his own political, religious, and social background. It also enables us to make sense
of what, in an English context, was far more problematic; namely, his ability to
associate with a broad range of men whose attitudes and beliefs often lay at oppo-
site ends of the religious and political spectrum. This is particularly evident in the
case of Greatrakes' business partners. In 1656, for example, he purchased, in partnership with Colonel Jerome (or Hierom) Sankey (1621–1686) and Sir Ames Meredith (1617–1669), the entire holdings of the corporation of Exeter in county
Tipperary. It is difficult to imagine two men more distant in terms of their religious
and political outlooks. Sankey was one of the most prominent figures in the
Cromwellian occupation and government of southern Ireland. He frequently used
his position of authority to shelter religious radicals, and by the Restoration was
firmly established as one of the leading lights in the thriving Baptist movement in
Ireland.[73] Meredith, on the other hand, possessed impeccable royalist credentials
having fought on the side of the King in Devon in the first Civil War. He appears
to have held no office under the governments of the Interregnum, but to have
concentrated instead on protecting and consolidating his English estates in Devon
and Cheshire as well as extending his investments in Ireland in collaboration with
Greatrakes.

Though subsequent references to Sankey in Greatrakes' life are rare, the business
relationship with Meredith clearly blossomed into something far deeper and more
personal. By the 1660s, Meredith was a constant companion of Greatrakes, ac-
companying him on his many healing missions, including that to England in

---

[72] For an overview of the aims and achievements of the Hartlib circle in Ireland, see T. C. Barnard,
Cromwellian Ireland: English Government and Reform in Ireland 1649–1660 (Oxford, 1975), 216–44;
T. C. Barnard, 'The Hartlib Circle and the Cult and Culture of Improvement in Ireland', in M. Green-
grass, M. Leslie, and T. Railor (eds), *Samuel Hartlib and Universal Reformation: Studies in Intellectual
Communication* (Cambridge, 1994), 281–97. Greatrakes' own connections with the English and Irish
members of the Hartlib circle are discussed more fully in Chapter 4 below.

[73] For Sankey, see especially W. T. Whitley, 'Colonel Jerome Sankey, M.P., Ph.D.', *The Baptist
Quarterly*, 4 (1928–9), 268–70; J. E. Auden, 'Sir Jerome Zankey (or Sankey) of Balderton Hall, co.
Salop, and of Coolmore, co. Tipperary', *Transactions of the Shropshire Archaeological Society*, 50 (1940),
171–8; A. J. Shirren, ' "Colonel Zanchy" and Charles Fleetwood', *Notes and Queries*, 198 (1953),
431–5, 474–7, 519–24.

1666, when, in typical seventeenth-century fashion, he shared his bed with the charismatic healer while travelling the country. With his unblemished royalist and Anglican credentials (his sister, Gertrude, was married to a future bishop, George Hall), Meredith played an important role in facilitating a smooth reception for Greatrakes in England in 1666 (see p. 73). He may also have helped to introduce Greatrakes to his first wife, Ruth, the daughter of a Cornish royalist, Sir William Godolphin (1605–1663).[74] Above all, Meredith, like Greatrakes, seems to have shared his young friend's ability to work and cooperate with men of different religious and political backgrounds. As a moderate and conciliatory royalist in the Civil War, he arranged the marriage of his ward, Sir William Courtenay, to a daughter of the Parliamentarian General, Sir William Waller, in 1645.[75] Later, in the 1660s, he was frequently to be found, with Greatrakes, in the company of Quakers like William Penn and the regicide, Robert Phaire, and retained life-long friendships with other important Cromwellians such as his Cheshire neighbour, Colonel Robert Venables (d. 1687), a leading figure in the government of Ireland in the 1650s.[76] Meredith, in other words, epitomised that much maligned species of mid-seventeenth-century English gentleman, who preferred pragmatic moderation to ideological intransigence and who, behind the scenes, laboured to effect a more lasting political solution to the nation's divisions based on economic necessity and common material concerns. In the process, he shared much in common with his young protégé, Valentine Greatrakes, who was similarly engaged in promoting Protestant unity and political harmony via commercial incentives rather than the sword.

Greatrakes' willingness and ability to transcend conventional partisan politics, like that of his friend and business partner, Sir Ames Meredith, enabled him to broker deals with a wide range of men, in military, civilian and mercantile circles. In an account book owned by Greatrakes, which survives for the crucial decade of

[74] Meredith's maternal grandmother, Judith, had married John Godolphin, the grandfather of Ruth, Greatrakes' first wife; F. W. Marsh, *The Godolphins* (1930), 19. During the sixteenth century, the Merediths (or Amerediths) were established at Exeter. Valentine Greatrakes and Ames Meredith may have exploited these connections in their purchase of the corporation's Irish lands in 1656. For the early origins of the Amerediths, see W. T. MacCaffrey, *Exeter, 1540–1640: The Growth of an English County Town* (Cambridge, MA, and London, 1975), 259–60. Ames's father, Edward, would appear to have been a typical representative of that festive culture despised by the puritans. His providential death at the hands of a vengeful God for sabbath-breaking and maypole dancing in 1634 formed part of a collection of similar acts of divine judgement published by the puritan martyr Henry Burton; H. Burton, *A Divine Tragedie Lately Acted, or A Collection of Sundry Memorable Examples of Gods Judgements upon Sabbath-Breakers* ([London], 1636), 26–7.

[75] DRO, PR 1508 M Devon/V 29, 10. Ames Meredith served in south Devon during the first Civil War under another royalist moderate, Sir Edward Seymour; I. Palfrey, 'The Royalist War Effort Revisited: Edward Seymour and the Royalist Garrison at Dartmouth, 1643–44', *TDA*, 123 (1991), 47, 48, 54; DRO, 1392 M/L 1644/15, 36. It is highly probable that Meredith first made Greatrakes' acquaintance in the 1640s, when both frequented royalist circles in the South Hams.

[76] I. Grubb (ed.), *My Irish Journal 1669–1670, by William Penn* (London, 1952), 26; *CSP Ireland, 1666–1669*, 700. Venables and his wife received small bequests in Meredith's will, which was also witnessed by Robert Phaire; TNA, PROB 11/336, fos 202v–203v.

the 1660s,[77] the importance of old army connections is confirmed by the appearance of the names of former officers and army colleagues with whom Greatrakes was engaged in financial and land transactions. Among those mentioned are the Quaker sympathizer, friend, and future Muggletonian, Colonel Robert Phaire, Major Robert Venables, and a host of lesser figures. These accounts also make it clear that Greatrakes had established close links in the 1650s with the London business community. During this period, for example, he employed an agent in London called King,[78] who may have assisted Greatrakes' consortium in the purchase of an interest in various estates in county Tipperary owned by John Kendrick (d. 1661), a noted puritan and republican sympathizer who served as Lord Mayor of London in 1652. Following his death in 1661, Greatrakes continued to act for Kendrick's heirs and, as we shall see, fought tirelessly to protect their Irish inheritance from the attempt by its original Catholic owners to seek repossession under the Act of Settlement.[79]

Another important business associate of Greatrakes in the 1650s was his brother-in-law, John Nettles (d. 1680), who seems to have acted as an agent in numerous transactions involving London-based investors in Irish land. Nettles' credentials for the role were impeccable. Descended from a Herefordshire family, Nettles had settled in Ireland in about 1630, and was granted Toureen Castle, a few miles south of Affane, in 1641 on the forfeiture of Lord Roche.[80] He rapidly rose to economic and political prominence in nearby Youghal, acting as bailiff in 1654 and mayor in 1657.[81] At the same time and in partnership with his brother-in-law,

[77] BL, Add. MS 25,692. Edited extracts from this manuscript were published by James Buckley in 1908; see Buckley, 'Selections from a General Account Book of Valentine Greatrakes, AD 1663–1679', *Journal of the Waterford and South-East Ireland Archaeological Society*, 11 (1908), 211–24.

[78] CH, Lismore MS 29, 2 November 1656. In all probability, Greatrakes' agent was John King, later Lord Kingston (*c.*1620–1676), a noted speculator in Irish land, who seems to have been acquainted with several prominent members of the Hartlib circle in Ireland in 1652. In that year, Hartlib records meeting 'one King of the North of Ireland', who thanked him for publishing the natural history of Ireland. Hartlib added that King possessed a particular interest in husbandry, and was well acquainted, among others, with William Petty and Benjamin Worsley, two noted Hartlibians who were involved in surveying Ireland in the 1650s in preparation for the Protestant resettlement of the island; see C. Webster, *The Great Instauration: Science, Medicine and Reform, 1626–1660* (London, 1975), 445; SUL, HP, 28/2/43A-B; Bottigheimer, *English Money and Irish Land*, 185, 205.

[79] A grocer, of Broad Street, London, Kendrick invested £700 in the Irish adventure in 1642, and later drew 1,555 acres in county Tipperary. As a prominent figure in the government of Interregnum London, he played a central role on a number of municipal and parliamentary committees set up to oversee the Irish adventure and to relieve poor and dispossessed Protestants. He left two sons, John and Thomas, who feature prominently in Greatrakes' account book. Greatrakes would appear to have been acting as an agent on the sons' behalf for these lands, and to have aggressively pursued their (and his own) interests in Tipperary over the claims of the original owners, the Catholic Prendergasts. The ownership of the Kendrick lands in Tipperary was finally confirmed by the Court of Claims in January 1668; A. B. Beaven (ed.), *The Aldermen of the City of London*, 2 vols (London, 1908–13), i, 75, 150; *CSP Adventurers, 1642–1659*, 104; R. Dunlop (ed.), *Ireland under the Commonwealth. Being a Selection of Documents Relating to the Government of Ireland from 1651 to 1659*, 2 vols (Manchester, 1913), i, 44n; K. Lindley, 'Irish Adventurers and Godly Militants in the 1640s', *Irish Historical Studies*, 29 (1994), 6, 10; BL, Add. MS 25,692, fos 4r, 5r and *passim*; JRL, Irish MS 125, fo. 39v.

[80] Nettles was married to Valentine's sister, Mary Greatrakes (d.1684). For background information on the origins of Nettles' family, see Hayman, 'Notes on the Family of Greatrakes', 85.

[81] Caulfield, *Council Book of Youghal*, 289, 301.

he invested heavily in the purchase of adventurers' estates and leases, including those belonging to a group of London businessmen and small merchants headed by Obadiah Weekes and Samuel Enderby.[82] Weekes, like John Kendrick, was a loyal Cromwellian. A tanner by trade, he swiftly ascended through the ranks of the corporation of Kingston-upon-Thames in Surrey and played a pivotal role in the Cromwellian purge of the borough in 1654. He was also an active supporter of the Puritan ministry, which he continued to uphold after 1660 and the return of Anglicanism.[83]

From the evidence of these and other transactions, it is evident that Greatrakes was a man who moved with relative ease across the sectarian and political divides of his day. Well acquainted with the needs and demands of the soldiery who settled in Ireland in the 1650s and alongside whom he had fought in the first half of that decade, he also belonged to a network of important connections that enabled him to accumulate large personal holdings of land, often in partnership with prominent London merchants and investors. These in turn were usually sublet to native Protestants or newcomers, many of whom saw Cromwellian Ireland in biblical terms as another Canaan, or land of milk and honey. It would be easy to conclude on the basis of this evidence that Greatrakes was little more than an opportunist, a man on the make, who carefully sought to profit from his position as a well-connected Anglo-Irish middleman in the redistribution of Irish land. To do so, however, is to risk an over-simplistic reading of the evidence. In particular, we need to remember that from Greatrakes' perspective, as well as that of his class, the future of Ireland was clearly best served by strong and dynamic government from the centre, particularly where this allowed Protestant communities to flourish and expand. As a result, and in line with many of his fellow co-religionists and countrymen, he experienced few qualms in supporting the government of the day, regardless of its specific religious and political orientation. Though such 'trimming' also occurred in post-Civil War England, the situation in Ireland was very different. Here, cooperation across religious and political boundaries that frequently inhibited social and economic collaboration in England was the rule, not the exception, and Greatrakes set out to exploit every opportunity to promote his own material interests regardless of the religious or political viewpoints of those Protestants with whom he did business.

---

[82] For Nettles' role in overseeing the legal transfer and sale of adventurers' lots in 1652, see *CSP Ireland, 1647–60*, 387. In 1661, Greatrakes and Nettles were described as tenants to Weekes, Enderby and Robert Child for 613 acres in the parish of Killohally in county Waterford. Greatrakes was also tenant to Weekes for smaller lots in several other parishes in the county; BL, Add. MS 4765, fo. 13r. It was presumably these lands that Lady Ranelagh, sister of Robert and Roger Boyle, was seeking to purchase, probably at the instigation of her elder brother, Richard, the second Earl of Cork, in 1658 when she wrote to her friend Samuel Hartlib asking him to act as an intermediary; see CH, Lismore Papers, vol. 31, nos 2, 11, 47.

[83] *Scandal on the Corporation: Royalists and Puritans in Mid-Seventeenth-Century Kingston, from the Kingston Borough Archives* (Kingston, 1982), xii-xiii. In his will of 1681, Weekes made several bequests to local nonconformist preachers who had been ejected at the Restoration; TNA, PROB 11/370, fos 187r–v.

Unlike many political pragmatists, however, Greatrakes did not subsequently abandon former acquaintances when the winds of political fortune shifted direction after 1660. As we shall see, one of the most notable features of Greatrakes' later life was the fact that he remained faithful to many of those who had befriended and supported him in the 1650s, even when it would have been politically expedient to have shunned and disowned such company. This is evident, for example, in the close bonds of friendship that Greatrakes forged with the radical Governor of Cork, Colonel Robert Phaire (d. 1682), in the early 1650s. After 1660, Phaire was a dangerous man to know. Not only had he played a prominent part in the execution of Charles I in 1649, but his later adoption of religious extremism (he was one of the first major converts to Quakerism in Ireland) marked him out as a potential enemy to the restored regime of Charles II. And yet, despite the obvious dangers, Greatrakes' relationship with Phaire remained warm throughout the troubled years of the Restoration, during which time the stroker frequently employed his curative powers on members of the Phaire household. These were not the actions of a cynical opportunist. On the contrary, they reflect what I believe constituted a sincere belief on Greatrakes' part that any settlement of Ireland, and by extension England, should be comprehensive and include men like Phaire who, despite their religious idiosyncrasies, remained at heart loyal and sincere Protestants.[84]

Another important formative element in Greatrakes' character, which helps to provide a more balanced picture of the man, is the fact that he was well equipped to view a wider world beyond the confines of his isolated Munster estates. This simple fact, frequently overlooked by the anglocentricity of historians of early modern Britain, has, I believe, an important bearing on our understanding of Greatrakes, who all too often in the past has been portrayed as a naïve outsider or innocent abroad and thus susceptible to the machinations of those who surrounded him. As we shall see, however, this characterization fails to do justice to the complex reality of life for Anglo-Irish settlers like Greatrakes in this period. He was, for example, a frequent visitor to England in the years after 1666 and, in his business dealings there, proved more than a match for his associates and partners. Moreover, his Anglo-Irish roots, most evident in the close links that he retained with his mother's native county of Devon, helped to underpin Greatrakes' self-confidence in this respect. It must also have made him acutely aware and appreciative of the deep-rooted religious, political, social, and economic links that existed between

---

[84] Phaire, like Greatrakes, came from a family that had suffered much during the rebellion of 1641. An active participant in the Cromwellian conquest of Munster, as well as an agent in the transportation of native Catholics to Connaught, Phaire was subsequently rewarded with large estates in counties Cork and Wexford amounting to almost 6,000 acres; TCD, MS 825, fo. 275; Bodl., Carte MS 44, fo. 474v. He married as his second wife, Elizabeth, the daughter of Sir Thomas Herbert, a leading Cromwellian civil servant in Ireland in the 1650s. Like Greatrakes, he too sought to attract wealthy English investors to Ireland, as for example in his scheme to establish an iron works and English colony at Enniscorthy in Wexford; W. H. Welply, 'Colonel Robert Phaire, "Regicide", His Ancestry, History, and Descendants', *Notes and Queries*, 12 (1923), 123–5, 143–6. For a summary of his later life and career during the Restoration, see the recent article by Toby Barnard in *ODNB*.

southern Ireland and south-west England at this time. It was surely no coincidence that many of the major investors in the Irish debenture scheme of the 1640s came from the English west country and included not only large corporations but also scores of individuals.[85]

We should not therefore be surprised to learn that a number of those who played such an important role in publicizing Greatrakes' cures in the early 1660s shared the stroker's west country roots. Some, such as John Lancaster of Cornworthy, who in 1665 was among the first to subscribe to Greatrakes' cures in print, were close kinsmen. Lancaster's will, written in 1684, provides further evidence for the way in which extended families in this period retained social and economic links across the Irish Sea. Lancaster had probably arrived in Cornworthy at about the same time as Greatrakes and the Tyntes, part of the general diaspora of Munster Protestants in the early 1640s. Although he, unlike his cousins, did not return to Ireland, he nonetheless remained in close contact with kin there, and was probably responsible for encouraging his brother-in-law, Andrew Woodley, to settle in Munster in the late 1650s or early 1660s.[86] Other advocates of Greatrakes' healing touch such as Lionel Beacher moved between southern Ireland and south-west England with apparent ease, the importance of trade networks between the two regions clearly facilitating such movement.[87] Greatrakes himself inherited lands and estates in Devon following the death of his mother in, or around, 1656. In that year, he visited Exeter in order to complete the paperwork on the purchase of the corporations' estates in southern Ireland.[88] Evidence of this nature should alert us to the

---

[85] The point is emphatically made by Stephen Roberts, who, citing the original work of Karl Bottigheimer, notes that 'Devonians were, after Londoners, the most important group of colonists participating in the accelerated plantation of Ireland between 1642 and 1660. Two hundred Devon men contributed £17,500 towards the scheme, and Exeter especially seems to have been a city of small investors willing to take a risk on the subjugation of Ireland'; S. Roberts, 'War and Society in Devon 1642–1646', *TDA*, 127 (1995), 92–3; Bottigheimer, *English Money and Irish Land*, 64–5, 159–60. The deep-rooted connections throughout the early modern period between Munster and south-west England are highlighted in M. MacCarthy-Morrogh, *The Munster Plantation: English Migration to Southern Ireland 1583–1641* (Oxford, 1986).

[86] In Lancaster's will, Woodley, who had been accused of using his royalist connections on behalf of Mary Greatrakes in Devon in the 1640s (see pp. 31–2), was described as a resident of county Cork. In May 1666 he petitioned the Lord Lieutenant, Ormond, in a plaint of debt in relation to lands at Inchy, county Cork; DRO, PR/A 821; Bodl., Carte MS 154, fos 82r–v. Lancaster also made bequests to other Irish cousins including Henry Tent or Tynte of Ballycrennan and Owen Silver. For the well-connected Silver, a kinsman of Greatrakes, see p. 70n.

[87] Beacher's life and subsequent career as a loyal retainer of the Boyle family is discussed in more detail below, pp. 68–70.

[88] There are a few traces of Valentine's mother, Mary Greatrakes, in the parish accounts for Cornworthy between 1650 and 1656, as is evident from the extracts collected by the clerk of the parish in the first half of the nineteenth century, and later published in 1893. Her death some time around 1656 is suggested by a note against her name in the poor book stating that in that year her contribution was 'discontinued'. Unfortunately the full accounts do not appear to have survived; see Rev. S. G. Harris, 'John Tucker, Parish Clerk of Cornworthy and Antiquary', *TDA*, 25 (1893), 475–81. The sale of Exeter's Irish lands and Greatrakes' role in the transaction are calendared in *HMC Records of the City of Exeter* (London, 1916), 329–30. The original documents from the Act Book of the chamber, of which these are a faithful transcript, can be found in DRO, ECA 10, fos 71r, 72v, 78r. The fact that Greatrakes styled himself 'of Cornworthy' in these transactions suggests he had recently come into his inheritance.

problems of viewing men like Greatrakes through the eyes of an older generation of historians who allocate to Ireland a largely peripheral role in the consciousness of seventeenth-century Englishmen. Indeed, one of the problems in analysing a figure such as Greatrakes is the real difficulty inherent in seeking to establish a firm identity or label for men of his background and social status. English, Irish, Anglo-Irish, none of these descriptions seem to do full justice to the rich complexity of the careers of men like Greatrakes and his social superior and mentor, Lord Broghill.[89]

In conclusion, what can we say of the formative years of Valentine Greatrakes? He was clearly a survivor, one who had been forced to learn from an early age the merits of flexibility and the need to adapt to the swiftly changing events of his era. As a young man, he pursued and acquired material interests in both England and Ireland, and seems to have moved easily between the two. He was undoubtedly an opportunist, but he must also have been keenly aware of the need to underpin the safety and security of his assets by supporting those government initiatives which most promised to safeguard the evolving Protestant ascendancy in Ireland. In the circumstances of the 1650s, there was little room in Ireland for ideologically driven partisanship, and although Greatrakes may have favoured monarchical government by upbringing, education, and personal preference, his political instincts dictated that he would loyally follow the various changes of regime foisted on Ireland by Cromwell. During the course of the 1650s, therefore, Greatrakes can usually be found propping up the status quo and cosying up to those in authority, particularly in those instances where his economic interests were at stake. This was amply illustrated in 1652, when his intimacy with the regicide lawyer and recently appointed Chief Justice of Munster, John Cook, led to accusations of jury-rigging in Greatrakes' favour in a case concerning his property rights in Affane (discussed more fully, p. 51) As the tenor of government moderated after 1655 with the appointment in Ireland of Henry Cromwell in place of the more radical administration of Lord Deputy Fleetwood, so too did Greatrakes, a point made clear in his dealings with Richard Boyle, second Earl of Cork, one of the few members of the Boyle family with whom Greatrakes' relationship was cool. Finally, by the late 1650s, with the writing on the wall for the declining republic, Greatrakes astutely sought the protection of his old mentor, Roger Boyle, Lord Broghill, whose patronage would provide Greatrakes and many of his closest associates with immunity from prosecution in the aftermath of the Restoration in 1660. In many respects, however, the greatest challenge for Greatrakes and so many others like him who had prospered on the back of the Cromwellian resettlement of Ireland

---

[89] This issue has recently received much attention among historians of early modern Ireland, as well as a new generation of British scholars eager to investigate the problem of identity and embryonic national consciousness in the British Isles in this period. For the disunity and lack of consensus among Irish Protestants as to their place and role in the wider world, see T. C. Barnard, 'Crises of Identity among Irish Protestants 1641–1685', *Past and Present*, 127 (1990), 39–83. The theme of identity is further explored in Barnard, 'Protestantism, Ethnicity and Irish Identities, 1660–1760', in T. Clayton and I. McBride (eds), *Protestantism and National Identity: Britain and Ireland, c.1650–c.1850* (Cambridge, 1998), 206–35.

was still to come. The first half of the 1660s was punctuated by political, religious, and economic crises in Ireland that threatened to destroy once and for all the material prosperity and political authority of men like Greatrakes. It is to this stage of Greatrakes' life that we must now turn if we are to understand fully the various factors that induced Greatrakes to take on the mantle of miracle healer in the early years of the Restoration.

3

Greatrakes, Ireland, and the Restoration, 1660–1665

About four years since I had an Impulse, or a strange perswasion in my own mind (of which I am not able to give any rational account to another) which did very frequently suggest to me that there was bestowed on me the gift of curing the Kings-Evil.

Valentine Greatrakes, *A Brief Account of Mr Valentine Greatrak's, and Divers of the Strange Cures By him Lately Performed* (London, 1666), 22.

NEGOTIATING THE RESTORATION

The Restoration of the Stuart monarchy in Ireland, as in England, was met with a mixture of widespread enthusiasm and optimistic expectation. Typically, bells were tolled, bonfires lit, and much wine drunk as the little-lamented Interregnum gave way to the return of Charles II in May 1660. In Dublin, as elsewhere in Britain, the passing Commonwealth was ritually mocked in a series of staged processions culminating in the funeral and incineration of a misshapen body without a head that was intended to represent the much-maligned Rump Parliament. Meanwhile, in the corridors of power preparations were made to reinstate the various organs of monarchical government and restore the body politic, with head now firmly back in place, to its former glories.[1] Beneath the surface, however, and despite the widespread protestations of loyalty, there were genuine concerns in Ireland as to the precise direction Restoration might take. In particular, there was the issue of land ownership and the possibility of a large-scale move to transfer property back to those Protestants and Roman Catholics who had remained loyal to Charles I. Uppermost, however, in the minds of those who had collaborated with the previous regime was the need to secure personal indemnity from prosecution in the event that the new regime should proceed to exact revenge for the regicide. As it happened,

---

[1] For a detailed account of the early stages of the process of restoration in Ireland, see especially A. Clarke, *Prelude to Restoration in Ireland: The End of the Commonwealth, 1659–1660* (Cambridge, 1999), 292–320. For the Restoration itself, see C. A. Dennehy (ed.), *Restoration Ireland: Always Settling and Never Settled* (Aldershot, 2008). I discuss more fully the use of organicist imagery invoking the disorderly nature of the body politic at this time in Chapter 5.

Valentine Greatrakes, unlike some of his former comrades in arms, was not greatly discomforted by the change of regime in 1660. Fortunately, he was able to call on the support of his former commanding officer, Roger Boyle, Lord Broghill, who had played a crucial role in negotiations surrounding the return of Charles II. Broghill himself was suitably rewarded when he was advanced to the peerage as the Earl of Orrery in September 1660. Thereafter, his star steadily rose so that by the middle years of the 1660s he was second only to James Butler, Duke of Ormond, in terms of the power and influence which he was able to bring to bear on events in Ireland. There is little doubt that Greatrakes continued to cultivate this important source of support and patronage during these years, the bond of friendship between the two men strengthened, as we shall see, by their shared interest in the occult and a deep-seated attachment to the role of providence in contemporary affairs.

The close relationship between Greatrakes and Orrery lies in sharp contrast to that which prevailed between the former and Orrery's older brother, Richard Boyle, second Earl of Cork (1612–1698), who had inherited the vast family estates in 1643. In the short term, this represented a potential obstacle to Greatrakes as it was now highly likely that the staunchly royalist and episcopalian Earl of Cork would use his newly acquired authority to reimpose seigneurial control over his vast estates, including those of Affane. Whether or not Greatrakes called on his ally, Orrery, to intercede on his behalf is not known. What is clear, however, from the evidence of the Earl of Cork's private papers is that he bore a substantial grudge against Greatrakes for what he perceived as numerous slights to his authority committed by him in the previous decade. Restored to his estates in the 1650s, the Earl had struggled to reassert authority over his father's former tenants in an attempt to secure power and revenues throughout Munster. Conflict had become inevitable, especially with 'new men' like Greatrakes, recently restored to his own family holdings at Affane, who were unlikely to cede without a struggle those rights they had accrued as a result of the political changes after 1649. Greatrakes held the upper hand and observed few scruples in maintaining that hard-earned position. In July 1652, for example, the Earl recorded in his diary an ongoing dispute with Lieutenant Valentine Greatrakes over the latter's attempt to rebuild a weir in the River Blackwater on land adjacent to his estate at Affane. In December, the case finally came to court and was heard before the radical judge and regicide, John Cook (1608–1660), who, according to Cork, was 'so partiall to Greatrakes that hee in Court privately bespoke Carwarden a Councellor to bee for Greatrakes...and besides by the favour of a jury was packt to decide for Greatrakes though it apeard that I had peacefully enjoyed the privilege of that river above forty years'.[2] Behind the scenes, Greatrakes had undoubtedly exploited his radical connections to good effect. The most likely source of advantage lay in the power wielded locally by

---

[2] CH, Lismore MS 29, 14 July 1652, 7 September 1652, 20 December 1652. Walter Carwardine was commissioner to the president's court in Munster and later served as a JP for county Cork; T. C. Barnard, *Cromwellian Ireland: English Government and Reform in Ireland 1649–1660* (Oxford, 1975), 271; H. F. Berry, 'Justices of the Peace for the County of Cork', *JCHAS*, 3 (1897), 59.

Greatrakes' close friend and commanding officer, Colonel Robert Phaire. Phaire was on intimate terms with Cook and acted as an intermediary for a number of Greatrakes' colleagues and acquaintances who were similarly entangled in legal disputes with the Earl. In another case, for example, between Cork and Greatrakes' friend and neighbour, Nicholas Pyne, the Earl claimed to have inside information that the jury had been 'packt and chosen by Coll.Phaire'.[3] The upshot was a prolonged period of coolness between Greatrakes and the Earl which did not begin to thaw until about 1656 when the former, in his new office as registrar for transplantations, was able to provide the Earl with inside information regarding land that had become available for purchase in county Tipperary. By late November 1656, Greatrakes was dining with the Earl and able to proffer further useful advice with regard to a rating dispute which involved the Earl's extensive ironworks in county Waterford.[4] Thereafter, frequent references to Greatrakes in Cork's diary suggest that he was trying hard to ingratiate himself with the Earl, as for example in May 1657 when he gave him two planks 'to make a shovel board table'.[5] The abiding impression of these entries, however, is of a business-like relationship between the two men, founded on mutual financial concerns, which seems to have survived the political turbulence generated by the Restoration. By then, of course, the Earl was able to exert much greater pressure on Greatrakes with respect to the latter's interests at Affane and elsewhere. Thus, in 1663, the Earl was able to overturn the original judgement of 1652 with respect to Greatrakes' weir on the Blackwater, as well as apply considerable pressure in relation to Greatrakes' other commercial interests in the neighbourhood.[6]

The evidence of Cork's private papers confirms the impression gleaned elsewhere that Greatrakes had weathered the storm of the Restoration tolerably well, even if he had been forced to concede valuable rights and control over some of his estates at Affane. A far greater threat to his well-being, however, was the looming spectre of a major redistribution of land in Ireland made likely by the terms of the Restoration settlement which promised compensation to those loyal Protestants

[3] CH, Lismore MS 29, 21 December 1652, 22 December 1652, 12 January 1652/3. For Pyne, see pp. 128–9.

[4] On this occasion, Greatrakes revealed his contempt for a local official, George Cawdron, a leading Baptist, who, he claimed, on the information of his agent in London, was guilty of both financial and moral improprieties. If Greatrakes was beginning to distance himself from the radical party in Munster politics, it may well have been prompted by political acuity on his part given the recent arrival of the moderate Henry Cromwell in Ireland in 1655, when he effectively took up the reins of power as *de facto* Lord Deputy in Fleetwood's absence; ibid. 27 August 1656, 2 November 1656. For Cawdron, see Barnard, *Cromwellian Ireland*, 66n.

[5] CH, Lismore MS 29, 25 May 1657.

[6] CH, Lismore MS 30, 15 June 1663, 7 November 1663, 18 September 1665; Lismore Papers, vol. 33, no. 3. Cork was also pressurizing Greatrakes at this time to fulfil what he believed to be an obligation on his tenant's part to supply him with lime for his ironworks. First mention is made of the demand in August 1659. Two and a half years later, Greatrakes was still dragging his feet, Cork's solicitor reporting that he had received from Greatrakes 'his answer about the Lime, which is; That his Business about the Earle of Clancarty's mortgage hath so troubled him, that (for this yeare) he shall not be able to compass the burning of a kill [i.e. kiln]; But desires your Lordships Pardon, & promiseth, that if your lordship shall have use of a thousand Barrells, the next yeare he will not fayle to furnish your Lordship with soe much'; Lismore MS 29, 27 August 1659; Lismore Papers, vol. 32, no. 85.

and Catholics who had lost their estates in the 1650s.[7] Here was an issue that had the potential to unite all strands of Protestant feeling in Ireland since many former royalists, including Greatrakes' close friend Sir Ames Meredith, as well as radicals and soldiers, had profited from the appropriation of Catholic property in the previous decade. Greatrakes himself, as we have seen, was a major beneficiary of this process. Consequently, he now faced the spectre of financial meltdown. During the 1650s, Greatrakes had exploited his position as registrar for transplantations to broker large-scale investments in alienated Catholic estates, most notably in county Tipperary, where he purchased the holdings of the corporation of Exeter as well as, in all probability, those of Dartmouth. These were then leased, either indirectly to English tenants or directly to pensioned soldiers, the rents going part of the way towards repaying the original purchase price of the lots. Unfortunately for Greatrakes, however, the income from such sources failed to keep pace with his other debts, so that by the mid-1660s he still owed large amounts of money on his original investments.[8] The prospect, therefore, of forfeiting some or all of these estates in a new land settlement in Ireland threatened financial oblivion for Greatrakes and many of his neighbours, associates, and fellow countrymen, as well as a host of private investors in England. Under the circumstances, it is impossible to exaggerate the extent to which the imminent imposition of such a settlement induced widespread communal anxiety and apprehension in the ranks of Protestant landowners like Greatrakes.

After much debate, the Act of Settlement of 1663 finally laid down the terms by which land was to be reallocated to those 'innocent' Catholics and sequestrated royalists who had remained loyal to the crown in the 1640s. Under the provisions of the Act, one-third of land now in the hands of adventurers, or their heirs, was to be set aside to settle the claims of the dispossessed which were to be adjudicated in the newly established Court of Claims at Dublin. For over three years, the Court heard evidence from claimants and defendants, Greatrakes among them, the legal process reaching its climax at the same time that Greatrakes' reputation as a miracle healer was at its height. The two events may not have been entirely unconnected. In the first place, Greatrakes himself explicitly requested that the money he was to receive for attempting the cure of Anne, Lady Conway, in England in 1666 should be used, in his own words, 'for the purchasing of the thirds which by the bill I am to lose'. And in the second, the precise timing of Greatrakes' visit to England in the spring of 1666 was specifically orchestrated in order to facilitate access to powerful interests in London which, Greatrakes hoped, might secure exemption from, or

---

[7] For general background to the Restoration land settlement in Ireland, see K. S. Bottigheimer, 'The Restoration Land Settlement in Ireland: a Structural View', *Irish Historical Studies*, 18 (1972), 1–21; L. J. Arnold, *The Restoration Land Settlement in County Dublin, 1660–1688* (Dublin, 1993). Also useful is K. McKenny, 'Charles II's Irish Cavaliers: the 1649 Officers and the Restoration Land Settlement', *Irish Historical Studies*, 28 (1993), 409–25; *idem*, 'The Restoration Land Settlement in Ireland. A Statistical Interpretation', in Dennehy (ed.), *Restoration Ireland*, 35–52.

[8] For the increasingly desperate attempts of the corporation of Exeter to redeem these debts, see *HMC Records of the City of Exeter* (London, 1916), 334–6. This 'long and troublesome business' (in the words of the Exeter scribe) was not finally resolved until 1675.

overturn, any adverse judgements made against him in the Irish Court of Claims. Thus in March 1666, at the height of Greatrakes mania in London, it was reported in one of the newsletters that the Irish healer's 'petition for the Settlement of certaine Lands he had in Ireland... is rejected in [the Privy] Counsell'.[9] Despite this setback, Greatrakes refused to accept the verdict, and in June 1666 Lord Conway, husband of Lady Anne, wrote to a senior figure in the Dublin administration, Sir Edward Dering, requesting that he intervene personally on Greatrakes' behalf with respect to his claim then pending in the Court of Claims.[10] The outcome is unknown, but one conclusion is inescapable. From the moment that Greatrakes had first received the impulse to heal, some time around 1662, the major preoccupation of his life had been to secure the fate of his recently acquired investments and holdings in Irish land. And what's more, many of those who flocked to him for cure in the early 1660s shared his concerns and anxieties on this critical issue.

What made the question of the redistribution of Irish land such an explosive issue in the 1660s was the religious and political dimension of the problem. For leading figures like Orrery as well as grassroots Cromwellian settlers and soldiers, it was difficult to disguise the process of land redistribution as anything other than a selling-out of the Protestant interest. Not surprisingly, the years immediately after 1660 were punctuated by fears of open rebellion and mass unrest within the Protestant community, particularly among those whose allegiance to the restored regime was never more than skin deep. In Munster, where Greatrakes was partly responsible for the oversight of justice and the maintenance of political order,[11] talk of plots and sedition was commonplace. In 1663, mass arrests were made throughout the south of Ireland in the wake of the abortive Dublin rising, the suspects including a number of Greatrakes' erstwhile allies and business associates.[12] The ambivalence that men like Greatrakes must have felt at times was echoed by others in power, including Greatrakes' mentor, the Earl of Orrery, whose fear of resurgent Catholicism made him an eloquent advocate for a policy of official moderation towards all segments of the Protestant community in Munster, including its radical

---

[9] *Conway Letters*, 267; TNA, SP 29/151/23, fo. 45r.

[10] *Conway Letters*, 274–5. Sir Edward Dering (1625–1684) was appointed one of the six commissioners to enact the Act of Settlement in Ireland in July 1662. An MP in the Dublin Parliament for Lismore, he gained the respect of the Lord Lieutenant, Ormond, and, according to a correspondent of Orrery's writing in June 1666, was considered 'Orrery's very real servant'; Henning, i, 208–12; E. MacLysaght (ed.), *Calendar of the Orrery Papers* (Dublin, 1941), 44.

[11] In 1663, for example, he served as sheriff of county Waterford, and was a JP in county Tipperary in 1681. In 1663, as part of his shrieval duties, Greatrakes acted as receiver for the hearth money in county Waterford. In October of that year, he was provided with an armed escort to bring in the collected revenues to Dublin; Bodl., Carte MS 165, fos 55v, 145; CH, Lismore MS 30, 15 June 1663; Bodl., Carte MS 59, fo. 247.

[12] One of the most notable victims in this respect was his former business partner, Jerome Sankey. Initially sympathetic to the aims of the restored regime, Sankey studiously avoided sectarian politics. By 1663, however, he, 'like many other old soldiers... found reason to think that the new government did not mean to play fair, and that little by little the soldier-settlers were to be ousted'. As a result, he joined in the Dublin plot and suffered as a result; W. T. Whitley, 'Colonel Jerome Sankey, M.P., Ph.D.', *The Baptist Quarterly*, 4 (1928–9), 270. Richard Greaves, however, suggests that there was 'no hard evidence' linking Sankey to the Dublin plot; R. L. Greaves, *Deliver Us From Evil: The Radical Underground in Britain, 1660–1663* (New York & Oxford, 1986), 258n.

fringe. Men like Orrery knew only too well that the future of Ireland was dependant upon the support and acquiescence of all strands of Protestant opinion, a view which even an ex-royalist such as Ormond was able to empathize with from time to time. Faced with the loss of some or all of their estates, and the reinstatement of former Catholic owners, it is little wonder that many of those who did threaten to take up arms against the Crown in the early 1660s did so in the belief that they were acting as Protestant patriots rather than rebels.

By 1663, the province of Munster was awash with rumours of impending insurrection. In that year, the Mayor of Waterford reported to Sir George Lane, secretary to the Lord Lieutenant, Ormond, that the soldiery in the city were murmuring about an imminent Presbyterian uprising to be followed by the replacement of Orrery as Lord President of Munster.[13] In neighbouring Tipperary, where numerous soldiers had settled in the late 1650s, similar discontent had led many to speculate openly about taking up arms again in defence of the 'good old cause'. One, Charles Minchin, a former soldier under Ludlow, was reported in 1662 as saying that he would rather 'that the souldiers that served Oliver Cromwell in Ireland had not sould their Estates to the Officers, and that if they had kept them, neither the Kinge nor the Duke of Ormond durst trye their Quallification'.[14] Greatrakes himself had extensive interests in county Tipperary, and later served as a JP on the county bench. He could not fail to have been aware of the growing discontent, particularly as a number of colleagues and associates were implicated in the rumoured plotting. In June 1663, for example, the house of Thomas Batty in Clonmel was raided and searched, and an itinerant nonconformist minister, Zephaniah Smith, was arrested on suspicion of preaching insurrection. In 1658, Batty had acted as an intermediary in various business transactions involving Greatrakes and the Earl of Cork.[15] As those in authority repeatedly noted, the chief cause of discontent among the soldier-settlers was the widespread fear that they would lose some or all of their estates in the process of land redistribution that was fully under way by 1663. The point was well made by Michael Boyle, Bishop of Cork, in a letter to Ormond in 1663, in which he refers to the disaffected nature of the 'English' in the city and county of Cork. According to Boyle, 'they begin to tamper

[13] A week later, the mayor, William Bolton, had tracked down the origin of these rumours to 'three younge Girles of Anabaptisticall Education'; Bodl., Carte MS 32, fos 483, 521.

[14] Bodl., Carte MS 31, fo. 592. Three years later, Minchin was indicted at Clonmel assizes for malicious and scandalous words; NLI, MS 4908, fos 4r, 7r–v, 8r.

[15] Bodl., Carte MS 32, fols 527, 530; CH, Lismore MS 29, 24 May 1658; NLI, MS 6256, 24 May 1658. Batty had served as Treasurer for the precinct of Tipperary under the Commonwealth regime from 1650 to 1658. Part of his job was to receive and reimburse moneys to the soldiery in his precinct, work that probably brought him into contact with officers like Greatrakes. In 1661, he also acted as a middle man for Colonel Jerome Sankey and the earl of Cork, who clearly trusted Batty; BL, Egerton MS 1762, fo. 203r; *CSP Ireland, 1660–1662*, 461, 481; NLI, MS 11,959, 110; Allen Library, Dublin, Jennings MSS, J2/Box 263, no. 17; CH, Lismore Papers, vol. 32, no. 14. The minister Smith, originally from New England, was recruited by the Government to establish a preaching ministry in Ireland in the 1650s. Immediately prior to his arrest in 1663, he had stayed at Cappoquin. He subsequently admitted to having visited numerous disaffected officers and ministers in the neighbourhood of east Cork, including Colonel Phaire and Major Jasper Farmer, who had assisted Greatrakes in the rendition of Cappoquin in 1649; Bodl., Carte MSS 32, fo. 530; 66, fos 250r–v, 252r–v.

much with the soldiers and give out that they are sure of the generality of the English to joyne with them upon the great apprehension which they have of the loss of their estates unto the Irish'. The same day, the Bishop wrote a further letter to Ormond pleading that some provision might be made in the land settlement to appease this section of the population. Not only did he believe that this would undermine the ringleaders, among whom he listed Greatrakes' close friend and associate, Colonel Robert Phaire, but, he reassured Ormond, it would also appease the majority of the loyal populace whose condition he described as 'desperat'.[16]

In addition to Phaire, who was ordered to appear before Orrery,[17] numerous other close associates of Greatrakes came under suspicion in the summer of 1663 in the aftermath of the abortive Dublin plot. Two MPs in the Dublin Parliament, Sir Anthony Morgan and Sir Thomas Stanley, were implicated in the rising, and both subsequently wrote obsequious letters to Ormond, the principal target of the would-be insurgents, protesting their innocence and pledging their allegiance to the Lord Lieutenant and the Crown.[18] Stanley is an interesting figure who clearly retained the confidence of Greatrakes. In late December 1665, as Greatrakes made final preparations for his journey to England in order to cure Lady Conway and impress the English court, he instructed Sir George Rawdon that the payment of £155 for his services was to be forwarded to Sir Thomas Stanley, 'a Parliament man, now in Dublin', the money to be used 'for the purchasing of the thirds which by the bill I am to lose'.[19] Stanley, like Greatrakes' close friend and confidante, Sir Ames Meredith, was a native of Cheshire. During the 1650s, he had served as governor of Clonmel, and was rewarded for his services to the state with a knighthood in January 1659, as well as extensive estates in counties Tipperary, Waterford, and Louth. In the same year, with the support of the Earl of Cork, he was elected MP for Tipperary and Waterford.[20] At the Restoration, he seems to have returned to England

---

[16] Bodl., Carte MS 32, fos 437, 494; cf. Carte MS 45, fo. 135. For similar fears expressed in a letter to Ormond in 1662, see Bodl., Carte MS 32, fo. 141. Among those who were fearful that the soldiery might be excluded from the land settlement was Greatrakes' attorney in the Court of Claims, Major Samuel Bull; BL, Add. MS 25,692, fo. 25v; Bodl., Carte MS 228, fos 35–6. A former Cromwellian, Bull was rewarded 'for his loyal help in the Restoration' with the post of sub-commissioner for the King's Declaration and Instructions for the Settlement of Ireland. As an attorney in the Court of Claims, he also acted on behalf of the Earl of Orrery and his brother Robert Boyle; *CSP Ireland, 1660–1662*, 246, 414; WSxRO, MS 13,223, nos 5, 6 and 9; Bodl., Carte MS 228, fos 14–15 and *passim*; M. Lennon, 'Winston Churchill, 1662–1668', *Dublin Historical Record*, 43 (1990), 105.

[17] Phaire sent his apologies to Orrery, claiming that he could not attend at such short notice 'in regard he is out of money & cloathes at present'; Bodl., Carte MS 32, fo. 653. The Irish economy was suffering acute depression at this time and thus added to the general sense of anxiety that all landowners were then experiencing.

[18] Bodl., Carte MSS 32, fos 542, 575; 214, fo. 512. The moderate bishop of Killaloe Edward Worth (c.1620–1669) had earlier proposed to Ormond that Stanley be added to the commission of the peace for the county of Tipperary, a strategy intended to bolster Stanley's fragile loyalty through the use of persuasion rather than force; Bodl., Carte MS 214, fo. 458. Stanley had been suspected of plotting at Clonmel in October 1660; *CSP Ireland, 1660–1662*, 45.

[19] *Conway Letters*, 267. Stanley, pardoned with Greatrakes and others in 1661, was apparently acting on the stroker's behalf in the Court of Claims in early 1666; see *CSP Ireland, 1660–1662*, 316; *CSP Ireland, 1666–1669*, 16, 44.

[20] CH, Lismore MS 29, 6 January 1659. He was also admitted a burgess for the city of Waterford in May 1660; S. Pender, 'Studies in Waterford History V', *JCHAS*, 53 (1948), 44.

where he actively pursued a baronetcy from the King. However, he met with fierce opposition from numerous members of the Cheshire county gentry, who remembered only too well his role in crushing Booth's rebellion and other disloyal acts against the Crown. Rebuffed in England from securing the rewards that he felt were due to a man of his rank, Stanley returned to Ireland, where it was reported in February 1661 that he planned to 'plant and settle his lands'. He was subsequently returned as MP for Tipperary and Louth in the Parliament of 1661 (opting to represent the latter), and retired to his estate at Tickincarr in county Waterford.[21]

There can be little doubt then that the single most important issue facing the vast majority of Munster Protestants in the first half of the 1660s was the impending Act of Settlement that aimed to resolve the complex web of claims and counter-claims that emanated from various competing groups in the province. Most threatened were those Cromwellian soldiers, who had decided to settle their lots in lieu of unpaid wages in the 1650s, but equally at risk were the holdings of a large number of investors and adventurers, some of whom were new settlers, but many of whom, like Greatrakes, came from second or third generation planter families. The beneficiaries of any such redistribution—if beneficiary is the right word to describe those who had been so ruthlessly dispossessed of their lands in the 1650s—were those so-called 'innocent' Catholics who could prove that they had played no part in the 1641 rebellion or its aftermath. The attempt to indemnify this group, above the claims of others, was almost certainly responsible for the revival of a virulent strain of anti-Catholicism among the Protestant population in the early 1660s. It might also have played, as I suggest below, an important contributory role in the genesis of Greatrakes' claims to heal the sick of a multitude of diseases in his native Munster.

Greatrakes himself, as we have already noted, later claimed in 1666 to have always acted honourably with regard to the Catholic population in the 1650s, despite his role as an agent of the Cromwellian state in the transportation of Munster Catholics to Connaught. As a loyal Protestant and JP, who claimed to have 'endeavoured to convert as many Papists to Protestantism as I could', he protested that he had 'never molested any that was known, or esteemed to be innocent, but suffered them to continue in the English Quarters, and that without prejudice'.[22] The claim is extraordinary for one of his class, whose family, kin, and friends had suffered at the hands of Catholic rebels in the 1640s. And like other statements made by Greatrakes in his autobiographical account, it deserves to be treated with both caution and suspicion. Other sources, for example, provide a very different picture of Greatrakes' attitude toward Irish Catholics and suggest in the process that his self-proclaimed moderation was either highly superficial, or

[21] *CSPD, 1660–1661*, 132, 133, 364–5, 409–10; *CSP Ireland, 1660–1662*, 223; *Notes and Queries*, 199 (1954), 545; Bodl., Carte MS 67, fo. 71v. Stanley, like Sir Anthony Morgan, was a witness to Greatrakes' therapeutic powers. In 1667, Sir Edmund Berry Godfrey alluded to a passage in one of Greatrakes' letters, where reference is made to cures performed by the stroker in the house of Sir Thomas Stanley, who, it was said, was willing to provide a glowing testimonial; NLI, MS 4728, 10–11. (See p. 218).

[22] Greatrakes, *Brief Account*, 20, 21.

part of a stratagem designed to reassure an English audience (and more specifically pro-Catholic elements within the court) of his eirenic intent, or both.

The historical record then would not appear to corroborate Greatrakes' image of himself as a friend to the native Catholic population. In January 1655, for example, one Cornet Greatrakes (specifically identified in another source as Valentine Greatrakes) was accused by several Catholic prisoners of having taken money and goods from them following the storming and capture of Ballybranagh Castle in county Cork.[23] More conclusive, however, is the evidence of the protracted legal battle waged by Greatrakes and his associates on the one hand, and the Catholic Prendergast family on the other, in relation to disputed property rights in county Tipperary in the early 1660s. The land in question lay in the vicinity of Mullough Abbey, near Newcastle, in the south-eastern corner of the county, where Greatrakes acted as the legatee of the adventurer, John Kendrick (see p. 44). In November 1661, Edmund, the eldest son of James and Ann Prendergast, subscribed a series of depositions and affidavits to the effect that Greatrakes and his associates (mostly tenants, to whom Greatrakes had sub-let the Kendrick estates) were systematically cutting down the woods of lands previously owned by his father but since lost in the great land redistribution of the 1650s. According to an order of 9 January 1661 (reaffirmed in September 1662), all tree-felling was to cease until the Court of Claims had determined rightful ownership of the lands in question. Prendergast asserted, however, that Greatrakes and his friends offered only violence in response to his frequent requests that they desist from cutting immediately and obey the law. Greatrakes in particular, according to Prendergast, treated him with total contempt and threatened to 'crop his ears'.[24] In the following year, the Greatrakes' camp retaliated when the heirs of John Kendrick brought a suit against the Prendergasts in the Irish court of Chancery, the object of which was to prove once and for all their entitlement to these lands. Subsequently referred to the Court of Claims in Dublin for adjudication, the Prendergasts appear to have issued a counter-writ in Chancery against Greatrakes and others for intruding upon and despoiling their lands.[25]

[23] NLI, MS 11,959, 378–80. Cornet Greatrakes claimed that a Catholic priest was hiding in the castle. In every other reference to Greatrakes in the first half of the 1650s, when he was serving as a soldier in Munster, he is referred to as holding the rank of lieutenant; see, for example, BL, Egerton MS 212, fo. 16r. However, an extract from a no longer extant order book specifically refers to the accused as Cornet Valentine Greatrakes; Allen Library, Dublin, Jennings MSS J2/Box 263, no. 12, 13. The matter was subsequently referred for judgement to a triad of officers that included Major Thomas Stanley (verdict unknown).

[24] King's Inns Library, Dublin, Prendergast Papers, vol. 2, 951–4. The Prendergasts were an old English Catholic family that had traditionally dominated this remote part of county Tipperary lying in the shadow of the Knockmealdown mountains. The family almost certainly looked to their 'protector', the Duke of Ormond, to support them in their claims to the ownership of these estates; W. J. Smyth, 'Making the Documents of Conquest Speak: The Transformation of Property, Society, and Settlement in Seventeenth-Century Counties Tipperary and Kilkenny', in M. Silverman and P. H. Gulliver (eds), *Approaching the Past: Historical Anthropology Through Irish Case Studies* (New York, 1992), 258, 283.

[25] *Sixth Report of the Deputy Keeper of the Public Records in Ireland* (Dublin, 1874), 61, 68; Bodl., Carte MS 67, fo. 44v.

In 1664, amidst further legal wrangling, Edmund Prendergast made the claim that his father, James, who had died in January 1661, was in full possession of the lands of Mullough Abbey and surrounding estates at the time of his death. Claiming rightful inheritance, he protested that his family were never transplanted, and that his father was an 'Innocent papist', who was provided with a certificate confirming his peaceable conduct from, among others, the Duke of Ormond, the Earl of Inchiquin, and the Earl of Kingston. The judges ordered restitution, but the defendants, including Greatrakes, continued to dispossess them, 'by what pretence of right they cannot conceive'. Greatrakes for his part responded by affirming that he held these lands as the rightful legatee of the adventurer, John Kendrick, alderman of London, who had been in full possession of them since 1656. The Prendergasts were reduced, according to Greatrakes, to a cabin and a single acre of land, for which they paid rent to another of Greatrakes' former army colleagues, Cornet Alexander Deane. Greatrakes did admit that the plaintiffs had successfully indicted him for a forcible entry and had been granted a writ of restitution. This, however, he asserted only applied to a small remnant of the Prendergast holding (presumably the single acre), for which offence he was acquitted at Clonmel assizes in 1661.[26]

As the religious and political temperature rose in Ireland in the wake of the Dublin plot and amid growing fears of a new bout of land redistribution, it was only natural that those who stood to lose from the implementation of the Act of Settlement should lay the blame at the door of their Catholic neighbours. In Munster itself, Greatrakes' patron, the Earl of Orrery, led the chorus of disapproval against any measures designed to allow the Catholic majority a greater stake in the economic, religious, and political life of the province. Meanwhile, rumours of another Catholic uprising were rife. In Wexford in 1663, news circulated of a Catholic plot to seize lands formerly lost in the 1650s. Three years later, immediately following Greatrakes' arrival in England, information was passed to the Government concerning an intended Catholic insurrection in Munster followed by a French invasion of Ireland. The Government's informant was none other than Richard Williams, of Bideford, in north Devon, the stepson of Lionel Beacher, who, as we shall see, had been one of the first to promote Greatrakes' cures in print.[27] Shortly after these events, Beacher entered the service of Roger Boyle, Earl of Orrery. Under the circumstances, it is probably not too far-fetched to conclude that the hand of the Lord Deputy of Munster lay behind the scare. If so, Orrery's plan to provoke a reaction in governing circles against the Catholic population seems to

---

[26] *Sixth Report*, 68; King's Inns Library, Dublin, S. Prendergast, Viscount Gort, 'The Prendergasts of Newcastle, Co. Tipperary, AD 1169–1760', 112–13. Alexander Deane lived at Lismore, where he was a tenant to several properties owned by the earl of Cork. He, too, had assisted Greatrakes in the capture of Cappoquin in 1649. It was while visiting Deane at Lismore in Easter 1665 that Greatrakes first became fully convinced that God had granted him the gift of healing the sick, crippled, and lame. In 1669, he walked the bounds of Greatrakes' estate at Affane. He is also referred to in the latter's account book as a tenant of the Kendricks, paying rent to Greatrakes, in the mid 1670s; NLI, MS 6259, 30; Bodl., Carte MSS 66, fo. 252r; 68, fo. 150r; Greatrakes, *Brief Account*, 26; NLI, MS 8143, 24 May 1669; BL, Add. MS 25,692, fo. 18r.

[27] Bodl., Carte MSS 33, fo. 138; 34, fos 632, 634.

have been partially successful. In February 1666, Ormond wrote to Arlington in London claiming that Orrery and the wife of an army officer had information relating to a Catholic design to raise a disturbance in the province. Two months later, he was still in a quandary as to how to proceed, and insisted on arresting only those suspects against whom there was definite proof of plotting. It is difficult to escape the conclusion that all of this was part of an elaborate plan on Orrery's part to instigate a backlash against the native Catholic population, coinciding as it did with the culmination of the work of the Court of Claims in Dublin.[28] Fears of a Catholic revival, then, were widespread in Munster, as throughout much of the rest of Ireland, in the years immediately after the Restoration. Greatrakes seemingly shared these fears and, despite public protestations to the contrary, was content to prosecute and harass Catholics when his own material interests were threatened. Anxieties surrounding a land settlement that might reward 'innocent' Catholics thus helped to unite all strands of Protestant opinion in Ireland. They also helped to create a strong sense among the settler community of a disordered body politic, which required the careful ministration of those 'state physicians' newly appointed by the Crown to oversee the Restoration settlement. This, then, was the context in which Greatrakes, himself a magistrate and minor limb of the Irish body politic, discovered and publicized his miraculous gift of healing.

DISCOVERING THE GIFT OF HEALING

Greatrakes first began to heal the sick some time around 1662, when he claimed to have received an 'impulse, or a strange perswasion in my own mind' instructing him that he had received the gift of curing the king's evil, or scrofula. From the outset, he was convinced that the inner voice he experienced was divine in origin and, despite his wife's sceptical protestations, he proceeded to make trial of his gift on the diseased and disfigured bodies of neighbours, most of whom were tenants of the Earl of Cork.[29] Initially, Greatrakes' practice, restricted to cases of the king's evil, involved little else other than the laying on of hands on those parts affected by the disease, followed by a blessing. By Easter 1665, however, he had become convinced of his ability to cure a wide range of diseases through the same means, and shortly thereafter his fame as a miracle healer spread rapidly through the neighbourhood, his house at Affane being besieged with visitors seeking relief

---

[28] Bodl., Carte MS 51, fos 135r, 166r. Orrery returned to the same fears time and time again, as for example in 1679 when he claimed that there were plans for an imminent Catholic uprising in Munster to be followed by the obligatory French invasion; Bodl., Carte MS 118, fos 182–3.

[29] Among those locals cured by Greatrakes was the wife of Stephen Bateman, a long-standing friend and business partner of the stroker. A tenant of the earl of Cork, he assisted Greatrakes in the rendition of the garrison of Cappoquin in 1649 and was later involved with his neighbour in the despoliation of the Prendergast lands in county Tipperary; Greatrakes, *Brief Account*, 25; CH, Lismore Papers, vol. 22, no. 47; T. Fitzpatrick, *Waterford During the Civil War 1641–1653* (Waterford, 1912), 107–8, 112; Bodl., Carte MS 66, fo. 250r; NLI, MS 6259, 7; BL, Add. MS 25,692, fo. 4r; *Sixth Report*, 68; King's Inns Library, Dublin, Prendergast Papers, vol. 2, nos 952, 953; NLI, MS 4908, fo. 10v.

from their ailments. From a historical perspective, the timing of these events is clearly critical. Greatrakes himself later provided various reasons as to why he believed God had granted him the gift of healing at this particular time. These included conventional explanations focused on the goodness and beneficence of God, who acted in part to confound that growing band of 'wits' and unbelievers in 'this Age of Atheism'. But it also sprang, according to Greatrakes, from a need to 'abate the pride of the Papists that make Miracles the undeniable Manifesto of the truth of their Church'.[30] Resurgent Catholicism, as we have seen, was a major issue for Protestants of all denominations in Restoration Ireland. Greatrakes was no different, and there seems little doubt that his mission to heal the sick was born, in the first instance, from a need to counter similar claims made by Irish Catholic healers, most notably those of an obscure parish priest, James O'Finallty of Tuam.

O'Finallty provided both a useful role model for Greatrakes as well as a catalyst to initiate his own gift of healing. He first came to prominence in the late 1650s, when according to the influential Franciscan, Peter Walsh (*c.*1618–1688), he drew vast crowds, 'not only Catholicks but Protestants', and was said to heal all manner of ailments. Initially enthusiastic and willing to suspend his disbelief, Walsh grew increasingly sceptical, particularly when he was informed that O'Finallty had claimed that all his patients were diabolically possessed or obsessed and that 'all kinds even of the most seeming corporall or natural diseases' were attributed by him to the 'special effects of the Devils really Possessing, or obsessing the bodies of the sick'.[31] Walsh again crossed paths with O'Finallty in 1662, when he was asked by the Duke of Ormond, recently restored as Lord Lieutenant, to investigate further claims relating to his ability to cure the sick. Both Walsh and Ormond were eager to disprove the priest's claims and to expose him as a fraud, since both were concerned that such overt attempts at proselytizing would backfire on moderate Catholics, eager, like Walsh, to reach some form of accommodation with the new regime.[32] In the event, O'Finallty, discouraged by the low level of support he received from the Catholic hierarchy, both lay and ecclesiastical, turned his attention

[30] Greatrakes, *Brief Account*, 22–31.

[31] P. Walsh, *The History & Vindication of the Loyal Formulary, or Irish Remonstrance, So Graciously Received by his Majesty, Anno 1661, Against all Calumnies and Censures in Several Treatises* (Dublin?, 1674), 710–36 [quote at 712]. For a summary of O'Finallty's career, see A. Faulkner, 'Father O'Finaghty's Miracles', *Irish Ecclesiastical Record*, 104 (1965), 349–62; C. Parker, 'Father Finaghty, Valentine Greatrakes, and Attitudes to the Miraculous in Seventeenth-Century Ireland and England', MA thesis (National University of Ireland, Maynooth, 1997).

[32] Walsh, *History and Vindication*, 710–17. Among those who offered early support and encouragement to O'Finallty was Richard Bellings (1613–1677), a Leinster gentleman and Catholic, who claimed the priest had cured his gout. He subsequently approached Ormond, his kinsman, in order to secure a pass for O'Finallty to come to Dublin and perform his miraculous cures there. Ormond, however, attempted to dissuade him on the grounds that if he failed it would discredit all his co-religionists and undermine his own attempts to secure a measure of religious and political freedom for moderate Catholics; Walsh, *History and Vindication*, 714–15. Interestingly, in 1674, Bellings again wrote to Ormond advertising the miraculous feats of another Catholic healer, who, it was said, numbered among her patients Lord Carlingford and the bishop of Meath. She was said to be well known to Ormond's sister, Lady Clancarty, though Bellings also observed that some sceptical (Protestant?) physicians attributed her success to witchcraft; Bodl., Carte MS 243, fo. 156.

to England, and like Greatrakes, appeared at court where he performed more of his cures before Charles II's new wife and Catholic Queen, Catherine of Braganza. Some time in 1663 he returned to Dublin, his reputation enhanced by the support which he received from influential lay Catholics in England such as John Digby, and here he once again plied his trade gaining a growing reputation among Protestants and Catholics, as well as aristocrats and senior clergy.[33]

O'Finallty, however, was finally exposed, according to Walsh, when he was confronted by the sceptical rationalism of the Protestant natural philosopher, Sir William Petty (1623–1687). Petty challenged the Irish priest to a healing contest, his confidence bolstered by the assumption that if one gathered enough sick people together in one place, the law of averages dictated that a significant number would recover without any external intervention or medical assistance. O'Finallty declined the challenge, and shortly afterwards was persuaded by Walsh and others to return to his native Connaught. It was at this point in Walsh's narrative that he pointedly commented on the fact that as O'Finallty's star waned so that of Greatrakes first emerged in the firmament:

> [N]o sooner had this Roman-Catholic, Irish Priest Finachty, been so discovered at Dublin, but at Cork…starts up one…Gratrix, an English Lay-Protestant, to supply the formers place, by making people believe himself too had a Gift from God to Cure all diseases by Praying and Stroaking, and accordingly practises everywhere on many, even also at London, whither he came at last to Cheat the World, as the former was thought to have done.[34]

There were in fact strikingly close parallels between the careers of the two Irish miracle workers. O'Finallty first rose to prominence among the exiled Catholic community in Connaught following a series of dispossessions that he performed in the mid-1650s. His cures were widely acclaimed and acted as a rallying point for influential and sympathetic lay supporters such as Richard Bellings and Geoffrey Browne.[35] Moreover, O'Finallty, like Greatrakes, subscribed to the view that the illnesses from which many of his patients suffered were essentially demonic in origin and that his cures thus constituted a form of dispossession. Unlike O'Finallty, however, Greatrakes was a layman, whose brand of Protestantism defies easy categorization. Nevertheless, in seeking to rally Protestant opinion through espousing a message of religious moderation and accommodation, Greatrakes, it could be

[33] [J. Digby], *Miracles Not Ceas'd* (London, 1663); *idem, The Reconciler of Religions: Or, a Brief Decider of all Controversies in Matters of Faith* (London?, 1663). For the relationship of Digby, the son of the Catholic royalist, Sir Kenelm Digby (d.1665), to O'Finallty, see R. Gillespie, *Devoted People: Belief and Religion in Early Modern Ireland* (Manchester, 1997), 67–8.

[34] Walsh, *History and Vindication*, 736.

[35] Browne (d. 1668) was convinced by O'Finallty after watching him cure a cripple at Galway in Cromwell's time. A Roman Catholic lawyer, he was elected to the Irish House of Commons for the borough of Tuam in 1661, but subsequently lost his seat at a re-election. In the same year, his lands, like those of his confederate Bellings, were ordered to be restored to him as a loyal sufferer for the royalist cause in Ireland; Walsh, *History and Vindication*, 714; Barnard, *Cromwellian Ireland*, 70n; *CSP Ireland, 1660–1662*, 217.

argued, shared the ecumenical aims of his Catholic rival. Both men were clearly keen to promote the virtues of religious unity and harmony within their separate confessions, while also engaging, to a certain degree, in making new converts to their respective faiths. Ultimately, both too failed in this respect as they proved unable to convince those in authority of the genuine nature of their divine callings. In Greatrakes' case, as we shall see, opponents from within the Anglican Church, both in Ireland and England, as well as some nonconformists, were quick to argue that his putative cures were little more than an elaborate ruse and a cover for sedition. We shall examine these claims in a little more detail shortly. In seeking to understand what motivated his urge to cure, we need nonetheless to remind ourselves that throughout this period Greatrakes remained a pillar of the local community, who served various offices in county government and drew support for his cures from a wide religious and political cross-section of the Protestant population. Stubbe's later depiction of him as the 'miraculous conformist' was, in this respect, both accurate and informative. By education, temperament, and family background, Greatrakes inclined to religious and political conformity, a stance that could only have been reinforced by his marriage in the early years of the Restoration to Ruth Godolphin, the daughter of the Cornish gentleman, Sir William Godolphin (1605–1663).[36]

Greatrakes' new father-in-law was a die-hard royalist, who had commanded a regiment of foot for Charles I in the first Civil War and subsequently claimed to have lost the staggering sum of £10,000 as a result of the King's defeat. The loyal credentials of Sir William and his family were thus beyond reproach. They may also, indirectly, have provided Greatrakes with a potential role model for his future career as a miracle healer. Given their prominence in Cornwall as supporters of the crown, they were no doubt familiar with the saintly figure of the young Cornish maid Anne Jefferies, who in 1647 was widely lauded in royalist circles as a worker of miracle cures. Sir Edward Hyde (1609–1674), who as the Earl of Clarendon was later to serve as chief minister to Charles II, related how there was 'much discourse here of the Prophesies of a Maide in Cornwall, who heales the Kings Evill, broken Joynts, Agues . . . by touch only'. She also predicted the imminent restoration of Charles I to the throne in the wake of his recent defeat and capitulation in the first Civil War.[37] Stories about Jefferies were clearly circulating in royalist circles in the west of

[36] Greatrakes' marriage to Ruth may have been facilitated by his close friend, Sir Ames Meredith, a relative of the Godolphins. Equally, however, it may owe something to his father-in-law's cordial relations with the Boyles following his enforced stay at Lismore in 1625–6, when, with others, Sir William was entertained there by the first earl of Cork. In 1663, shortly before his death, he wrote to the countess of Cork, recounting his earlier happy sojourn at Lismore and thanking her for the many kindnesses that she had performed for his daughter, Ruth, since her (recent?) arrival in Ireland. He concluded by expressing the hope that he might one day return to Lismore 'whereof no man was ever more a child of favour to be a servant to it whilest I live'. Godolphin died in 1663. In his will, made shortly before his death, he left Ruth Greatrakes 'my yellow watch, & my golden case containeing my lady Cromptons picture . . . as also my Lozeng diamond Ring sett in gold & black' as well as the 'wearing apparrell' of his late wife, Grace (d.1663) which he had purchased in France; Henning, ii, 407; *Calendar of Treasury Books*, i, 40, 259; Green, *CPCC*, ii, 1559; Grosart, ii, 173, 177; BL, Althorp MS B6; Cornwall Record Office, G 652/1–2.

[37] Bodl., Clarendon MS 29, fos 102, 148v, 165r.

England at this time, making it highly likely that the Godolphins in Cornwall were aware of her cures and prophecies, and may conceivably have played some part in promoting them.[38] It would probably be a mistake, however, to conclude that Greatrakes was indebted to any single source of inspiration for his gift of healing. In addition to the example of Catholic thaumaturges like O'Finallty, and the recollections of his in-laws, he may equally have drawn on his own experiences in the 1650s when he came into close contact with a wide range of radical groups, many of whom practised forms of miracle healing. Greatrakes' business partner Jerome Sankey, for example, was a lay Baptist preacher who, it was alleged, had attempted to exorcise an acquaintance by resorting to fasting and prayer. Greatrakes, as we shall see, was convinced that his own 'stroking' was a form of dispossession.[39]

SPREADING THE WORD

Greatrakes himself, though, was clearly no radical. In all the early accounts of his cures, he was uniformly praised as a modest and charitable man, who sought no financial reward and acted solely for the benefit of the commonweal. In the first such description, dating from July 1665, he was reported by those who knew him well to be a 'very civil, franck, and well humour'd man, conformable to the discipline of the Church'. A fortnight later the same newspaper focused on the fact that he was 'Master of a competent Estate', who took 'neither Mony nor Present for his Cures'. His credibility and good intent were further bolstered by the fact that among his leading admirers and supporters were lawyers and gentlewomen, including one described as 'a prudent and a very excellent person'. Significantly, later testimonials would allude to the fact that 'in the ordinary course of his life he appears to be a person of a friendly sociable humor, and free from that popularity and ostentation, which commonly attends men of his pretensions'.[40] From a very early

---

[38] In a later account, published in 1696 when Anne was still alive, it was alleged that her cures by 'stroking' attracted prospective patients from all over Cornwall, and even from as far afield as London; M. Pitt, *An Account of One Ann Jefferies... and of the Strange and Wonderful Cures She Performed... In a Letter from Moses Pitt to... Dr Edward Fowler, Lord Bishop of Gloucester* (London, 1696), 14, 16. For a recent account of this case, and its use by bishop Fowler in the late seventeenth-century campaign against atheism, see P. Marshall, 'Ann Jeffries and the Fairies: Folk Belief and the War on Scepticism in Later Stuart England', in A. McShane and G. Walker (eds), *The Extraordinary and the Everyday in Early Modern England: Essays in Celebration of the Work of Bernard Capp* (Basingstoke, 2010), 127–41. I discuss Fowler's interest in such matters within the context of his latitudinarian beliefs below, pp. 139–40.

[39] W. Petty, *Reflections upon Some Persons and Things in Ireland, by Letters to and from Dr Petty. With Sir Hierome Sankey's Speech in Parliament* (London, 1660), 101–2. Petty, as we have already seen in the case of the priest O'Finallty, would appear to have relished exposing fraudulent healers. In Sankey's case, there is little doubt that Petty's mocking denunciation of his methods was partly inspired by a desire to denigrate an old political enemy. Unfortunately, his opinions of Greatrakes' cures have not survived, though he was certainly acquainted with Valentine and his brother, William; see pp. 166–7.

[40] *The Newes*, 13 July 1665, 27 July 1665; *The Intelligencer*, 21 August 1665. These reports also included the testimonial of an acquaintance of Greatrakes, 'a very intelligent and sober person, a counsellor at law', who claimed that the stroker was so popular he was forced to leave his home at Affane and set up surgery at Youghal. Here, boatloads of expectant patients from England vied for Greatrakes' attention and on their return spread the word of the stroker's miraculous gift.

stage then, Greatrakes' credibility as a healer was augmented by his gentlemanly status and demeanour. Unlike so many other run-of-the-mill seventh sons and mountebanks who proliferated in early modern Britain, there was nothing vulgar or mercenary about Greatrakes. His gentility and dispassionate charity bestowed authority and legitimacy upon his gift of healing, echoing what some have perceived as the essential components of the public persona of one of Greatrakes' foremost admirers, the eminent natural philosopher, Robert Boyle.[41]

A particularly illuminating account of the wide respect in which Greatrakes was held, as well as of the manner of his curing and general demeanour, can be found in the autobiography of the future Astronomer Royal, John Flamsteed (1646–1719). Born in 1646, Flamsteed had suffered from birth with a weak physical constitution and various crippling ailments. So bad were the inflammations in his joints that he was unable to attend university, his home-based study interspersed by bouts of long and largely unsuccessful courses of medical treatment.[42] In 1665 news began to reach Derbyshire of the Irishman's miraculous cures, and at his father's instigation Flamsteed was sent on the long journey to Ireland to seek help at the hands of the celebrated stroker. On his arrival in Ireland in September 1665, Flamsteed discovered that Greatrakes' routine was to heal on Sundays (after the sermon), Tuesdays, Thursdays, and Saturdays. He was subsequently stroked on three separate occasions, seemingly without success, but he was none the less struck by the charismatic demeanour of his new physician. Recalling their first meeting, Flamsteed recounts how when he met Greatrakes in his yard, overseeing his cattle, 'he had a kind of majestical, yet affable, presence, a lusty body, and a composed carriage'. Others would make similar allusions to his physical presence, charm and sociable demeanour. In Flamsteed's case, it was sufficiently attractive to cause him to revisit Greatrakes for a further bout of stroking at Worcester in the following year.[43]

Initially, Greatrakes' thaumaturgical claims would appear to have provoked little overt concern or opposition in his native Munster. For three years, he practised his gift without alarming the authorities. The first sign of trouble arose in the summer of 1665, when he was cited to appear in the local church court at Lismore accused, according to one witness, of unspecified but 'horrid crimes, destructive to his own and others salvation'. On this occasion, however, the charges against him were

---

[41] See especially S. Shapin, *A Social History of Truth: Civility and Science in Seventeenth-Century England* (Chicago, 1994).

[42] His father's nonconformity may also have played a part in the decision not to send the young Flamsteed to Oxford or Cambridge. As an example of his father's attraction to the dissenting interest, in 1664 he placed his son under the care of Luke Cranwell (d.1683), an ejected Derbyshire minister, who achieved some fame in local dissenting circles for his medical prowess; see F. Baily (ed.), *An Account of the Revd John Flamsteed, the First Astronomer Royal* (London, 1835), 8, 11; *Cal. Rev.*, 142.

[43] Baily, *Account*, 16, 21. Flamsteed's admiration for Greatrakes, like that of so many of his supporters (see Chapter 4), may have stemmed from his eirenic, latitudinarian leanings in the 1660s, which Michael Hunter has discerned from his reading in this period; see M. Hunter, 'Science and Astrology in Seventeenth-Century England: An Unpublished Polemic by John Flamsteed', in Hunter, *Science and the Shape of Orthodoxy: Intellectual Change in Late-Seventeenth-Century Britain* (Woodbridge, 1995), 252.

either dropped or reduced, as he subsequently claimed that the only offence with which he now stood charged was that of practising medicine without a licence from the local bishop. Inhibited from stroking, Greatrakes himself may now have deliberately raised the stakes for, according to the same informant, he utterly refused to countenance the need to request or receive any such authorisation for his healing activities. In typically forthright fashion, he argued that his gift derived either from God or the Devil, and effectively challenged the Church to prove the case one way or the other.[44] Depending on which source one believes, Greatrakes was now either ordered to appear before the recently installed Archbishop of Dublin, Michael Boyle (1609–1702), or requested such a meeting in order to clear his name. The two men subsequently met in Dublin in July 1665, when Greatrakes was subjected to what would appear to have been a severe interrogation at the hands of the sceptical Archbishop. Boyle, a hardline episcopalian, soon became convinced that Greatrakes' healing was some form of subterfuge that represented a coded criticism of the Restoration settlement in Ireland. His former association with known radicals in the 1650s was invoked during this inquisition, although Boyle was willing, possibly as a sop to other members of his family such as the Earl of Orrery, to entertain the view that Greatrakes was merely a dupe in this business, the victim of more sinister forces seeking to subvert the restored regime.[45]

The archbishop also hinted, in a letter to Lord Conway, that others shared his scepticism. Greatrakes, it would appear, was indeed attracting criticism and not just from the upper echelons of the restored Church. The Congregational preacher Samuel Mather (d. 1671), a leading figure in dissenting circles in Dublin, became convinced, like Michael Boyle, that the stroker's claims to heal the sick were either fraudulent or diabolical in origin, and should be publicly exposed as such. He later wrote that he found Greatrakes 'a Man of Whim [with] a strong Imagination' and repeated the rumour, also reported by the Archbishop, that he had previously dabbled in illicit magic having fallen under the influence of infamous magicians like Cornelius Agrippa (1486–1535) from whom he had 'got his Abracadabra'. Indeed, so incensed was Mather that according to Edmund Calamy he wrote 'a Discourse against his Pretensions... to prevent the People from running to him'. The work in question, however, was never published. After Mather had shown it to 'some Persons of Figure', it was subsequently commended 'but not allow'd to be Printed,

---

[44] Greatrakes, *Brief Account*, 36–7; RS, EL/M1/36.

[45] *Conway Letters*, 262–3. Michael Boyle was a cousin of Richard Boyle, second earl of Cork, who shared his religious conservatism, loyalty to the Stuarts, and distrust of Greatrakes; *ODNB*. In all probability, his instinctive dismissal of Greatrakes was based on a long standing knowledge of the man and the circles he frequented in the 1650s. In January 1653, for example, Michael Boyle informed his cousin that one Poole had escaped a charge of blasphemy when he appeared before the Lord Chief Justice of Munster, John Cook, and was then seen the following evening dining with the judge at the house of Colonel Robert Phaire. Also present was a radical minister, Thomas Royle. Two years later, in June 1655, Lieutenant Valentine Greatrakes certified that in conference with Royle he heard him utter 'divers blasphemous expressions'. Royle was also accused of atheism and being married to a bigamist; CH, Lismore MS 29, 24 January 1653; RCBL, Dublin, GS 2/7/3/20, 24, 81–4, 89; Barnard, *Cromwellian Ireland*, 110n; S. D. Seymour, *The Puritans in Ireland 1647–1661* (Oxford, 1969), 64.

because of the Author's Character'.[46] A manuscript version of that treatise, however, almost certainly survives in the Sloane manuscripts in the British Library.[47] This suggests that on balance Mather's analysis of Greatrakes' cures was even harsher than that of the Archbishop. In addition to rehearsing the standard arguments of Protestant theologians against men who claimed a special dispensation to effect miracles (these, he argued in orthodox fashion, had ceased since the day of the apostles), Mather went further by suggesting that Greatrakes' healing derived from his immersion in the works of the mystic Jacob Boehme (d. 1624) and other 'magical' authors. In Mather's eyes, Greatrakes was either a naïve dupe or a clever charlatan. Regardless of his real intentions, however, or those of his supporters, Mather became convinced of one thing: namely, that Greatrakes did not possess the true ability to heal and that if any real benefit accrued to his patients, it was in all likelihood achieved through the intercession of the Devil and not God.

Greatrakes then undoubtedly divided Protestant opinion in Ireland. From the outset, he seems to have attracted supporters and opponents from across the religious spectrum in equal measure. Not all nonconformists, for example, shared Samuel Mather's negative estimation of the man and his cures, a fact fully attested by the circumstances surrounding the publication of *Wonders If Not Miracles* (1665), the first full-length account of his cures to appear in England.[48] The prov-

---

[46] E. Calamy, *An Abridgement of Mr Baxter's History of His Life and Times*, 2 vols (London, 1713), ii, 417. A possible factor in Mather's disinclination to accept the reality of Greatrakes' cures may be found in the fact that shortly after these events he preached a sermon in Dublin justifying withdrawal from the Church of Ireland and urging instead greater cooperation and union among the various dissenting sects and factions. It would appear that those nonconformists who did endorse Greatrakes' claims were far more likely to have favoured continuing dialogue with their persecutors (for examples of which see Chapter 4). For Mather, see his entry in the *ODNB*, which makes no reference to his encounter with Greatrakes. He was probably the source of his brother Increase's depiction of Greatrakes as that 'late miracle monger or Mirabilian stroker', whom he accused of attempting to cure an ague by using the word 'Abrodacara'. Like Samuel, Increase also castigated the evil influence of the works of Agrippa; I. Mather, *An Essay for the Recording of Illustrious Providences* (Boston, 1684), 182, 258.

[47] BL, Sloane MS 1926, fos 1–10. Internal evidence strongly suggests that the anonymous author of this small treatise was a learned cleric, well versed in theological argument and a committed Calvinist. If Mather was the author, then the reference to a colleague who had witnessed Greatrakes blaspheme, a 'godly Minister' identified only by his initials T. J. (fo. 5r), was probably an allusion to Mather's American co-religionist Thomas Jenner, who like Mather had been encouraged to settle in Ireland in the 1650s as part of the evangelising mission undertaken by the Cromwellian authorities; Barnard, *Cromwellian Ireland*, 138. Jenner was minister to an independent congregation at Carlow at the time of Greatrakes' visit to Dublin. Mather's authorship is also suggested by the derogatory references to Agrippa (fo. 2r), as well as his description of Greatrakes and others like him as 'Mirabiliarians' (fo. 4r). One final piece of circumstantial evidence in favour of Mather as the author is suggested by the writer's comment that 'I have not my Library heere with mee' (fo. 7v). Forced to leave Ireland in 1660, Mather settled in Lancashire, where he was ejected shortly afterwards. He was back in Ireland in 1664, but may well have left his personal belongings, including his books, in England; *Cal. Rev.*, 344.

[48] *Wonders If Not Miracles or a Relation of the Wonderful Performances of Valentine Gertrux of Affance near Youghall in Ireland* (London, 1665). This short work largely consists of a letter written by one Lionel Beacher of Youghal, prefixed by a celebration of Greatrakes' cures as attested by three Devon gentlemen, John Lancaster, John Pley and Henry Hatsell of Plymouth. The author also notes that 'all that were of his [i.e. Greatrakes'] acquaintance in these parts while he lived here, do give the character of a very sober, discreet, civil Gentleman'; ibid. 5. Two copies of Beacher's letter, dated 18 May 1665, with very slight modifications, survive in the archives of the Royal Society. They probably represent copies forwarded by John Beale to Robert Boyle in September 1665; RS, EL/M1/36; EL/B1/106; Boyle, *Correspondence*, ii, 522.

enance of this interesting pamphlet is unclear, but it was probably published by a cabal of close friends and acquaintances of the stroker, all with connections to Devon. At least one of the four men mentioned in the tract, Captain John Lancaster, was a close kinsman of Greatrakes (see pp. 31–2). The other three had all played a conspicuous part in the government of Devon during the Interregnum. Captain Henry Hatsell (d. 1667), described in error as Haslell in the pamphlet, was a Cromwellian naval commissioner and JP, who, it was widely rumoured in the early 1660s, was involved in plots against the restored King. Originally from Minehead, he had served in the armies of Parliament, assisted the naval preparations for the convoy of troops to Ireland after 1649, and had benefited from the purchase of sequestrated estates and forfeited Crown lands in Somerset and Cornwall in the 1650s.[49] Hatsell's former naval colleague, Captain John Pley, was likewise a marked man, having acted as vice-admiral for the county in the 1650s. He also sat briefly as a local MP and chaired the committee for sequestrations.[50] The bulk of the pamphlet, however, consists of a letter written by one Lionel Beacher, from Youghal in Ireland, who claimed to have witnessed at first hand Greatrakes' cures of various patients, including those suffering from the king's evil, fits, deafness, and other chronic complaints.

Beacher is an interesting character whose early life and career has some intriguing parallels with that of the subject of his letter. Like Greatrakes, the young Beacher owed an important debt of patronage to the Boyle family, and in particular the first Earl of Cork. He first appears as a retainer on the Boyle payroll in

---

[49] F. Hancock, *Minehead in the County of Somerset. A History of the Parish, the Manor, and the Port* (Taunton, 1903), 73, 75, 278; I.J. Gentles, 'The Debentures Market and Military Purchases of Crown Land, 1649–1660', PhD thesis (London, 1969), 293; *CSPD, 1651*, 577 [where payment was made to Captain Henry Hatsell for 'his pains, travel, and service in the reducing of Scilly']. Hatsell's career as a committed Cromwellian JP, severe on Quakers, tipplers and other 'enemies of the state', can be followed in the calendared state papers for the 1650s. It is quite possible that he may have met Greatrakes during the course of his duties. He was in Exeter, for example, for the assizes in April 1656, at about the same time that Greatrakes was concluding the purchase of the city's Irish lands; *CSPD, 1655–1656*, 524, 526, 532. As a naval commissioner, he was also in contact with the Irish ports, including Youghal. After the Restoration, he retired to his estates at Saltram, just outside Plymouth. Despite rumours of his plotting, there does not appear to be any surviving evidence linking Hatsell with overt opposition to the restored regime; S. K. Roberts, *Recovery and Restoration in an English County: Devon Local Administration 1646–1670* (Exeter, 1985), 154; cf. TNA, SP 29/449/90, where Hatsell's name is included in a list of 'Persons most likely to make Insurrecion in Devon: Somersett & Cittie of Exon'. According to newspaper reports he was arrested, along with Thomas Mall, in the wake of Venner's rising in January 1661; see pp. 192–3.

[50] Pley, along with Lancaster and Greatrakes, had connections to Cornworthy in Devon, where the three men were business partners in 'a parcel of land'; *Wonders If Not Miracles*, 4. In 1655, he was active in the parish as an overseer of the poor and the church's accounts, an office he shared with Lancaster until 1672; Rev. S. G. Harris, 'John Tucker: Parish Clerk of Cornworthy and Antiquary', *TDA*, 25 (1893), 480. Like Greatrakes, he too used his military and political contacts in order to act as an agent or middle man in the purchase of adventurers' lots in Ireland. In December 1656, he wrote to Colonel Clarke, an admiralty commissioner in London, who had served in Ireland and sat as an Irish MP in Barebones, reporting that he had approached several adventurers in Dartmouth with the intention of purchasing their recently allocated lots of Irish land. Few, however, were willing to sell; *CSPD, 1656–1657*, 483. It seems highly likely, therefore, that he was part of Greatrakes' network of investors and agents who were busily brokering deals in Irish land.

December 1638, and he continued to serve the Earl until June 1640, when he departed his service to serve in the Bishops Wars in Scotland.[51] By 1642 he was back in Ireland and eager to serve both the Earl and the Protestant cause in general in the aftermath of the Catholic uprising. In June of that year, for example, he wrote a long letter to the Earl, recounting skirmishes and enemy troop movements in the vicinity of Lismore, as well as a shortage of arms and munitions among the defenders of Lismore Castle. Beacher was finally rewarded for his loyalty to the Boyles in November 1642 when, with the Earl's assistance, he married the wealthy widow of one Captain Thomas Williams.[52] Beacher's fortunes, however, were soon to take a turn for the worse. As a prosperous merchant with useful contacts, he was expected to play his part in supplying the Protestant ports and garrisons of Munster with wheat and other vital provisions. Accordingly, in 1643, he saddled himself with a huge debt of over £1,000, incurred in the service of the state, which he spent the next twenty years attempting to reclaim. Although he continued to trade for a brief period in Youghal, where he was made a freeman in October 1644, he deserted Ireland shortly thereafter and, like the young Greatrakes, sought refuge in Devon, where he was soon active in support of the parliamentary cause.[53]

During the 1650s, Beacher rose rapidly to political prominence in the small borough of Bideford, where he was able to exploit the well-established commercial and social ties that linked the north Devon port with settlements on the other side of the Irish Sea. Throughout this period he acted as an agent of the Cromwellian government, eventually rising to the position of mayor. At the same time he came into close contact with other well wishers to the commonwealth regime in Devon, including Hatsell and Pley.[54] At the Restoration, Beacher returned to Ireland, where he clearly hoped to avoid the inevitable recriminations for his past services to the Interregnum regime. In a penurious condition, he threw himself upon the mercy of the Boyle family with whom, as in Greatrakes' case, there were long-established connections.[55] Through the intercession of Roger Boyle, now Earl of Orrery, Beacher's fortunes steadily improved. In 1664 he was appointed clerk to

[51] Grosart, v, 68, 101, 142. Beacher's outstanding wages were not paid in full until the summer of 1642; NLI, MS 6900, accounts, weeks ending 8 January 1642 and 18 June 1642.

[52] CH, Lismore Papers, vol. 22, no. 132; vol. 23, no. 74; Grosart, v, 217; BL, Egerton MS 80, fos 12r–v.

[53] Ibid. fo. 12v; Bodl., Rawlinson MS A 110, fos 74r–v; R. Caulfield (ed.), *The Council Book of the Corporation of Youghal* (Guildford, 1878), 249, 250; NLI, MS 6900, disbursements, weeks ending 26 October 1644, 9 November 1644.

[54] Bideford was particularly reliant upon trade with south-west Ireland. Among other services to the Interregnum state, Beacher acted as a government agent in the town organizing the transportation of horses, men, and supplies to Ireland in connection with the Cromwellian conquest in 1651. He was also closely involved with Hatsell and Pley in impressing sailors for the Cromwellian navy; *CSPD, 1651*, 548–9; *CSPD, 1655–1656*, 157. As a lay magistrate, Beacher conducted civil marriages under new legislation brought in by the Cromwellians; North Devon Record Office, W. H. Rogers, 'Notes on Bideford', 3 vols, iii, 53–5.

[55] In August 1661, Beacher was back in Youghal, from where he wrote to Orrery's brother, the second earl of Cork, seeking a post in the customs in return for past services and favours; CH, Lismore Papers, vol. 32, no. 32.

the trustees responsible for managing the affairs of the 1649 Officers before the Court of Claims.[56] Two years later, Beacher was serving as a burgess in his native Youghal, as well as holding the customs post of land waiter.[57] At about the same time, he entered the service of the Earl of Orrery as a steward at the Earl's new residence at Charleville in county Cork, a post which he continued to hold for many years and one that led him into frequent conflict with the countess, who clearly did not share her husband's faith or conviction in his abilities. Beacher none the less remained a loyal servant of the Boyles, and may well have shared his patron's religious and political prejudices. In 1666, for example, as previously noted (see p. 59), he and his stepson informed the Government of a suspected Catholic uprising and French invasion of Ireland, fears that were widely shared by Beacher's patron, Orrery.

Under the circumstances, then, it is reasonable to speculate that Beacher's role in publishing the first pamphlet advertising the wondrous cures of Greatrakes may have owed something to Orrery, who was always eager to bolster the cause of a broad-based Protestant ascendancy in Munster in opposition to the Catholic majority and their lukewarm abettors within government circles.[58] At the same time, it is worth noting the role played by another of Greatrakes' English-based admirers, Benjamin Worsley, in dispersing copies of Beacher's letter to various figures close to Orrery's brother, Robert Boyle, including the physician Thomas Sydenham and clergyman John Beale. Worsley was well placed to act as an intermediary, given his connections in both Devon and Ireland, as well as his long-standing acquaintance with Boyle and his sister Lady Ranelagh.[59] His response to the Restoration also suggests some striking parallels with that of Greatrakes.

[56] NLI, MS 816, fo. 30. Another important intermediary who acted on Beacher's behalf in securing this post was Owen Silver (d.1688), a Youghal lawyer and solicitor for the 1649 Officers in the Court of Claims. Silver had served as a soldier under Cromwell in Ireland and had secured substantial holdings in the counties of Waterford, Kerry, Tipperary, Leitrim and the cities of Dublin and Waterford. He was appointed MP for Youghal in 1661 and town clerk of the borough for life in 1664 (as well as recorder in 1671). He was clearly well known to both Orrery and Greatrakes. In 1669, Beacher proposed Silver to Orrery as a referee in his attempt to secure the post of surveyor of the customs farm at Youghal. He recommended him as one 'knowne to your Lordship'. Silver also appeared in the wills of his kinsmen, Valentine Greatrakes and John Lancaster of Cornworthy. The former described Silver as 'my faithful friend and kinsman', while the latter, in his will of 1683, referred to him as his cousin, to whom he left £100 as well as a gift of land to his eldest son; ibid. fo. 32; Bodl., Carte MS 145, 276; JRL, Irish MS 125, fos 22v, 33r; *Fifteenth Report of the Irish Record Commission Respecting the Public Records in Ireland* (Dublin, 1825), 67, 101; Bodl., Carte MS 67, fo. 69v; C. M. Tenison, 'Cork MPs', *JCHAS*, 2 (1896), 276; WSxRO, MS 13,223 (10); RCBL, MS 80/B2/2, 285; DRO, PR/A 821.
[57] Caulfield, *Council Book of Youghal*, 314. It is possible that Beacher was sitting as a burgess on the town council of Youghal before 1666. Unfortunately the borough records do not survive for the critical period from 1659 to 1666.
[58] MacLysaght, *Calendar of the Orrery Papers*, 83 and *passim*; Bodl., Carte MS 34, fos 632, 634. For a brief account of Beacher's later life and service at Charleville, see T. C. Barnard, 'The Political, Material and Mental Culture of the Cork Settlers, 1649–1700', in P. O'Flanagan and N. G. Buttimer (eds), *Cork: History and Society. Interdisciplinary Essays on the History of an Irish County* (Dublin, 1993), 341.
[59] For Worsley, see T. Leng, *Benjamin Worsley (1618–1677): Trade, Interest and the Spirit in Revolutionary England* (Woodbridge, 2008).

Like the stroker, Worsley had played an important role in the Cromwellian land settlement in Ireland, both in his capacity as chief surveyor as well as his role in planning the transportation of native Catholics to Connaught. Moreover, he too had profited from this process, acquiring land and office, and was thus faced with a similar dilemma in 1660 when political change threatened his material and other interests in Ireland. Worsley responded by seeking accommodation with the new regime. In November 1661, he wrote to Lady Clarendon asking her to intercede on his behalf with her husband, now chief advisor to Charles II. Worsley's petition makes interesting reading, projecting an image not dissimilar from that adopted by Greatrakes in his published account of 1666. The tone of the petition is partial, subjective, and conciliatory, and provides further evidence of the convoluted nature of the politics of survival in early Restoration Britain. Worsley had first served in Ireland in the early 1640s in his capacity as surgeon to the English forces there. At no point, however, did he admit to taking sides in the quarrel between King and Parliament. Of the crucial period between 1647 and late 1649, he wrote:

> I can with much faithfullnesse, and Integrity affirme, I never so made my selfe of any Party, as to hold Intelligence about any publicke Concerne, with any single person eyther of the Kings side or of the Parliaments side... but preserved my selfe (at least as to any matter of Acting) as a Person wholly disengaged, though using the liberty of my owne privatt judgement, as I saw there was most ground for it.[60]

Furthermore, on his return to Ireland in 1650, Worsley claimed never to have signed any public address, protestation, or engagement, nor 'tooke any Oathe [to Cromwell], And upon the passing of the Petition and Advise I declared so much dissatisfaction as that upon his Sonnes being made Deputy of Ireland [Henry Cromwell] or soone after my place of surveyor generall was given to another privattly.' He subsequently retired to his estates in Queen's County where, like Greatrakes in Waterford, he was responsible, as a local JP, for supervising the transportation of local Catholics to Connaught and reallocating the vacant lands to soldiers and adventurers. As a result, echoing Greatrakes' experience, he faced financial ruin at the Restoration as it became increasingly likely that much of the land he had acquired in the 1650s would be returned to its original owners or granted to loyal royalists. His petition to Clarendon should thus be seen as part of a wider strategy to secure his financial future through the spurious claim that he had played little active part in the government of Ireland in the 1650s. Worsley's petition, moreover, also fails to mention the extent to which his political isolation in the late 1650s was due to his radical religious and political views that fell out of favour after 1655 following the appointment of Henry Cromwell as lord deputy. It was during this period that he became increasingly disenchanted with mainstream denominational worship and began to agitate for a broad-based programme of ecumenical church reform that would have tolerated all Protestant

---

[60] Bodl., Clarendon MS 75, fo. 300r.

sectaries, including the Quakers, sentiments that he wisely chose to omit from his biographical sketch of 1661.[61]

It would be a mistake, however, to attribute Worsley's new-found moderation in 1661 purely to the demands of political pragmatism. Men did change their minds in the seventeenth century for reasons other than expediency, a fact often overlooked by historians who too frequently assume ideological consistency at the expense of messy pragmatism. In Worsley's case, his theological outlook, experimental and not easily pigeon-holed at the best of times, did not so much undergo a transformation, but rather evolved toward a position wherein he could see little value in continued disputes over the outward trappings of religion. In September 1660, for example, he wrote a letter to Samuel Hartlib that was largely concerned with the contemporary and heated debate over the form the liturgy should take in the restored Anglican Church. Typically, he contended for the middle way, arguing for a policy of coexistence that would have enabled those who objected to the forms of worship prescribed in the old Book of Common Prayer to worship side by side with those who laboured for its reintroduction. Echoing Greatrakes, he therefore argued that men's private consciences, and not external forces, should act as the final arbiter in such matters:

> Lett them therefore that will commend it to the people see to it: and see that they do rightly approve themselves to their great Master in nursing the people by it, and that they are careful heeders and observers of his worke & Providences among us that they do not mistake. Lett them on the other hand who scorne it and deride it and condemne it see that they do performe a service to god that is truly more righteous & spirituall & acceptable then it, That they change not that forme to take up another for Ostentation...And lett both...see that they do approve themselves and their hearts unto God in all the Worship they performe...and then I know nothing they need to feare from mans judging of them.[62]

---

[61] Ibid. fos 300r–v. For Worsley's career in Ireland, see G. Aylmer, *The State's Servants: The Civil Service of the English Republic 1649–1660* (London & Boston, 1973), 270–2; Barnard, *Cromwellian Ireland*, 215–22, 229–33; Leng, *Benjamin Worsley*, 18–19, 80–90. Worsley left Ireland permanently in 1659 when Lady Ranelagh, a close friend and supporter, described him as 'a diligent solicitor for that poor country'. Worsley's friendship with Lady Ranelagh may explain why he sought the intercession of Clarendon at the Restoration. Ranelagh was on good terms with the Clarendons, who, it has been suggested, may have been sympathetic to her 'puritan, but essentially pietistic religious views'. In 1666, Worsley was engaged with both Robert Boyle and his sister in a scheme for financing the commercial cultivation of senna; CH, Lismore Papers, vol. 31, no. 50; Bodl., Clarendon MS 75, fos 300r–v; Leng, *Benjamin Worsley*, 136, 146; P. Seaward, *The Cavalier Parliament and the Reconstruction of the Old Regime, 1661–1667* (Cambridge, 1989), 29; K. Dewhurst, *Dr Thomas Sydenham (1624–1689). His Life and Original Writings* (London, 1966), 32–3. For a useful summary of Worsley's religious worldview and his relationship with Robert Boyle, see C. Webster, 'Benjamin Worsley: Engineering for Universal Reform from the Invisible College to the Navigation Act', in M. Greengrass, M. Leslie and T. Raylor (eds), *Samuel Hartlib and Universal Reformation: Studies in Intellectual Communication* (Cambridge, 1994), 213–35.

[62] SUL, HP, 33/2/15A–B. Significantly, perhaps, this letter was signed from Dartmouth in Devon, where Worsley was staying with friends. It is possible therefore that his acquaintances in this part of the west country included men like Captain John Pley, a resident of Dartmouth and an associate of Greatrakes (see note 50). Worsley's connections with Dartmouth probably arose from his marriage in 1656 to Lucy, the daughter of William Cary, who was a resident of the Devon port.

It is impossible to establish the full extent to which Greatrakes collaborated with those who first promoted his cures to a wider audience in 1665, but it seems highly probable that he played some part in the management of his public image in the summer of 1665, when, as we shall see, he was already planning to extend his healing mission to England. Given his close connections with men like Lancaster and Beacher, he must have approved of the general tenor of *Wonders If Not Miracles*, which may have been prompted by a desire on his part to counter misinformation and falsehoods then circulating ostensibly in support of his claims. Hints of such thinking appear in a letter which Greatrakes wrote to George Hall, Bishop of Chester, in September 1665. Here, he provides a brief summary of the early origins and manner of his healing gift, something which he felt constrained to repeat and defend because 'unhappy have I been to have my letters published, and misprinted'.[63] By this date, news had probably reached England of the doubts that were being voiced by some members of the Anglican establishment in Ireland as to the potentially seditious intent of Greatrakes' mission and those who lauded his cures. His interrogation at the hands of the Archbishop of Dublin had led to much heated speculation as to his real motives in claiming to heal diseases such as the king's evil. Fearful of bad publicity, Greatrakes, ever the 'moderate conformist', thus went to great length in his letter to Bishop Hall to disavow any such subversive aims or ambitions. In appealing to Hall, whose religious moderation and concern for a broad-based settlement in ecclesiastical affairs mirrored Greatrakes' own, the Irish stroker undoubtedly hoped to cultivate powerful friends in England who might provide *bona fide* testimonials on his behalf and thus smooth the way to wider recognition and approval at the centre of government within the English court.[64]

Greatrakes' healing in Ireland prior to his departure for England in early 1666 thus formed part of a carefully orchestrated campaign in which he sought to allay fears among his fellow countrymen and women that God had not deserted the cause of Irish Protestantism, and that He remained active as a providential deity in the daily lives of ordinary believers. In many respects, Greatrakes was ideally placed to play the role of God's deputy and to take on the added mantle of 'state physician' to the ailing body politic. By temperament and upbringing, he straddled the

---

[63] 'A Copy of Mr Valentine Greataricks Letter to the Bishop of Chester [Dr Hall] Touching his Cures by Stroakinge', in Bodl., V.15.8 Linc. [inserted between items 1 and 2]. Greatrakes was belatedly replying to a letter from Hall, written on 19 August 1665, but not received by him 'till the 12th of this instant'.

[64] Greatrakes' choice of Hall as a mediator in this matter was guided by familial and social ties as well as religious concerns. The bishop's wife, Gertrude, was related to Greatrakes' wife, Ruth Godolphin. She was also the sister of Greatrakes' close friend and business partner, Sir Ames Meredith, who was almost certainly acting as Greatrakes' advocate and apologist in England at this time. In his letter to Hall, the stroker suggests that if he needs any further assurances concerning the manner or authenticity of his cures he need only consult the anonymous gentleman and bearer of the letter, who had been an eye witness to these 'wonderfull things'. Sir Ames was a frequent visitor to his Cheshire estates, and was, in all likelihood, Greatrakes' go-between in this matter. For the family ties of the Godolphins, Merediths and Halls, see J. L. Vivian (ed.), *The Visitations of Cornwall...1530, 1573, and 1620* (Exeter, 1887), 184; *idem*, *The Visitations of the County of Devon...1531, 1564, and 1620* (Exeter, 1895), 13; DRO, PR/A 338.

complex religious and political divisions of his day. A member by birth of the old Protestant establishment, he mixed with members of the local aristocracy and governing classes, while his economic interests led him to socialize and collaborate with many of the more humble Protestant settlers, some of them former soldiers under Cromwell, who formed the backbone of the Irish economy. In religion, too, Greatrakes was well placed to steer a middle path, consistently advocating tolerance towards those whose religious views he did not share as long as they were not inimical to good government or subversive of the state.[65] He may even have extended such moderation to Roman Catholics, though his treatment of the Prendergasts argues otherwise. Greatrakes, moreover, consistently posed as a true and loyal member of the restored Episcopalian Church, which, he argued, ought to 'comprehend' or include the vast majority of Protestants regardless of their personal or private beliefs. Greatrakes was at heart an eirenicist; that is, one who promoted religious peace and harmony, whose mission to heal the sick in body extended to a wider aspiration to cure the spiritual sicknesses under which so many of his compatriots, many patients, now laboured. Above all, he saw himself as a witness, under divine favour, to the sickening divisions which threatened to tear apart the body politic in Ireland in the early years of the Restoration. In seeking to cure the physical manifestations of those divisions, we thus catch a unique glimpse of the response of one man, albeit that of a prominent and well-respected member of his local community, to the anxieties engendered by two decades of warfare and civil strife which, as Greatrakes was all too aware, had their ultimate origin at the centre of power in England. Under such circumstances, it is hardly surprising then that in the late summer of 1665 he should now seriously contemplate journeying to England, where, if the opportunity arose, he might demonstrate his curative powers before the highest authorities in the land.

---

[65] In his autobiography, Greatrakes the magistrate claimed that he never committed 'any one for his Judgment or Conscience barely; so it led him not to do anything to the disturbance of the civil Peace of the Nation'. Elsewhere, he lamented the onset of political corruption in Interregnum Ireland, which he saw as the inevitable by-product of the sectarian divisions initiated by the Civil War; Greatrakes, *Brief Account*, 20–2.

4

'An Exemplar of Candid and Sincere Christianity': Greatrakes' Mission to England, 1666

It being a time of great Expectations among all men, and of strange Impressions upon very many, the very imagination of strange alterations in the world, makes strange alterations upon men's thoughts and spirits; it's no wonder, when all men look for a year of Miracles, that one man should attempt to begin it.

[David Lloyd], *Wonders No Miracles; Or, Mr. Valentine Greatrates Gift of Healing Examined* (London, 1666), 11-12.

YEAR OF EXPECTATION: GREATRAKES' ARRIVAL IN ENGLAND, 1666

As interest in Greatrakes was reaching its peak in Ireland and stories of the Irishman's miraculous cures began to circulate in English newspapers, the first of many approaches was made to the Irish healer in an effort to persuade him to travel to England in order to exercise his gifts on Lady Anne Conway (1631–1679), a chronic sufferer from paralysing migraines. Many others had tried but failed, including some of the leading lights of the English medical establishment such as William Harvey (1578–1657) and Thomas Willis (1621–1675). The appeal to Greatrakes thus represented something of a high-risk strategy given the unorthodox nature of his healing methods and the taint of sectarianism that dogged his footsteps. However, this was not the first time that the Conways had dabbled with miracle healers. In 1654, Lady Anne entered into a lengthy correspondence with the London cleric Robert Gell (1595–1665) and her close friend Henry More (1614–1687) concerning the merits of a miracle healer called Matthew Coker.[1] There were strong similarities between Coker's approach to curing the sick and that employed by Greatrakes. Both, for example, claimed to heal by touch or stroking,

---

[1] *Conway Letters*, 98–104. Robert Gell was appointed rector of the rich London living of St Mary Aldermary in 1641 and remained undisturbed at the Restoration. His religious stance was decidedly heterodox. A firm believer in astrology, he was accused in 1658, amongst other things, of being an Arminian, a well-wisher to seekers and Quakers, and over-fond of allegorizing the scriptures. Like Coker, whom he greatly admired, he too advocated a broad-based and tolerant resolution of the country's religious divisions; *ODNB*; [R. Gell], *EIPHNIKON: or, a Treatise of Peace Between the Two Visible Divided Parties* (London, 1660).

and both encouraged the view that their sanative powers were divine in origin. In addition Coker, like Greatrakes, attracted the support of powerful patrons, including aristocrats such as the Earl of Pembroke, who shared his eirenic aspirations. Coker's miraculous gift, as reported by More, was thus accompanied by a prophecy in which Coker alleged that 'there will be at last such a time, as names of division will cease and that there will be no higher nor more gratefull style then that of Christian'.[2] Such a message was certain to prove attractive to a woman like Lady Conway, who, despite her aristocratic background, demonstrated an unusually broad-minded approach to the religious and philosophical novelties of the 1650s. Steeped in the writings of men like the Silesian mystic Jacob Boehme (d. 1624), she was later to convert to Quakerism, her home at Ragley Hall in Warwickshire becoming a haven for persecuted members of that sect.[3]

Anne's husband, Edward Lord Conway first became aware of Greatrakes' gift of healing in July 1665, when he wrote excitedly to his close friend, Sir George Rawdon, with news of the stroker's successful cures, and asked him to act as an intermediary in order to arrange for Greatrakes to visit his ailing wife at Ragley. No expense was to be spared. At the same time, he wrote to two other acquaintances in Ireland, Philip Tandy and Michael Boyle, Archbishop of Dublin, asking for their opinion as to the veracity of the claims made on Greatrakes' behalf. The latter's reply was, as one might expect, profoundly negative. The archbishop, who had summoned and interrogated Greatrakes for an hour (see p. 66), depicted him as an insubordinate and surly radical, who voiced a strong disinclination to kowtow to aristocrats and whose chief supporters were drawn from the ranks 'of those who were on the same side with him in the last wars'. Under the delusion that he was now living in the last days, he dreamt, according to Boyle, of 'converting the Jew and Turk'. Under no circumstances could he be prevailed upon to cross the Irish Sea, expressing himself 'somewhat rudely upon this accompt'.[4]

Unperturbed by this reverse, Conway continued to pursue his original plan of bringing Greatrakes to England via another go-between, his friend the Irish cleric,

[2] *Conway Letters*, 99, 101. Philip Herbert, fifth Earl of Pembroke (1621–1669), fought for Parliament during the Civil War and briefly held the post of President of the Council of State in the summer of 1652. He soon made his peace with the restored regime of Charles II in 1660, but following a short period as councillor for trade and navigation he retired from public life. Like Greatrakes' patient Lady Conway, he was also attracted to the radical fringe and the ideas of the Silesian mystic Jacob Boehme; *ODNB*. Coker, of whom little is known, was the author of three short pamphlets in which he advertized his cures and promoted an end to religious divisions: *A Propheticall Revelation Given from God Himself unto Matthew Coker of Lincoln's Inne* (London, 1654); *A Short and Plain Narrative of Matthew Coker* (London, 1654); and *A Whip of Small Cords, to Scourge Antichrist* (London, 1654).
[3] *Conway Letters*, 381–3. For a synopsis of the medical history of Lady Anne Conway, her friendship with Henry More, and later introduction to the Quakers via Francis Mercury van Helmont (1614–1699), the son of the celebrated physician, Joan Baptista van Helmont, see Sarah Hutton, 'Of Physic and Philosophy: Anne Conway, F. M. van Helmont and Seventeenth-Century Medicine', in O. P. Grell and A. Cunningham (eds), *Religio Medici: Medicine and Religion in Seventeenth-Century England* (Aldershot, 1996), 228–46.
[4] *Conway Letters*, 260–3. It is not known if Philip Tandy played any further role in the approach to Greatrakes. Tandy, who was Lady Conway's preferred choice for go-between, was far more likely to have been conducive to Greatrakes' taste. A friend and correspondent of the philosopher Thomas Hobbes, he had served for much of the 1650s as a servant of the Cromwellian state in England, and

George Rust (*c.*1628–1670). He may also have been helped in making these plans by his burgeoning friendship with Roger Boyle, Earl of Orrery. In a letter to an unknown recipient that was probably written in early August 1665, Conway described Orrery as 'particularly acquainted' with Greatrakes, who, it was alleged, had undertaken to cure the Earl of gout.[5] These approaches evidently bore fruit for in December 1665 Greatrakes wrote to Sir George Rawdon agreeing to travel to Ragley in order to attempt the cure of Lady Conway. Terms were agreed, and on this occasion Greatrakes insisted on the payment of a substantial fee (he normally cured *gratis*) that, as we have seen, was intended to cover any legal costs sustained in the attempt to retain his threatened lands in the Irish Court of Claims.[6] Whether it had always been part of his long-term plan, or whether this represented an unwelcome diversion from his normal activities, is uncertain. However, the weight of evidence would appear to point towards the timing of this journey as a calculated move on Greatrakes' part, both to capitalize on the millennial fervour and excitement surrounding the date of his arrival in England (January 1666) as well as to pursue his personal and material interests which, as we have seen, stood at a critical juncture at this time.[7]

The mood of apocalyptic thinking was of course heightened by the fact that large areas of England were then suffering from the ravages of the last great outbreak of bubonic plague. In the summer of 1665, most university-educated doctors had fled London for the countryside in the belief that there was little that they could do to allay the terrible disease. There, they were joined by their wealthy patients while the vast bulk of the population was left to fend for themselves as best they could. In many respects the medico-political crisis engendered by the plague epidemic played into Greatrakes' hands and may well have encouraged prospective patients to shun the orthodox therapies of discredited physicians and to place their

was twice accused of profiteering from his privileged position in government. In 1657, he determined to return to his native Ireland and set up as a minister. A year later, George Rawdon wrote to his friend Lord Conway extolling Tandy's merits as a preacher and stating that he was well liked by his new parishioners. Like Greatrakes, he was a large investor in Irish lands and subsequently suffered financial hardship as a result of the Act of Settlement of 1666; BL, Add. MS 32,553, fos 1–2, 3; G. Aylmer, *The State's Servants: The Civil Service of the English Republic 1649–1660* (London, 1973), 231–2; *CSPD, 1657–1658*, 141–2; *CSP Ireland, 1647–1660*, 673; RCBL, GS 2/7/3/20, 61; *CSP Adventurers, 1642–1659*, 9, 95, 343–4; *CSP Ireland, 1666–1669*, 22. The London goldsmith, Charles Doe, whose son John was cured by Greatrakes in London in 1666, assigned his allocated lot of Irish lands to Tandy, then of Westminster, in the 1650s; Greatrakes, *Brief Account*, 54–5; *CSP Adventurers, 1642–1659*, 9.

[5] *Conway Letters*, 266. Conway first became acquainted with Orrery in 1665. In June of that year, he described the Earl to his brother-in-law as 'a person of the greatest honor and merit that ever I was acquainted with in my life, and you will finde yourselfe more happy under his protection, then if you had had the choice of all the court, for his Power and readiness to oblige is greater then any mans'; ibid. 240.

[6] Ibid. 266–7.

[7] The heightened millennial excitement surrounding the year 1666 is well captured by Michael McKeon, who discusses Greatrakes in a chapter entitled 'Ideologically Problematic Prophecy' in his *Politics and Poetry in Restoration England: The Case of Dryden's* Annus Mirabilis (Cambridge, MA, 1975), 209–15. There is a further clue, albeit cryptic, to official attitudes to Greatrakes prior to his departure for England in a comment made by Father Patrick Maginn in February 1666. Maginn, who was a close confidante of the King and confessor to his Portuguese wife, Catherine of Braganza, was reported to have said that 'if [Greatrakes] had stayd a little longer in Ireland, your grace [the Duke of Ormond] would have comprehended him'; Bodl., Carte MS 46, fo. 257v.

faith in his hands.[8] Greatrakes himself was often critical of the medical establishment and orthodox therapeutic methods, castigating the failure of physicians to cure a whole range of diseases (discussed further on p. 83). He was not alone as a critic of mainstream, educated medicine. In 1665, an attempt to challenge and overthrow the medical monopoly exercised by the College of Physicians in London was launched by a group of practitioners who advocated a new system of practice based on the iatrochemical principles of Paracelsus (1493–1541) and Joan Baptista van Helmont (1579–1644). Greatrakes' appearance in England in 1666, therefore, represented one of a number of challenges to orthodox medicine that was welcomed by many who were becoming increasingly disaffected with the costly and ineffectual treatments advocated by the purveyors of traditional Galenic therapies. Moreover, this disdain for medical orthodoxy and willingness to try alternative cures was not limited to those who were unable to afford the services of the medical elite. The rich and well connected, as much as the poor, were willing to employ a diverse range of medical personnel, regardless of their educational qualifications or social status. The newly restored King, Charles II, engaged and elevated a host of mountebanks and medical charlatans, as did members of his court and entourage, many of whom supported the Society of Chemical Physicians in its rivalry with the collegiate physicians in 1665.[9] Greatrakes had thus chosen an opportune moment in which to visit England and display his miraculous healing talents. Fear of plague and disenchantment with orthodox medicine created a mood of intense expectation that was fuelled further, as we shall see, by growing discontent among the population at large with the unfolding religious and political settlement in England after 1660. To many, including the Conways, it must have seemed as though Greatrakes' gift was an act of special providence in an age in which miracles and divine intervention in the affairs of men were once again widely anticipated.

In the event, Greatrakes, who arrived at Ragley Hall in late January 1666, was unable to alleviate the pain of Lady Conway's headaches.[10] Within a fortnight of his arrival, Lord Conway reported the Irishman's failure to cure his wife. Like others, however, he enthusiastically recounted his efficacious handling of hundreds of other patients in the vicinity of Ragley Hall. At the same time, he remained firmly of the opinion that Greatrakes's thaumaturgical abilities were not miraculous in origin, but rather proceeded from 'a *sanative* virtue and a *natural* efficiency'.[11] Within a very short time, Greatrakes had become the talk of the neighbourhood. At Ragley itself,

---

[8] There is a large literature on the plague epidemic of 1665–6. The best recent account is to be found in A. L. Moote and D. C. Moote, *The Great Plague: The Story of London's Most Deadly Year* (Baltimore, 2004).

[9] I discuss the social and ideological origins of the Society of Chemical Physicians in my *Medicine and the Politics of Healing in Seventeenth-Century Britain* (forthcoming).

[10] Greatrakes arrived in England, via Dublin, toward the end of January 1666. He initially disembarked at Bristol, not Chester, from where he travelled into Somerset. A contemporary newspaper account describes flocks of people descending on him from Bristol and adjacent areas, and 'of wonderful Cures wrought by him'. He must have departed soon after for Ragley; *Intelligencer*, 29 January 1666.

[11] *Conway Letters*, 268. In the same letter, Lord Conway expressed concern for Greatrakes' pressing financial concerns, which he felt were being neglected, and asked Rawdon to intercede with Sir Thomas Stanley to do all in his power to assist.

he was introduced to a wide circle of influential scholars and luminaries, many of whom were only too eager to authenticate Greatrakes' claims to heal the sick as well as sympathize with his wider religious and political aspirations. As his fame spread, accompanied by growing excitement and expectation, he was invited in February by the mayor of nearby Worcester to demonstrate his efficacious gift of stroking in that city. Details of Greatrakes' visit survive in the city's accounts as well as in the controversial pamphlet which the physician and former radical Henry Stubbe (1632–1676) published in March under the provocative and deliberately ambiguous title of *The Miraculous Conformist*. From these sources it is apparent that the chief promoters of his cures emanated from those sections of local society which were, for one reason or another, dissatisfied with the Restoration settlement. In Worcester itself, he was entertained by Richard Withie, a local barrister, who had been ousted from a number of civic posts sometime before 1662, and lodged with one Richard Smyth, a leading citizen, who had been purged from the aldermanic bench in 1660.[12] In addition, the mayor, Edward Cooksey (d.1693), and his assistant, Nicholas Baker, who were jointly responsible for inviting Greatrakes to Worcester, would later become prominent supporters of the Whig cause in the city.[13] Similarly, many of those whom Greatrakes treated were drawn from those sections of Restoration society who had suffered most from the draconian religious policies of the new regime. Among those stroked by Greatrakes at Worcester were the prominent Quaker sympathizer, Henry Bromley (*c.*1626–1667),[14] and one Mrs Reynolds, 'a shopkeeper's wife from Alcester', who was almost certainly married to the mercer John Reynolds (d. 1671), one of the leading Presbyterians in that town.[15]

[12] WRO, Shelf A 10, Box 3, vol. 3, *supra* Accounts 1666; H. Stubbe, *The Miraculous Conformist: Or An Account of Severall Marvailous Cures Performed by…Mr Valentine Greatarick* (Oxford, 1666), 32; WRO, Shelf A 14, fos 5, 7, 8, 12v, 17r, 21r, 26v, 31v, 35r, 36v, 38r, 40r, 44v. Withie was first appointed as attorney in the Common Pleas in Worcester in 1640, and held the post in every year until ousted in 1662. Smyth was almost certainly a nonconformist. In 1677 he and his wife were cited to appear in the consistory court for failing to attend their parish church of St Helen's and for refusing to pay their parish dues; WRO, 795.02/BA2302/28/6192. One of this name also signed a letter on behalf of the nonconformists of Worcester to Richard Baxter in 1664; N. H. Keeble and G. Nuttall (eds), *Calendar of the Correspondence of Richard Baxter*, 2 vols (Oxford, 1991), ii, 42.

[13] C. A. F. Meekings, 'The Chamber of Worcester—1679 to 1689', *Transactions of the Worcestershire Archaeological Society*, 8 (1982), 8, 12, 13, 21n. Cooksey was elected a permanent alderman of Worcester in January 1677, but was removed from office in May 1683. While he played no overt part in the political conflict engendered by the Exclusion Crisis, his various sons-in-law were active at the heart of the Whig movement in the city, as was his own son Edward. He died on 16 March 1693 and left numerous legacies to the poor of the city's parishes, all of which were to be dispensed annually on the politically sensitive anniversary of the Gunpowder Plot (5 November); *CSPD, 1680–1681*, 175; TNA, PROB 11/414, fos 133v–134v.

[14] Stubbe, *Miraculous Conformist*, 29. Bromley was a close friend of the Conways who stimulated Anne Conway's early interest in the Quakers; see *Conway Letters*, 278–80. For his brother, Thomas, who was attached to the circle of the Behmenist mystic, John Pordage, at Bradfield in Berkshire and also attested to one of Greatrakes' cures in London; see page xxxx.

[15] Stubbe, *Miraculous Conformist*, 32. Mrs Reynolds' sister was married to Samuel Ticknor, the former minister of the town, who had been ejected in 1662. The house of John Reynolds was the site of a Presbyterian conventicle in 1669 and 1671; *Cal. Rev.*, 486; WRO, 712 BA 3965, 28. In his will of November 1670, Reynolds made numerous bequests to local dissenting ministers, as well as the widows of two others. It does not, however, mention his wife who had presumably predeceased him; TNA, PROB 11/335, fos 214r–215r.

Greatrakes' visit to Ragley and Worcester was cut short, however, when he was summoned to the court of Charles II at Whitehall in the middle of February 1666. Royal interest in Greatrakes' cures may have been stimulated by the King's curiosity, particularly given the Irishman's declared penchant for curing the king's evil.[16] The King himself had only recently returned from Oxford, having suspended the ceremonial of the royal touch following the outbreak of the plague in the late summer of 1665. As a result, his royal office was certainly susceptible to interlopers like Greatrakes, who may have been perceived by Charles II and some of his entourage as a political threat. It is equally possible, however, that Greatrakes' call to court was engineered by his influential and well-connected brother-in-law, William Godolphin (1635–96), a protégé of the Secretary of State, Henry Bennet, Lord Arlington (1618–1685).[17] Godolphin was not only familiar with Irish politics and leading figures such as Orrery,[18] but he also owned vast estates in the west of Ireland, which he had secured in 1665 as a reward for loyal service to the crown. In late 1666, he left England for Spain, where he remained for much of the rest of his life. During his absence his Irish lands were leased in 1668 to his brother-in-law, Greatrakes, an arrangement which suggests that the latter may have played some role in the first instance in securing these estates for his wife's well-connected brother. Whatever the case, relations between Greatrakes and Godolphin were still sufficiently warm by the end of the 1660s for the former to be mentioned in the latter's will, though whether their relationship survived Greatrakes' growing financial crisis in the 1670s and Godolphin's subsequent conversion to Roman Catholicism is impossible to judge.[19]

Regardless of the precise origins of Greatrakes' call to court in February 1666, it seems inconceivable that Lord Arlington, who issued the summons, was unaware of Greatrakes' relation to his protégé, Godolphin, which in turn must have raised

---

[16] This is the view of Harold Weber, who has suggested that Charles II was largely indifferent to what others have seen as the subversive potential of Greatrakes' ministrations, and that 'intellectual curiosity and love of novelty... characterized the royal response to Greatrakes'; H. Weber, *Paper Bullets: Print and Kingship under Charles II* (Lexington, 1996), 76–7. According to Stubbe, Greatrakes received his summons to attend on the King on 15 February; Stubbe, *Miraculous Conformist*, 42.

[17] For a brief biography of Godolphin, see Henning, ii, 407–8. He was elected MP for the Cornish seat of Camelford in 1665, but probably never took his seat in the Commons.

[18] A warm relationship between Orrery and Godolphin is evident from as early as 1663, when the former attempted to circumvent Sir Henry Bennet by encouraging his agent, William Shaen, to dine with Godolphin. Three years later, in January 1666, Orrery requested that all intelligence from Ireland should pass direct to Godolphin; NLI, MS 32, fo. 40; Rev. T. Morrice, *A Collection of the State Letters of the Right Honourable Roger Boyle* (London, 1742), 105. Godolphin was also a member of the Royal Society, though he does not appear to have been an active participant in its deliberations; M. Hunter, *The Royal Society and Its Fellows, 1660–1700: The Morphology of an Early Scientific Institution* (Oxford, 1994), 168–9; Boyle, *Correspondence*, ii, 415.

[19] *HMC House of Lords MSS 1697–1699* (London, 1905), 123. Godolphin was granted nearly 5,000 acres in county Limerick, land that was formerly in the possession of the Cromwellian financier and speculator, Samuel Avery, of London. In an undated and unsigned letter to Ormond, Avery was described as receiver of the customs in London during the 1650s who was now in debt to the state to the tune of £20,000. The anonymous informant, probably Godolphin, advises that the King would be perfectly entitled to take possession of Avery's Irish lands in lieu of his outstanding debts. Godolphin's claim to ownership of the lands was confirmed by the Court of Claims in Dublin in 1666; Bodl., Carte MSS 43, fos 437r–438v; 44, fo. 439; 60, fo. 114; JRL, Irish MS 125, fo. 5v. Greatrakes' tangled relationship with his brother-in-law is discussed more fully on pp. 169–70.

the Irish healer's hopes that he would be warmly received. In the event, however, his reception was a mixed one. At court, he conducted numerous healing sessions in the royal presence, as well as before other luminaries including the King's cousin, Prince Rupert. But the King, so we are told, was not impressed, perhaps as a result of his failure to cure the distracted courtier-poet, Sir John Denham (d.1669).[20] Outside the confines of the court, however, interest in Greatrakes, and support for his cures, was growing daily. During the course of the next few months, Greatrakes performed thousands of cures by the laying on of hands, or stroking, in and around the city of London, attracting patients from as far afield as Cheshire.[21]

Before he departed the capital at the end of May, he opted to publish a defence of his thaumaturgical skills that necessarily involved a brief autobiographical account of his life to-date. This appeared in the form of a letter addressed to the celebrated natural philosopher Robert Boyle and was largely intended as a rejoinder to a pamphlet that had appeared anonymously on 13 March under the title *Wonders No Miracles* (see Fig. 6).[22] At the same time, Greatrakes managed to secure numerous testimonials from grateful patients and eyewitnesses who were willing to corroborate his successful cures and which he appended to this work. Supplemented

[20] Denham, who had the reputation of a court wit and one who 'despised religion', was said in April 1666 to suffer from fits of distraction and to rave of 'nothing else' but religion. Others reported that his madness was caused by the 'rough stroking' of Greatrakes, who treated Denham in early March 1666; *CSP Ireland, 1666–1669*, 52; *HMC Manuscripts of the Marquess of Ormonde* (London, 1904), 217; *HMC Sixth Report*, Part 1, *Report and Appendix* (London, 1877), 339. George Walsh (*c*.1621–1692), the source of the rumour that Greatrakes had caused Denham's madness, was a loyal courtier and JP, who had suffered greatly for his loyalty to the Stuart cause in the 1650s; Green, *CPCC*, iii, 2226; TNA, LS 3/2; *CSPD, 1661–1662*, 386; R. Kingston, *Pillulae Pestilentiales: or a Spiritual Receipt for Cure of the Plague* (London, 1665), epistle dedicatory; *Calendar of Treasury Books*, i (1660–7), 119; Henning, i, 401–2; iii, 665.

[21] On 1 March 1666, George Tipping of Bowden, Cheshire, testified before the Board of Greencloth that he had come to London to be cured by 'Mr Gratterick' of 'dimness of sight and lameness'; *CSPD, 1666–1667*, 543. Newsletters and diaries further attest to the wild scenes that greeted the stroker's appearance in London, where he became the talk of the coffee houses; *CSPD, 1665–1666*, 281, 300; BL, Add. MS 10,117, fo. 157v; J. Glanvill, *Saducismus Triumphatus, or, Full and Plain Evidence Concerning Witches and Apparitions* (London, 1681), i, 90. During this period, Greatrakes administered to patients at a number of venues both in and outside the city of London. David Lloyd refers to his presence at Whitehall, St James' Palace, Lambeth, Westminster, Fleet Street, Bread Street, Cheapside and Foster Lane. He also set up a temporary base at Charterhouse Yard in Lincoln's Inn Fields, where he attended on patients five days a week for several weeks in March. There, his main host was Captain John Cressett (for whom, see p. 102 and n.). He also conducted cures at the homes of Lady Ranelagh in Pall Mall, Edmund Berry Godfrey in Westminster, John Owen at Mortlake, the Countess of Devonshire at Roehampton and Captain William Wildey at Stepney; [Lloyd], *Wonders No Miracles*, 22, 23; Greatrakes, *Brief Account*, 9, 32, 65–6, 79.

[22] This pamphlet was ostensibly occasioned by Greatrakes' failure to cure several patients at the Charterhouse in London. It was also clearly intended, in part at least, as a rejoinder to Stubbe's *Miraculous Conformist*, which, as its title suggests, gave credence to those who saw Greatrakes' gift as an act of divine inspiration. David Lloyd (1635–1692), a diehard royalist and Anglican clergyman, who was reader in the Charterhouse at the time, was identified by Greatrakes as the author in his *Brief Account*, 5. He was the author of numerous works in favour of the Restoration and restored Church of England, biographies of members of the royal family, and a pseudonymous account in 1664 that berated the consistent disloyalty and plotting of the nonconformists; for details of Lloyd's career, which omits discussion of his authorship of *Wonders No Miracles*, see *ODNB*.

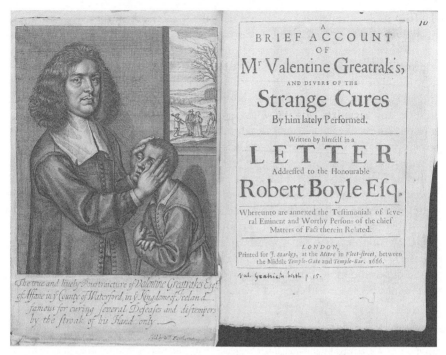

Fig. 6. Frontispiece to Valentine Greatrakes, *A Brief Account of Mr Valentine Greatrak's, And Divers of the Strange Cures By him Lately Performed* (London, J. Starkey, 1666). Engraving by William Faithorne. Bodleian Library, Oxford.

by accounts of other cures performed by Greatrakes extracted from miscellaneous sources, it has been possible to identify more than 200 individuals who were either cured by Greatrakes or witnessed and commented upon his practice. While this represents only a tiny percentage of those with whom Greatrakes came into contact, it nonetheless provides a valuable sample from which to assess the impact and appeal of the charismatic Irishman upon Restoration society. The vast majority of these testimonials were, after all, elicited freely in the knowledge that Greatrakes was likely to publish them. It seems fair to conclude therefore that if Greatrakes did appeal to specific interest groups in British society that these ought to be apparent from close analysis of the lives of those who chose to publicly authenticate his cures.[23]

At first sight, there is little homogeneity in the profiles of our sample, particularly in relation to those who sought physical relief from the Irishman's stroking. Despite the malicious attempt by critics such as David Lloyd to suggest that the majority of Greatrakes' patients were women and children, who were 'not capable of understanding how they are cured', the surviving evidence strongly suggests otherwise; Greatrakes cured the young and the aged, male and female, with no

[23] For a complete list, with brief descriptions of those not discussed in the text, see Appendix 2.

apparent bias towards social status or background.[24] However, closer inspection of those who proffered corroboratory evidence of Greatrakes' success in healing the sick reveals an interesting pattern of common allegiances and interests. A disproportionate number of these witnesses, for example, were men of some social standing in their respective communities whose professional and occupational status was high. Physicians, clergymen, magistrates, politicians, scholars, and wealthy merchants all figure prominently among the ranks of Greatrakes' most enthusiastic supporters.

'THIS ANTICHRIST OF PHYSICIANS'

The disproportionate presence of medical men willing to offer their support is perhaps surprising given both Greatrakes' marked antipathy toward the profession and the delight which he would appear to have taken in curing those on whom the specialists had given up. His criticism of the established medical profession was all-embracing, invoking the complaints of an earlier generation of would-be reformers in the interregnum. Opponents reported, for example, that he 'declaimes much against Physicians . . . as if it were not a Lawfull and Usefull Calling, or as if there were not Worthy and Learned men of that profession'. He was particularly critical of the excessive fees that learned physicians charged their patients, contrasting their greed and self-interest with his own largesse in practising *gratis*.[25] Such views were bound to alienate many within the medical profession, who were clearly stung by his criticisms and unconvinced of his method and motives. At least one anonymous pamphlet, sadly no longer extant, appeared under the hand of an anonymous physician in which the stroker's deceitful aims were laid bare. It was soon followed, however, by a rejoinder in the form of a ballad that depicted the average doctor as immoral and obsessed with money and status. Other medical men soon followed suit, offering impressive moral and intellectual support in the form of glowing testimonials attesting to the success of Greatrakes' stroking. Despite his thinly veiled contempt for the profession, there can be little doubt that Greatrakes himself valued such support, commenting gleefully to Lord Conway in April 1666 that 'I have hardly a testimonial but there is the hands of 3 or 4 doctors of physic to it'.[26]

---

[24] [Lloyd], *Wonders No Miracles*, 30. Lloyd's aim in focusing on what he saw as Greatrakes' bias towards the treatment of women was clearly part of a wider strategy that aimed to question the Irishman's moral probity and suggest a sexual element to his stroking of women's bodies; ibid. 17. Occasionally, Greatrakes' patients objected to intimate, physical contact; Stubbe, *Miraculous Conformist*, 29.

[25] BL, Sloane MS 1926, fo. 5r; Boyle, *Correspondence*, iv, 102. For Greatrakes' specific condemnation of one Dr Anthony and his excessive regard for fees, see Bodl., 15.8.Linc. Anthony, physician to the Earl of Orrery at Charleville, was present when Greatrakes conducted one of his first cures, that of Margaret Macshane, who suffered from the King's evil; Greatrakes, *Brief Account*, 23–4; RS, EL/M1/36; E. MacLysaght (ed.), *Calendar of the Orrery Papers* (Dublin, 1941), 64–5.

[26] *Rub for Rub: or, An Answer to a Physicians Pamphlet, styled, The Stroker Stroked* (London?, 1666); *Conway Letters*, 272.

Significantly, many of those medical practitioners who did corroborate Great-rakes' cures were, to a large degree, enthusiasts for medical reform who espoused the new chemical-based therapies associated with Paracelsus and van Helmont. Jeremiah Astel and Thomas Williams were signatories of the ill-fated petition to create a Society of Chemical Physicians.[27] Others, such, such as Daniel Coxe (1640–1730),[28] Albertus Otto Faber (1612–1684),[29] and Benjamin Worsley[30] were passionate advocates of chemical medicine. Interest in the new methods of the chemical physicians was not, moreover, limited to the medics among Greatrakes' supporters. The clergyman John Beale and, most famously, Robert Boyle, were equally contemptuous of established medicine and the efficacy of Galenic reme-dies, and may well have been attracted to Greatrakes because they shared his an-tipathy toward traditional methods of healing. In November 1663, for example, Beale wrote to Boyle, lamenting the contemporary state of medicine in England.

---

[27] Greatrakes, *Brief Account*, 91–4, 46–7. Astel, who was licensed to practise medicine in the dio-cese of London in March 1663, was on friendly terms with Robert Boyle. He ministered to plague victims in London in 1665–6 and was subsequently rewarded with a gift of inscribed silver plate by the city authorities in 1666; T. O'Dowde, *The Poor Man's Physician* (London, 1665), appendix; G. Starkey, *Liquor Alcahest, or a Discourse of that Immortal Dissolvent of Paracelsus and Helmont... Pub-lished by J[eremiah] A[stel] Pyrophilus* (London, 1675), epistle dedicatory by Astel to Boyle; Boyle, *Correspondence*, ii, 235; W. G. Bell, *The Great Plague in London in 1665* (London, 1951), 290; Bloom and James, 45. Williams (*c*.1612–1712), who was acquainted with Boyle, played a central role in promoting the aims of the chemists. Following the failure of their petition in 1665, he entered royal service as chemical physician to Charles II and was paid handsomely for his work in the royal labora-tory at Whitehall. At the same time, he entered politics, was briefly an MP, and became involved in various intrigues at court. He eventually suffered the loss of all his posts following the deposition of James II; O'Dowde, *Poor Man's Physician*, appendix; Henning, iii, 726–7; TNA, C 10/477/110; Boyle, *Correspondence*, iii, 2–14; *CSPD, 1673–1675*, 605; TNA, LC 3/24, fo. 16; 3/26, fo. 145; 3/30, fo. 42; *CSPD, 1668–1669*, 73, 98, 224, 245, 315; F. Harris, 'Lady Sophia's Visions: Sir Robert Moray, the Earl of Lauderdale and the Restoration Government of Scotland', *The Seventeenth Century*, 24 (2009), 144, 146; TNA, PC 2/68, 231, 237.

[28] Greatrakes, *Brief Account*, 46–7; Boyle, *Correspondence*, iii, 82–90. Initially sceptical, Coxe became a great admirer of Greatrakes. He did not, however, subscribe to the view that his cures were miraculous. Rather, he argued that they were purely physical or mechanical in nature, a product of the stroker's extraordinary physical constitution. Coxe was on close terms with a number of Greatrakes' other admirers. In addition to his close friendship with Robert Boyle, he was acquainted with John Wilkins, who proposed him for membership of the Royal Society in 1665, and was lodging with John Cressett (for whom, see p. 102 and n.) at the Charterhouse at the time of Greatrakes' visit to London. He later became a prominent dissenter and Whig, who signed the Exclusion petition in 1679–80 and was arrested in 1685. Coxe was also on close terms with John Locke, who shared his passion for Hel-montian iatrochemistry; *ODNB*; Hunter, *Royal Society and Its Fellows*, 172–3; Oldenburg, *Correspond-ence*, ii, 460n; Boyle, *Correspondence*, iii, 82–90; M. Knights, 'Petitioning and the Political Theorists: John Locke, Algernon Sidney and London's "Monster" Petition of 1680', *Past and Present*, 138 (1993), 105 and n; TNA, SP 29/421/160.

[29] Greatrakes, *Brief Account*, 46, 52–3, 76, 76–7, 89. For Faber's topsy turvy career in England, punctuated by spells of imprisonment for his support for the Quakers, and concluding with his ap-pointment as chemist to Charles II, see *ODNB*; J. L. Nickalls, 'Albertus Otto Faber, the German Doctor', *Journal of the Friends Historical Society*, 32 (1935), 54–7; H. Sampson, 'Dr Faber and His Celebrated Cordial', *Isis*, 34 (1942–3), 472–96; TNA, LC 3/27, fo. 48. Faber's interest in chemistry remained undimmed to the end of his life. In the year of his death, he enthusiastically endorsed the alchemical endeavours of a friend and alchemical colleague in a work dedicated to Robert Boyle; J. S. Weidenfeld, *Four Books... Concerning the Secrets of the Adepts* (London, 1685).

[30] For Worsley's commitment to Paracelsian and Helmontian methods of cure, see C. Webster, *The Great Instauration: Science, Medicine and Reform 1626–1660* (London, 1975), 278, 301, 378–9.

While quick to extol the work of the physician *per se*, which he compared to that of the 'good magistrate' who 'gives life to the people' and presides over an orderly and healthy body politic, he was scathing in his condemnation of those who filled that office. 'Never was there any such cruel and merciless tyrant on earth, as in an unskilful or dishonest physician', averred Beale, who 'to consume our substance, and to fill their own purses, they tear our flesh, corrode our bones, and torture us in all our parts and vitals for days, weeks, and months together'. Moreover, that Beale had in mind the established medical profession, and not the world of moun- tebanks, empirics, and charlatans, is evident from the praise that he went on to lavish on amateur healers such as the countess of Kent, whose cures, he insisted, represented a singular manifestation of divine providence. Elsewhere, he demon- strated a consistent and marked preference for unconventional treatments, includ- ing the use of a dead man's hand to cure wens, and consistently belittled the achievements of Galenic physicians and their remedies, preferring instead the chemical remedies of van Helmont and the pills and nostrums of empirics such as Richard Matthews (d. 1661).[31] Beale's disdain for orthodox medicine may well, therefore, have helped to sow the seeds of his early interest in Greatrakes, an out- come strongly advertized by his observation to Boyle in 1663 that some men and women were granted 'an extraordinary guift of healing' by God in order 'to prevent the crueltyes of Lucrative, and dishonest practitioners'.[32]

Beale's animus against traditional physic was shared by his friend Boyle, who expressed a distinct, though typically guarded, ambivalence toward the established medical profession, its monopoly of practice and over-dependence upon Galenic methods of healing.[33] His views, moreover, were almost certainly shared by other

---

[31] Boyle, *Correspondence*, ii, 203–4, 158–66, 198–205. The medical observations that Beale sent to Boyle in 1663 may have been the same as those described by Samuel Hartlib in a letter to Boyle in September 1657, where he discusses his admiration for Beale's 'addition of health'. Beale continued to provide his friend Boyle with medical advice, much of which betrayed his continuing antipathy for con- ventional medicine. In January 1664, for example, he recommended water cures to Boyle as a cheaper and more effective alternative to those offered by physicians and surgeons. Three years later, he suggested that recent experiments with blood transfusions might be successfully applied to the cure of lunatics and epi- leptics and thus save them from 'the more cruell handlings of Chirurgeons, & Physicians'. Beale clearly had in mind members of the medical elite here. Elsewhere in the same letter he caustically refers to the actions of the 'Colledge-butchers'. Beale's comment is highly redolent of that uttered by Samuel Hartlib on hearing of the death of Dr Arnold Boate in 1653, when he lamented that his friend had died at the hands of physicians, 'those common butchers of human kind'; ibid. i, 156–7, 233; ii, 239; iii, 283.
[32] Beale was careful to add, however, that such divinely gifted practitioners healed 'perchance nott in the same vigour as in the Apostolicall age'; ibid. ii, 200, 205.
[33] For a good synopsis of Boyle's views on medicine and his antipathy toward Galenism and other aspects of contemporary practice, see M. Hunter, 'Boyle Versus the Galenists: A Suppressed Critique of Seventeenth-Century Medical Practice and Its Significance', in *idem, Robert Boyle (1627–1691). Scrupulosity and Science* (Woodbridge, 2000), 157–201. This work also contains trenchant criticisms of earlier attempts to analyse Boyle's medical thinking. Boyle himself was an early admirer of the thera- peutic methods of van Helmont. Evidence of his disdain for orthodox Galenic physic is neatly cap- tured in his comment to John Mallet in 1651 that he was restored to health by the Helmontian George Starkey 'without the wonted Martyrdome of Physicke'; Boyle, *Correspondence*, i, 104. Given Boyle's views on medicine, it is possible that the John Lancaster who dedicated his translation of the Italian iatrochemist Leonardo di Capua (1617–1695) to Boyle in 1684 was the same man as Great- rakes' cousin, who was among the first to promote his cures in print in 1665 (see p. 68); L. Di Capua, *The Uncertainty of the Art of Physick* (London, 1684).

members of his family, including those who keenly supported Greatrakes' thaumaturgical mission. Boyle's sister and Beale's close confidante, Lady Ranelagh, was
thus not averse to medical experimentation, much preferring to 'take Physick
rather upon Experience than upon a fine reasoning discourse'. Such open-mindedness almost certainly made her receptive to the ministrations of empirics. In 1649,
for example, she and her brother Robert wrote to Samuel Hartlib with details of
her recent cure at the hands of an Irish gentleman named Kertcher, who treated her
for toothache. In a manner reminiscent of the methods later used by Greatrakes,
he was also said to cure a range of agues as well as the plague by a form of stroking.
Not surprisingly, Lady Ranelagh also demonstrated a distinct aversion to those
evacuative methods favoured by the Galenists such as phlebotomy, recalling in
1652 how an Irish neighbour and kinsman had been killed by the unseasonable
use of bloodletting. A few years later she played a prominent role in supporting the
attempt of the Helmontian William Rand (d.1663) to establish an alternative
medical society for London in opposition to 'the more ambitious, covetous, domi-
neering, and selfish sort of Physitians [who] will evermore joine to the old
Colledge'.[34] Likewise, her brother and Greatrakes' patron, Roger Boyle, Earl of
Orrery, showed little faith in the ability of London's finest physicians to cure his
gout, refusing 'to hearken to his friends in this matter'. Not surprisingly, he resorted to Greatrakes for relief, as did his brother-in-law, Charles Rich, Earl of
Warwick (1616–1673), who suffered from the same complaint and was stroked by
the Irish healer at the home of Lady Ranelagh in 1666.[35]

The Boyles' aversion to orthodox Galenic medicine and its practitioners was also
shared by another prominent supporter of Greatrakes, and associate of Beale and
Robert Boyle, Henry More. Physicians, he pronounced, 'very seldom cure, but
where nature by ordinary country meanes and abstinence would cure itself'.[36]
Others among Greatrakes' entourage who may have shared an antipathy for con-

---

[34] CH, Lismore Papers, vol. 31, no. 2; SUL, HP 28/1/2A, 2A–B; Boyle, *Correspondence*, i, 137;
SUL, HP 42/10; Webster, *Great Instauration*, 307–8, 533–4. Lady Ranelagh's pronounced preference
for alternative forms of medical therapy, particularly those favoured by the iatrochemists, is strongly
suggested by her patronage of continental physicians such as Johann Sibertus Küffeler and Johann
Brün, alias Unmussig. Among other things, she tried to encourage the latter, who settled in Ireland in
the 1650s, to take up a position as physician to her older brother, Richard, the second Earl of Cork;
Boyle, *Correspondence*, i, 163–4, 334.

[35] BL, Sloane MS 4227, fos 92r–v; Boyle, *Correspondence*, iii, 86. It is highly likely that the medical
unorthodoxy exhibited by the Boyle siblings may have owed something to the prejudices of their
overbearing father Richard Boyle, the first Earl of Cork, who also eschewed conventional physic in
favour of chemical medicines and other home-grown remedies such as sea water and the healing properties of stone bottles; N. Canny, *The Upstart Earl: A Study of the Social and Mental World of Richard
Boyle, First Earl of Cork 1566–1643* (Cambridge, 1982), 137, 148; CH, Cavendish MS 78, vol. 2,
40–1, 137.

[36] *Conway Letters*, 103. More's friend and fellow admirer of Greatrakes, Joseph Glanvill, was equally
dismissive of the efficacy of traditional medicine, which he claimed 'never brought the world so much
practical, beneficial knowledge, as would help towards the cure of a cut finger'; J. Glanvill, *Plus Ultra;
or the Progress and Advancement of Knowledge Since the Days of Aristotle* (London, 1668), 7–8. In the
same work, he promoted the usefulness of chemistry which he believed would produce real advances
in medicine and society if shorn of its 'phantastick, unintelligible and delusive' elements; ibid.
10–12.

ventional physic include the celebrated clinician Thomas Sydenham (1624–1686),[37] a close associate of Boyle, in whom he confided in 1668 that he was sneered at and ostracized by the medical establishment, as well as Ezekiel Foxcroft (1629–1674)[38] and John Ward (1629–1681),[39] who were both drawn toward iatrochemistry and related ideas in the 1660s. Chemistry, moreover, also offered a naturalistic explanation for the efficacy of Greatrakes' stroking. Thomas Willis' theory of fermentation, for example, lay at the root of Stubbe's approach, while Boyle's own corpuscularian theories underpinned his attempt and that of others like Henry More and Daniel Coxe to explain the 'sanative virtue' inherent in Greatrakes' handling of his patients.

GREATRAKES, LATITUDINARIANS, AND THE ACCOMMODATION OF DISSENT

The interest generated by Greatrakes among the medical fraternity is perhaps unsurprising. Many, no doubt, were intrigued to understand more about the man and his method of cure as part of a wider and growing fascination in medical circles with natural philosophy and the new science. The foundation of the Royal Society in 1662 encouraged renewed speculation and interest in a whole range of natural phenomena, including the prodigious and unexplained, into which category of the 'preternatural' the Irish stroker's cures were readily assimilated. While this aspect of the Greatrakes affair has attracted much interest among historians of science, far less attention has been paid to the wider political significance of the stroker's appearance in England in 1666. Here, close analysis of our sample provides some interesting insights into this broader issue, suggesting distinct patterns of religious and political outlook among Greatrakes' most committed supporters. In religion, for example, the latter would appear to have been dominated by men and women who, broadly speaking, favoured moderation and accommodation with regard to the religious divisions of the post-Restoration era. Generally speaking, they were dominated by those who advocated a non-dogmatic and non-doc-

---

[37] Boyle, *Correspondence*, iv, 55–7; Appendix 2.

[38] For Foxcroft's promotion of Greatrakes, see Stubbe, *Miraculous Conformist*, 32–44; Greatrakes, *Brief Account*, 83; BL, Harleian MS 3785, fo. 111. For his interest in chemistry and the occult, a passion he shared with his mother Elizabeth, see *Conway Letters*, 323; C. Rosencreutz, *The Hermetic Romance, or The Chymical Wedding. Translated by E. Foxcroft* (London, 1690). The Foxcrofts were also on close personal terms with Robert Boyle. Ezekiel's brother, Nathaniel, corresponded with Boyle, providing him with natural observations of India in 1664, while three years later his mother, Elizabeth, wrote to Boyle thanking him for interceding on behalf of her beleaguered husband, who as governor of Fort St George in India was accused of speaking treasonous words; Boyle, *Correspondence*, ii, 421–3; iii, 221–34.

[39] D'Arcy Power, Diary of John Ward, iii, 606, 609, 629–30, 631. Ward's diary provides a fascinating glimpse into the often shady world of chemical operators and alternative medical practitioners in early Restoration London. Ward himself was clearly attracted to the idea of a career as a chemical physician, but ultimately entered the church, serving as vicar of Stratford-upon-Avon from 1662 until his death in 1681; R. G. Frank Jnr, 'The John Ward Diaries: Mirror of Seventeenth-Century Science and Medicine', *Journal of the History of Medicine and Allied Sciences*, 29 (1974), 147–79.

trinaire approach to ecclesiological issues, whose specific denominational affiliations rarely correspond to the narrow and overly simplistic nomenclature to be found in traditional accounts of the Restoration church. Most were conforming Anglicans, who, despite assenting to the prescribed doctrines and liturgy of the recently restored Church of England, were actively engaged in the pursuit of ecclesiastical reconciliation with the majority of their excluded, nonconformist brethren. Essentially moderate and conciliatory in their religious outlook, they were representative of what some have opted to describe as the latitudinarian wing of the Anglican Church, an influential force in the 1660s, even if, as has recently been suggested, they lacked the institutional unity and ideological consistency which one might expect of an organized religious party, sect, or group.[40]

Greatrakes' first contact with the English latitudinarians was made at Ragley Hall. Here, at the behest of Lady Conway, who was herself possessed of a remarkably tolerant and broad-minded approach to the search for religious truth, Greatrakes encountered a close-knit group of friends, scholars, and acquaintances whose eirenic instincts were fully in tune with his own. Among those who wrote approvingly of Greatrakes' cures were Henry More (1614–1687), Benjamin Whichcote (1609–1683), Ralph Cudworth (1617–1688), George Rust, and Ezekiel Foxcroft (1629–1674), all of whom shared a profound commitment to the revived Platonism of Interregnum and Restoration Cambridge. The religious outlook of this intellectual coterie was typically moderate and conciliatory, and it was this aspect of Greatrakes' persona that underpinned the group's confidence in his ability to heal the sick. Henry More, for example, praised him as a man who 'gave himself up wholly to the study of Godliness and sincere mortification, and through the whole course of his life, shew'd all manner of specimens of a Christian disposition'. In particular, More emphasized that Greatrakes:

> did nothing but what carried an Air of Justice and Equity in it, and a general good will towards all: insomuch that, though he did most heartily embrace the Reformed Religion, yet he would persecute no Sect upon the Score of Religion, not even the Papists ... nor could I discover any thing in him that was contemptuous or immoral towards the spiritual or secular Magistrate. And truly he seem to me such an Exemplar of candid and sincere Christianity, without any pride, deceit, sourness or superstition.[41]

---

[40] J. Spurr, '"Latitudinarianism" and the Restoration Church', *The Historical Journal*, 31 (1988), 61–82. For a recent attempt to downplay the extent of partisan religious conflict in urban England after 1660, and to focus instead upon a vast middle ground of opinion that encouraged accommodation of moderate dissent, see J. Miller, *Politics and Religion in English Provincial Towns 1660–1722* (Oxford, 2007), Chapter 6.

[41] Henry More, 'Scholia on *Enthusiasmus Triumphatus*', appended to '*Enthusiasmus Triumphatus*: or, a Brief Discourse of the Nature, Causes, Kinds, and Cure of Enthusiasm', in *A Collection of Several Philosophical Writings of Dr Henry More* (London, 1712), 53. More's friend and former colleague, George Rust, provided a similarly positive assessment of Greatrakes' temperament and character, concluding that he was 'a person of an honest and upright mind, a free and open spirit, a cheerful and agreeable humour ... of large and generous principles ... that carries on no design of faction or interest'; Greatrakes, *Brief Account*, 60. Rust's testimonial was later reprinted in Glanvill, *Saducismus Triumphatus*, i, 90–2. This view of Greatrakes was apparently shared by many of his Irish supporters. In July 1665 an anonymous newsletter reported that most people found him free of 'endeavouring by this advantage to propagate any faction or private opinion'; BL, Add. MS 4182, fos 29v–30r.

To what extent the latitudinarian aspirations of More and his circle of friends at Ragley and Cambridge and their championing of Greatrakes were shared by others within the restored Anglican Church is not easy to determine. The Irishman's cures certainly provoked great interest in clerical circles, particularly among those with Cambridge connections. In February 1666, William Sancroft (1617–1693), former master of Emmanuel College and Dean of York and St Paul's, was receiving regular updates on Greatrakes' activities at Ragley from former associates at Cambridge, who, like More, were keen to witness at first hand the Irish thaumaturge.[42] Moreover, Cambridge-educated clergy and scholars, including physicians such as James Fairclough (d. 1685), were disproportionately represented in the sample of Greatrakes' adherents, providing further evidence, perhaps, linking support for the Irish healer with latitudinarian elements in the restored Church of England. Cambridge, it has been argued, was widely perceived then and now as the spiritual home of latitudinarianism.[43] Many of these men, as we shall see, were broadly sympathetic to the aims of the latitudinarians. They were also closely connected, through kinship and other networks. Henry More, for example, may have actively encouraged current and former students to either observe or seek assistance from Greatrakes. Peter Fullwood (d. 1705), a medical student at Cambridge in the 1660s who More took under his wing, and Edward Sleigh (d. 1675 or 1676), a former student of More's from the previous decade, were both witnesses to Greatrakes' cures at Ragley and London, respectively, in 1666.[44] In time, interest in Greatrakes waned at Cambridge, although he remained an object of discussion for many years to come. As late as 1676, Richard Salter (d. 1705), a former Fellow of Jesus College, reported in a letter to an old college friend, John Strype (1643–1737), that the Irishman's cures were still the subject of debate at Cambridge, though Joseph Glanvill's recent defence of the same had received a cool response.[45]

Cambridge, moreover, was not the only outlet for the expression of latitudinarian aims. It could also be found in the upper echelons of the restored Church, even among the episcopate, many of whom became powerful advocates of Greatrakes in the 1660s. George Hall (1613–1668), bishop of Chester, and his successor, John Wilkins (1614–1672), both attested to Greatrakes' sincerity and loyalty to the Church of England, which underpinned their own faith in the efficacious nature of his cures. Like many of his fellow latitudinarians, Hall had been a passionate advocate of a moderate *via media* in religion since the 1650s. As minister for St Botolph's, Aldersgate, in London, he had preached and subsequently published in 1655 a powerful sermon in defence of religious moderation in which he made a

[42] BL, Harleian MS 3785, fos 109, 111r–v. For Sancroft's correspondents, John Felton and Samuel Foster, both former Fellows of Caius, see Appendix 2.
[43] J. Gascoigne, *Cambridge in the Age of the Enlightenment: Science, Religion and Politics from the Restoration to the French Revolution* (Cambridge, 1989), Chapter 2. For Fairclough (d. 1685), who provided testimonials for twenty-eight of Greatrakes' patients but about whom we know disappointingly little, see Appendix 2.
[44] BL, Harleian MS 3785, fo. 111; Greatrakes, *Brief Account*, 52–3. For Fullwood and Sleigh, see Appendix 2.
[45] CUL, Add. MS 1, no.26. For Salter and Strype, see Appendix 2.

plea for mutual tolerance, forbearance and understanding in spiritual matters. He classified his opponents as 'the rigid Punctilio men, both of the right hand and of the left', who revelled in petty distinctions and name-calling, and called for an end to 'those ill-invented Differential Terms, whereby we have been distinguished from each other'. He concluded that 'there must be Abatements and Allowances of each other, a coming down from our Punctilio's, or we shall never give up a good account unto God'.[46] These were precisely the same views that John Wilkins, his successor to the See of Chester, would seek to implement a decade later under the altered circumstances of the Restoration, and they were shared by other leading clerics and admirers of Greatrakes such as Herbert Croft (1603–1691), Bishop of Hereford, whose efforts to promote and secure an ecumenical and comprehensive religious settlement in the 1660s demonstrated a remarkable personal empathy for the plight of those moderate nonconformists who had been excluded from the restored church.[47] At the parish level, one can also see evidence for the practical appeal of such thinking in the cordiality that often characterized relations between restored ministers and those nonconformists whom they displaced. Again, such activity is evident in the sample of Greatrakes' most dedicated admirers. John Pinckney (c.1619–1680), for example, who was ejected from the vicarage of Longstock in Hampshire, regularly attended his parish church after 1662 where his successor read sermons from a volume that was lent to him by Pinckney.[48]

What these high-ranking ecclesiastical supporters of Greatrakes shared was not a common theology or ecclesiology, but rather a general desire to see peace and harmony restored to the Church in the wake of the religious anarchy and bitter divisions unleashed by the Civil War and Interregnum and now continued into the Restoration. Above all, what united them was a deep-seated attachment to the attainment of this goal through peaceable means rather than the coercive methods laid down in the penal Clarendon Code. At the heart of this eirenic approach was the willingness of moderate voices within the restored Church to keep open the channels of communication with their dissenting and excluded brethren, and to continue the search for

[46] G. Hall, *Gods Appearing for the Tribe of Levi: Improved in a Sermon Preached at St. Pauls, Nov. 8 to the Sons of Ministers, then Solemnly Assembled* (London, 1655), sig. A3v; 25.

[47] Wilkins was present on numerous occasions when Greatrakes effected his cures; Greatrakes, *Brief Account*, 56–7, 67–8, 73. For his personal tolerance, religious eirenicism, and role in promoting a comprehensive settlement in the Church of England, see *ODNB* and B. Shapiro, *John Wilkins, 1614–72: An Intellectual Biography* (Berkeley, 1969), 61–70. Croft was reported to have said of Greatrakes' cures that they were 'to his owne certaine knowledge, beyond all the power of nature'; E. M. Thompson (ed.), *The Correspondence of the Family of Hatton*, 2 vols (London, 1878), i, 49. For Croft's pronounced support for a moderate and comprehensive resolution of ecclesiastical affairs, see J. Spurr, *The Restoration Church of England 1646–1689* (New Haven, 1991), 70–1. Croft's moderate colleague William Nicholson (1591–1672), Bishop of Gloucester, encouraged one of his prebends to seek cure from Greatrakes, though his assessment of the miracle healer is unrecorded; *Conway Letters*, 268; Stubbe, *Miraculous Conformist*, 28.

[48] *Cal. Rev.*, 390. Pinckney witnessed Greatrakes' cure of one of his former parishioners in London in March 1666; Greatrakes, *Brief Account*, 81–2. He later received a licence to preach as a Presbyterian in his house at Longstock in 1672. It is tempting to speculate that Pinckney's interest in Greatrakes may have been spurred by what Calamy described as his fascination with the Jews. Others in Greatrakes' entourage, including the stroker himself, demonstrated a keen interest in various prophetic utterances at this time that included belief in the imminent conversion of the Jews.

common ground that might form the basis of a lasting and comprehensive religious settlement. The appearance of Greatrakes in England in 1666 seemed to offer an opportunity for the expression of such views, and it was one that was equally welcome to many on the other side of the religious divide who found themselves, much to their horror and shame in many cases, excluded from the body of the established church.

Given the presence of so many moderate, conformable voices among Greatrakes' support, we shouldn't perhaps be too surprised to find representatives from the dissenting communities in the same sample. They are by no means, however, a homogenous group. Greatrakes' eirenic mission to heal the sick and lame attracted men and women from across the religious spectrum whose affiliations and beliefs defy simple categorization. Among those who claimed either to have been cured by Greatrakes, or to have witnessed and authenticated his cures, were the son of the former fifth monarchist Arthur Squibb,[49] the Quaker sympathizer and chemical physician Albertus Otto Faber, the Muggletonians, Robert Phaire and John Denison,[50] and the Behmenist Thomas Bromley (1630–1691), a member of John Pordage's circle at Bradfield in Berkshire.[51] In addition, one of the earliest surviving accounts of Greatrakes' cures in Ireland was secured by the prominent Devon Congregationalist Thomas Mall, who travelled to Ireland in the summer of 1665 to observe at first hand Greatrakes' thaumaturgical powers.[52] We also know of at least one former Baptist, Thomas Morris, who was persuaded to conform after witnessing Greatrakes' miraculous feats of healing.[53] Such examples might appear at first

---

[49] Greatrakes, *Brief Account*, 77–8. Arthur Squibb Snr (d. 1679 or 1680) was an MP in the Barebones Parliament, who served the commonwealth in numerous capacities. He was appointed a Commissioner for Compounding, JP, and held a reversion to a tellership in the Exchequer. He invested some of the profits in Irish land, purchasing the lot of George Foxcroft, father of Ezekiel (above), in county Meath. There is no evidence to suggest that he or his son, also Arthur, were actively engaged in resistance to the Restoration regime. Indeed Arthur Jnr eventually entered the church, serving as Vicar of Netherbury in Dorset from 1674 until his death in about 1697. His father, however, may have been a reluctant conformist. He was prosecuted in 1664 for failing to attend his parish church at Farnham in Surrey, and was again arrested in 1671. A year later, however, he was granted a licence to preach as a Baptist at his house in Chertsey; *ODNB*; Aylmer, *State's Servants*, 216–18; *CSP Adventurers, 1642–1659*, 32, 78, 344; *CSP Ireland 1647–1660; Addenda, 1625–1660*, 403, 419, 557; WSA, D5/21/1/39; D5/9/2, fo. 2v; D. L. Powell and H. Jenkinson (eds), *Surrey Quarter Sessions Records… 1663–1666* (Frome and London, Surrey Rec. Soc., 16, 1938), 166.

[50] Greatrakes, *Brief Account*, 27; BL, Add. MS 4291, fos 150v, 151 r–v; BL, Stowe MS 747, fo. 113; *Notes and Queries*, 9 (1884), 62.

[51] For the mystical Behmenist Bromley and his association with the Pordage circle, see *ODNB*. It is tempting to speculate that another colleague of Pordage, the physician William Boreman, was the same as the Mr Boreman with whom Edmund Squibb corresponded in April 1666 regarding Greatrakes' cures; Greatrakes, *Brief Account*, 77–8; Appendix 2. Edmund Squibb, half-brother of the fifth monarchist Arthur Squibb, was living with his aunt, Dame Ursula Verney (d.1668), in Covent Garden at the time of his cure. At the Restoration, he attempted unsuccessfully to petition for his father's reversion of the tellership in the Exchequer, an outcome that probably owed much to his earlier loyalty to the Cromwellian regime; TNA, PROB 11/326, fos 116r–v; *CSPD, 1654*, 272; *CSPD, 1655*, 193; *CSPD, 1663–1664*, 121; *CSPD, 1667*, 534; Sir J. Tremaine and J. Rice, *Placita Coronae, or Pleas of the Crown* (London, 1723), 684–8.

[52] RS, EL/M1/36; Boyle, *Correspondence*, ii, 522; Appendix 2. Mall was arrested in January 1661, along with Captain Hatsell, in the wake of Venner's rising; *Mercurius Publicus*, 24–31 January 1661; *The Kingdomes Intelligencer*, 28 January–4 February 1661.

[53] ESxRO, FRE MS 4223, fos 153–202, esp. fos 172r–v. For Morris, see Appendix 2.

sight to offer some support to those who have suggested that Greatrakes' activities represented little more than a covert exercise designed to undermine the Restoration regime. It should be stressed, however, that at the time of Greatrakes' visit to England, the vast majority of his supporters drawn from dissenting circles were not engaged in active opposition to the Government or the established Church. Some, such as Robert Boyle's close friends and acquaintances, Daniel Coxe and Benjamin Worsley, were particularly anxious to avoid controversy if for no other reason than to secure royal patronage and government posts.[54] Others, such as Colonel John Owen (d.1679), who entertained Greatrakes at his home at Mortlake in Surrey, denied official accusations of nonconformity or, as in the case of the Quaker sympathizer, Henry Bromley, retreated into a state of resigned quietistic pacifism.[55]

Obviously, there are real difficulties for the historian in attempting to take a snapshot of the religious beliefs of a large group of men and women, many obscure, at any given moment in time. The religious views and opinions of early modern English men and women were rarely constant, often fluctuating with the ebb and flow of official policy and the inconsistent implementation of the penal code against both Catholics and dissenters. This was particularly the case in the period immediately following the re-establishment of the Anglican Church in the 1660s, when individuals were forced to reassess and reaffirm their personal faith in the light of a rapidly changing religious and political atmosphere. Although positions were to harden in the late 1670s, especially in the wake of the Popish Plot and Exclusion Crisis, they remained very fluid throughout the 1660s. As a result, the goal of creating a more moderate, inclusive, state church—sentiments usually associated with the latitudinarian wing of the Anglican Church—was seen as a real possibility in the 1660s. Within a decade the dream had faded, and with it the hopes of a number of those who had previously empathized with the eirenic aspirations of Greatrakes. Simon Patrick, Joseph Glanvill and John Beale all fall into this category. At the same time, nonconformists too fluctuated in their reactions to the established church, one moment actively encouraging plans which might lead to re-integration, and at other times withdrawing from contact with the spokesmen of official Anglicanism. The years immediately following the restoration of Charles II were therefore punctuated by moments of hope and interludes of pessimism, but for much of this period many people continued to believe in the feasibility and desirability of a more comprehensive solution to the religious problems of the age, one which might appeal to all but the most recalcitrant of sectaries and Roman Catholics.

The appeal of a united, national church thus remained high on the agenda of many conformists and dissenters in the 1660s, none more so than among those

---

[54] Coxe was appointed physician in ordinary to the King in October 1665. His father was a Cromwellian administrator and the family were closely tied to the circle of the radical general, John Lambert; *CSPD, 1665–1666*, 37; TNA, C 7/216/48; D. Farr, *John Lambert, Parliamentary Soldier and Cromwellian Major-General, 1619–1684* (Woodbridge, 2003), 224–6. Worsley, who served the governments of the Commonwealth in various capacities, was anxious to pursue a career as an adviser to the crown on colonial and economic policy after 1660; T. Leng, *Benjamin Worsley (1618–1677): Trade, Interest and the Spirit in Revolutionary England* (Woodbridge, 2008), 138–84. Both men's religious views placed them outside the established church.

[55] For Owen, see pp. 94–5. For Bromley, see p. 96.

who inhabited parishes where the impact of religious division and conflict was felt most keenly. For many on both sides of the new religious divide, but particularly for those who refused to conform to the liturgy and doctrines of the restored Anglican Church, the religious settlement created unbearable tensions and anxieties. In effect, the implementation of the Clarendon Code excluded from participation in the body politic large numbers of dissenters, many of whom considered themselves eminently qualified, by birth, education, and rank, to govern their respective communities. Indeed, for the previous two decades many had ruled the country. Now, they were 'purged' from office and pulpit and, in the case of many ministers, forced to fend for themselves and their families as best they could. Under such circumstances, and given the fact that many of the same people subscribed to a providential world view that linked the physical well-being of individuals with that of the health of the wider environment, including the political realm, it is tempting to speculate that some of Greatrakes' admirers and patients saw their sicknesses, like the plague, as a punishment for political failure.[56] Indeed, as I argue in Chapter 5, such failure may ultimately have become manifest in the very symptoms displayed by some of Greatrakes' patients and others in the dissenting community, as for example in those cases of suspected bewitchment and diabolical possession which Greatrakes routinely diagnosed in his day-to-day practice. In his pioneering study of madness in early modern England, Michael MacDonald noted that communities in which the violent passions of religious conflict were most marked were more likely to produce larger numbers of patients suffering from a range of mental and related ailments. Many of Greatrakes' patients would appear to have come from similar communities.[57] At Shinfield in Berkshire, for example, the home of Peter Noyes (d. 1666), a patient of Greatrakes in 1666, the preceding years had witnessed unprecedented levels of religious division and strife, so bad in fact that the Bishop of Salisbury declared it one of the two most disaffected parishes in the whole diocese.[58] Other Berkshire parishes blighted by similar conflict provided Greatrakes with large numbers of patients and associated testimonials. The living of Shaw-cum-Donnington, for example, was held by Henry Pierce (c.1624–1680),

---

[56] It is interesting to note, in this respect, that two of Greatrakes' admirers clearly perceived a link between the plague and righteous judgement for the sins of the nation. In his will of August 1665, Edwin Brewns (d.1668), a common councilman in London with a home at Mortlake, made frequent reference to the recent visitation and the 'calamitous tymes which God hath most iustly sent amongst us for our ill returnes of mercys received'; TNA, PROB 11/327, fos 360v–362r. Lady Ranelagh was sufficiently exercised by the subject to write a manuscript treatise on the plague, which she saw as a divine punishment for the persecution of dissent and an argument in favour of liberty of conscience; R. Connolly, 'A Manuscript Treatise by Viscountess Ranelagh', *Notes and Queries*, 53 (2006), 170–3. For Brewns, see Appendix 2.
[57] M. MacDonald, *Mystical Bedlam: Madness, Anxiety, and Healing in Seventeenth-Century England* (Cambridge, 1981), 68–9.
[58] Greatrakes, *Brief Account*, 87–8; *CSPD, 1651*, 503; TNA, SP 29/43/68, fo. 125v; SP 29/43/84, fos 152r–v; SP 29/43/108, fo. 197r; WSA, D1/39/2/13, fo. 3v. Noyes and his family were almost certainly sympathetic to dissent. Peter and his brother John (d. 1668) played an import role after the Restoration in the affairs of their 'loving uncle', Dr Robert Wild (d.1679), a nonconformist minister and satirical poet. The brothers would also appear to have either employed or supported other local ministers ejected at the Restoration; Berkshire RO, D/A2/c 132, fos 30–2; E. Calamy, *A Continuation of the Account of the Ministers...Ejected and Silenced*, 2 vols (London, 1727), i, 514–15; *Cal. Rev.*, 297; Birmingham City Archives, MS 3415/42; TNA, PROB 11/328, fos 192v–193v; 243r–244r.

who testified to Greatrakes' cure of a Buckinghamshire market gardener in 1666. Two years earlier, the village had been riven by disputes between its two leading parishioners over the implementation of the Act of Uniformity, a conflict that was fought out in the neighbouring town of Newbury, where both men held civic office.[59]

Particularly intriguing in this respect are Greatrakes' frequent visits to Mortlake in Surrey between March and May 1666. His host on at least three separate occasions was Colonel John Owen, a wealthy London merchant with an estate in the Surrey village. Owen, whom Greatrakes cured of an unspecified ailment, was undoubtedly a nonconformist sympathizer, if not an outright dissenter, who struck up a very close relationship with the Irish healer.[60] At Owen's invitation, Greatrakes visited his house in Mortlake, a notorious centre of nonconformist activity which the Government was closely monitoring.[61] While there, he continued to perform his daily routine of stroking which excited much local interest. Particularly intriguing are the testimonials provided by two prominent members of the London Dutch merchant community, Sir Abraham Cullen (1624–1668) and his brother-in-law, William Rushout (d.1671), who witnessed the cures of two local people. Both men possessed close links with the mercantile nonconformist community in London while at the same time figuring prominently in the activities of the Dutch Reformed Church in the city and its various provincial satellites.[62] One such satellite was the Dutch congregation at Mortlake which, two years earlier, in 1664, was thrown into religious turmoil by the provocative utterances of its minister, Peter

---

[59] Greatrakes, *Brief Account*, 83; L. A. B. Harrison, 'A Vanished Berkshire Family', *The Berkshire, Buckinghamshire and Oxfordshire Archaeological Journal*, 37 (1933), 96. Given the disproportionate number of patients and witnesses drawn from Berkshire and the surrounding area, it is tempting to conclude that Greatrakes must have passed through this area on his way from Worcester to London in February 1666. In addition to Shinfield and Shaw, Greatrakes stroked patients from Windsor, Newbury, Swallowfield, Chievely and Thatcham in the county of Berkshire.

[60] Greatrakes, *Brief Account*, 55–6, 74–5, 86–7, 90. Owen, a London grocer with strong links to the former Cromwellian regime, was prosecuted for nonconformity in the secular courts in 1664, 1667, and 1677. The strongest evidence for his dissenting sympathies, however, are contained in his will, where he left legacies for several congregational ministers, including his namesake (and probably relation), John Owen (1616–83) and David Clarkson (d. 1686), who suffered ejection from the living of Mortlake at the Restoration. Owen was also fined for his refusal to disavow the covenant and serve as alderman in 1666; Powell and Jenkinson (eds), *Surrey Quarter Sessions Records… 1663–1666*, 194; D. L. Powell (ed.), *Surrey Quarter Sessions Records… 1666–1668* (Kingston-upon-Thames, 1951), 178; SHC, QS 2/5/Epiphany 1673, m. 70; QS 2/5/Midsummer 1677, mm 15, 26; QS 2/5/Epiphany 1678, m. 163; TNA, PROB 11/359, fos 177v–179v; Corporation of London Record Office, SF 178, no. 15; J. R. Woodhead, *The Rulers of London, 1660–1689: A Biographical Record of the Aldermen and Common Councilmen of the City of London* (London, 1965), 124.

[61] Captain John Owen 'so commonly cald' was included in a list of suspected persons and fanatics living in the area in 1664 by a government spy; TNA, SP 29/104/64.

[62] Greatrakes, *Brief Account*, 55–6, 56. Cullen's brother-in-law was the dissenter and future whig, Sir John Lawrence, who served as lord mayor in 1664–5. Rushout left £50 in his will to Cromwell's former chaplain Peter Sterry (1613–1672), who established a quietist retreat for dissenters at nearby West Sheen after the Restoration. His brother John (d.1653) was eulogized by the Presbyterian Nathaniel Hardy (1619–70) in 1648; Henning, ii, 179–80; TNA, PROB 11/336, fos 99v–100r; N. Matar, '"Alone in our Eden": A Puritan Utopia in Restoration England', *The Seventeenth Century*, 2 (1987), 189–97; N. Hardy, *Faith's Victory over Nature* (London, 1648).

Tessemaker. Among other things, Tessemaker was accused of preaching in English against the King and in support of nonconformity, actions that threatened the special privileges enjoyed by the Dutch churches in Restoration England. In February 1664, the task of mending bridges with the local Anglican community and its irate vicar fell to none other than William Rushout. An embarrassed but no doubt sympathetic Rushout reprimanded Tessemaker for 'meddling with affairs which concern the State or Church-government of England'. At roughly the same time, Greatrakes' future host, John Owen, stood accused in the local courts of being a 'fanatic' for not attending his local parish church.[63]

What, we might ask, brought men such as Rushout, Cullen, and Owen together in the spring of 1666 to subscribe publicly to the therapeutic gifts of Greatrakes' stroking? Was it simply a shared faith in the authenticity of his actions? By now, it should be clear, that what I am arguing for in the case of Greatrakes goes beyond a simple chronicle of the fascination which contemporaries displayed for the feats of a putative miracle worker. Belief in the charismatic Irishman's ability to heal was founded for many on more than simply an evaluation of his success rate as a healer. It was also bound up with an estimation of the man himself, his personal character and moral standing, as well as related to the personal circumstances of those who observed him at work and testified to his cures. What they saw, if we are to trust the various descriptions bequeathed to posterity by his supporters, was an *exemplary* figure, a Christian gentleman and a godly magistrate, who might stand as both a rebuke and a pattern for the divided polity which constituted England and Ireland in the 1660s. Greatrakes, it should be remembered, was himself a magistrate in his native Ireland who, by his own confession and that of his followers, consistently practised what he preached, refraining from the use of coercion in the face of dissent. The discrete political message which his healing and general demeanour conveyed was thus one of moderation and forbearance. It was also implicitly critical of the powers-that-be, especially the government of Charles II, that periodically encouraged the persecution of dissent and thus engendered a general malaise in the body politic. Greatrakes, like the vast majority of his known supporters, did not, I believe, wish to assist in the overthrow of the monarchy or the re-establishment of the 'good old cause'. He did, however, consciously and consistently strike an exemplary figure in stark contrast to the present incumbent of the throne, a point that did not go unnoticed by many of Greatrakes' supporters who, like the stroker, held magisterial and political office in Restoration England and Ireland.

[63] Greatrakes, *Brief Account*, 55–6, 56; J. H. Hessels (ed.), *Ecclesiae Londino-Batavae Archivum*, 3 vols (Cambridge, 1887–97), iii, pt. 2, 2501, 2502–3; Powell and Jenkinson (eds), *Surrey Quarter Sessions Records... 1663–1666*, 194. For discussion of the background to events at Mortlake, and the catastrophic collapse of the tapestry works there after the Civil War, see O. P. Grell, 'From Persecution to Toleration: The Decline of the Anglo-Dutch Communities in England, 1648–1702', in O. P. Grell, J.I. Israel, and N. Tyacke (eds), *From Persecution to Toleration: The Glorious Revolution and Religion in England* (Oxford, 1991), 103–5.

GREATRAKES AND THE 'STATE'S PHYSICIANS'

A significant proportion of Greatrakes' adherents who publicly espoused his cause in the 1660s were drawn from the ranks of the governing classes. MPs, both English and Irish, and a host of London aldermen and common councilmen attested to his cures.[64] The vast majority echoed Greatrakes' abhorrence of the physical suppression of religious dissent, while many attempted to conciliate and counsel caution in their everyday work as magistrates. Henry Bromley, for example, who served as a JP in his native Worcestershire in the 1650s, had earlier attempted to practise religious moderation when entrusted with magisterial authority. In the crisis year of 1659, he was cited by the Quakers in Worcestershire as one of the few non-persecuting magistrates in the county whom they deemed worthy of retaining his post.[65] Others, such as Sir Thomas Bludworth, Edmund Godfrey, and Sir William Smith, were similarly well disposed to the plight of mainstream, peaceable dissenters in their capacities as magistrates in and around the capital.[66] A number of Greatrakes' Irish followers were also active in the judiciary. Sir Thomas Dancer, for example, whose wife was cured by Greatrakes in 1665, served as Mayor of Waterford in 1661 in which office he was instrumental in providing protection to leading Baptists in the town who might otherwise have faced prosecution.[67]

The charismatic appeal of the Irish healer often endured, as is evident in the close friendship which he formed with the London magistrate and merchant, Sir Edmund Berry Godfrey (1621–1678), who entertained Greatrakes in 1666. During the spring of that year, Godfrey became one of the Irishman's leading patrons in London, offering his home as both a base for his healing and a refuge from the crowds. Many of Godfrey's closest friends and acquaintances attested to the authenticity of Greatrakes' cures,[68] and when the stroker finally returned home in May 1666, the burgeoning

---

[64] Among those who were English or Irish MPs at the time of Greatrakes's appearance in London: Colonel John Birch, Sir Thomas Bludworth, Sir Abraham Cullen, Andrew Marvell, Sir Anthony Morgan, Sir George Rawdon, Sir William Smith, and Sir Thomas Stanley. Others had served as MPs in the Interregnum or earlier: Sir Roger Burgoyne, Henry Hatsell. London aldermen and common councilmen include: Sir Thomas Bludworth, Edwin Brewns, Sir Charles Doe, Sir Edmund Berry Godfrey, William Knight, Thomas Massam, Stephen Parkes, and Sir George Waterman.

[65] *CSPD, 1658–1659*, 359–60.

[66] Bludworth (1620–1682), who was Lord Mayor at the time of Greatrakes' visit and both hosted and attended several of the stroker's surgeries, was also an MP and JP in Surrey. He was not a rigid enforcer of the Clarendon Code and was on friendly terms with the leading London Presbyterian, William Love, whom he had displaced in 1662. Love himself was the brother-in-law of Sir Roger Burgoyne, another who eagerly anticipated the arrival of the Irish healer to England in 1666. Bludworth, who received widespread blame for his handling of the Great Fire in September 1666, later became a staunch Tory, his daughter Anne marrying the notorious judge, George Jeffreys; Henning, i, 670–1. For Smith, see p. 168 and Appendix 2.

[67] Oldenburg, *Correspondence*, ii, 496; S. Pender (ed.), *Council Books of the Corporation of Waterford, 1662–1700* (Dublin, 1964), 4, 6, 29, 39, 46, 76; *CSP Ireland, 1660–1662*, 304, 319, 470; Bodl., Carte MSS 144, fo. 1v; 67, fo. 72v. Dancer, who was pardoned along with Greatrakes in 1661, was elected MP for New Ross in county Wexford in the same year.

[68] These included Richard Mulys and Colonel George Weldon (d. 1679), both of whom subsequently gave evidence to the parliamentary enquiry into the murder of their friend, Godfrey. Mulys, an auditor by profession, was described in 1666 as employed in this capacity in the service of the Countess Dowager of Devon. He later served the Duke of Ormond, Lord-Lieutenant of Ireland, when

friendship between the two men continued until Godfrey's tragic death in 1678. The strength of Godfrey's feelings for Greatrakes is abundantly clear from the surviving correspondence between the two men, Godfrey's letters frequently bordering on the homoerotic.[69] Greatrakes reciprocated by naming his second son, Edmund, in honour of his friend. Godfrey in turn remembered this and other acts of kindness when he left a small bequest to his Irish friend in 1677.[70] Godfrey, of course, was to achieve lasting historical fame following his widely rumoured 'murder' in 1678, as did another of Greatrakes' influential supporters, the poet and politician, Andrew Marvell (1621–1678). Marvell, along with his nephew, William Popple (1638–1708), and cousin, Thomas Alured (c.1633–1708), witnessed two of Greatrakes' cures in 1666, those of the Cambridge bookseller, Anthony Nicholson (1601–1667), and the Berkshire woman, Dorothy Pocock.[71] Marvell's sympathy for the plight of the moderate dissenters in Restoration England, like that of Godfrey, is well documented, and was shared by his nephew, Popple, who, in the 1680s was to write a series of pamphlets (including a translation of his friend, John Locke's *Letter Concerning Toleration*) advocating complete liberty of conscience as the bedrock of a civilized society.[72] Marvell's precise religious and political position in the 1660s is the

---

he was warned by Godfrey, shortly before his death, that his master's life was in danger. As the uncle of the Cromwellian adventurer Charles Alcock of Clonmel, county Tipperary, whom Mulys named as joint executor of his will, he was well placed to give a good account of Greatrakes. Alcock and Greatrakes were co-defendants in the Chancery trial of 1664 brought by the Catholic Prendergasts (see pp. 58–9); Greatrakes, *Brief Account*, 52–3, 53–4, 66, 68, 81–2, 82 –3, 89; *Commons' Journal*, ix (1667–87), 520; *HMC Eleventh Report, Appendix, Part II. Manuscripts of the House of Lords 1678–1688* (London, 1887), 47–8; Bodl., Carte MSS 215, fo. 506; 50, fo. 111; *HMC Ormonde Manuscripts*, 317, 338, 338–9; *CSPD, 1680–1681*, 350–1; TNA, PROB 11/450, fos 127r–128r; 11/454, fos 216r–v; *CSP Adventurers, 1642–1659*, 175; *CSP Ireland, 1647–1660*, 505, 510; *Sixth Report of the Deputy Keeper of the Public Records in Ireland* (Dublin, 1874), 68; W. P. Burke, *History of Clonmel* (Waterford, 1907), 109, 228, 230, 324–5. For Weldon, see Appendix 2.

[69] NLI, MS 4728. A complete transcript of Godfrey's letters, as well as those of other acquaintances of Greatrakes, forms Appendix 1 (see pp. 211–37). Their significance is discussed more fully in Chapter 6.

[70] TNA, PROB 11/359, fo. 357v.

[71] Greatrakes, *Brief Account*, 83–5. Thomas Alured was the second son of the regicide, John Alured, an adventurer in Irish lands. In 1662 his brother, John, was arrested, having been spotted lurking in the vicinity of the palace of Whitehall. Thomas, however, seems to have avoided political controversy after the Restoration and retired to his native Beverley in Yorkshire. As nonconformist recorder of that town, he later supported the plans of James II to restructure the corporation of Beverley in 1688; Venn, i, 216; J. Foster (ed.), *The Register of Admissions to Grays Inn, 1521–1889* (London, 1889), 274; *CSP Adventurers, 1642–1659*, 313, 349; J. P. Prendergast, *The Cromwellian Settlement of Ireland* (Dublin, 1922), 442; King's Inns Library, Dublin, Prendergast MSS, v, 114 [in error as 104]; R. L. Greaves, *Deliver Us From Evil: The Radical Underground in Britain, 1660–1663* (New York & London, 1986), 88; W. D. Pink, 'Alured of the Charterhouse, co. York', *Yorkshire Genealogist*, 1 (1888), 8–9; P. Burdon, 'Marvell and His Kindred: The Family Network in the Later Years. 1. The Alureds', *Notes and Queries*, 31 (1984), 379–85; J. Dennett (ed.), *Beverley Borough Records 1575–1821* (Wakefield, Yorkshire Arch. Soc., 84, 1932), 107, 178.

[72] For Popple, see especially C. Robbins, 'Absolute Liberty: The Life and Thought of William Popple, 1638–1708,' *William and Mary Quarterly*, 24 (1967), 190–223. Fiercely anticlerical in outlook, Popple decried religious dogmatism and laid much of the blame for the civil disturbances of the Restoration at the door of the Anglican clergy. In place of Anglican orthodoxy, he called for a renewal of Christian faith based on the light of reason and the evidence of Christian revelation. Like Robert Boyle, whom he greatly admired, Popple 'found in miracles the most readily comprehensible proof of Christianity' and a bulwark against deism; ibid. 215–23.

subject of much debate. A loyal servant of various commonwealth governments, he was nonetheless equivocal in terms of his ideological commitment to the Cromwellian republic. As an MP in the Restoration Parliament of 1661, he displayed a growing empathy for the plight of moderate nonconformists who found themselves excluded from office in church and state. Religious persecution ultimately drove him into outright opposition to the government of Charles II, though we should not assume from the stance that he adopted in the 1670s that he was implacably opposed either to the monarchy or the Anglican Church.[73] In the last resort, Marvell is probably best described, in the words of Gerald Aylmer, as a 'de factoist', a description that has also been used in connection with another of Greatrakes' celebrated clients, Sir Bulstrode Whitelocke (1605–1675), who argued strenuously throughout his life for liberty of conscience and an end to religious persecution.[74]

Another signatory to Greatrakes' manifesto in 1660 who later advocated a broad tolerance on the part of the magistrate toward Protestant dissent was the former royal physician, William Denton (1605–1691). At the height of the heated debate surrounding the Exclusion Crisis in 1681, Denton argued that:

> There is no such Contrariety between the different Opinions of the Assenters and Dissenters, in point of Liturgies and things indifferent, but that some moderation and connivance may be indulged to the Dissenters without peril of Inconvenience to the Government, and that without it, these petty differences and trifles may accidentally foment Divisions and disturb the quiet State of the Kingdom, and therefore the more prudent and safe way were to connive (at least by a prudent Neutrality between the Contrarieties) and take care that none do Condemn the other, nor yet the present Government, but that they all do live peaceably and Piously together.[75]

---

[73] On the basis of the admittedly fragmentary evidence that survives, it is probably fair to conclude with Professor Kenyon that Marvell was never actively engaged in nonconformity, despite his sympathy for the plight of moderate dissenters. Kenyon has also alluded to Marvell's 'disgust and disillusionment with the Restoration settlement' as demonstrated by his correspondence with Popple in the 1660s; J. Kenyon, 'Andrew Marvell: Life and Times', in R. L. Brett (ed.), *Andrew Marvell: Essays on the Tercentenary of his Death* (Oxford, 1979), 20, 22–3; H. M. Margoliouth (ed.), *The Poems and Letters of Andrew Marvell*, 2 vols (Oxford, 1952–67), ii, *passim*. The recent biography of Marvell by Nigel Smith largely confirms this image of the poet-politician.

[74] Aylmer, *State's Servants*, 174. Greatrakes stroked Whitelocke's son, Stephen, on three separate occasions in May 1666; R. Spalding (ed.), *The Diary of Bulstrode Whitlocke, 1605–1675* (Oxford, 1990), 704. Whitelocke was a close friend of Roger Boyle, Earl of Orrery, whom he greatly admired, and an acquaintance of his sister, Lady Ranelagh. In January 1670, in company with Robert Boyle, he dined at the home of Lady Ranelagh, where he recorded there was 'private discourse about Liberty of Conscience'. Seven years earlier, Charles II had requested his opinion as to the best solution to the religious problems of the time. Whitelocke advised the King to use his prerogative powers as head of the Church of England to extend liberty of conscience to dissenters; Whitelocke, *Diary*, 78, 249–50, 292, 663–4, 750–1; BL, Add. MS 21,009. Whitelocke consistently opposed the power of the state and the established church to persecute those of a different religious persuasion, and eschewed doctrinal controversy, both in the Cromwellian and Restoration Church. According to Blair Worden, theology for Whitelocke 'was a guide to behaviour', a position that sat comfortably with the moral imperatives favoured by Restoration latitudinarians; B. Worden, 'Toleration and the Cromwellian Protectorate', in W. J. Sheils (ed.), *Persecution and Toleration* (Oxford, 1984), 228–33.

[75] W. Denton, *Jus Caesaris et Ecclesiae Vere Dictae. Or A Treatise of Independency, Presbytery, the Power of Kings, and of the Church...Wherein the Use of Liturgies, Toleration, Connivance, Conventicles...are Debated* (London, 1681), 154; Denton also appealed to his fellow countrymen to avoid

As these examples suggest, what linked the vast majority of those powerful and well-connected laymen who lauded Greatrakes' cures was not their adherence to a single religious party or a specific political or ideological outlook, but rather a shared, though ill-defined, belief in the idea that the religious and political settlement of the 1660s had failed to unify the country. Sympathy for those excluded from that settlement came in many shapes and forms, and those who championed the cause of moderation and bridge-building did so for a bewildering range of motives and reasons. All are represented in the sample of Greatrakes' advocates and supporters. Some, perhaps the majority, were particularly concerned that the religious settlement had failed to steer a sufficiently middle course between extreme Protestant dissent on the one hand and recalcitrant Roman Catholicism on the other. Others, especially those drawn from the ranks of the London business community, may have inclined towards greater leniency toward nonconformity out of concern for the damaging effect to trade which many saw as the consequence of the implementation of the Clarendon Code. In certain cases, fear of Roman Catholicism and concern for economic well-being fused to produce a groundswell of sympathy for the fate of fellow Protestants faced with expulsion from the body politic and persecution at the hands of vindictive former enemies who now held the reins of power. In Ireland, of course, the situation was further complicated by the fact that many who held such views also stood to lose wealth and property with the impending implementation of the recommendations of the Court of Claims in the Act of Settlement.

It is worth noting in this context that a number of Greatrakes' English adherents were facing a similar prospect. Among those who stood to forfeit part of their newly-acquired Irish estates in order to appease sequestrated Irish royalists and Catholics were three city aldermen, Sir Charles Doe, William Knight (d. 1683), and John Owen.[76] Knight and Owen were assigned lots in county Tipperary, where, as we have seen, Greatrakes had considerable interests of his own as well as managing those of other non-resident investors. Doe, who drew

---

using terms like 'separatist' and 'schismatick' because 'they all hold the Truth in Righteousness'. Elsewhere, his political moderation, despite his avowed royalism, is evident in his comment on the passage of the revised Triennial Bill in 1664, when he lamented the failure of the opposition to halt the bill, 'all in vaine, the Bill is ingrossed, marcht upp to the Lords, & soe farewell Magna Charta'. He later developed political arguments that look distinctly Lockean in character, while advocating a religious viewpoint that favoured Erastian anticlericalism; ibid. 185; F. P. Verney and M. M. Verney (eds), *Memoirs of the Verney Family*, 4 vols (London, 1892–9), ii, 201; M. Knights, *Representation and Misrepresentation in Later Stuart Britain* (Oxford, 2005), 95–6; J. A. I. Champion, *The Pillars of Priestcraft Shaken: The Church of England and Its Enemies, 1660–1730* (Cambridge, 1992), 94–7.

[76] Doe and Knight, whose children were stroked by Greatrakes, were goldsmiths, neighbours, and business partners. Their partnership broke up acrimoniously as a result of losses incurred during the fire of 1666. They also served as aldermen, Knight being nominated by the dissenter Sir John Lawrence; Greatrakes, *Brief Account*, 54–5, Woodhead, *Rulers of London 1660–1689*, 61, 103; A. B. Beaven, *The Aldermen of the City of London*, 2 vols (London, 1908–13), ii, 42, 66; BL, Add. MS 5064, nos 69, 115.

lands in county Antrim, sold them on to Philip Tandy (for whom, see p. 76n.4), while his friend and business partner, the Presbyterian John Lane (d. 1670), left £100 from the sale of his Irish lands to Greatrakes' associate Charles Alcock.[77] These men thus shared Greatrakes' plight and may well have been attracted to him in the first instance through networks of mutual acquaintances and intermediaries. Similar motives may have impelled Anne Waring, the daughter-in-law of the London merchant and Cromwellian investor, Richard Waring (d. 1669), to seek relief from the stroker in 1666. Waring was a business partner of Greatrakes' neighbour and friend, Nicholas Osborne of Cappagh in Waterford.[78] In addition to these well-connected London businessmen, numerous former soldiers, civil servants, and others who had invested in the Irish adventure can be found among the ranks of those who attested to Greatrakes' curative powers. The loyal Cromwellian soldier Humphrey Mackworth (d. 1654), for example, whose widow Mary travelled to Affane in 1665 to seek the stroker's assistance, acquired vast estates in Ireland which, as a supporter of the regicide, were declared forfeit at the Restoration.[79] Other beneficiaries of the Cromwellian land settlement included Benjamin Worsley and Sir Anthony Morgan (d.1668), who both played an important role in overseeing the actual process of redistribution and allocation of confiscated lands, as well as lesser

[77] *CSP Adventurers, 1642–1659*, 9, 34, 327–8; JRL, Irish MS 125, fo. 39v; Prendergast, *Cromwellian Settlement of Ireland*, 389, 428, 446; TNA, PROB 11/334, fos 59v–61v.

[78] Greatrakes, *Brief Account*, 86. Anne Waring was the daughter of John Christopher Meyerne (d.1679), a wealthy merchant and large investor in East India Company stock, and wife of Sampson Waring (d.1671). Her father in law Richard Waring had played a prominent role in puritan politics in the capital throughout the 1640s and 1650s, and alongside other members of his family suffered harassment and deprivation of office after the Restoration. He was also the brother-in-law of the puritan preacher Cornelius Burgess (d.1665); K. Lindley, 'Irish Adventurers and Godly Militants in the 1640s', *Irish Historical Studies*, 29 (1994), 9; Bodl., Carte MS 44, fo. 439; Beaven, *Aldermen of London*, ii, 102; *CSP Adventurers, 1642–1659*, 77, 210, 353, 384; Greaves, *Deliver Us From Evil*, 31; *CSPD, 1660–1661*, 2; *CSPD, 1663–1664*, 325, 334; J. B. Heath, *Some Account of the Worshipful Company of Grocers of the City of London* (London, 1829), 113–14. Nicholas Osborne was the son of the parliamentarian Sir Richard Osborne (d.1667). Like Greatrakes, he was a tenant of the Earl of Cork and was pardoned with the stroker in 1661. His entitlement to his Irish lands, which he partly held with Richard Waring, were confirmed in 1666–7. In 1663, he was chosen by Greatrakes as a referee in his dispute with the second Earl of Cork over the rights to erect a weir on the Blackwater. More importantly, Greatrakes sold on the vast bulk of those lands purchased from the city of Exeter in 1656 to Osborne, whose failure to reimburse Greatrakes was the chief cause of the latter's severe cash flow problems in these years; NLI, MS 6900, 31 October–6 November 1641; *CSP Ireland, 1660–1662*, 318; JRL, Irish MS 125, fos 13r, 38r; *Fifteenth Report of the Irish Record Commission* (Dublin, 1825), 145; CH, Lismore MS 30, 7 November 1663; BL, Add. MS 25,692, fo. 34r [inverted].

[79] *Conway Letters*, 267; *ODNB*, sub Mackworth, Humphrey; *CSP Adventurers, 1642–1659*, 286, 354; *CSP Ireland, 1647–1660, Addenda 1625–1660*, 456, 480, 508, 536, 599, 652; *CSPD, 1661–1662*, 262; Prendergast, *Cromwellian Settlement of Ireland*, 439. Mary Mackworth's interest in Greatrakes may have been stimulated by her nephew, Colonel Robert Venables (d.1687), a business associate of the stroker and friend and neighbour in Cheshire of Sir Ames Meredith and George Hall, bishop of Chester. Venables played a key role in the subjugation of Ireland in the early 1650s; BL, Add. MS 25, 692, fo. 24v; TNA, PROB 11/336, fos 202v–203v; 11/330, fos 222v–223r; *ODNB*, sub Venables, Robert.

figures such as Richard Christmas (1615–1679),[80] Sir Thomas Dancer,[81] Ezekiel Foxcroft, Nathaniel Sibley (d. 1688), and Arthur Squibb.[82]

ACCOMMODATING THE PAST: THE SHADOW OF CROMWELL

In focusing on the religious allegiances of Greatrakes' English and Irish supporters, it has become evident that recourse to conventional historical labels that posited a simple divide between Anglican conformists and Puritan dissenters fails to reflect the complex reality of religious attitudes in the early years of the Restoration. The same proviso applies to any attempt to discern a common political standpoint among the mass of his followers. This, of course, did not stop his opponents from mud slinging and name calling. Greatrakes' decision to publish a defence of his cures before returning to Ireland in May 1666 was, in part, intended as a rejoinder to those who had raked up his past career as a soldier and administrator in Cromwellian Ireland, as well as hinting at his earlier involvement in radical politics and religion. In particular, Greatrakes was eager to counter the slanderous claims made in pamphlets such as *Wonders No Miracles*, where it was alleged that he had been:

> Bred up in loose times, and a more loose way, *a Souldier*, having prostituted *his under-standing* to a variety of Opinions and Errors, for he hath been in his time of most of the Factions that were lately extant; and now pretends himself a *Latitude-man*, that is, one that *being of no Religion himself, is indifferent what Religion others should be of.*[83]

Despite Greatrakes' protestations of loyalty to the new regime and attempts to distance himself from past allegiances, it was nonetheless the case that both he and the vast majority of those who freely testified to his gift of healing were tainted by their association with the Cromwellian regime. Many had served in one capacity

---

[80] Christmas, a Bristol Presbyterian who was frequently prosecuted for nonconformity, witnessed several of Greatrakes' cures in the city in the summer of 1668. As the older brother of Thomas Christmas, mayor of Waterford in 1664 and sheriff of the county in 1678, he possessed close links with Ireland. His entitlement to lands in county Waterford were confirmed under the Act of Settlement and Explanation. He also left £10 to the poor of Bandon Bridge in county Cork in his will of 1678; Boyle, *Correspondence*, iv, 100; R. Hayden (ed.), *The Records of a Church of Christ in Bristol, 1640–1687* (Bristol, Bristol Rec. Soc., 27, 1974), 286; Bristol Record Office, 04447/1, fo. 147r; 04447/2, fos 107v–108r; EP/V/3, sub 1674; *Fifteenth Report*, 51; King's Inns Library, Dublin, Prendergast Papers, vol. 2, 399; TNA, PROB 11/360, fos 308r–310r.

[81] Dancer held various posts as an administrator in the Cromwellian conquest and settlement of Ireland. He was rewarded with a grant of lands in county Tipperary, which were confirmed in 1666; E. MacLysaght (ed.), 'Commonwealth State Accounts Ireland, 1650–1656', *Analecta Hibernica*, 15 (1944), 270–1; R. Dunlop (ed.), *Ireland under the Commonwealth*, 2 vols (Manchester, 1913), ii, 632n–633n; *Fifteenth Report*, 170.

[82] For Foxcroft and Squibb, see note 49. In 1663, Lord and Lady Conway were busy attempting to secure a post in the Irish customs for the young Ezekiel Foxcroft; *Conway Letters*, 217. For Sibley, see Greatrakes, *Brief Account*, 75–6; Prendergast, *Cromwellian Settlement of Ireland*, 416; *CSP Ireland, 1647–1660; Addenda, 1625–1660*, 408, 523; Essex Record Office, D/AEW27/285 and note 88.

[83] [Lloyd], *Wonders No Miracles*, 9.

or another in either the military or civil administration of the 1650s, or, failing that, had acquiesced, with little apparent unease, in its rule. Some, like Greatrakes, had served the state both as soldier and governor. Captain John Cressett (d. 1707), Colonel John Owen, and Captain William Wildey (d. 1679), who all provided Greatrakes with hospitality and a base from which to work his cures in 1666, were likewise pensionaries of the Cromwellian state. Cressett, whose Puritan father Edward was an important figure in the administration of the 1650s, was employed by the state in numerous minor roles. Owen served as stationer to the Council of State, while Wildey, a godly naval captain, served as a vice admiral in the parliamentarian and Cromwellian fleets.[84] Others who held lucrative and prestigious posts under Cromwell include Sir Nathaniel Hobart (1600–1674), appointed as a Master in Chancery in 1652, and the young physician Thomas Sydenham, who was made Comptroller of the Pipe in the Upper Exchequer in 1655.[85] A number of these men, moreover, would almost certainly have been known to Greatrakes as a result of their employment as servants to the Cromwellian state in Ireland in the 1650s. Sir Anthony Morgan, for example, who ran confidential missions for Henry Cromwell in Ireland, had been involved in the transportation of native Irish Catholics to Connaught as well as being responsible for the drawing of lots for adventurers' and ex-soldiers' lands in the 1650s. Similarly, Benjamin Worsley, who like Sydenham was a close associate of Robert Boyle and his sister, Lady Ranelagh, in this period, played a pivotal role in the survey of Irish lands in the early 1650s as a necessary prelude to their redistribution in the latter half of that decade.[86]

---

[84] For Wildey, see Greatrakes, *Brief Account*, 79; B. S. Capp, *Cromwell's Navy: The Fleet and the English Revolution* (Oxford, 1992), 31, 166. Cressett and Owen (see note 60) continued to foster close links with the nonconformist community after the Restoration. Both attended conventicles, the former, a lawyer, performing a vital role in procuring licences for dissenting clergy in the wake of the Declaration of Indulgence. Cressett was also an acquaintance of Andrew Marvell and acted as advisor to Philip, Lord Wharton, in respect of his Irish lands, in 1666. In the same year, he was informed against as the improbable ringleader of an unlikely plot to assassinate the King; Greatrakes, *Brief Account*, 7–8; [Lloyd], *Wonders No Miracles*, 23; Aylmer, *State's Servants*, 415n; G. L. Turner (ed.), *Original Records of Early Non-Conformity*, 3 vols (London, 1911–14), iii, 478–80; Margoliouth (ed.), *Poems and Letters of Andrew Marvell*, ii, 161, 164, 240, 242–4; Bodl., Carte MSS 228, fo. 13; 103, fo. 257; *CSPD, 1665–1666*, 593. Owen's immersion in London dissent is further suggested by his close relationship with fellow stationer and admirer of Greatrakes, Alexander Merreal (d. 1707), whom he delegated to act as a trustee on behalf of various Independent and Baptist congregations in London. Merreal himself later left money to similar causes; Greatrakes, *Brief Account*, 91; Corporation of London Record Office, SF 178, no. 15; TNA, PROB 11/359, fos 177v–179v; 11/494, fos 9v–11r.

[85] For Sydenham, see *ODNB* and Appendix 2. Hobart was a member of the Verney-Denton circle whose daughter, Dorothy, married Greatrakes' admirer, and later business partner, Sir William Smith. In company with Smith, he witnessed numerous of Greatrakes' cures; see Appendix 2.

[86] For Morgan, see Greatrakes, *Brief Account*, 77–8; *ODNB*; Barnard, *Cromwellian Ireland*, 223, 237–8; Dunlop (ed.), *Ireland under the Commonwealth*, ii, 404, 428, 499–500, 544. He was pardoned at the Restoration, along with Greatrakes and others, at the behest of Roger Boyle. In 1663, a warrant for his arrest *in absentia* was issued in connection with the Dublin Plot. He subsequently decided to settle in England, where, in the spring of 1666, he was busily engaged in 'the managdement of all the Adventurers Concernes here in England' and was consulted, among others, by John Cressett (above note 84); *CSP Ireland, 1660–1662*, 46, 316; MacLysaght, *Calendar of the Orrery Papers*, 15–16; *CSPD, 1663–1664*, 163; Bodl., Carte MSS 32, fo. 542; 67, fos 70r, 71r, 73r; 214, fo. 512; 228, fo. 13. For Worsley in Ireland, see Leng, *Benjamin Worsley*, 80–94.

Even more striking perhaps are the Cromwellian connections of the clergymen to be found in our sample. All, without exception, either found preferment in the Cromwellian Church or accepted, apparently without scruple, the legitimate nature of that Church. Moreover, though many were far from what we might term 'puritan' in orientation, they none the less made common cause with the prevailing 'puritanism' of the time. In the 1660s, high church critics of such men would charge them with the crime of collaboration, while some of their erstwhile 'puritan' colleagues reacted to their subsequent conformity by deriding them as unprincipled time-servers. Regardless, many survived the onslaught and went on to secure preferment in the restored church. Typical in many respects was the career path of George Evans (1631–1702), a fellow of Jesus College, Cambridge, in the 1650s, who was later described by a former colleague as a 'zealous presbyterian'. He nonetheless conformed at the Restoration, and in 1663 acquired the rich living of St Benet Fink in London. Further preferment followed, including the award of a Cambridge DD, but throughout these years Evans retained some of his old 'puritan' fervour, refusing, for example, to bow to the altar, even in the presence of the King. Accused by some of cynically abandoning the godly cause for material gain, Evans offered hope to others who laboured for reconciliation and renewed dialogue with those brethren excluded in 1662.[87] Others, whose careers in the university and church mirrored that of Evans, include the brothers John (1632–1695) and Simon Patrick (1626–1707), and Clement Sankey (d. 1707), all products of Interregnum Cambridge who hitched their wagon to the latitudinarian cause after 1660.[88] Some of

[87] Greatrakes, *Brief Account*, 63–4; *ODNB*; G. C. Moore Smith (ed.), 'Extracts from the Papers of Thomas Woodcock (*ob.* 1695)', in *Camden Miscellany 11* (London, Camden Soc., 13, 1907), 62–3. Evans was a close friend of the moderate divine John Worthington (d.1671), who frequently officiated for him in his London parish. Interestingly, a number of Greatrakes' supporters, lay and clerical, shared links to Worthington. One of his parishioners, Edmund Barcock, who was cured by Greatrakes in the presence of Benjamin Whichcote and Ralph Cudworth, left him a small bequest in his will of 1670; Greatrakes, *Brief Account*, 66–7; TNA, PROB 11/335, fos 260r–v. Sir Charles Doe (see p. 76 and n.) borrowed money from Worthington; Worthington, *Diary*, ii, 247. In addition, Worthington was closely involved with the circle of Henry More and the Cambridge Platonists, whose religious and philosophical outlook he shared. He studied under Benjamin Whichcote and later married his niece; *ODNB*, sub Worthington, John.

[88] Greatrakes, *Brief Account*, 56–7, 61–3, 80. Simon Patrick, of course, who had been an early admirer of the Cambridge Platonists and was one of the original spokesmen for the latitudinarian cause, later 'recanted' his moderate views on church government, though his brother John was widely admired in dissenting circles; see p. 142 and n. Sankey was a protégé of another of Greatrakes' episcopal admirers, John Wilkins, the two men attesting to three cures performed by the stroker in 1666. At the time, Wilkins was living in the London parish of St Clement's, Eastcheap, where Sankey had recently been made rector. On Wilkins' elevation to the see of Chester in 1668, Sankey succeeded to the bishop's old prebend of South Newbald in Yorkshire; J. M. Horn and D. M. Smith (eds), *Fasti Ecclesiae Anglicanae 1541–1857. Vol. 4 York Diocese* (London, 1975), 49; *CSPD, 1665–1666*, 350. A number of Greatrakes' lay supporters would appear to have shared the moderate instincts of the latitudinarian clergy. Sir Roger Burgoyne (1618–1677), a member of the Verney circle, was a patron in the early career of Edward Stillingfleet (1635–1699); *HMC Seventh Report*, 464; *ODNB*, sub Stillingfleet, Edward. Joseph Sibley (d.1690), father of Nathaniel, left a bequest in his will to one of the most conciliatory of Restoration clerics, Edward Fowler (1632–1714). He served as a common councilman in London both before and after 1660 and was another member of the capital's business community to invest in the Irish adventure (above note 82); Woodhead, *Rulers of London, 1660–1689*, 149; TNA, PROB 11/403, fos 134r–136v.

these men, however, clearly struggled to shake off the stigma of their Cromwellian past and suffered accordingly. This was particularly true of the Cambridge Platonists, More and Cudworth, who, it is clear from the former's correspondence with Lady Conway, were in constant fear of losing their prestigious teaching posts at Christ's College in the early 1660s.[89] Their friend and colleague, George Rust, avoided a similar fate by removing to Ireland, where loyal and able churchmen were in short supply. In retrospect then, we can see that what linked the clerical supporters of Greatrakes was not so much doctrinal or ecclesiological consistency, as evoked by their somewhat vague latitudinarian aspirations, but rather the fact that they were all, in one way or another, products of the Cromwellian era. As a result, they were also to various degrees tainted by their acquiescence, overt or otherwise, in the republican regime of the 1650s, which cast a long shadow over their subsequent careers, especially in the volatile atmosphere of the early years of the Restoration.

In summary then, we can conclude that on the evidence of an in-depth analysis of our sample of Greatrakes' most committed supporters, the Irish healer appealed to a wide range of people who for a variety of reasons shared a common concern and anxiety for the fate of church and state in Restoration England. His dramatic appearance in England in 1666 should not be seen, therefore, as part of a concerted effort to destabilize the restored regime of Charles II. If one were to produce a composite picture of the type of man most likely to react favourably to Greatrakes' mission to heal the sick and maimed, it would not take the form of a radical zealot pining for the 'good old cause'. On the contrary, the typical proponents of Greatrakes' cures were men, or the relations of men, who had served the republic but now wished, for whatever reason, to seek accommodation with the restored regime. More often than not, these men had suffered financially from the change of government through loss of office, land or patronage, or a combination of all three. Others, if they had not already suffered financial loss, stood to do so with the imminent passage of the Irish Act of Settlement and Explanation. In some cases, moreover, it seems likely that the pain of financial loss was exacerbated by the damage to reputation and credit that ensued as a result of official scepticism in governmental circles aimed at those who had formerly served the Cromwellian state but who now professed loyalty to the crown and the Anglican Church. Such thinking, for example, seems to have underscored Sir Anthony Morgan's decision to quit Ireland in 1664, where, in the previous year, he had been falsely implicated in the Dublin plot. Similar motives may have impelled Greatrakes' friend and colleague, Sir Thomas Stanley, to move in the other direction following his failure to secure a baronetcy in England, where he was widely derided in his native Cheshire for the role that he played in crushing Booth's Rebellion.[90]

[89] *Conway Letters*, 220, 238, 242, 243. In July 1665, More remarked, in the context of a letter regaling yet again the attempts by Cudworth's enemies to have him removed from the Mastership of Christ's, that '[t]hey push hard at the Latitude men as they call them, some in their pulpits call them sons of Belial, others make the Devill a latitudinarian...I believe to all sober men such thinges cannot but be unsavoury'; ibid. 243.
[90] In the 1650s, Morgan had aligned himself with the moderate faction, which included Henry Cromwell and Roger Boyle, Lord Broghill, in promoting the offer of the crown to Cromwell; P. Little, *Lord Broghill and the Cromwellian Union with Ireland and Scotland* (Woodbridge, 2004), 134–5, 158–9.

What the vast majority of these men desired, above all else, was a stake in the new regime. Many of them were to petition the King and Council in the 1660s for place and patronage. All seemingly believed that reconciliation and accommodation was not only feasible but desirable. Many, Greatrakes included, continued to seek or hold important offices in local and national government after 1660, often in order to engineer a healing of the wounds of the past. From this perspective, a lasting religious and political settlement could only be achieved by an avoidance of religious dogmatism and political coercion, though how this might be brought about in practice proved both elusive and controversial. Given Greatrakes' professed opposition to the agency of persecution as the foundation of a godly commonwealth, it is hardly surprising that his feats of healing found a ready audience in the divided communities of Restoration England and Ireland. But if one were to look for a single individual whose attitudes and beliefs were most in tune with those of Greatrakes' own, one need look no further than the man whom the Irish stroker seemed to admire above all others and to whom he dedicated his parting gift, his autobiography, in 1666, the eminent natural philosopher Robert Boyle.

GREATRAKES AND BOYLE: MORAL EXEMPLARS IN AN AGE OF CONFLICT

Greatrakes' relationship with Boyle has been the subject of much debate, particularly with regard to the precise status (natural, preternatural, supernatural) that Boyle was willing to accord Greatrakes' acts of healing.[91] Here, however, I wish to discuss another aspect of their relationship that has hitherto received little attention, focusing in particular upon common concerns which until recently have been thought to relate only tangentially to matters of science and the empirical validation of healing by touch. What I wish to explore here is the extent to which Greatrakes the healer and Boyle the natural philosopher sought to project an image of themselves as moral exemplars or model citizens, whose gentlemanly attributes were widely perceived at the time as the bedrock upon which Restoration society and government was built. In short, the health of the body politic was dependant upon such men who laboured tirelessly in their own ways to re-establish social, political and intellectual harmony in the wake of civil war and the threat of further discord. Boyle's search for scientific truth, like Greatrakes' mission to heal the sick, can thus be seen as part of a far grander project that aspired to heal the divisions of the past and offer new certainties upon which to build consensus. The close relationship that the two men forged in the spring of 1666 (and which was reanimated two years later following Greatrakes' return to the capital) was a reflection of this mutual obsession, one that was undoubtedly reinforced by the fact that both men shared a common cultural heritage and social background shaped by the tragic events of the previous two decades.

[91] See pp. 15–16.

On a personal basis, the two men shared much. Born a few miles apart and within two years of each other, both suffered the loss of their fathers in the same year, 1643. Thereafter, they were forced to live as refugees in temporary exile, their educations fractured and unconventional for men of gentle origins. As adults, an obvious area of common ground between the two was the attachment which they both shared to their native homeland, even if in Boyle's case he now resided permanently in England.[92] Boyle retained close links with Ireland both through family connections and the correspondence of friends and colleagues, many of whom, like Greatrakes, had been active in the Cromwellian 'pacification' of Ireland in the 1650s. He also continued to draw an income from his Irish estates. Through these channels, he must have been fully aware of the controversial and divisive nature of the imminent land settlement that threatened to destabilize Protestant rule in his native land. Ireland, it is probably fair to conclude, was never far from Boyle's thoughts.[93] As we have seen, general fears for the safety and future of Protestant Ireland, particularly in relation to the outcome of the impending land settlement, reached a peak in the mid-1660s when Greatrakes' fame was at its height. To add to the uncertainty surrounding this process, another development in Anglo-Irish relations threatened to destabilize yet further the position of Irish landowners, namely, a move in the English parliament to place strict controls on the export of cattle from Ireland to England. Such was the magnitude of the issue that, for one of the few times in his life, Boyle was roused to set aside his private, scientific work and to espouse publicly a political cause dear to the hearts of his fellow countrymen.

The immediate spur to action came from the proposal, first mooted at Westminster in 1663, to impose a wholesale ban on the export of cattle from Ireland to England. Not only did this measure threaten the livelihoods of the vast majority of the rural population of Ireland, but it was also deeply unpopular in southwest England, where ports such as Minehead, Barnstaple, and Bideford were

---

[92] For Boyle and Ireland, see especially M. Hunter, 'Robert Boyle, Narcissus Marsh and the Anglo-Irish Intellectual Scene in the Late Seventeenth Century', in M. McCarthy and A. Simmons (eds), *The Making of Marsh's Library: Learning, Politics and Religion in Ireland, 1650–1750* (Dublin, 2004), 51–75. For Boyle's brief return to the land of his birth in the early 1650s, see Hunter, *Boyle: Between God and Science*, 87–91.

[93] In particular, Michael Hunter has stressed the degree of mental anguish suffered by Boyle in 1662 in relation to doubts that had arisen in his mind as to his right to receive the impropriations to abbey lands and other bequests made to him by his father. Despite taking counsel from a leading casuist, Robert Sanderson, he remained troubled by such scruples for the rest of his life; see M. Hunter, 'Alchemy, Magic and Moralism in the Thought of Robert Boyle', *British Journal for the History of Science*, 23 (1990), 392–3; idem, 'Casuistry in Action: Robert Boyle's Confessional Interviews with Gilbert Burnet and Edward Stillingfleet, 1691', *Journal of Ecclesiastical History*, 44 (1993), 83–4. Both works cited here have since been reprinted in Hunter's *Robert Boyle 1627–1691: Scrupulosity and Science*, 72–118. Boyle and his sister Lady Ranelagh also maintained a life-long interest in the project to translate the Bible into Irish; R. E. W. Maddison, 'Robert Boyle and the Irish Bible', *Bulletin of the John Rylands Library*, 41 (1958), 81–101; Hunter, 'Robert Boyle, Narcissus Marsh and the Anglo-Irish Intellectual Scene'; B. F. Taylor, 'Conversion, the Bible and the Irish Language: The Correspondence of Lady Ranelagh and Bishop Dopping', in M. Brown, C. I. McGrath, and T. P. Power (eds), *Converts and Conversion in Ireland, 1650–1850* (Dublin, 2005), 157–82.

hugely dependant upon trade with southern Ireland.[94] Throughout the autumn of 1665, as the first reports began to reach Boyle of the wonders performed by Greatrakes in Youghal and surrounding places, he was busy lobbying parliament in an attempt to prevent the passage of what he, and many others, saw as a potentially disastrous piece of legislation. Networking with friends and associates on both sides of the Irish Sea, Boyle worked assiduously to 'hinder poore Ireland from being utterly undone'. As he explained in a letter to Henry Oldenburg in October 1665, Boyle was acting out of 'the Duty I ow to a pore sincking Country', sentiments echoed by Lord Conway, who foresaw that the implementation of such an Act would merely compound the already grave problems posed by the imminent imposition of the Act of Settlement.[95] Given this combination of circumstances, as well as Greatrakes' close connections with the Boyles in Ireland, it is probably not too far fetched to suppose that Boyle's warm reception of Greatrakes in London in early 1666 was motivated in part by his deep-seated sympathy for the plight of the Irish Protestant landowning classes in general, and for Greatrakes in particular, whose moderation, charity and moral rectitude were exemplary in Boyle's eyes.[96]

We do not know for sure how, precisely, Greatrakes became so closely attached to Boyle's household in London in the spring of 1666. It seems highly probable, however, that old family connections, in particular Greatrakes' debt to his mentor and patron, Roger Boyle, Earl of Orrery, provided the initial opportunity for the Irish stroker to bring his gifts to the attention of the celebrated natural philosopher. Orrery, we know, shared his younger brother's concern for a moderate and peaceable solution to the religious divisions which had beset Britain since the end of the Civil War. During the 1650s, he had played a prominent part in the attempt of the Cromwellian Government to effect a lasting and broad-based settlement of church affairs. For much of the 1660s and 1670s he laboured to promote this design, and to encourage dialogue across sectarian and party divisions, albeit against the backdrop of a much-altered political scene. Orrery also

---

[94] The background to the various proposals and measures in parliament that culminated in an Act to prevent the importation of all Irish cattle into England in 1666 is fully explored in C. A. Edie, 'The Irish Cattle Bills: A Study in Restoration Politics', *Transactions of the American Philosophical Society*, 60 (1970). It is probably no coincidence that among those willing to substantiate Greatrakes' cures at Minehead in 1668 were various customs officers and merchants in the town whose employment and prosperity was directly linked to trade with Ireland; see Appendix 2, sub Samuel Crockford, Captain John Maurice, and Captain John Norris.

[95] Oldenburg, *Correspondence*, ii, 573, 577, 580. For the concerted efforts of men like Boyle, Conway and William Petty to obstruct and prevent the passage of the Irish Cattle Bill, see Bodl., Carte MSS 34, fos 442r–v, 448r; 46, fos 211r–v. Robert Boyle was well known to the Conways. In 1664, Lady Conway was making trial of one of his medicines, *ens veneris*; *Conway Letters*, 225, 226, 228–9, 230.

[96] It should be pointed out that Greatrakes himself, like so many of his fellow countrymen, was likely to suffer from the imposition of the Act. In describing his visit to Affane in 1665, Flamsteed referred to meeting the stroker 'in his own yard, looking at his cattle'; F. Baily (ed.), *An Account of the Revd John Flamsteed, the First Astronomer Royal* (London, 1835), 16. In addition, the Act would have severely affected the economic viability of local ports like Youghal, which functioned as a major point of export for Irish cattle to the western counties of England in this period; D. Woodward, 'The Anglo-Irish Livestock Trade of the Seventeenth Century', *Irish Historical Studies*, 18 (1972–3), 489–523.

shared Robert Boyle's (and Greatrakes') strong faith in providentialism, as well as his interest in supernaturalism and the spirit world, beliefs which, I argue in the next chapter, constituted a central plank in ecumenical attempts to restore unity in the Church after 1660. It is highly likely therefore that Greatrakes came to Robert Boyle highly recommended in March 1666, especially if, as seems likely, Boyle heeded the advice of his close friend John Beale, who in September of the previous year had written to him commending Greatrakes' cures and advising him to write to his acquaintances in Youghal and Lismore for confirmation of their authenticity.[97]

At the home of his sister, the pious blue-stocking, Lady Ranelagh, Boyle conducted a series of 'experiments' on his guest which rapidly confirmed his opinion that Greatrakes' cures were authentic. In arriving at this judgement, however, it should be noted that Boyle employed a wide range of criteria, some of which look out of place given Boyle's reputation as one of the leading exponents of the new empirical science. He thus drew up a series of notes and queries that were intended to reveal a vast array of information, much of it concerned with the healer's personal attributes and beliefs rather than devoted to a systematic analysis of his method of cure or patients' health. Among those items listed for examination, one in particular stands out as central, not only to Boyle's evaluation of Greatrakes' credibility, but also to that of his clientele, namely 'Whether Mr Greatrakes be able to cure Men of differing Religions, as Roman Catholics, Socinians, Jews, &c as also Infants, Naturals, or destracted Persons to whose recovery ye faith of ye Patient cannot concurre'.[98]

The implication behind the query is transparent. If Greatrakes was able to cure only those of a certain sect or party, as some had suggested, then his credibility as a healer would suffer a damaging blow. Alternatively, if he was able to cure men and women irrespective of their specific religious orientation, then his status as a performer of divinely sanctioned wonders, or even miracles, was assured. As Boyle and his learned contemporaries were only too aware, recent history had furnished plentiful examples of other putative miracle workers who turned out on closer inspection to be little more than frauds or evangelists for specific religious sects or causes. A number of the early Quakers, for example, including George Fox and the future schismatic Charles Bayly, were widely reputed to have performed a range of miraculous cures upon their co-religionists. Typically, however, their successes were all too readily dismissed on the grounds that their supposed gifts rarely extended to those of other denominations and that, according to their opponents, they frequently failed even among their own. Charles Bayly, for example, was widely de-

---

[97] Boyle, *Correspondence*, ii, 521–2. As Lord Broghill in the 1650s, and the Earl of Orrery after 1660, Roger Boyle was a consistent proponent of schemes designed to heal the breaches between the various mainstream Protestant groups in England and Ireland; see for example Little, *Lord Broghill*, 230–5; Spalding (ed.), *Diary of Bulstrode Whitelocke*, 749–53; R. Baxter, *Reliquiae Baxterianae or Mr Richard Baxters Narrative of the Most Memorable Passages of his Life and Times Faithfully Publish'd... by Matthew Sylvester* (London, 1696), iii, 109–40.
[98] RS, RB/3/3/14.

rided by the Baptists for failing to cast out a devil from one of his Kent congregation.[99] The exposure of such cases did not stifle optimism or belief in the theoretical authenticity of such claims, which remained high in the minds of men like Boyle and his immediate circle whose outlook was so conspicuously shaped by an expectant providentialism. They certainly figure prominently in the thoughts of many of those who were inspired by Boyle. In March 1667, for example, Samuel Colepresse, a correspondent and admirer of Boyle, wrote to him from Devon lauding the practice of a local woman who cured a range of ailments by stroking the affected parts in a manner highly reminiscent of that used by Greatrakes. Colepresse later experimented with some success on his sick father, though at a cost, as he claimed to have suffered from a transference of the pain to his own body.[100] He too, like Boyle, favoured a corpuscularian explanation for the success of such methods, a view that seems to have proved attractive in some medical circles. In 1683, for example, the 'empiric' Samuel Haworth, the son of an ejected minister, invoked the corpuscularian arguments favoured by Boyle, and echoed by John Beale in the *Philosophical Transactions*, in explaining the cures done by 'some Private Persons, who have been famous for Stroaking or Rubbing the Parts, and have been thought to have an Extraordinary or Divine Gift'.[101]

Given what we know of Boyle's personal religious faith, it is difficult to escape the conclusion that his interest in, and support for, Greatrakes in 1666 was founded, in part at least, upon an underlying empathy for the eirenic message

---

[99] H. J. Cadbury (ed.), *George Fox's Book of Miracles* (Cambridge, 1948); K. L. Carroll, 'From Bond Slave to Governor: The Strange Career of Charles Bayly (1632?–1680)', *Journal of the Friends Historical Society*, 52 (1968), 19–38. Bayly's alleged cures were mentioned in the same breath as those of other Quakers, Baptists, and Greatrakes himself by Thomas Morris in his correspondence with the Rye nonconformist Samuel Jeake the elder in 1666; ESxRO, FRE MS 4223, fo. 172r. In addition to these and other widely publicized cases (Matthew Coker, O'Finallty), a host of lesser-known figures were also active at this time such as the Worcestershire woman Eleanor Burt and the Baptist preacher James Wilmot of Hook Norton, Oxfordshire. Burt was questioned by JPs in May 1660 as to the origin of her call to heal the sick. In reply, she echoed Greatrakes in stating that 'shee did not take upon her soe to doe But Confesseth that when diverse have come to her that had Aches in their heads and other Infirmitys shee had and hath a gifte from god by good prayers and laying her hands upon theyr heads or faces often tymes to Recover and heale them of their Diseases'; WRO, QS 100/97/60. She may be the woman of the same name who was arrested at a conventicle at Great Comberton in Worcestershire in 1673; WRO, 100/110/36. John Ward recorded in his diary that Wilmot was famous locally for curing the king's evil in the early years of the Restoration. He subsequently suffered imprisonment and legal harrassment for his religious beliefs; D'Arcy Power, Diary of John Ward, ii, 475; T. Crosby, *The History of the English Baptists, from the Reformation to the Beginning of the Reign of George I*, 4 vols (London, 1738–40), iii, 124–5.

[100] Boyle, *Correspondence*, iii, 303, 308–9. The old woman concerned told Colepresse that she had been practising the same method publicly for about ten years and that she had learned it from a Dutch surgeon imprisoned at Plymouth (presumably during the First Anglo-Dutch War); ibid. 303–4.

[101] Samuel Haworth, *A Description of the Duke's Bagnio, and of the Mineral Bath and New Spaw Thereunto Belonging with an Account of the Use of Sweating, Rubbing, Bathing, and the Medicinal Vertues of the Spaw* (London, 1683), 48–9. Haworth was the author of numerous medical works, the contents of which belie crude descriptions of him as merely an 'empiric'. His greatest debt, however, was to Boyle, 'the mirrour of our Age', whose corpuscularianism formed the basis of his own original medical practice and theory as well as providing a bulwark against atheism and irreligion; Haworth, *Description*, 36–7. For accounts of Haworth that stress his empirical credentials, see *ODNB* and E. L. Furdell, *The Royal Doctors 1585–1714: Medical Personnel at the Tudor and Stuart Courts* (Rochester, NY, 2001), 188.

implicit in the Irish gentleman's vocation to cure the sick. His ability to heal those drawn from all sectors of Restoration society—something which Boyle must have witnessed at first hand—carried a potent political message in the mid-1660s. It promised religious and political reconciliation in the body politic and provided a template for a new dispensation in church and state. Moreover, Boyle's personal search for such a solution, based on what Professor Jacob has described as 'the eirenic healing doctrine of the harmony or unity of truths', was fully in keeping with the aspirations of both his brother Roger, sister Lady Ranelagh, and others of their circle. To some extent this was a template or prospect for change rooted in millennial expectation, though not of the kind favoured by some of the more extreme and radical sects. On the contrary, the Boyles' vision of renewal was essentially conservative in character, 'a reform of conduct and not of institutions', that was limited to the intellectual, moral and spiritual spheres.[102] As such, it was also a vision of the future to which many of those moderates both within the restored church as well as others excluded from its protection might happily subscribe. In the event, Greatrakes' mission, alongside other attempts to promote religious reconciliation, proved a false dawn. A series of new political crises after 1666, culminating in the Popish Plot and Exclusion Crisis, finally put paid to any lingering hopes of a peaceable resolution of the nation's problems. Greatrakes himself retreated from public view and returned to the relative obscurity of his estates in Ireland. There historians have been content to take their leave, reserving judgement on the limited significance of his place in the history of the early Restoration. In the final chapter, I seek to redress this image of Greatrakes as well as trace the final years of his life as he continued to make a small, but significant, impact upon his world. In order to make such an assessment, however, it is first necessary to address one final aspect of the Greatrakes affair that was central not only to his own understanding of his career as a miracle healer, but also that of others who clamoured to authenticate his cures. It is time now to turn to Greatrakes' role as physician to the body politic, and to examine more closely his desire to exorcize the demons afflicting Restoration society while at the same time administering a form of 'spiritual physic' to those who had fallen prey to the Devil.

---

[102] J. R. Jacob, 'Boyle's Circle in the Protectorate: Revelation, Politics and the Millennium', *Journal of the History of Ideas*, 38 (1977), 131–40. However, I am indebted to Professor Michael Hunter, for pointing out that Boyle's conservatism did not preclude engagement with the radical sectaries as originally suggested by Jacob in this article and elsewhere. Indeed, Hunter suggests that Boyle's ambivalence on this issue parallels that experienced by Greatrakes, which I discuss more fully in relation to the latter's continuing contact with radical groups after 1666. For Boyle and the sects, see especially M. Hunter, 'How Boyle Became a Scientist', in *idem, Robert Boyle (1627–91): Scrupulosity and Science*, 15–57, especially 51–7. This article originally appeared in *History of Science*, 33 (1995), 59–103.

5

Healing, Witchcraft, and the Body Politic in Restoration Britain

The Devill is a name for a Body Politick, in which there are different Orders and Degrees of Spirits, and perhaps in as much variety of place and state, as among our selves.

Joseph Glanvill, *Saducismus Triumphatus: Or, Full and Plain Evidence Concerning Witches and Apparitions* (London, 1681), i, 35.

RESTORATION, SICKNESS, AND THE BODY POLITIC

Recollecting a conversation in a London bookshop with the natural philosopher Robert Boyle, the Cambridge Platonist Henry More reaffirmed his conviction that the Irish gentleman's power of healing was directly related to the 'regenerate' nature of the stroker's body. Everything about his mien, character, and posture indicated that Greatrakes was a prodigious figure whose cures, if not true miracles, were nonetheless in keeping with Protestant sensibilities, and were thus to be accorded the status of 'the special Gifts of God in Nature'. In support of this claim, More, who had met and conversed with Greatrakes at Ragley on numerous occasions, recalled his piety, morality, and moderation, which he exercised both as a private man but also in his public capacity as an active member of the governing classes. In More's eyes, he was a truly exemplary figure, whose personal demeanour and public actions provided a template for government in the restored body politic. At the same time, he emphasized that Greatrakes' external appearance to the world mirrored an inner regeneracy that was physical or somatic in nature, and from whence he drew his therapeutic powers. Indeed, such was the powerful nature of his regenerate body that he not only healed by stroking with his hands, but also by applying his spittle and urine to the affected or diseased parts of his patients' bodies. If anyone should doubt the veracity of More's claims, they only had to smell the Irish stroker, for 'it was well known, that his Body as well as his Hand and Urine, had a sort of Herbous Aromatic Scent'.[1]

---

[1] H. More, 'Scholia on Enthusiasmus Triumphatus', appended to 'Enthusiasmus Triumphatus; or, a Brief Discourse of the Nature, Causes, Kinds, and Cure of Enthusiasm', in *A Collection of Several Philosophical Writings of Dr Henry More* (London, 1712), 51–3. More was not alone in commenting on the fragrant odours given off by Greatrakes' body. According to Henry Stubbe, both George Rust and Viscount Conway reported the same phenomena, while Robert Boyle set out to establish whether 'the Effluvia of [his] Body are well sented'. Boyle also experimented with the notion that Greatrakes' cura-

Greatrakes' bodily odour was widely cited by his supporters as evidence of the 'saintliness' of the man and helped convince many that his cures were genuine. It was also emblematic of the huge significance that contemporaries, both learned and un-learned, invested in physical or somatic signs. There currently exists a vast literature concerned with the history of the body, much of which stresses the unique way in which early modern Europeans experienced their bodies, and how they constructed meaning, both literal and symbolic, from bodily gestures and attributes. Drawing as it does on a broad range of related disciplines, including history, anthropology, soci-ology, literary studies, and art history, the body, in the words of one commentator, would now appear to have achieved the status of 'a new organizing principle within Anglo-American intellectual activity'.[2] Belief in the special significance attached to the human body has thus prompted a great deal of speculation among scholars as to how early modern men and women understood and experienced the notion of cor-poreality. In particular, it has proved hugely attractive to recent generations of literary scholars eager to explore how the human body might be construed or 'read' as an-other kind of 'text', and thus act as a commentary on various aspects of contempor-ary life. At the same time, historians of science and medicine have proved equally amenable to such studies in their attempt to write a social history of the culturally constructed body. Regenerate or saintly bodies, for example, as in the case of Great-rakes, have provided one source of fascination and enquiry. Of equal interest are the 'signifiers' that early modern men and women attached to unregenerate, or degener-ate, bodies, the apprehension and punishment of which increasingly required judi-cial intervention on the part of the state. This is the period, for example, in which criminal bodies were, for the first time, subject to medical scrutiny, the cadavers of convicted felons frequently offered up by the state for medical and scientific research in the new anatomy theatres of early modern Europe.[3] The bodies of the victims of crime were similarly scanned for signs that might help to convict those responsible

---

tive powers might be conveyed to articles of clothing, such as his gloves; H. Stubbe, *The Miraculous Conformist: Or, An Account of Several Marvailous Cures Performed by . . . Mr Valentine Greatarick* (Oxford, 1666), 11; BL, Add. MS 4293, fo. 52r. For discussion of this and related investigations into regenerate bodies at this time, see S. Schaffer, 'Regeneration: The Body of Natural Philosophers in Restoration England', in C. Lawrence and S. Shapin (eds), *Science Incarnate: Historical Embodiments of Natural Knowledge* (Chicago, 1998), 83–120, especially 105–15. According to Robert Crocker, More's natural-istic approach to Greatrakes's cures owed everything to his Platonic understanding of the stroker as a providentially gifted and spiritually refined individual, who was able to transmit the pure and curative effluvia of his highly spiritualized body to those who were sick; R. Crocker, 'A "Sanative Contagion": Henry More on Faith Healing', in M. Pelling and S. Mandelbrote (eds), *The Practice of Reform in Health, Medicine and Science, 1500–2000. Essays for Charles Webster* (Aldershot, 2005), 107–23.

   [2] M. Jenner, 'Review Essay: Body, Image, Text in Early Modern Europe', *Social History of Medicine*, 12 (1999), 143.

   [3] For a good, general introduction to this subject, see G. Ferrari, 'Public Anatomy Lessons and the Carnival: the Anatomy Theatre of Bologna', *Past and Present*, 117 (1987), 50–106; K. Park, 'The Crim-inal and Saintly Body: Autopsy and Dissection in Renaissance Italy', *Renaissance Quarterly*, 47 (1994), 1–33. For anatomised bodies as texts, see A. Carlino, *Books of the Body: Anatomical Ritual and Renais-sance Learning* (Chicago, 1999), pp. 187–225. The investigation of the bodies of convicted and exe-cuted felons might serve a variety of purposes (social, intellectual, political) as illustrated in England by the case of the hanged (but subsequently resuscitated) Englishwoman Anne Greene at Oxford in 1650;

for acts such as murder, though the methods used were often alien to modern forensic medicine. The popular belief, for example, shared by many medical experts, that the bodies of murder victims bled afresh in the presence of the perpetrator of the crime was widely accepted as evidence of guilt in the courts of sixteenth- and seventeenth-century Europe.[4]

Specific crimes left their marks on the bodies of perpetrators, which in turn required skilled experts to decipher. Guilt in cases of infanticide, for example, was commonly established by the judgement of a panel of matrons or midwives who examined the body of suspected women for signs of an interrupted pregnancy.[5] Similar panels were used to examine the bodies of suspected witches, who were widely believed to carry the stigmata of their crimes. In Britain, for example, the search for the witch's mark—an extra teat or bodily excrescence, usually located in the 'secret parts' of the body—was commonly cited as evidence of guilt in cases of witchcraft. The female witch, of course, represented the archetypal figure of the unregenerate body in early modern Europe. Every aspect of her physical being and demeanour betrayed the sinfulness of her intentions. Indeed, contemporary medical knowledge underpinned the stereotype of the witch as old, cold, dry, and sterile. Unable to menstruate, her blood was black and putrid, and her character, in line with contemporary psychology, peevish and revengeful. She was also widely believed to be incapable of shedding tears or showing remorse for her actions.[6] Betrayed at every stage by her outward physical appearance, the witch thus represented the antithesis of the saintly body as exemplified by the charismatic healer. This is evident in numerous ways, but none more so than in the methods that witches and miracle healers commonly used in plying their trade. Greatrakes' own approach to curing the sick, for example, was itself a direct inversion of that used by witches to inflict harm and physical suffering on their victims. Typically, witches

see L. Gowing, *Common Bodies: Women, Touch and Power in Seventeenth-Century England* (New Haven, 2003), 48–50; S. Mandelbrote, 'William Petty and Anne Greene: Medical and Political Reform in Commonwealth England', in Pelling and Mandelbrote (eds), *Practice of Reform in Health*, 125–49.

[4] See, for example, the numerous examples of cruentation cited in M. Gaskill, 'Reporting Murder: Fiction in the Archives in Early Modern England', *Social History*, 23 (1998), 1–30. The phenomenon was subjected to serious scrutiny by the physician John Webster in his *The Displaying of Supposed Witchcraft* (London, 1677), 302–8.

[5] Gowing, *Common Bodies*, 41–2. For examples from early modern England and Germany, see D. Harley, 'Provincial Midwives in England: Lancashire and Cheshire, 1660–1760', in H. Marland (ed.), *The Art of Midwifery: Early Modern Midwives in Europe* (London, 1993), 38–9; M. E. Wiesner, 'The Midwives of South Germany and the Public/Private Dichotomy', in Marland (ed.), *Art of Midwifery*, 87–8; U. Rublack, *The Crimes of Women in Early Modern Germany* (Oxford, 1999), 176–80.

[6] U. Rublack, 'Fluxes: the Early Modern Body and the Emotions', *History Workshop Journal*, 53 (2002), 7. Rublack cites the example of a German witchcraft trial in which medical expertise was invoked to demonstrate the physiological explanation that underlay the witch's inability to shed tears. For another German example, see L. Roper, *Witch Craze: Terror and Fantasy in Baroque Germany* (New Haven, 2004), 199. The ability to shed tears, it should be noted, was considered a sign of genuine contrition in the act of penitence; see for example M. Todd, *The Culture of Protestantism in Early Modern Scotland* (New Haven, 2002), 160n. For a broader analysis of contemporary understanding of the witch's body, and the role which it played in both protecting and exposing those accused of witchcraft, see D. Purkiss, *The Witch in History: Early Modern and Twentieth-Century Representations* (London, 1996), 119–44.

infected their victims by physical contact, either through breath, the evil eye, or touch. It was reported, for example, by the American colonial governor John Winthrop (1588–1649) that the white witch, Margaret Jones, had such 'a malignant touch, as many persons…whom she stroked or touched with any affection or displeasure…were taken with deafness, or vomiting, or other violent pains or sickness'.[7] Likewise, Henry More, commenting on the case of the Irish witch, Florence Newton, was reminded that in this relation there was 'an eximious example of the magical venom of witches, (whence they are called *Veneficiae*) in that all the mischief this Witch did, was by kissing, or some way touching the party she bewitched, and she confest unless she touched her, she could do her no hurt, which may be called a Magical Venom or contagion'.[8]

Given the prominent role played by Greatrakes in the trial of Florence Newton (discussed more fully below pp. 127–32) and his obsession with demonology, it may not be too fanciful to suggest that he may have modelled his own method of healing by touch, albeit in an inverted form, on the malevolent practices of women like Newton. Other aspects of his practice also bear comparison with the activities ascribed to witches. Various observers noted, for example, that those who suffered from the falling sickness immediately fell into fits on encountering Greatrakes, in much the same way as the victims of witchcraft were often said to have fallen into uncontrollable fits in the presence of their diabolical tormentors. Moreover, Greatrakes' tendency to conflate epilepsy with diabolical possession undoubtedly helped to convince him that the source of his therapeutic skills was miraculous and that his cures were on a par with those performed by Christ.[9] In the last resort, however, the debate over the precise nature of Greatrakes' cures was largely academic. For the vast majority of those who either received relief at his hands, or attested to the veracity of his cures, Greatrakes' appearance at this time provided clear evidence of the providential ministrations of a caring God who used the bodies of men like Greatrakes to advertise His will and hopes for mankind. In a similar vein, the bodies of witches and their victims, like those of Greatrakes and his patients, attested to the eternal conflict in society between the forces of good and evil, and

[7] J. K. Hosmer (ed.), *Winthrop's Journal History of New England, 1630–1649*, 2 vols (New York, 1966), ii, 344–5. Among the evidence adduced at her trial was that derived from a strip search of her body, upon which were found several suspicious teats in 'her secret parts'.

[8] J. Glanvill, *Saducismus Triumphatus: Or Full and Plain Evidence Concerning Witches and Apparitions* (London, 1681), ii, 189. In the same work, More's colleague Glanvill had attempted to provide a scientific rationale for attributing the cause of the physical harm to the witch alone, and not the Devil or evil spirit, by recourse to corpuscularian theories of infection. Sometimes this involved the passage of venomous and malign ferments through the air. On other occasions, however, More believed that it was quite conceivable that 'some kinds of fascination are perform'd in this grosser and more sensible way, as by striking, giving Apples, and the like, by which the contagious quality may be transmitted, as we see Diseases often are by the touch'; ibid. i, 23–4. The source of the contagious ferment was nonetheless diabolical, transferred to the witch by suckling imps or devils. More's insight that Greatrakes' curative powers represented an inversion of the methods used by witches in 'poisoning' their victims is discussed more fully in R. Crocker, *Henry More, 1614–1687: A Biography of the Cambridge Platonist* (Dordrecht, 2003), chapter 9.

[9] As well as curing demoniacs, Felton alleged that Greatrakes, like Christ [John 9:6], had cured a blind man with his spittle; BL, Harleian MS 3785, fo. 110r.

both provided important opportunities for contemporaries to explore their under-standing of the forces at work in the body politic. In such instances, the body became a site of contention, fought over by the instruments of God and the Devil, the outcome frequently providing spectators with valuable insights into the mind-set of the Creator. At the same time—as I have suggested in the case of the eirenic Greatrakes—the bodies of charismatic healers, as well as those of their sick patients, were widely observed to provide a divinely sanctioned commentary on the religious and political preoccupations of the day, although the precise meaning contempor-aries attached to such events was, more often than not, hotly debated.

It was much the same for other extraordinary bodies, such as monstrous births, which attracted the interest of scholars and social commentators as well as provid-ing an endlessly fascinating spectacle for the wider public.[10] Alexandra Walsham's analysis of such phenomena is particularly helpful here as she demonstrates how early modern commentators often felt that God 'encoded a particular message in the contorted limbs and tumorous growths of these unfortunate infants, projecting onto their diminutive bodies a silhouette of the sins which had infested the body politic'.[11] What is crucial here for my analysis of Greatrakes, and his relationship to the religious and political events of the Restoration, is the explanatory authority that contemporaries attached to the semiotics of bodies and their relationship to the wider body politic. Although Walsham was writing of the period before the Civil War, it is evident from what follows that such concerns did not expire with the onset of that conflict, nor its conclusion, and that the idea of a close correlation between events in the microcosm, or human body, and those in the wider world, or macrocosm, continued to inform both learned and popular belief for decades after 1660. Indeed, Greatrakes' emergence as a charismatic healer was simply one of numerous examples of the genre, the most famous and celebrated being reserved for the 'miraculous' Restoration of Charles II in 1660.

The collapse of the Republic amid growing fears of a return to religious and political anarchy in 1659–60, followed by the return of the Stuarts, was widely celebrated through recourse to the language of the body politic and associated tropes. The failure of the restored Rump, for example, provided a wealth of op-portunities for opponents to associate republican rule with disordered bodies, be they monstrous, excremental, diabolical, or a combination of all three.[12] By early

---

[10] There is a burgeoning literature on the early modern European preoccupation with monsters and teratology which owes much to the pioneering work of Jean Céard, Katharine Park, and Lorraine Daston. For recent examples of case studies in relation to England, see especially K. Park and L. J. Daston, 'Unnatural Conceptions: The Study of Monsters in France and England', *Past and Present*, 92 (1981), 20–54; K. M. Brammall, 'Monstrous Metamorphosis: Nature, Morality and the Rhetoric of Monstrosity in Tudor England', *Sixteenth Century Journal*, 27 (1996), 3–21; D. Cressy, 'Monstrous Births and Credible Reports', in *idem*, *Travesties and Transgressions in Tudor and Stuart England: Tales of Discord and Dissension* (Oxford, 2000), 29–50; *idem*, 'Lamentable, Strange and Won-derful: Headless Monsters in the English Revolution', in L. L. Knoppers and J. B. Landes (eds), *Monstrous Bodies/Political Monstrosities in Early Modern Europe* (Ithaca, NY, 2004), 40–63.

[11] A. Walsham, *Providence in Early Modern England* (Oxford, 1999), 195.

[12] See especially M. Jenner, 'The Roasting of the Rump: Scatology and the Body Politic in Restor-ation England', *Past and Present*, 177 (2002), 84–120.

1660, the vast majority of the population, regardless of office and status, were united in the conviction that the only solution to the manifold ailments afflicting the body politic lay in the restoration of the curative authority of the Stuarts. By restoring Charles II to his rightful place at the pinnacle of the social and political pyramid, it was confidently expected that order and propriety would return to the rest of the realm, the head once again firmly ruling the subordinate members of the body politic. In sermon after sermon in the immediate wake of Charles II's return to England, ministers, many of them Puritans who chose not to conform after 1662, invoked traditional medical metaphors that stressed the benevolent and hierarchical nature of royal government and the corresponding malaise and disorder associated with republican rule. Typical was the Dorset puritan John Hodder (d. 1680), who informed his congregation that 'we have been like a body beheaded, for which no other head will serve, how artificially soever it be set on'.[13] In a similar vein, Henry Hibbert, in a sermon preached at St Paul's on the day of Charles II's coronation, compared England under the commonwealth to a sick patient 'tossing to every side the bed for ease', the victim of what other clergymen and commentators consistently labelled as the new 'state physicians' or 'mountebanks' of the 1650s.[14]

Diagnoses in the pulpit of the nation's ills differed only in degree, not in substance. All concurred that Britain laboured under some providential malaise, punishment no doubt for the sins of its people. And all were uniformly unequivocal in arguing, at least in the early years of Charles II's reign, that the cure of these distempers lay in the healing hands of the restored monarch. In this context, Charles II was frequently likened to a sanctified physician, who, like Christ, was expected to heal both the physical as well as the spiritual maladies of his subjects.[15] This was most literally the case with respect to the disease commonly known as the king's evil, or scrofula, which English, as well as French, kings had claimed to heal by application of the royal touch since the Middle Ages.[16] Largely overlooked by the

---

[13] A. Short, *God Save the King: Or, A Sermon Preach'd at Lyme Regis May 18 1660 at the Solemn Proclamation of His Most Excellent Majesty Charles II* (London, 1660), B1r [preface by John Hodder]. Speaking no doubt for many of his Presbyterian colleagues, Hodder added: 'we are weary studying the meaning of Common-wealth, and although we have had the name beaten into us, yet cannot possibly understand the thing'; B2r. Both Hodder and Short were ejected in 1662; *Cal. Rev.*, 269–70, 440–1.

[14] H. Hibbert, *Regina Dierum: Or, The Joyful Day in a Sermon* [29 May 1661] (London, 1661), 12. A month earlier at Dublin, Thomas Bramhall used precisely the same conceit to convey the sense of England as a sick man, 'that can take no rest in his bed, but is continually tossing, and turning from side to side'; T. Bramhall, *A Sermon Preached at Dublin* [23 April 1661] (Dublin, 1661), 22.

[15] See for example J. Lyngue, *Davids Deliverance: Or A Sermon Preached at the Sessions Holden at Maidstone… being the Day of the Coronation of King Charles the II* (London, 1661), 22. Lyngue was vicar of Yalding in Kent. The Restoration sermons of the long-suffering royalist preacher, Matthew Griffith (d. 1665), are similarly replete with medical allusions and analogies designed to demonstrate Charles II's credentials as a healer of the nation's political divisions; see for example his *The Fear of God and the King. Press'd in a Sermon* [25 March 1660] (London, 1660), 104–5; *Christian Concord: Or, S. Pauls Parallel between the Body Natural and Mystical. Exemplified in a Sermon* [13 January 1661] (London, 1661); *The Catholique Doctor and his Spiritual Catholicon to Cure Our Sinfull Soules* [26 May 1661] (London, 1661), 10, 11, 12, 21. *Christian Concord* was dedicated to Sir Edward Nicholas (1593–1669), whom Griffith described as one who laboured to make 'a sick Bodie politick, a sound one'; A3r.

[16] For an excellent overview of the historical significance of the practice of touching for scrofula, see M. Bloch, *Les Rois Thaumaturges* (Paris, 1924), published in English as *The Royal Touch: Sacred Mon-*

first two Stuarts, Charles II immediately revived the practice on returning to England and is calculated to have touched approximately 100,000 of his subjects in the course of his twenty-five year reign.[17] Not surprisingly, those welcoming the return of Charles II in 1660 repeatedly did so by comparing the symptoms of the nation's ills in the previous two decades to those of scrofula, which left its sufferers badly disfigured. William Sancroft (1617–1693), for example, fervently hoped and prayed that the restoration of the King's gift of healing would be a prelude to 'the healing of the Church's and the People's Evils, as well, as of the King's'.[18] Likewise, the Presbyterian Richard Eedes (d. 1686), who was to be ejected in 1662, diagnosed the sickness of the body politic in 1660 as that of the king's evil, the cure for which was vested in the special powers of the person of the monarch for 'His Majestie is now become a Physitian, and the Lord make him a healer of his People [so that] I may say to every one that is sick of this Evil… The King touches you. The King touches you, and with so gentle an hand would be set all broken bones in joint again.[19]

One of the fullest treatments of this kind can be found in the work of the Presbyterian John Bird, whose *Ostenta Carolina* (1661) provides a detailed analysis and comparison of events in the interrelated worlds of politics and medicine in the 1650s. In common with many of his co-religionists, Bird alludes throughout to his former allegiance to the cause of godly reformation, while at the same time distancing himself from the excesses of parliamentary government, particularly the execution of the King in 1649. In a manner typical of

archy and Scrofula in England and France (London, 1973). For an earlier account, see R. Crawfurd, *The King's Evil* (Oxford, 1911).

[17] Charles I's belated resurrection of the royal ceremony of touching for the king's evil in the 1640s may have been little more than an act of political expediency on his part. For Charles I's reluctance to practise the gift of healing for much of his reign, see J. Richards, '"His Nowe Majestie" and the English Monarchy: The Kingship of Charles I before 1640', *Past and Present*, 113 (1986), 86–94. For an alternative view that stresses Charles' overwhelming regard for order and decorum as the principal motivation behind his attempt to reform procedures relating to the touch (one effect of which was to restrict access to the king according to a rigidly controlled timetable), see S. Brogan, 'The Royal Touch in Early Modern England: Its Changing Rationale and Practice', Ph.D. thesis (London, 2011), 87–97. I am extremely grateful to Stephen Brogan for sharing his knowledge of this and other aspects of the royal touch in early modern England.

[18] W. S[ancroft], *A Sermon Preached at St Peter's Westminster on the First Sunday in Advent* (London, 1660), 33. Sancroft, it should be noted, took a keen interest in the exploits of Greatrakes; see Appendix 2.

[19] R. Eedes, *Great Britains Resurrection. Or England's Complacencie in Her Royal Soveraign King Charles the Second. A Sermon Preached… at Gloucester, June 5, 1660* (London, 1660), 33; *Cal. Rev.*, 180. The royalist lawyer Giles Duncombe, commenting on the ruinous state of the body politic in early 1660, claimed that 'we are all sick of the kings evil, therefore nothing but the touch of his sacred Majesties hands can cure us'; Cimelgus Bonde [i.e. Giles Duncombe], *Scutum Regale The Royal Buckler, or, Vox Legis, a Lecture to Traytors, who Most Wickedly Murthered Charles the I* (London, 1660), 387–8. Similar sentiments pervade many of the poetic encomiums and ballads written in 1660 to celebrate the return of the king; see for example, *Anglia Rediviva: A Poem on His Majesties Most Joyfull Reception into England* (London, 1660), 1–2; *Iter Boreale. Attempting Somthing upon the Successful and Matchless March of the Lord General Monck, from Scotland, to London… Printed on St. Georges Day, Being the 23d of April, 1660* (London, 1660), 8; J. P., *The Loyal Subject's Hearty Wishes to King Charles the Second* (London, 1660?).

many of his Presbyterian colleagues, he sought to interpret the Interregnum, and the subsequent slide towards political and religious radicalism, as a manifestation of biblical prophecy. Citing Isaiah, Chapter 1, as his source, Bird claimed that the afflictions of the Jews described by the Old Testament prophet were directly comparable to those experienced by his fellow countrymen in the 1650s:

> and as under the Type of a disease in the same Chapter the Prophet describes al-legorically their sins and sufferings, so hath the Lord God miraculously by two Diseases of the Body of man described unto us mystically, the people of England, and such as resemble the Diseases set down in the Text, our sins, and our calamities.[20]

The two diseases that Bird had in mind were rickets and the king's evil. These two were 'nothing else but in every part and circumstance living pictures of what we have done and suffered, and but Metaphorical names of the very things'. Using some very intricate and ingenious word-play, Bird went on to explain how the word rickets derived from the same root as the word for regents. Consequently, he was able to explain how in the very name of the disease were prefigured 'the AUTHORS of our late CALAMITIES; for according to the Name of the Disease they were not Kings, but such as took upon them REGAL AUTHORITY'. Bird even noted the fact that the disease was referred to in the plural, thus indicating that there was more than one involved in the usurpation of the throne.[21] Bird's employment of recent medical terminology was not simply a literary or rhetori-cal trope that was devoid of deeper meaning or significance. On the contrary, his own medical training and experience, combined with his deep-seated religious and political convictions, meant that he envisaged a real, as well as a metaphori-cal, correspondence between events in the body politic and the physical com-plaints suffered by the King's subjects, including new afflictions such as the rickets. Bird was confident therefore that Charles II would not only 'cure those wounds and putrified sores, which our State Physicians . . . have made and caused', but that in time he would also eradicate its physical equivalent, the rickets and scrofula, the symptoms of which he systematically described and compared with those ills that had afflicted the body politic in the previous decade.[22] Bird even brought the latest techniques of archival research to bear upon the problem when

---

[20] J. Bird, *Ostenta Carolina: or the Late Calamities of England with the Authors of Them. The Great Happiness and Happy Government of K. Charles II Ensuing, Miraculously Foreshewn by the Finger of God in Two Wonderful Diseases, the Rekets and Kings-Evil* (London, 1661), 27. The preface to the reader is dated 24 January 1661 at Sion College, London.

[21] Ibid. 52–3.

[22] Ibid. 51, 54–65, 70. Bird was not alone in promoting the royal touch after 1660. In 1662, the Norwich physician Robert Bayfield (1630–1690) claimed that scrofula was 'commonly cured by the hand of the Prince and otherwise therefore, seldomer striven withal amongst us'. Thirty years later, the Presbyterian Richard Baxter was loathe to dismiss the reality of the divine gift of the royal touch, though he argued strongly for the idea that the power to heal resided in the office of monarchy and was not inherent in the constitution of individual rulers; R. Bayfield, *Tractatus de Tumoribus Praeter Naturam. Or, A Treatise of Preternatural Tumors* (London, 1662), 147; R. Baxter, *The Certainty of the Worlds of Spirits* (London, 1691), 212–13.

he claimed that rickets first manifested itself in England three years after the birth of Charles II 'as I have found by search in the Parish Clerkes Register kept in their Hall'[23]

In all these accounts, there is an underlying emphasis upon the idea that the English body politic had been subjected to the experimental regime, or regimen, of counterfeit 'state-physicians' or 'mountebanks', whose so-called cures of the nation's ills have in fact turned out to be worse than the original disease. 'How did those Mountebancks and Quacksalvers of State that had the body Politick in cure, try all conclusions,' enquired one apologist for the Restoration. Such men, he went on, would do anything to avoid the return of the King:

> prescribing sometimes the strong Purges of illegal Sequestrations: sometimes the fasting Spittle of pretended Humiliations: sometimes the letting blood of a High Court of Justice: constantly the Weapon-Salve of a domineering army? And what did all availe us? All could see at last and acknowledge the King's Evill was the Disease which we were sick off, and his hand onely could work the cure, and him God gave us.[24]

Echoing these sentiments, the Presbyterian minister Edward Willan referred in 1661 to those 'new State Physicians' who applied 'cruel phlebotomie' to Charles I and thus deprived the nation of its chief source of health.[25] In sermon after sermon, the execution of the King was repeatedly described as an act endowed with medical, as well as political, significance. Not only were his judges alleged to have mocked the King with the cry of 'Now Stroaker cure thy self', but further indignities were heaped upon his headless cadaver when, according to one royalist divine, his body was subjected to a political autopsy that was designed to demonstrate the rottenness of both his body and that of the kingdom he ruled over:

> [After his execution] they delieevered the body to be unbowelled to an infamous Empirick of the Faction, together with the rude Chirurgions of the Army . . . who were all most implacable enemies to His Majesty, and commanded them to search . . . whether

---

[23] Bird, *Ostenta Carolina*, 78. In the preface to John Hall's *Select Observations on English Bodies* (London, 1657), Bird described himself as 'Medicinae Praelector Linacerianus' in the University of Cambridge. He may be the same as the John Bird, a graduate of Merton College, Oxford, who was repeatedly hauled before the London College of Physicians in the 1630s for practising medicine illegally; Foster, i, 127; RCPL, Annals, iii, 248, 255, 272, 425; *CSPD, 1639–1640*, 85; TNA, PC2/51, fos 29r, 41r. He may also be the man of the same name who in April 1662 was described as a former sequestrator, a combatant at Worcester (1651) and 'a notorious enemy to His Majesty during the late wars, and to his restoration'. If so, then the publication of *Ostenta Carolina* was clearly an attempt to ingratiate himself with the new government; *CSPD, 1661–1662*, 347. For research on rickets as a specifically puritan medical project, see W. J. Birken, 'The Dissenting Tradition in English Medicine of the Seventeenth and Eighteenth Centuries', *Medical History*, 39 (1995), 205.

[24] R. Meggott, *The New-Cured Criple's Caveat: Or, England's Duty for the Miraculous Mercy of the King's and Kingdome's Restauration* [19 May 1662] (London, 1662), 29.

[25] E. Willan, *Beatitas Britanniae: Or, King Charles the Second, Englands Beatitude, as Preached to the Incorporation of the Honour of Eye, in the County of Suffolk, March 31 1661 Being the Lords Day before the Election of Their Burgesses, and the Week before the Choice of Knights for the County* (London, 1661), 27. Willan would appear to have renounced his earlier commitment to Presbyterianism at the Restoration and subsequently conformed. The political significance of the occasion of this and similar sermons reinforces the importance attached by contemporaries to the notion of the body politic in the early years of the Restoration.

they could not find in it symptoms of the French disease, or some evidences of Frigidity, and natural impotency: that so they might have some colour to slander him who was eminent for Chastity; or to make his Seed infamous.[26]

According to those who now celebrated the return of the monarchy, instead of curing the nation's ills, the 'state physicians' who were responsible for the murder of Charles I had simply succeeded in undermining the general health and well-being of the nation. The country was sick and distempered, and subject to a whole range of maladies, many or most of which lay beyond the power of conventional physic and physicians to cure. Alongside the king's evil, one other malady in particular stands out in the various sermons and panegyrics issued after 1660 to encapsulate this sense of a diseased body politic. In countless sermons and pamphlets, critics of the Cromwellian regime consistently reiterated and reworked the idea of England as a nation bewitched. Thomas Reeve (d. 1672), for example, in a series of sermons preached at Waltham Abbey in Essex in 1661, repeatedly inveighed against the actions of those 'state witches' and state-wizards' who had cast a spell over the people of England and induced them to rebel. Invoking the notion of a country and a people languishing in a state of diabolical bewitchment, Reeve was now convinced that the return of Charles II had effectively dispossessed the nation. Thus in one sermon dedicated to prominent figures in the restored judiciary, he lamented:

> What a chase hath there been in this Land? ye have gone a Pilgrimage from your Courts of Justice. The whole Land hath been possessed with evil spirits, and Westminster-hall hath been a Demoniack.... But I trust that this Hericano [Hurricane] is over and that this Devil is exorcized out of the Body of the Law.[27]

In a similar vein, in February 1660 John Gauden (d. 1662) repeatedly invoked the image of England as a nation possessed, the Cromwellian rulers and clergy variously depicted as medical empirics, Paracelsians, wizards, and cunning men, who:

> fly to their inchantments, as if they would heal by charmes, and cure by Philters or amulets, as by carrying Bibles in their hands, by using much Scripture phrase and

---

[26] H. King, *A Sermon Preached the 30th of January at White-Hall 1664* [i.e. 1665] (London, H. Herringman, 1665), 41; [R. Perrinchief], *The Royal Martyr: Or, The Life and Death of Charles I* (London, 1676), 206. According to Perrinchief, the surgeons were prevented from reporting evil things of Charles' body by the intervention of 'a Physician of great Integrity and Skill', who also 'published that Nature had tempered the Royal Body to a longer life than commonly is granted to other men. And as His Soul was fitted by Heroick Virtues to Eternity, so His Body by a Temperament almost *ad pondus* made as near an approach to it as the present condition of Mortality would permit'; ibid. 206–7.

[27] T. Reeve, *England's Backwardness or A Lingring Party in Bringing Back a Lawful King Delivered in a Sermon at Waltham Abbey Church in the County of Essex, at a Solemne Fast* (London, 1661), A3v–A4r. Other contemporary works by Reeve that play on similar themes include: *England's Beauty in Seeing King Charles the Second Restored to Majesty* (London, 1661), 23, 31; *The Man of Valour, or the Puissance of Englands Great Champion. Delivered in Three Sermons, in the Parish Church of Waltham Abbey, Upon Duke Albemarle's Coming Up to London, and Declaring for a Free Parliament* (London, 1661), 'The Man of Valour', 71–2; 'Sheba's Head Cast Over the Wall', A3r; 'England's Restitution or the Man, the Man of Men', 28, 53, 84. Reeve, whose sermons are suffused with demonological language, also alluded to the king's evil, prior to 1660, as a form of national suffering; 'England's Restitution', A3v.

expression, by affecting an odd kind of canting way of writing and speaking...by crying up providences and successes, by conjuring up strange fears and hopes, jealousies and expectations, like so many Ghosts and Goblins, to scare and amuse the common people.

The populace under such a government were like 'Demoniacks, or possessed', their cure resting in the counter-magic inherent in the person of the monarch.[28] Similar statements invoking contemporary demonological beliefs can be found in countless sermons dating from this period. William Creed (d. 1663), for example, in a thanksgiving sermon preached in the summer of 1660 drew an explicit parallel between the actions of witches and those of rebels. Citing 1 Samuel 15:23, he claimed that the sins of both were 'very nigh of kinne' for 'the one sets up another God, or Gods; and the other a new King, or severall Princes, and the Devil, the Master and the Governour, rules alike in both. He, with his Sorceries and Inchantments, doth equally bewitch them; and there is no getting out of the snare, without Gods great mercy, grace and goodness'.[29]

The meaning of Creed's sermon was transparent. God, acting through Charles II, had restored the nation to its former health and exorcized the kingdom of its demonic usurpers. It was precisely this kind of thinking that informed the elaborate ceremonies devised by the city of London for the King's coronation on 23 April 1661.[30] En route for Westminster Abbey, Charles was entertained by the city fathers, who erected in his honour four triumphal arches. The first of these was clearly intended to symbolize the return of the kingdom to peace, justice, and harmony following the turmoil of rebellion, civil war, and general discord. As Charles approached the arch from its north side, he was confronted by a terrifying figure in the form of a woman dressed in the garb of a classical witch 'personating

---

[28] J. Gauden, *ΚΑΚΟΥΡΓΟΙ sive Medicastri: Slight Healings of Publique Hurts Set Forth in a Sermon* [29 February 1659/60] (London, 1660), 39–40, 64, 66–7, 78, 85. Such thinking is also implicit in W. Bartholomew, *The Strong Man Ejected by a Stronger than He. In a Sermon Preached at Gloucester* [15 May 1660] (London, 1660). Gauden was not alone in equating support for the 'good old cause' with those who championed Paracelsianism; see T. Reeve, *A Dead Man Speaking or the Famous Memory of King Charles I. Delivered in a Sermon upon the 30th of Ian. Last, in the Parish Church of Waltham Abbey* (London, 1661), 15; *A Mirror: Wherein the Rumpers and Fanaticks...may see their Deformity...Sent in a Letter by a Friend, to a Votary and Follower of that Faction* (London, 1660), 1, 2, 7, 11. Likewise, John King, Dean of Tuam in Ireland, saw Charles II as the healer of the nation's ills and castigated the regicides as 'State-emperiques [who] have practised upon the body politique'; J. King, *A Sermon on the 30th of January* (London, 1661), 59.

[29] W. Creed, *Judah's Return to their Allegiance: And David's Returne to his Crowne and Kingdom* (London, 1660), 29. Creed was Regius Professor of Divinity at Oxford from 1660 till his death in 1663. Shortly before his death, Joseph Glanvill reported that John Mompesson, a Wiltshire gentleman, had sent Creed full details of the case of the demon drummer of Tedworth, a demonological *cause célèbre* in early Restoration England. Glanvill's associate, Henry More, was firmly of the opinion that Creed was about to publish a full account of the case prior to his death; Glanvill, *Saducismus Triumphatus*, ii, 110; *Conway Letters*, 218–19. For a fresh analysis of this affair, and Creed's role in it, based on the evidence of recently discovered letters between Mompesson and Creed, see M. Hunter, 'New Light on the "Drummer of Tedworth": Conflicting Narratives of Witchcraft in Restoration England', *Historical Research*, 78 (2005), 311–37.

[30] For the coronation as 'an exercise in political theater', see C. A. Edie, 'The Public Face of Royal Ritual: Sermons, Medals and Civic Ceremony in Later Stuart Coronations', *Huntington Library Quarterly*, 53 (1990), 313–18.

REBELLION, mounted on a Hydra'. She in turn was accompanied by her attendant, 'CONFUSION, in a deformed Shape', who was dressed in 'a Garment of severall ill-matched Colours, and put on the wrong way'. A brief dramatic interlude followed in which the witch-figure, Rebellion, addressed the King as follows:

> Would you know what Int'rest I have here?
> Hydra I ride: great Cities are my Sphear:
> I Sorcery use, and hang Men in their Beds,
> With Common-wealths, and Rotas fill their Heads,
> Making the Vulgar in Fanatique Swarms
> Court Civil War, and dote on horrid Arms;
> 'Twas I, who, in the late unnatural Broils,
> Engag'd three Kingdoms, and two Wealthy Isles:
> I hope at last, to march with Flags unfurl'd,
> And tread down Monarchy through all the World.[31]

The speech concluded, Charles marched triumphantly through the open arch and in that instant, metaphorically at least, the kingdom was disenchanted. A few hours later, with the King safely ensconced on his new throne, the process of restoration was complete. Again, it would be easy to dismiss this kind of spectacle as little more than a popular dramatic device designed to celebrate and propagandize the Stuart cause. Contemporaries, however, as we have seen, were not so 'rational' in their view of sacred monarchy and its charismatic blessings. Amongst the many benefits that some ascribed to Charles' return was the overthrow and defeat of actual diabolical witchcraft. There may even have been a link between the decline of prosecutions for the crime of witchcraft in the Restoration period and the re-establishment of monarchical government. One of the more notable features of the post-Restoration era was the growing propensity of Charles' judges to dismiss or ignore the threat of witchcraft while at the same time actively seeking out and prosecuting those 'surrogate witches', religious and political dissidents, who were widely stigmatized in loyalist circles as acolytes of the devil.[32] The preacher John Douch (d. 1676), for example, in a sermon of 1660, was quick to assert that there were 'never more Witches in England since Monarchy and Hierarchy lay in the dust'. In similar vein and in the same year, the Presbyterian George Starkey (1628–1665) welcomed the return of the King by comparing the regicides and Cromwellians unflatteringly with those witches who, he hinted, had been unjustly

---

[31] J. Ogilby, *The Entertainment of His Most Excellent Majestie Charles II, in His Passage Through the City of London to His Coronation* (London, 1662), 13, 15, 47. The association between witchcraft, rebellion, disorder, and the language of inversion is fully explored by Stuart Clark in his ground-breaking *Thinking With Demons: The Idea of Witchcraft in Early Modern Europe* (Oxford, 1997), 69–79. Many of the themes discussed here were also prominent in much of the verse celebrating the Restoration; see for example J. Collop, *Itur Satyricum: In Loyall Stanzas* (London, 1660), 4, 10.

[32] I use the term 'surrogate witches' to describe the way in which the Quakers were demonised both before and after 1660 in my '"Saints or Sorcerers": Quakerism, Demonology and the Decline of Witchcraft in Seventeenth-Century England', in J. Barry, M. Hester, and G. Roberts (eds), *Witchcraft in Early Modern Europe: Studies in Culture and Belief* (Cambridge, 1996), 145–79.

put to death in East Anglia during the trials instigated by Matthew Hopkins in the 1640s.[33] In the minds of many loyal preachers, eager to celebrate the return of the Stuarts, the crime of witchcraft was consistently linked with civil war and political disorder, a point forcefully made by John Riland (d. 1673), archdeacon of Coventry, in 1661 when he claimed that:

'Tis recorded of the Civill Wars in France, that they produced 30,000 witches, and above a Million of Atheists; what the Effects of ours hath been upon us in particular we know not, but 'tis much to be feared, there hath been a greater increase of such Monsters, then good Christians...And generally we find that's a shrewd Proverb, when War begins, Hell opens: for be sure then some Customers will be coming; but especially, if they be Civill Wars: those being Hell's huge Fair daies, when others are but ordinary Markets.[34]

That rebellion and witchcraft should be linked in this way is hardly surprising. Ever since the outbreak of the Civil War in the 1640s, royalist preachers and propagandists had unstintingly reminded their loyal compatriots of the words of the prophet Samuel: 'For rebellion is as the sin of witchcraft, and stubbornness is as iniquity and idolatry' (1 Samuel 15:23). Evidence of the extent to which such thinking had percolated down to the masses can also be found across Britain in the various acts of popular street theatre that were devised to celebrate the Restoration. The King's birthday (29 May 1661), for example, was the occasion of popular rejoicing at Sherborne in Dorset and Oundle in Northamptonshire, where effigies of notorious witch-rebels such as Cromwell and the Marquess of Argyll were ritually desecrated and burned. Similar events were recalled by the Presbyterian James Kirkton (d. 1699) at Linlithgow in Scotland.[35] Allusions to 1 Samuel 15:23 continued to pepper loyal sermons throughout the period after 1660, more often than not on occasions of acute political sensitivity such as the anniversary of the regicide or a meeting of the assizes, reaching a crescendo in the wake of the Exclusion Crisis and Rye House Plot. One product of this offensive was the creation in the minds of many of Charles' subjects of a clear association between the crime of witchcraft

[33] J. Douch, *Englands Jubilee: Or, Her Happy Return from Captivity: In a Sermon, Preached at St Botolphs Aldersgate, London* (London, 1660), A3v; G. Starkey, *Royal and Other Innocent Bloud Crying Aloud to Heaven for Due Vengeance* (London, 1660), 41. For the chemical physician Starkey's pro-royalist pamphlets as a sincere expression of his long-held Presbyterianism, see W. R. Newman, *Gehennical Fire: The Lives of George Starkey, an American Alchemist in the Scientific Revolution* (Cambridge, MA, 1994), 191.

[34] J. Riland, *Elias the Second His Coming to Restore All Things: Or Gods Way of Reforming by Restoring...In Two Sermons* (Oxford, 1662), 'Moses the Peace-Maker', 41.

[35] *Mercurius Publicus*, 30 May–6 June 1661; *Kingdomes Intelligencer*, 3 June 1661; C. K. Sharpe (ed.), *The Secret and True History of the Church of Scotland, From the Restoration to the Year 1678 by the Rev. Mr James Kirkton* (Edinburgh, 1817), 126–7. At Sherborne, where there had been a witch scare in the previous year involving a group of Quakers, the marquess was tried by a mock court of justice alongside 'a woman-Witch'. Both effigies were decked in radical accoutrements, including the Solemn League and Covenant. The woman was also wearing a copy of the Anabaptists' creed on her breast, along with '2 pamphlets which were, not long before, taken from 2 notorious Phanaticks of this place'. The rumour that the rebel Covenanter Argyll had consulted with witches, subsequently burned at Edinburgh, had reached rural Worcestershire by 20 May; J. W. Willis-Bund (ed.), *Diary of Henry Townsend of Elmley Lovett 1640–1663*, 2 vols (London, 1915–20), i, 74.

and that of opposition to divine right government. Some, like Douch, even went so far as to declare that 'Rebellion *is* the sin of witchcraft'. He went on to warn his audience that 'if you hearken to [rebels], or come near them, they will inchant you, and (like Conjurors) raise such and such spirits in against God, and his Vicegerent, that 'tis not all the Orthodox Preaching can allay them'. Similar claims were later made by John Fell (1625–1686) during the Exclusion Crisis: 'But that rebellion is the sin of witchcraft one would wonder, by what enchantment men should be persuaded to disturb at once their own and the public peace'.[36]

EXORCIZING THE DEMONS OF THE PAST: GREATRAKES THE DEMONOLOGIST

Historians, like many of Greatrakes' contemporaries, have been eager to explain, or in some cases explain away, the nature and success of the Irish stroker's 'miraculous' gift. Few, however, have given serious consideration to Greatrakes' own explanation as to what he believed he was doing when he stroked the sick and lame. However, if one listens to the voice of the chief actor in this drama, as well as the informed comments of spectators, one discovers interesting clues and insights into the origin and purpose of Greatrakes' practice. Perhaps the most striking, in the light of what has been said about the widespread resort in the early 1660s to the language of diabolical witchcraft, was Greatrakes' own view that many of his cures were in fact forms of dispossession. In a passage from his autobiographical *Account* that has rarely been quoted, he hinted strongly at a demonic element in his thaumaturgical operations:

> I hope you will pardon me when I relate to you my own Observations, and what my Experience inclines me to believe, in saying that I have met several Instances which seemed to me to be Possessions by dumb Devils, deaf Devils, and talking Devils, and that to my apprehension, and others present, several evil Spirits one after the other have been pursu'd out of a Woman, and every one of them have been like to choak her...before it went forth.... There have been others that have faln down immediately as soon as they have seen me...many, when they have but heard my voice, and have been tormented in so strange a manner that no one that has been present could conceive it less then a Possession.[37]

Numerous other sources confirm Greatrakes' self-image as a Christ-like figure, capable of healing the sick in mind as well as body, many of whom were suffering, in Greatrakes' eyes, from preternatural or demonically inspired maladies. Thus the physician Henry Stubbe alluded to his ostensible cure of demoniacs. In an appendix to his *Miraculous Conformist*, he included the testimonial of the Cambridge scholar Ezekiel Foxcroft, who witnessed at first hand Greatrakes' attempt to cure

---

[36] Douch, *Englands Jubilee*, 17 [my emphasis]; J. Fell, *A Sermon Preached Before the House of Peers on December 22 1680. Being the Day of Solemn Humiliation* (Oxford, 1680), 3. Douch was minister at Stalbridge in Dorset, and had played a minor role in the early education of Robert Boyle.

[37] Greatrakes, *Brief Account*, 32–3.

the daughters of one Mrs Bickeridge or Vicaridge of Tewkesbury in Gloucestershire. The Irish stroker, Foxcroft alleged, was convinced that one of the girls was suffering from an incursion of 'some Evill spirit gotten into the Body of the Child'. Greatrakes' diagnosis, it would appear, almost certainly confirmed the worst fears of the children's parents. Shortly after departing Worcester, Susan Vicaridge relapsed into her former fits. Various measures were subsequently tried to alleviate the fits, including legal sanctions against a local woman suspected of bewitching the children, but no outcome or verdict is recorded.[38] Foxcroft also noted Greatrakes' diagnosis of possession in the case of the Malvern schoolmistress, Mrs Walling, who suffered, like the Vicaridge children, from the falling sickness.[39]

On other occasions, Greatrakes was approached by sufferers who were clearly convinced that they were bewitched, and that the Irishman would be able to effect their cure. In 1668, for example, Greatrakes described in a letter to Robert Boyle how, on a return visit to England, he was approached at an inn between Ragley and Bristol by a woman whose fourteen-year-old daughter was in a pitiful state:

> the most absolute Skelliton that ever was seen who was dumbe, & by her Mother thought to be bewitched, on whom I lay my hand's, & though she could not speake, yet she heard well, & directed me when her paines flew, which I pursued from place, to place, till I drove them out, & then it pleased God that her speech was restored to her, now what that paine was which caused her to be dumbe, & caused her to pine away in such a manner, I leave you to judge of, & how it should be possible that a paine in her foote, or hande should stopp her tongue from speakeinge, which presently as soone as it went out, she did perfectly pray tell me if you can by your philosophy.[40]

Two years previously, Greatrakes had regaled the sceptical Boyle and his sister, Lady Ranelagh, with a similar but more detailed account of his approach to such cases, which he clearly believed to be demonic in origin. On 15 April 1666 Boyle

[38] The case excited much local interest, as well as eliciting comment from further afield. In an undated letter addressed to the Gloucestershire JP John Smyth the younger, Conway Whithorne, a fellow magistrate and loyal Anglican, described the examination of the suspected witch, Isabell Sheene. He, along with other JPs, concluded that there was 'little or no thing but groundless suspitions'. Nonetheless, he reported that she was placed under the roof of Mrs Vicaridge for three days 'to be searched and watched as she pleased... where she was treated after the wilde method of witchfinders and returned home in a condition, more like to die then live and recovered not in several weekes'. At the same time, the Oxford antiquarian Anthony Wood noted in his diary that in the summer of 1666 the eleven year old child of Mr John Viccaridg, living 'within a mile of Tewkesbury', had become 'strangly possest'; Stubbe, *Miraculous Conformist*, 32–5; GRO, Smyth of Nibley Papers, vol. 15, no. 93; vol. 16, no. 57; A. Clark (ed.), *The Life and Times of Anthony Wood*, 5 vols (Oxford, 1891–1900), ii, 53–4; Extracts from some of the material in the Nibley Papers, which provides details of the witnesses against Isabell Sheene, are discussed and reproduced in D. C. Beaver, *Parish Communities and Religious Conflict in the Vale of Gloucester, 1590–1690* (Cambridge, MA, 1998), 58–9, 343–4.
[39] Stubbe, *Miraculous Conformist*, 40–1. In this instance, however, Greatrakes' patient clearly did not share his enthusiasm for a demonic diagnosis. At the suggestion that she was obsessed, she indignantly replied in Latin that it was not the Devil that bothered her, but flatulence! The latter was seized upon by the hostile Anglican cleric David Lloyd as a further example of the fraudulent conduct of the Irish stroker; [D. Lloyd], *Wonders No Miracles; Or, Mr Valentine Greatrates Gift of Healing Examined... in a Letter to a Reverend Divine* (London, 1666), 45.
[40] Boyle, *Correspondence*, iv, 99.

reported that Greatrakes 'thinks most Epileptick Persons to be Daemoniacks notwithstanding what I could say to ye contrary'. In all these cases, the symptoms of the patients echoed those commonly associated with diabolical possession and Greatrakes' method of cure was specifically designed to drive out the evil spirits from one of the body's extremities. Typically, as in his diagnosis of the disease known as the 'suffocation of the mother', Greatrakes sought the source of the pain, and then chased it from 'place to place till it be quite expeld'.[41] It seems likely, moreover, that Greatrakes had long held the view that the majority of those who came to him for assistance were in fact suffering from some form of diabolically induced illness. In the summer of 1665, he reportedly told one onlooker that the reason why pain was driven from the bodies of sufferers following his stroking was because 'the Divell has a hand in all Diseases, tho much more in some than in others; and therefore such, as were afflicted with the falling sicknes, and such like diseases, in Christ's time, were called daemoniacks'.[42]

The fact that Greatrakes conceived of so many of his cures as a form of dispossession is, I believe, intimately related to his self-proclaimed role as an expert on psychic phenomena and manifestations of the demonic. This aspect of his healing mission was, as we have seen, noted at the time and continued to elicit comment more than thirty years later. In 1696, for example, the Yorkshire cleric and antiquarian Abraham de la Pryme (1671–1704) recorded an encounter with an old man who claimed to have been present at Ragley and London when Greatrakes performed his cures. Something of a sceptic, he described the Irishman as a 'strange conceited fellow', who believed 'strange things of devils, spirits, and witches'. Likewise, the French writer and courtier, Charles Saint-Evremond (1613–1703), who claimed to have witnessed Greatrakes in action at the residence of the French ambassador in London, wrote of him that he 'ascribed all Indispositions to Spirits; and all Infirmities to him were possessions'. In short, Saint-Evremond concluded that 'he knew everything that related to Spirits [and] was acquainted with their Numbers, their Ranks, their Names, their Employments and Functions; nay, he boasted that he understood the Intrigues of Demons, much better than the Affairs of Men'.[43]

---

[41] BL, Add. MS 4293, fos 50v–51r. The term 'suffocation of the mother' was often applied by sceptical physicians to certain hysterical conditions that others saw as demonic in origin; see M. MacDonald (ed.), *Witchcraft and Hysteria in Elizabethan London: Edward Jorden and the Mary Glover Case* (London, 1991), vii–lxiv.

[42] RS, EL/M1/36.

[43] C. Jackson (ed.), *The Diary of Abraham de la Pryme, the Yorkshire Antiquary* (Durham, 1869), 90–1; C. Saint-Evremond, *The Works of Mr de St Evremont*, 2 vols (London, 1700), ii, 79–81. Saint-Evremond claims that these events took place at the house of the French ambassador, the Count de Comminges, who tried to engage Greatrakes in a theoretical discussion of his cures by citing the authority of van Helmont and Bodin. De Comminges, however, was ambassador from 1662 to 1665, and Saint-Evremond was in Holland from 1665 to 1670. It seems likely, therefore, that Saint-Evremond based his description of Greatrakes' cures on second-hand accounts, probably emanating from sceptical acquaintances at the court of Charles II. For the freethinker Saint-Evremond, see *ODNB*; H. T. Barnwell, 'Saint-Evremond: A French Political Exile in Seventeenth-Century London', *Proceedings of the Huguenot Society of London*, 18 (1952), 449–63.

The most telling evidence for Greatrakes' immersion in both the practice and theory of demonology is suggested by the central role that he played in the trial of the accused witch, Florence Newton of Youghal, in 1661, one of the few well-documented cases of witchcraft in Ireland to survive from the seventeenth century.[44] Several experiments were tried to test the guilt of the accused witch, including the following proposal made by Greatrakes and an accomplice, Edward Perry (d. 1696). At the subsequent trial, Perry testified that he and Greatrakes:

> had read of a way to discover a Witch, which he would put in practice. And so they sent for the Witch, and set her on a Stool, and a Shoemaker with a strong Awl endeavoured to stick it in the Stool, but could not till the third time. And then they bad her come off the Stool, but she said she was very weary and could not stir. Then two of them pulled her off, and the Man went to pull out his Awl, and it dropt into his hand with half an inch broke off the blade off it, and they all looked to have found where it had been stuck, but could find no place where any entry had been made by it. Then they took another Awl and put it into the Maids hand, and one of them took the Maids hand, and ran violently at the Witches hand with it but would not enter it, though the Awl was so bent that none of them could put it straight again.[45]

On another occasion, Greatrakes, in company with one Mr Blackwall, who had also assisted in the earlier experiment, performed a further series of tests designed

[44] Glanvill, *Saducismus Triumphatus*, ii, 179–83. Glanvill's account is based on what looks like a transcript of the trial compiled by the judge, Sir William Aston (d.1671). How it got into Glanvill's hands is not known for certain. However, it seems highly probable that the intermediary in this instance was Robert Boyle. In 1678, Boyle informed Glanvill that he knew of a number of Irish cases of witchcraft that would 'accommodate your Designe'. In particular, he mentions one that occurred in Munster some time during the Presidency (1660–72) of his brother Roger, Earl of Orrery, and of his acquaintance with a number of the 'chiefe Witness's mentioned in it' (including, presumably, Greatrakes). He specifically refers to receiving an account from the judge in this case via his brother Orrery, an account shortly before the Restoration like that reprinted by Glanvill in which Aston's signature appears at the end of each set of depositions. The original survives in Boyle's papers in the library of the Royal Society, though for reasons unknown Glanvill decided to reverse the order of the manuscript and to exclude small sections, including the final witness statement of an English trooper named George Lowther. I am extremely grateful to Louis Caron for pointing out these omissions in the published version of the Newton trial; Boyle, *Correspondence*, v, 20; RS, RB 37/1/5, fos 96r–102v. The judge in the Youghal case, Sir William Aston, a member of the Convention Parliament in Dublin, was sent to England shortly before the Restoration to welcome the King and protect the interests of the soldiers and adventurers. He was subsequently rewarded with a judgeship and served as 'Counsel for the Commonwealth' in the Court of Claims. In the same year as the trial of Florence Newton, Aston found in favour of Greatrakes at the Clonmel assizes in his dispute with the Catholic Prendergasts over lands in county Tipperary (see pp. 58–9); F. E. Ball, 'Some Notes on the Irish Judiciary in the Reign of Charles II', *JCHAS*, 7 (1901), 215–16; A. Clarke, *Prelude to Restoration in Ireland: The End of the Commonwealth, 1659–1660* (Cambridge, 1999), 196; King's Inns Library, Dublin, Standish Prendergast, Viscount Gort, *The Prendergasts of Newcastle, Co. Tipperary A.D.1169–1760*, 113. The case of Florence Newton was widely publicised by Greatrakes. Glanvill's editor, Henry More, refers to the fact that 'this Witch of Youghal is so famous that I have heard Mr Greatrix speak of her at my Lord Conway's at Ragley'; Glanvill, *Saducismus Triumphatus.*, ii, 189. He may well have referred to it in his meetings with Boyle in either 1666 or 1668.

[45] Ibid. ii, 179.

to prove the witch's guilt. These were based on the well-established principle that the victims of witchcraft were likely to suffer fits and seizures in the presence of those who caused their affliction.[46] Greatrakes' prominent role in the trial of Florence Newton suggests that he was widely considered as something of an expert in such cases among his Protestant neighbours in Munster. As a local magistrate, there may have been numerous further opportunities for him to demonstrate his skill in detecting witches. Whatever the case, this was certainly not an isolated instance. On at least one other occasion he claimed to have taken part in psychic experiments in the house of his patron, Roger Boyle, Earl of Orrery, at Charleville in county Cork. Here, he investigated the case of a man who claimed to be haunted by a spectre or spirit that threatened to carry him off (see Fig. 7). Glanvill repeated the story, told to him by Henry More, that the man:

> was kept in a large room, with a considerable number of persons to guard him, among whom was the famous stroker Mr Greatrix, who was a neighbur... [A]t length he was perceived to rise from the ground, whereupon Mr Greatrix and another lusty Man clapt their Arms over his shoulders, one of them before him, and the other behind, and weighed him down with all their strength. But he was forcibly taken up from them... and for a considerable time he was carried in the Air to and fro over their heads.[47]

The trial of Florence Newton, Greatrakes' role in it, and his subsequent enthusiasm in publicizing details of the case, merit closer scrutiny as they provide important insights into the wider political context that gave rise to witch trials, and confirmed belief in witchcraft, after 1660.[48] Witchcraft was a peculiarly sensitive barometer of religious and political instability for much of this period, witch panics often arising within communities that were experiencing extraordinary periods of conflict and tension. That which took place at Youghal in 1661 certainly fits this description. Greatrakes, as we have previously noted, had strong links with the town of Youghal. He owned property in the borough, regularly transacted business there, and was well acquainted with a number of its most prominent citizens, including the master of one of Florence Newton's alleged victims, John Pyne.[49] Nicholas Pyne (d. 1670), a relation, who provided much of the evidence against Newton in 1661, was an old associate of Greatrakes, the two men appearing as

---

[46] Ibid. ii, 183. Greatrakes' acccomplice, Mr Blackwall, was in all probability, Thomas Blackwell, a sequestrated Church of Ireland minister who sought reinstatement at the Restoration; Clarke, *Prelude to Restoration*, 284n. A Thomas Blackwell, 'preacher of Gods word', was admitted a freeman of the town of Youghal on 20 September 1650, but had been resident there as a jurat since at least September 1644. He probably practised medicine in the 1650s; in 1659, Thomas Blackwell, doctor of physick, was listed as resident in the town; R. Caulfield (ed.), *The Council Book of the Corporation of Youghal from 1610 to... 1800* (Guildford, 1878), 249, 285; S. Pender (ed.), *A Census of Ireland, Circa 1659* (Dublin, 1939), 200.

[47] Glanvill, *Saducismus Triumphatus*, ii, 247–8.

[48] For a recent analysis of the trial from the perspective of gender studies, see M. McAuliffe, 'Gender, History and Witchcraft in Early Modern Ireland: A Re-Reading of the Florence Newton Trial', in M. G. Valiulis (ed.), *Gender and Power in Irish History* (Dublin, 2009), 39–59.

[49] Glanvill, *Saducismus Triumphatus*, ii, 168, 175–6. Pyne would appear to have assisted in the relief of Youghal during the troubled years of the early 1640s when it was besieged by Catholic forces; Caulfield, *Council Book of Youghal*, 280.

Fig. 7. Frontispiece to Joseph Glanvill, *Saducismus Triumphatus* (2nd edn, London, T. Newcomb for S. Lownds, 1682). Bodleian Library, Oxford. The scene in the bottom left hand corner almost certainly depicts a case of demonic levitation described in the book that took place at the home of the Earl of Orrery and which featured Greatrakes as a participant and witness.

co-defendants in the 1650s in a long-running legal dispute with the Earl of Cork over property rights in the area. Moreover, like Greatrakes, Pyne applied a series of novel tests to the suspected witch designed to establish her guilt, including one that demonstrated her inability to read or hold a bible without it being thrust from her hand by an invisible force.[50] Pyne's prominence within the town was matched

---

[50] Glanvill, *Saducismus Triumphatus*, ii, 171–2, 176, 178–9. For Pyne's earlier friendship with Greatrakes in opposition to the Earl of Cork, see p. 52. Pyne's relationship with the Boyles was both long-standing and frequently punctuated by ill feeling and animosity. His father, Henry (d.*c.*1627),

by other witnesses, such as the mayor, Richard Mayre or Myers, who threatened to apply the 'Water Experiment' to the suspect witch, Florence Newton, and two others whom she had implicated. He also testified that 'there were three Aldermen in Youghall, whose Children she had kist as he had heard them affirm, and all the Children died presently after'. More to the point, he was convinced that Newton had killed his own daughter, Grace; so convinced in fact that he ordered an autopsy, carried out by 'persons of judgement', which failed to reveal any 'Inwarde Imperfection or defect' in the child's body.[51] Mayre's successor as mayor, Nicholas Stoute, was another leading citizen with a checkered past who gave evidence against Newton (he tried the test of the Lord's Prayer which she repeatedly failed). A neighbour of Greatrakes at Affane, Stoute was elected a bailiff of Youghal in 1655 where he held the patent of Customer and Collector of the Port. However, about the time of the witch trial, Stoute was suffering financial problems with possible political connotations, when he was suspended from his duties as a port officer for certain unspecified misdemeanours. In all probability, he was under a cloud because of his earlier attachment to the parliamentary and Cromwellian cause.[52] Similar com-

who first came to Ireland with Raleigh in the late 1580s, held an estate at Mogeely in county Cork. A former business associate of the first Earl of Cork, he later fell out with Boyle amid bitter recriminations that continued to blight relations between the two families for the next four decades. In 1642, for example, Nicholas was accused by the Earl's son, Lord Broghill, of various misdemeanours including a reluctance to supply victuals for his troops as well as calling his father 'a fool and an ass'. Arrested in 1643 for these and other 'outrages', he later served on a council of war at Youghal, where he was appointed a jurat in 1645. Like Greatrakes, he was apparently on friendly terms with the radical Colonel Robert Phaire, who acted as trustee of the marriage settlement between his daughter, Catherine, and Captain John Wakeham. Phaire no doubt assisted Pyne in his on-going dispute over land with the second Earl of Cork in 1652 (finally settled in 1663). Under the circumstances, it is reasonable to suppose that Pyne was experiencing great anxiety at the Restoration given his former relations with the Boyles and his previous 'collaboration' with the Cromwellian authorities in Munster; H. F. Morris, 'The Pynes of Cork', *The Irish Genealogist* 6 (1985), 696–710; CH, Lismore Papers, vol. 1, fo. 318; vol. 2, fos 77, 120, 255; vol. 3, fos 66, 76–81, 99r–100r, 155; vol. 5, nos 130–137, 141; vol. 8, no. 77; vol. 22, no. 178; vol. 23, nos 71, 78, 81, 83, 108; Grosart, v, 222; BL, Add. MS 25,287, fo. 31r; Caulfield, *Council Book of Youghal*, 254.

[51] Glanvill, *Saducismus Triumphatus*, ii, 184–5; RS, RB 37/1/5, fos 101v–102r. Mayre or Myers had served as commissary at Youghal in 1643, having been appointed a bailiff of the borough in the previous year. He first served as mayor of the borough in 1647. In 1662 he was serving as comptroller of the ports of Youghal and nearby Dungarvan; Bodl., Rawlinson MS A 110, fos 74r–v; *CSP Ireland, 1660–1662*, 526. For reasons unknown, Glanvill excluded the reference to the death of Mayre's child in his published version of the case. I would like to thank Wanda Henry for alerting me to this omission.

[52] Glanvill, *Saducismus Triumphatus*, ii, 174–5; Caulfield, *Council Book of Youghal*, 301–2, 619; Bodl., Carte MS 154, fo. 27v; *CSP Ireland, 1660–1662*, 485. Stoute's connections with Affane probably date to the period of the late 1630s and early 1640s, when his name and that of his mother ('widow Stoute') appear regularly on the rentals of the Earl of Cork. Forced to leave these lands in the aftermath of the Catholic uprising, he seems to have retired to Youghal, where he was in trouble with the royal customs officer in 1642 for withholding moneys. Despite an order for his arrest, he was still at large in July of that year, when it was alleged that he owed over £1,000. His reluctance to pay probably stemmed from his support for the parliamentary cause. In 1646 he undertook a recoinage at Youghal, and was prominent thereafter in the town's affairs; NLI, MS 6239, 17; MS 6247, *sub* Aughmane [i.e. Affane]; MS 6249, 17; MS 6900, *sub* Ballyneigh and other properties; BL, Egerton MS 80, fos 23v, 26v, 28v; BL, Add. MS 25,287, fo. 34v.

ment probably applies to yet another of Newton's tormentors, Edward Perry, who, along with Greatrakes and Mr Blackwall, devised a variety of tests to prove the witch's guilt. Admitted as a freeman of the borough of Youghal in 1655, he subsequently served as bailiff (along with John Pyne) in 1664 and mayor in 1674.[53]

It is difficult to avoid the conclusion that the prosecution of Florence Newton for witchcraft in 1661 was the product, in part at least, of the acute religious and political tensions then afflicting the borough. Many of those most active in the proceedings against Newton came from prominent and prosperous families who stood to lose not only political office and influence as a result of the Restoration, but, like Greatrakes, were threatened with the loss of their lands and livelihoods. Compromised by their earlier allegiance to the Cromwellian regime, many must have feared that they would soon fall victim to the widepread purges of the corporate boroughs that were either mooted or already occuring throughout England in the spring of 1661. While most survived, some did pay the price for their republican and puritan associations. James Wood, for example, the congregational minister of the town who provided expert testimony to support Greatrakes' elaborate tests for witchcraft, refused to conform in 1662 and was subsequently ejected. In the following year he was arrested and imprisoned in the wake of the Dublin Plot.[54] The body politic of Youghal, like the minds and bodies of many of its godly citizens, was thus in a tortured state in the early years of the Restoration facing as it did the twin threat of sectarian subversion and Catholic revival. Baptists, Quakers, and even Ranters had found a congenial home in the town since the early 1650s and continued to pose a threat to godly order there in the early years of the Restoration. Their presence however was probably of minor significance when

---

[53] Glanvill, *Saducismus Triumphatus*, ii, 179–80, 181–2; Caulfield, *Council Book of Youghal*, 302, 620; Grosart, v, 285. Perry claimed to have acquired a sure-fire method of proving the guilt of witches from one William Lap while attending the assizes at Cashel.

[54] Glanvill, *Saducismus Triumphatus*, ii, 182–3. Wood was first appointed as preacher at Youghal in 1650, but did not arrive from England until September 1652. He was made a freeman of the borough on 19 September 1656. Walter Gostelow described him as one 'whom the parliament power had put in Preacher...and settled upon him an handsom sallery of some an hundred and twenty pounds per annum'. He added caustically that '[h]is name implies he may be Timber, though some suspect he is not yet fitted for the building up the House of God'. Wood was equally disliked by the town's Quakers who accused him of hypocrisy. His comeuppance arrived in 1663 when he was gaoled for holding a conventicle in the town. At the same time he was widely suspected in Munster of involvement in the plot to overthrow the Dublin government. Thereafter, he continued preaching illegally while earning a living as a schoolteacher in county Tipperary; RCBL, GS 2/7/3/20, 13, 78; Caulfield, *Council Book of Youghal*, 303; W. Gostelow, *Charls Stuart and Oliver Cromwell United, or, Glad Tidings of Peace to all Christendom* (London?, 1655), 120; J. Sicklemore, *To All The Inhabitants of the Town of Youghal who are Under the Teaching of James Wood* (1657?); CH, Diary of Richard Boyle, second Earl of Cork, 25 May 1663; Lismore Papers, vol. 33, no. 20. Wood, who like Greatrakes was educated as a schoolboy in Devon, probably returned there in 1688. In that year, one James Woode preached a sermon as 'minister of the Gospel' at Bideford in which he attempted to defend the nonconformists' right to accept the recent Declaration of Indulgence issued by the Catholic James II; J. Woode, *A Sermon Preach'd at Bideford, in the County of Devon on the Fifth of November, 1688* (London, 1689); *Some Reflections on Mr Wood's Sermon on St Matthew 7.20* (London, 1690). He eventually separated from the Congregational church in Bideford following a scandal involving an Irish girl in 1693, and set up his own meeting in the High Street. He died sometime around 1698; A. Brockett (ed.), *The Exeter Assembly: The Minutes of the Assemblies of the United Brethren of Devon and Cornwall, 1691–1717, as Transcribed by the Reverend Isaac Gilling* (Torquay, 1963), xiii, 14–15, 16, 21–2, 28, 42.

compared to the state of heightened anxiety created by the fear of a sudden incursion of Irish Catholics, many of whom had been exiled and dispossessed in the previous decade as part of the Cromwellian land settlement. An indication of the way the wind was blowing came in November and December 1660, when the appearance of an Irish Catholic sea captain in the town, threatening various revenges on the 'English', created widespread panic. A few months later, and immediately prior to the arrest of Florence Newton for witchcraft, the fears of the 'English' were brought to fever pitch by news of a royal declaration in which the King restored the lands and estates of loyal papists and royalists in the town in order that 'the said natives and inhabitants may freely and indifferently without contradiction, live, trade, and cohabit together with the Protestant inhabitants...without distinction'.[55] The anxieties of the leading citizens of Youghal can only have been exacerbated by other government proclamations issued at this time. In January 1661, all meetings of Presbyterians and Independents were declared illegal and their pastors were prohibited from appointing days of humiliation and thanksgiving. Four months later, the Irish Parliament ordered everyone to return to Anglican worship, including use of the Book of Common Prayer. At the same time, all corporate bodies were ordered to burn the Solemn League and Covenant, while those clergy who had taken it were required to publicly renounce the same.[56] Under the circumstances, it is tempting to conclude that here, as elsewhere in Restoration Britain, the arrest and punishment of a universally loathed figure, the witch, provided an opportunity for the godly citizens of Youghal to channel those communal fears generated by the Restoration and, by removing evil from its midst, to promote a renewed sense of unity and wellbeing in the body politic.

WITCH-HUNTING, THE PRETERNATURAL, AND THE PURSUIT OF RELIGIOUS PEACE IN SEVENTEENTH-CENTURY BRITAIN

Greatrakes' interest in witchcraft and demonology, and that of his Youghal neighbours and friends, was also shared by many of those who were most ardent in offering support and providing testimonials for his acts of healing. This is most obviously apparent in the case of the Boyle family, whose interests, as we have seen, often intersected with those of the stroker. Indeed, it is quite possible that Greatrakes' early interest in witches and spirits may have owed a debt to his patron, Roger Boyle, whose own fascination with such matters predated the Restoration.

---

[55] Gostelow, *Charls Stuart*, 263–4, 265–6; *CSP Ireland, 1660–1662*, 116–17, 218. The activities and utterances of the Catholic sea captain, George Codd, were reported to the government by an alarmed mayor, Richard Mayre. His colleague and witch-hunting associate, Nicholas Stoute, was responsible around the same time for imprisoning the Quaker, John Browne, who had recently been put out of his place as master gunner at Youghal; *CSP Ireland, 1669–1670; with Addenda 1625–1670*, 374.

[56] T. Harris, *Restoration: Charles II and His Kingdoms 1660–1685* (London, 2005), 90–1.

In 1656, for example, during his period as Lord President of the Council in Scotland, he examined a suspected witch at Edinburgh.[57] On this occasion, immediately prior to his departure from Scotland, he demonstrated commendable open-mindedness by advising 'those that were left to be her Judges to be moderate in their Censures'. Ten years later, however, in his capacity as Lord President of Munster, he used his executive authority to overturn a decision of the assize judges to release a suspected witch following the testimony of Lord Kerry, who alleged that his wife was a victim of fits induced by the woman.[58] Roger Boyle's lifelong interest in witchcraft and related phenomena also extended to the collection of providential occurrences, many of which he later communicated to his friend, the nonconformist divine Richard Baxter, who incorporated them into his published work on witchcraft in 1691. In addition, in January 1659, he regaled his older brother, Richard, the second Earl of Cork, with the details of 'a great fire in the sky, which soon fell and divided into 2 parts', an event which he claimed to have personally witnessed. On other occasions, as the testimonies cited in Glanvill's famous defence of witchcraft demonstrate, his residence at Charleville was frequently the site of psychic investigations and discussions.[59] Roger Boyle's deep-seated interest in such matters was shared by other members of his family. His father, Richard, the first Earl of Cork, eagerly anticipated news of celebrated cases of witchcraft in

[57] This case, which echoes that of the Frenchman, Martin Guerre, is described in some detail in BL, Sloane MS 4227, fos 60v–61v. The manuscript itself was copied from Orrery's private papers in the eighteenth century and was heavily edited prior to publication in 1743. This section, as well as that detailing the bewitchment of Lady Kerry some time around 1665 (fo. 81r), are crossed through in the original and did not appear in the published version, a reflection perhaps of the growing antipathy exhibited by Enlightenment audiences to such stories and beliefs. Similar omissions and deletions in Orrery's manuscript and printed works are discussed by his most recent biographer; see P. Little, *Lord Broghill and the Cromwellian Union with Ireland and Scotland* (Woodbridge, 2004), 2–4. There are striking parallels here, of course, with the fate of the papers of Orrery's brother, Robert Boyle, at the hands of his eighteenth-century editors. The role played by the natural philosopher's eighteenth-century editor Henry Miles in seeking to 'purge his manuscript remains' of the taint of 'credulity' is discussed in M. Hunter, 'Magic, Science and Reputation: Robert Boyle, the Royal Society and the Occult in the Late Seventeenth Century', in *idem, Robert Boyle 1627–1691: Scrupulosity and Science* (Woodbridge, 2000), 238–9.

[58] BL, Sloane MS 4227, fos 61v, 81r. William Fitzmaurice, Lord Kerry (1633–1697), was the son of the turncoat Patrick Fitzmaurice (d.1660), who converted to Protestantism and lived in London throughout the 1640s and 1650s. He married Constance (d.1685), the daughter of William Long, whose sufferings at the hand of a witch from county Cork are preserved in the Orrery manuscripts.

[59] Baxter, *Certainty of the Worlds of Spirits*, 57–8; CH, Lismore Papers, vol. 30, no. 63; Glanvill, *Saducismus Triumphatus*, ii, 245–50. Broghill was also suspectible, it would seem, to belief in the power of prophecy. In 1651, he was encouraged to fight a battle against royalist insurgents in Ireland as a result of hearing a prediction from some native inhabitants that he would win if he fought at Knocknaclashy; R. Gillespie, *Devoted People: Belief and Religion in Early Modern Ireland* (Manchester, 1997), 141. In stressing Roger Boyle's interest in witchcraft and other preternatural phenomena, as well as his importance as a patron of Greatrakes' healing and psychic investigations, I dissent from the view of Patrick Little, who downplays his and the rest of the Boyle family's interest in signs, wonders, and portents; Little, *Lord Broghill*, 229–30. For Boyle's long-standing friendship with the eirenicist Baxter, whom Little regards as one of the chief influences shaping Boyle's religious outlook, see ibid. 227. In 1658, Baxter recorded conversations with Boyle (then Lord Broghill) regarding the devil of Mascon (see note 61).

England in the 1630s,[60] while his brother, Robert, and his sister, Katherine, Lady Ranelagh, were both actively engaged in exploring and promoting the wider significance of preternatural phenomena in the body politic.

Robert Boyle's sustained interest in witchcraft and the demonic has proved something of an embarrassment to many historians of science, eager to promote his image as a leading figure in the scientific revolution of the seventeenth century. In 1677, he wrote to Joseph Glanvill, praising him for his efforts in collecting verifiable and authentic accounts of witchcraft and similar phenomena. Not only did he request further information about certain cases of suspected witchcraft, but he also seems to have provided numerous instances of his own. Like his brother Roger, Robert's interest in, and attempts to publicize, accounts of spectral and related activity predated the Restoration. In 1658, for example, he played a leading role in promoting the publication of the celebrated case of the devil of Mascon, which was translated into English by Pierre du Moulin the younger (1601–1684). In the preface to this work, Boyle relates how his 'setled indisposedness to believe strange things' was fully overcome by the conversations he had with the original author, the French Calvinist pastor, François Perreaud (1572–1657), when he was resident in Geneva as a young man in the early 1640s.[61] Boyle's interest in such matters continued until the end of his life. In the early 1690s, for example, he intended to publish a sequel to his collection of 'Strange Reports', appended to his *Experimentae et Observationes Physicae* (1691), which would have included material on premonition and other supernatural phenomena such as apparitions and witchcraft.[62]

Underpinning Boyle's approach to such matters was his profound sense of the importance of verifiable witchcraft testimonies as evidence for the providential work of God in everyday life and as a bulwark against atheism. In an age that to

[60] CH, Lismore Papers, vol. 18, no. 13. Earlier, a correspondent of the Earl had regaled him with news of the departure of Prince Charles from Spain which he described as taking place amid 'a most tempestuous and cruell storme...the lyke havinge not beene seene in them parts before, in soe much as it it thought the Witches or divells of Spayne were in action'; CH, Lismore Papers, vol. 14, no. 171.

[61] F. Perreaud, *The Devill of Mascon, or, A True Relation of the Chiefe Things which an Unclean Spirit did, and said at Mascon in Burgundy in the House of Mr Francis Pereaud* (Oxford, 1658). The author had presented Boyle with a manuscript copy of the complete work prior to its publication as *Démonographie, ou Traité des Demons* (Geneva, 1653). The translator Pierre du Moulin the younger (1601–1684) was chaplain in Ireland to Boyle's brother, the second Earl of Cork, for much of the 1650s. He was also on friendly terms with Richard Baxter, whom he revered 'above all the divines of this age'. Baxter himself frequently cited *The Devill of Mascon* in his own work on witchcraft; CH, Lismore MS 29, 15 January 1651, 20 March 1653, 11 March 1655; Gostelow, *Charls Stuart*, 33, 86–7; Baxter, *Certainty of the Worlds of Spirits*, 2, 18–19; N. H. Keeble and G. F. Nuttall (eds), *Calendar of the Correspondence of Richard Baxter*, 2 vols (Oxford, 1991), i, 312–13, 316–17.

[62] M. Hunter, 'Alchemy, Magic and Moralism in the Thought of Robert Boyle', *British Journal for the History of Science*, 23 (1990), 395. This material is unfortunately no longer extant. Boyle's interest in Scottish witchcraft and second sight, as well as his wider fascination with the preternatural, is discussed further in *idem, The Occult Laboratory: Magic, Science and Second Sight in Late Seventeenth-Century Scotland* (Woodbridge, 2001), 2–10. Boyle's diffidence in discussing or promoting such topics publicly, which Hunter relates to Boyle's canny recognition that '[c]redulity...was ill at ease with the decorum and judgement which formed part of the preferred image of the gentleman', is discussed more fully in his 'Magic, Science and Reputation', 223–50 [quote at 234].

men like Boyle, Baxter, and Glanvill seemed increasingly susceptible to various forms of unbelief, authentic accounts of demonic activity provided a vital prop to religion, morality, and godliness. Providentialism also formed the bedrock of Lady Ranelagh's religious and political worldview and, like her eminent brother Robert, stimulated her interest in visions and apparitions as well as the 'miraculous' cures of Greatrakes in London in the spring of 1666. Much of Robert Boyle's scrupulous and painstaking examination of the Irish healer's practice took place at the London home of his sister in Pall Mall.[63] Her providentialist frame of mind at this time is also evident in a letter which she wrote to her older brother, Richard, in September 1665, in which she referred to the recent outbreak of the plague as 'more destructive than any…ever was before'. She went on to chide him with the observation that:

> a servant of yours did often tell you we were by our practices making some terrible Judgments inevitable to us. & I doubt you will find that opinion too sadly Confirmed by effects this being but a beginning of many other mysteries that wilbe the natural consequences thereof unless it have a speedy stop put to it which we appear not at al in the way of getting donn.[64]

It is clear then, from a wide range of sources, that the Boyle family was attracted to various providentialist accounts of God's interaction with men and women, many of which frequently invoked exploration of demonic, preternatural, and super-natural phenomena. Roger, Robert, and Katherine also shared a common religious outlook, one that shunned sectarian extremism while at the same time promoting the need for unity and spiritual harmony among Protestants. In the case of Kath-erine, Lady Ranelagh, the two themes came together as early as 1647 when she became closely involved in the celebrated case of the child prodigy, Sarah Wight. Sarah's extraordinary fasting, illness, and religious conversion soon attracted the attention of a wide range of spiritual advisors, as well as physicians, many of whom were keen to establish the authenticity of her claim to act as a messenger of God. A central feature of Sarah's revelations was an appeal to the various religious fac-tions then contending for power in London to compose their differences and seek some form of rapprochement.[65] Indeed, one of the most striking features of this

---

[63] For Boyle's notes on the cures performed by Greatrakes at the house of his sister at Easter 1666, including his stroking of a number of Lady Ranelagh's servants and one of her daughters, see BL, Add. MS 4293, fos 50r–53v. As early as 1658, Lady Ranelagh and her brother, Robert, were exchanging tales of spirits and apparitions with Samuel Hartlib; Hunter, 'Magic, Science and Reputation', 227 and n.

[64] BL, Althorp MS B4, 2 September 1665. It is possible that the 'servant' of her brother who prophesied terrible judgements was Walter Gostelow, who persistently showered both Richard and Roger Boyle in the 1650s with stories of impending doom should his fellow countrymen fail to imple-ment a peaceful resolution of the nation's religious and political differences. A moderate royalist and Anglican, Gostelow even foretold on one occasion that unity would ensue following the marriage of Lady Boyle to the exiled King. Moreover, he was not averse to invoking the language of witchcraft to get his message across; Gostelow, *Charls Stuart*, 78, 149. Walter's brother, Leonard, was secretary to the Earl.

[65] The chief source for the events surrounding Sarah Wight was a pamphlet produced by the Baptist preacher Henry Jessey entitled *The Exceeding Riches of Grace Advanced* (London, 1647). For discussion of this case, see B. R. Dailey, 'The Visitation of Sarah Wight: Holy Carnival and the Revolution of the Saints in Civil War London', *Church History*, 55 (1986), 438–55; C. Scott-Luckens, 'Propaganda or

episode concerns the way in which it parallels many of the events surrounding Greatrakes' own appearance in London in 1666. Not only were a number of those directly involved in the questioning of the maid, Sarah Wight, later active in promoting Greatrakes' cures (Lady Ranelagh was accompanied by her friend, the physician Benjamin Worsley), but the religious aspirations of both patient (Wight) and healer (Greatrakes) were remarkably similar. Like Greatrakes, Wight too professed to shun religious divisions and disputes. And just as his healing acted as a metaphor for the spiritual recovery of the nation, so too did Wight's ministry serve as a stimulus to those in attendance to seek the path of religious reconciliation in the wake of the civil and ecclesiastical divisions unleashed by civil war. In the words of Barbara Ritter Dailey, 'the visitors to Sarah Wight's bedroom entered another dimension of reality separate from the confrontational world surrounding them'. In the process, 'she had conquered her devil, and she now had the special knowledge of the blessed to give insight to worldly insanity'.[66]

Interestingly, Ritter concludes her study of this episode in Civil War sectarian politics by comparing the context in which Sarah Wight's prophetic utterances were accorded credence with those of other young women whose trancelike states and pronouncements were frequently attributed to witchcraft and diabolical possession. There was nothing new about this phenomenon. Since the late sixteenth century, cases of alleged witchcraft and possession had frequently provided an opportunity or vehicle for the expression of partisan religious or political ends. Generally speaking, these formed part of a wider debate between contending groups, parties, or sects, such as that provoked by the ministry of the Puritan exorcist John Darrell (*c*.1562–*c*.1607). It would be a mistake, however, to construe belief in witchcraft as amounting to little more than a form of propaganda or adjunct to the confessional debates of the period, or indeed as a crass manifestation of the superstitious and persecutory nature of early modern society. On many occasions, as for example at Youghal in 1661, it was invoked as a medium for uniting and healing divided or conflicted communities. There is, for example, a case to be made for comprehending the activities of another charismatic witchfinder, Matthew Hopkins (d. 1647), in a similar light; that is, as an act of communal healing, in which an attempt to purge the war-torn and divided communities of East Anglia of witches

---

Marks of Grace? The Impact of the Reported Ordeals of Sarah Wight in Revolutionary London, 1647–52', *Women's Writing*, 9 (2002), 215–32; V. J. Camden, 'Attending to Sarah Wight: Little Wonder of God's Wonders', *Bunyan Studies*, 11 (2003–4), 94–131. For Lady Ranelagh's involvement in the questioning of the young maid, see Jessey, *Exceeding Riches*, 9, 85–8. Jessey, of course, was later responsible for collecting and publishing a three-volume edition of prodigies and providential events (1660–2) that was largely designed to discredit the restored ministers of the Anglican Church and to bolster the spirits of those who refused to conform.

[66] Dailey, 'Visitation of Sarah Wight', 452. Although Sarah Wight did not practise healing as such, she did proffer 'spiritual physic' to many of the women who visited her and were suffering similar pangs of conscience. A further point of similarity between the two cases concerns the way in which the two accounts of Wight and Greatrakes were publicised in the press with the testimonials of witnesses attached. Seventy individuals, for example, are named in Jessey's pamphlet, which Dailey suggests make his book read like 'a kind of petition'; ibid. 452.

was welcomed by many, including local ruling elites, as part of a wider campaign devoted to the moral regeneration of society.[67]

What holds for East Anglia in the mid-1640s, is, I feel, equally applicable to the divided communities of Restoration Britain. It may also provide further clues as to the meaning which a large number of Greatrakes' supporters attached to his gift of healing. We have already seen, for example, how Greatrakes himself was keen to promote a view of his cures as exorcistic acts, as well as chronicling his own involvement in witchcraft trials and psychic investigations in the 1660s. We have also witnessed how such concerns were shared by numerous members of the Boyle family, some of whom were to play a conspicuous part in promoting his therapeutic abilities. Interest in such matters, however, was not limited to Greatrakes and the Boyles. One of the most striking features of the Greatrakes affair is the extent to which those who openly supported and authenticated his 'miraculous' cures shared his obsession with witchcraft and the supernatural. This was true not just of men like Henry More and Joseph Glanvill, who published widely on the subject, citing in the process the testimony of men like Greatrakes. But it was also a consistent concern of many of Greatrakes' friends and supporters who were equally keen to vindicate belief in the existence of spirits and demons. The latitudinarian clergyman, Simon Patrick, for example, who was stroked by Greatrakes, attested to several of his cures, and provided a glowing testimonial of his religious and political conformity, was also an avid collector of illustrious providences.[68] In November 1661, Samuel Hartlib wrote to John Worthington informing him that Patrick had recently sent him 'a large account concerning some Illustrious Providences', which he was forwarding to his friend. Worthington acknowledged receipt of the papers in February 1662. These contained two accounts of supernatural phenomena, both emanating from sources at Cambridge. The first was a classic ghost story in which a recently departed father returned from the dead to reassure his daughter of certain future events. The other was told to Patrick by a student, 'a person of piety and veracity', who provided a detailed description of recent poltergeist activity at his family home. Three years later, in December 1665, Patrick wrote to Lady Gauden with the latest news concerning the haunting of the house of Mr Mompesson in Wiltshire.[69]

---

[67] For a highly nuanced and sensitive account of the Darrell case, which stresses the extent to which he was as much the victim and instrument of others, as the protagonist and architect of the dispute with Samuel Harsnet, see M. Gibson, *Possession, Puritanism and Print: Darrell, Harsnett, Shakespeare and the Elizabethan Exorcism Controversy* (London, 2006). Her attempt to rehabilitate Darrell and remove the 'thick dusting of abuse' which has adhered to him for over four hundred years, alongside her depiction of his godly supporters as 'neither insincere, revolutionary or devious', mirror my own evaluation of Matthew Hopkins and his supporters in East Anglia in the 1640s; ibid. 27, 56. I discuss these ideas more fully, particularly in relation to the Hopkins' trials in East Anglia in the 1640s, in my forthcoming *Witchcraft, Witch-Hunting and the Body Politic in Early Modern Britain*.

[68] Greatrakes, *Brief Account*, 61–3; CUL, Add. MS 20, fos 31r–v. Patrick is widely credited as the author of the earliest latitudinarian manifesto, *A Brief Account of the New Sect of Latitude-Men Together with Some Reflections upon the New Philosophy* (London, 1662).

[69] Worthington, *Diary*, ii, 71, 102; CUL, Add. MS 19, fo. 11. Two copies of Patrick's account, entitled 'Of Illustrious Providences', unsigned but dated Battersea, 14 November 1661, are in CUL,

During the early 1660s, Patrick was closely connected to the circle of the Cambridge Platonists, many of whom gathered at Ragley and subsequently generated a vast reservoir of support for the thaumaturgical mission of Greatrakes. He was introduced to Samuel Hartlib, for example, through the good offices of the celebrated Cambridge Platonist, Benjamin Whichcote, who, like Patrick, was both cured by the Irish healer and provided fulsome testimonials as to his methods of cure and exemplary religious and political disposition.[70] Other Cambridge acquaintances of Whichcote who gathered at Ragley in February 1666 to witness at first hand Greatrakes' exploits included Ralph Cudworth, Henry More, George Rust, and Whichcote's nephew, Ezekiel Foxcroft. All were united by a shared passion for the preternatural and the investigation of psychic phenomena that defied natural or conventional explanation. Cudworth, More, and Rust, for example, assisted Glanvill in the compilation of trustworthy accounts, or 'matters of fact', relating to demonic and spectral activity that later found their way into print.[71] The exceptional interest of these men in such matters, moreover, seems to have infected a number of their younger colleagues and students in Cambridge. George Rust's protégé, Henry Hallywell (d. *c*.1703), published a defence of witchcraft in 1681.[72] Ezekiel Foxcroft's mother, Elizabeth, was fascinated by the stories of witchcraft retold at Ragley by Greatrakes and others. In all probability, she was responsible for

MS Dd.III.63, fos 68r–69v; Dd.III.64, no. 67, fos 150r–151r. Some time after 1678, the well-connected nonconformist Thomas Woodcock reported that Patrick had told a colleague that the ghost of the recently murdered justice, Sir Edmund Berry Godfrey, had appeared before his kinswoman, Mrs Lamb; G. C. Moore Smith (ed.), 'Extracts from the Papers of Thomas Woodcock', in *Camden Miscellany 11* (London, Camden Soc., vol. 13, 1907), 70. For Mr Mompesson and the case of the demon drummer of Tedworth, see note 29 above.

[70] Greatrakes, *Brief Account*, 8–9, 64, 66–7. Patrick was introduced to Hartlib by Whichcote in late 1661; Worthington, *Diary*, ii, 66–7. In October 1661, Worthington wrote to Hartlib concerning the recent publication of *Mirabilis Annus*, a collection of strange prodigies and extraordinary occurrences that was designed to elicit sympathy for the plight of those who were either unable or unwilling to subscribe to the restored Anglican church; Worthington, *Diary*, ii, 66. For the interest of Hartlib and his circle in the collection of illustrious providences, especially witchcraft, see pp. 143–51.

[71] Glanvill, *Saducismus Triumphatus*, ii, 198, 229, 230–1, 238–45, 253, 289–92. Benjamin Whichcote also verified another story of an apparition told him by the clergyman John Bretton; ibid. ii, 241.

[72] H. Hallywell, *Melampronoea: Or A Discourse of the Polity and Kingdom of Darkness. Together with a Solution of the Chiefest Objections Brought Against the Being of Witches* (London, 1681). In addition to translating and publishing Rust's *A Discourse of the Use of Reason* (London, 1683), Hallywell was responsible for editing his mentor's collected works; see G. Rust, *The Remains of that Reverend and Learned Prelate, Dr George Rust* (London, 1686). Hallywell's interest in witchcraft predated the publication of *Melampronoea*. In *A Private Letter of Satisfaction to a Friend* (1667), written in June 1665, he described how demons took on material form by employing natural ingredients such as the air, and alluded to the practice of familiars and imps 'who make themselves a kind of Teat in some part or other of the bodies of their accursed Consorts, whereby they exhaust their blood and spirits, and render their visages for the most part horrid and gastly, like themselves'; ibid. 54, 56–7. For Hallywell's cordial relationship with Henry More, see Christ's College Library, Cambridge, MS 21, no. 31. Hallywell's theological writings also received the approval of another member of the Ragley circle, Elizabeth Foxcroft, the sister of Benjamin Whichcote; *Conway Letters*, 293.

inculcating an early interest in her son in other aspects of occult natural philosophy, including alchemy.[73]

Another associate of this group with strong Cambridge connections and latitudinarian leanings was the clergyman Edward Fowler (d. 1714), who supplied Henry More with various accounts of spectral activity that were later published under Glanvill's name.[74] The nonconformist physician Henry Sampson (d. 1700) described Fowler as 'a great Collector of such storys & others of like importance to prove the Being of Spirits', and passed on such accounts to leading dissenters such as John Howe (1630–1705).[75] Fowler's interest in such matters continued for the

---

[73] Shortly after Greatrakes' departure from Ragley in February 1666, Henry More, in a letter to Lady Conway, alluded to various stories of ghosts and apparitions that were sparked by Elizabeth Foxcroft's discussion of such matters with her friends, including Greatrakes, at Ragley; *Conway Letters*, 270–1. More continued for the next eight years to regale Lady Conway with stories of witches and preternatural occurrences; see ibid. 294 [spirit of a murdered boy at Sheffield and pregnant woman bewitched at Yarmouth], 341–2 [witches in Scotland], 344–5 [a Scottish Presbyterian minister burned as a witch], 347 [whether good souls may leave the body, as well as the souls of witches who frequent 'conventicles'], 348 [nature of witches' nocturnal frolics], 385, 387 [apparition in Cornwall]. The chief source for this last proof of the existence of spirits was John Robartes, baron Robartes of Truro (1606–1685), a former Presbyterian and influential figure in Restoration government who advocated various policies and legal reforms designed to protect nonconformists from the full rigour of the Clarendon Code; see *ODNB*. More had acted as tutor to all his sons, including his other source mentioned here, the politician and natural philosopher, Francis Robartes (d. 1718).

[74] Glanvill, *Saducismus Triumphatus*, ii, 230–1, 238–42, 242–5, 247–8, 269–72 [mispaginated, should read 289–92]. Fowler, a pronounced religious moderate with close ties to the dissenters, owed his appointment as a prebend in Gloucester Cathedral in 1676 to his friendship with Henry More and the intercession of Lord Conway. Appointed Bishop of Gloucester in 1691, he later married the widow of 'that great Trimmer and Latitudinarian' Hezekiah Burton (1632–1681), who, like Fowler, assisted Glanvill and More in their psychic researches and supported John Wilkins' scientific and religious aims during the latter's brief stay at Cambridge in 1659–60; *ODNB*, Fowler, Edward and Burton, Hezekiah; Glanvill, *Saducismus Triumphatus*, ii, 228–30, 231–5, 235–7, 245; J. Gascoigne, *Cambridge in the Age of the Enlightenment: Science, Religion and Politics from the Restoration to the French Revolution* (Cambridge, 1989), 42–3. Fowler's interest in the occult may have been stimulated by his early association with John Worthington, who described him in his will as 'my very worthie friend' and asked him to act as executor in 1671; TNA, PROB 11/338, fo. 172v. Fowler and More were also closely linked in the eyes of their contemporaries. In the Bodleian copy of Fowler's anonymous, latitudinarian manifesto, *The Principles and Practices, of Certain Moderate Divines of the Church of England* (London, 1670), the original owner initially ascribed the work to Henry More; Bodl., Linc. 8°A 16.

[75] BL, Add. MS 4460, fos 54r–v. The leading nonconformist apologist John Howe was also partly responsible in 1676 for initiating a correspondence between Joseph Glanvill and Robert Boyle, in which the former outlined his plans to research and publish 'some modern well attested relations of fact, to prove the existence of witches and apparitions'. He may also have supplied Glanvill with particular instances of witchcraft; Boyle, *Correspondence*, iv, 460; v, 37–8. Howe's involvement in the psychic researches of Fowler and Glanvill reinforces a number of themes to be found throughout this chapter. A moderate Presbyterian and staunch Calvinist, Howe was of 'a truly eirenical spirit' and laboured throughout his life, both as a minister of the church of England before 1662, and as a dissenter thereafter (he was ejected from the living of Great Torrington in Devon), to find common ground between religious moderates of all persuasions. Like his friend Richard Baxter and John Beale, he played a leading role in establishing an association of Presbyterian and Congregationalist ministers in his county in the 1650s. After the Restoration, he laboured tirelessly for a comprehensive religious settlement. On being asked by Wilkins why a man of such obvious latitude should refuse to conform, he answered that it was his latitudinarian views that prevented him from assenting to the authority of a church that established terms of communion 'narrower than Christ made'. After 1688, he continued to promote greater union between the dissenters, but with only limited success. From his Cambridge days, he enjoyed a life-long friendship with Henry More, and was also on close terms with Ralph Cudworth. His *Gods Presence* (1677) was written in response to a query of Robert Boyle; *ODNB*, sub Howe, John.

remainder of his life. In 1696, for example, he promoted the publication of a pamphlet lauding the 'strange and wonderful cures' of the Civil War prodigy Anne Jefferies (for whom, see pp. 63–4). In the same year, Fowler preached a sermon before the House of Lords in thanksgiving for the safe deliverance of William III, who had recently survived an attempt on his life, in which he raised the issue of the problematic status of providential miracles, and the difficulties inherent in differentiating between these and purely natural events. He was left to conclude that 'ordinarily the Divine Concurrence with the free Actings of Men and with natural Agents, is not so discernible as that we are able to say, this is the Divine Part of the Event, and that the Humane, or merely Natural'. Nonetheless, he was keen to preserve a special intermediary category which fell between the everyday and the miraculous, and labelled the king's deliverance a 'Special Providence' that ranked alongside the Gunpowder Plot and the Restoration of Charles II.[76] Shortly after these events, Fowler began to bombard his friend and fellow latitudinarian John Sharp (d. 1714), Archbishop of York, with stories of apparitions and related phenomena. In 1699, for example, he was busy investigating claims of a haunted house belonging to a nonconformist minister at Deptford in Kent, as well as providing the Archbishop with 'expert' advice in the case of an apparition that appeared at Whitby in Yorkshire. Two years later, he agreed to investigate poltergeist activity in another house in the city of London.[77] If anything, his interest in such matters would appear to have grown with old age. In 1712, for example, he struck up a friendship with the like-minded Yorkshire antiquary Ralph Thoresby (1658–1725), whom he presented with a copy of John Beaumont's recent work on witchcraft. Thoresby, like Fowler, shared a deep-seated sympathy for the plight of moderate nonconformists. After much agonising, he eventually rejoined the Anglican fold in 1699, in the same year that he also acted as a conduit for his

---

[76] M. Pitt, *An Account of one Ann Jefferies... In a Letter from Moses Pitt to the Right Reverend Father in God Dr Edward Fowler, Lord Bishop of Gloucester* (London, 1696), 3; E. Fowler, *A Sermon Preached Before the House of Lords* [16 April 1696] *... Being a Day of Publick Thanksgiving... for the Most Happy Discovery and Disappointment of a Horrid Design to Assassinate His Sacred Majesty, and for Our Deliverance from a French Invasion* (London, 1696), 17–19.

[77] GRO, D 3549/6/2/4. These letters form part of a larger bundle of miscellaneous correspondence and other papers belonging to John Sharp, Archbishop of York, catalogued under the title 'Apparitions, miracles, prophecies and witchcraft, 1698–1705'. They include some fascinating material, including a manuscript account of a case of witchcraft at Ashford in Kent in 1698. In the case of the haunted house at Deptford, which also occasioned a published broadside, Fowler described the owner of the house as a long-standing acquaintance and nonconformist minister, who was also an old friend of Dr Benjamin Whichcote. The man in question was almost certainly Henry Godman (d.1702), who combined preaching with medical practice and had resided at Deptford since at least 1672 (the pamphlet refers to the owner of the house as a 'Mr G.'); *Cal. Rev.*, 225; *The Devil of Deptford* (London, 1699). Fowler also mentions as a visitor to the house, and one who would give full credence to the claims of spirit activity, Dr John Mapletoft (1631–1721), a former physician and associate of John Locke and Thomas Sydenham, who took holy orders in 1683 and was appointed to Benjamin Whichcote's old London living in 1686. He joined the newly founded Society for the Promotion of Christian Knowledge in 1699 and was known to have close connections with several leading latitudinarian divines; *ODNB*, Mapletoft, John. Bishop Fowler also offered support for, and praised the work of, John Beaumont in collecting and publishing evidence for the existence of spirits, demons, witches, and related beings in 1705; see *ODNB*, Beaumont, John.

friend, the Irish Presbyterian Joseph Boyse (1660–1728), in transmitting stories of Greatrakes' cures to leading fellows of the Royal Society, including John Evelyn.[78]

A common and notable feature of the religious outlook of all these men was their commitment to the pursuit of a broad-based religious settlement in the 1660s that, if implemented, would have overcome the bitter divisions engendered by the passage and imposition of the Clarendon Code. Most were clergymen or university teachers who served office under Cromwell but conformed at the Restoration. Typically, they retained and continued to foster close links with their nonconformist brethren after 1662, often interceding on a personal level to lessen the sting of coercion while at the same time promoting schemes of religious comprehension and reconciliation.[79] Many also possessed links with Ireland that may have helped to facilitate interest in, and support for, Greatrakes on his appearance in England in early 1666.[80] Above all, however, what linked this circle of clergy and scholars was a profound and shared interest in, and engagement with, scientific innovation

[78] J. Hunter (ed.), *The Diary of Ralph Thoresby, F.R.S.*, 2 vols (London, 1830), ii, 102–3. For Thoresby and Boyse, who shared the former's eirenic instincts and hoped that moderates on both sides of the Protestant divide might be the 'happy instruments of healing those breaches which persons of narrower judgements on either hand do unhappily widen', see *ODNB*. Thoresby's diary, it should be noted, contains numerous references to his fascination with witchcraft and related phenomena, much of it driven by a desire to confront and expose freethinkers such as Obadiah Oddy, whom he met in a London coffee house in 1712; ibid. ii, 118–19 and *passim*.

[79] The process also worked in reverse. When John Worthington was offered the vacant living of Barking in Suffolk in 1663 he received an effusive letter from the ejected incumbent John Fairfax (d. 1700), wholeheartedly welcoming his appointment and providing a useful guide to his new parish. Worthington was happy to reciprocate. According to the irate archdeacon of Suffolk, Laurence Womock, Fairfax repeatedly preached to his old congregation during Worthington's absences in London; Worthington, *Diary*, ii, 121–2; Bodl., MS Add. C 304a, fo. 60. For Fairfax, a leading member of a prominent dynasty of puritan and later nonconformist ministers, many of whom took up medicine after the Restoration, see *ODNB*; *Cal. Rev.*, 189. Collusion and cordiality frequently characterized relations between moderate Anglican clergy and their dissenting colleagues, a point frequently noted by historians of the Restoration church; see for example J. Spurr, '"Latitudinarianism" and the Restoration Church', *The Historical Journal*, 31 (1988), 77; J. D. Ramsbottom, 'Presbyterians and "Partial Conformity" in the Restoration Church of England', *Journal of Ecclesiastical History*, 43 (1992), 249–70; P. W. Jackson, 'Nonconformists and Society in Devon 1660–1689', Ph.D thesis (Exeter, 1986), 84–106.

[80] Simon Patrick, for example, married Penelope, the daughter of William Jephson, a prominent figure in the government of county Cork and a near neighbour of Greatrakes. Although they did not marry until 1675, they had first met ten years earlier; Rev. A. Taylor (ed.), *The Works of Simon Patrick, D.D.*, 9 vols (Oxford, 1858), ix, 58. George Rust, a fellow of Christ's College, Cambridge, in the 1650s, achieved rapid promotion in the Irish church after the Restoration, ending his career as bishop of Dromore; *ODNB*. His friend Ralph Cudworth, who was appointed Master of Christ's in 1654, had previously served as one of the fifteen trustees committed to the reform and remodelling of Trinity College, Dublin, in 1650. There, he served alongside a number of close associates of Greatrakes, including Colonel Hierom Sankey, Robert Venables, John Cook, and Bulstrode Whitelocke; T. C. Barnard, *Cromwellian Ireland: English Government and Reform in Ireland 1649–1660* (Oxford, 1975), 199n. Finally, Ezekiel Foxcroft was befriended by Lord Conway, a leading figure in the government of Restoration Ireland, who offered to secure him a post there in 1663. The Foxcrofts were seemingly in dire financial straits at this time 'in regard the losse of their estate', a reference no doubt to George Foxcroft's lands in Ireland, purchased in the 1650s when he held numerous administrative posts in the Cromwellian government of England; *Conway Letters*, 217; *CSP, Adventurers 1642–1659*, 32, 78, 344. Lord Conway, it should be noted, also offered More and Cudworth the hope of preferment in the Irish church as a way of extricating themselves from the increasingly hostile atmosphere of post-Restoration Cambridge; *Conway Letters*, 298–9.

and the new natural philosophy, which they sought to invoke as a bulwark against religious indifference and atheism. Many of the Cambridge Platonists, for example, shared Robert Boyle's enthusiasm for the new mechanical philosophy, even if, as in the case of Henry More, they might differ in their precise understanding of the nature and properties of matter and spirit.[81] Simon Patrick, in his latitudinarian manifesto of 1662, envisaged the new science as providing an antidote to all forms of atheism, enthusiasm, and superstition.[82] His passion for the new natural philosophy as expounded by men like Boyle was shared by his brother, John, who witnessed several of Greatrakes' cures and kept a commonplace book in which he copied extracts from 'Mr Boyles Experiments of the spring of Air'.[83] Others, such as John Wilkins, combined a commitment to the search for a peaceful resolution of the nation's religious divisions with a profound attachment to the work and principles of the newly founded Royal Society in the 1660s.[84] Natural theology, which lay at the heart of the approach of men like Boyle and Wilkins to science after 1660, was thus inherently compatible with the religious aims of the latitudinarians, who shared a common faith in man's ability to resolve ecclesiastical differences and understand the workings of the universe through the use of reason.[85]

Just as most of these men had begun their educational and clerical careers in the 1640s and 1650s, so too the majority owed their early interest in the new science to the various informal groups of like-minded friends and experimenters that

[81] For example, More's attempt at disproving Boyle's work on the vacuum and 'exploding that monstrous spring of the ayre' gave rise to a prolonged debate, much of it carried out in print, between the two men; ibid. 423. For discussion of the issues at stake, see J. E. Jenkins, 'Arguing about Nothing: Henry More and Robert Boyle on the Theological Implications of the Void', in M. J. Osler (ed.), *Rethinking the Scientific Revolution* (Cambridge, 2000), 153–79.

[82] P[atrick], *A Brief Account of the New Sect of Latitude-Men*, 19–24.

[83] CUL, Additional MS. 77, fos 11r–32r. At the time, Patrick was serving the cure of Battersea on behalf of his brother. Unlike Simon, however, who underwent a change of heart with regard to religious dissent in the late 1660s, John Patrick continued to evoke the admiration of many nonconformists for his conciliatory attitude toward their plight. Richard Baxter later claimed that his *A Century of Select Psalms* (London, 1679) had 'so far reconciled Non-conformists, that divers of them use his Psalms in their Congregations'; R. Baxter, *Poetical Fragments Heart-Imployment with God and It Self* (London, 1681), unpaginated 'To the Reader'.

[84] Greatrakes, *Brief Account*, 56–7, 67–8, 73. For Wilkins and the new natural philosophy, see B. Shapiro, *John Wilkins 1614–1672: An Intellectual Biography* (Berkeley, 1969). For Wilkins' use of experiments designed to test Greatrakes' claims, see p. 152. Wilkins was another latitudinarian divine who was seemingly intrigued by manifestations of spiritual or psychic activity. In February 1663, Abraham Hill, secretary of the Royal Society, reported that the future bishop of Chester was considering travelling to Tedworth in Wiltshire to investigate the case of the demon drummer; *Familiar Letters which Passed between Abraham Hill, Esq. and Several Eminent and Ingenious Persons of the Last Century* (London, 1767), 92. Wilkins had also engaged in discussion of witchcraft with the Somerset magistrate Robert Hunt, whose book of examinations later formed one of the chief sources for Glanvill's work on the subject; Boyle, *Correspondence*, iv, 461.

[85] The same point, confirming the validity of the term 'latitudinarianism', has recently been made by Scott Mandelbrote in his discussion of the role of natural theology in combating the dangers of atheism, enthusiasm and materialism in late seventeenth-century England; see his 'The Uses of Natural Theology in Seventeenth-Century England', *Science in Context*, 20 (2007), 457–8. As the example of Wilkins cited above suggests, however, I am not so readily convinced of his argument that there existed 'two different styles of natural theology' at this time with Wilkins firmly in the camp of those natural theologians who rejected the wondrous in preference for the regular, providential workings of the deity in the sublunary world.

sprung up in London and Oxford in the same two decades. A key figure here was the Polish émigré, Samuel Hartlib (*c.*1600–1662), who acted as a conduit for the communication of new scientific, technological, and philosophical research in the period immediately before 1660. Many of those who later featured prominently in the early history of the Royal Society had previously participated in Hartlib's abortive attempt to create a Baconian 'New Atlantis' in Interregnum England. In addition to the scientific aims of this group, many of its leading members also championed the cause of religious eirenicism and actively campaigned for schemes of Protestant unity throughout Europe. For many in the Hartlib circle, intellectual speculation was not to be limited or constrained by the intrusive dictates of contemporary religious conflict and debate. Instead, participants in the Hartlib circle actively sought to promote the new science as a potential instrument of religious reconciliation. Greater understanding of the divine creation, it was argued, would lead to a diminution of religious strife and pave the way toward reconciliation among the various branches and sects of the Protestant faith.[86] We should hardly be surprised therefore to discover that many of those who played such a vital role communicating with Hartlib and promoting his scientific and religious goals in the 1640s and 1650s were equally enthusiastic supporters of Greatrakes as well as keen students of the 'invisible world' of spirits, demons and witches.

JOHN BEALE: A CASE STUDY IN THE POLITICS OF THE PRETERNATURAL

Such themes are exemplified in the career of the clergyman and natural philosopher John Beale (1608–1683), whose interests and connections intersected with those of so many others who actively supported Greatrakes in the 1660s. Beale had played an important role in preparing the way for the Irish healer's reception within the Boyle household in London in 1666. As early as September 1665, he was acting as a conduit for highly favourable reports of Greatrakes' cures in Ireland, based on the testimonies of men familiar to, and highly respected by, Robert Boyle such as Thomas Sydenham and fellow Hartlibian Benjamin Worsley. Beale's motive in trumpeting Greatrakes's cures was decidedly religious in nature. Desperate to bolster the religious middle ground, he pleaded with Robert Boyle to make further enquiries in Ireland among his acquaintances there in the hope that further testimonials might be 'speedily published' and thus constitute 'convincing evidence of the powerful name of our Lord Jesus, in a season that needed some evidence, that all revelations were not fanatical'.[87]

---

[86] Thanks to the Hartlib Papers Project and the publication of the vast database associated with Hartlib, much new scholarship has appeared in recent years extolling the work of the Hartlib circle; see especially the various essays in M. Greengrass, M. Leslie, and T. Raylor (eds), *Samuel Hartlib and Universal Reformation: Studies in Intellectual Communication* (Cambridge, 1994). Still valuable however is the pioneering research of scholars such as George Turnbull and Charles Webster.

[87] Boyle, *Correspondence*, ii, 521–2.

Beale's suggestion that validation of Greatrakes' cures might somehow be used to buttress support for the established church in opposition to the forces of 'fanaticism' should not be interpreted as a straightforward assertion of Anglican intolerance in the face of dissent. As Beale must have known, all his sources were men with suspect religious and political backgrounds, who might easily fall into the category of 'fanatic' in the eyes of Beale's more hardline colleagues in the restored church. Beale's willingness to validate their testimonials of Greatrakes' cures almost certainly reflects his own desire at this time to act as a mediator between Anglicans and nonconformists, and to promote a broad-based religious and political consensus that would have excluded only the most extreme of radical sectaries whose implacable opposition to the Restoration threatened to destabilise and subvert the body politic. Like Beale, and so many others who supported Greatrakes in the 1660s, his informants were typically men who were tainted to some extent by their former association with the Cromwellian regime. Beale's willingness to indulge men like Worsley, for example, undoubtedly reflected his own misgivings about a religious settlement which, in his eyes, was insufficiently conciliatory toward moderate dissent. A life-long admirer of Erasmus, Beale was attracted from an early age to the 'rational, tolerant and simplified Christianity' that constituted the hallmark of the Great Tew circle. As early as 1640, he had drafted a tract on liberty of conscience which circulated at Oxford. By the 1650s, he was growing weary of the religious divisions of the day, and was increasingly attracted to the vision of a millenarian transformation of society that would bring an end to confessional strife and spiritual conflict. Throughout the 1650s he laboured to bring about such an outcome and was an active promoter of the scheme for ministerial association in Herefordshire. In order to preserve ecclesiastical unity, Beale understood that concessions to tender consciences were essential. In December 1658, he wrote to Hartlib lamenting the failure of Protestants to resolve their differences, unlike their Catholic opponents, and went on to outline his own vision of a reformed Christian polity:

> Ile tell you plainely in what notion I knit all Protestants together in my hearte. When I reade Pauls epistles to Corinthians &c I see him soe easy to take in corrupted Gentiles, even Idolaters & Magicians, drunkards & adulterers into the Covenant, & so gentle to beare with them that were not fully reclaimed nor satisfied concerning the resurrection, That hence, & from many other arguments I allowe a Nationall Church, Though by them the porch bee widened to admit of much unavoydeable pollution. And whether this church bee Episcopall, or Presbyteriall (soe both bee moderated & contempered from insolence & tyranny) I should refer it to changeable Vote...Each man may choose freely (according to his best information) for himselfe; but should not prescribe to others. And above all things, let God bee the sole determiner of Notions, & iudge of Understandings.[88]

---

[88] M. Stubbs, 'John Beale, Philosophical Gardener of Herefordshire. Part 1. Prelude to the Royal Society (1608–63)', *Annals of Science*, 39 (1982), 463–89, esp. 467–8, 477, 484; SUL, HP, 51/42A–B. For Beale's later career, see especially M. Stubbs, 'John Beale, Philosophical Gardener of Herefordshire. Part II. The Improvement of Agriculture and Trade in the Royal Society (1663–1683)', *Annals of Science*, 46 (1989), 323–63. Stubbs' articles provide a valuable synopsis of Beale's life and career.

Crucially for my analysis of the demonological dimension to Greatrakes' healing mission, Beale's fervent advocacy of a *via media* in religion, based on mutual tolerance and respect, coexisted alongside his equally profound interest in exploring, and seeking to vindicate, belief in a spirit world, interests, as we have seen, which he shared with the Cambridge Platonists and others within the Boyle circle. His voluminous correspondence with Samuel Hartlib is replete with animated discussions on the reality of supernatural manifestations designed to undermine the claims of materialists and atheists and prove the existence of a spiritual realm. As a child, Beale had read the Puritan demonologist William Perkins (1558–1602) and devoured local lore on magical charms and spells. During the 1650s, he was encouraged to undertake further research in this field through his reading of men like Henry More and John Worthington, both of whom were keen to collaborate with Hartlib in a wider design to uphold belief in the existence of spirits, demons, and devils. In an undated letter, probably written in the early 1650s, More had requested Hartlib's assistance in procuring 'as much of the true history of spirits as you can'. In particular, he requested:

> intelligence from any that have been ey witnesses of the late prodigies in Germanie, England or other parts such as men fighting in the ayr and such like, [for] it will gratify me in a double designe that I have in hand. I would desire also to be fully certifyde of the windes that the witches in Lapland and those northern parts which they are said to sell to merchants whether it be true or no. As also of the spirits that are sayd to appear in the stanneries in the west parts of England, and lastly an assurance that the Divell or some spirit dos visibly appear to the Americans. For the belief of spirits seeming so extremely ridiculous to many, it will be no les ridiculous to adventure to descant upon their nature, before we be assurd of their existence.[89]

It may well be that Beale was stimulated to pursue his own early interest in these and related topics in the late 1650s through contact with Hartlib and other corresponding members of his circle. Whatever the case, Beale was undoubtedly convinced of the providential nature of God's supervision of the sublunary world and of the reality of phenomena such as divine inspiration and diabolical possession. 'Too mea', he wrote, 'the visite of Angells, or the possession of Satan is as naturall, as the gusts of Winde'. 'Yea', he added, 'the Lord Almighty is as constant in Conferences with the Spirite of Man, as in causing the winds to blow & the

Oddly, however, they contain no mention of his role in the Greatrakes' affair, a curious oversight in the light of Beale's life-long interest in occult philosophy and preternatural curiosities. Like other members of the Hartlib circle, he also actively canvassed for the 'Plantation of Ireland with English' in the 1650s; see SUL, HP, 52/166.

[89] SUL, HP, 18/1/42A. In 1653, More's associate, John Worthington, informed Hartlib that Francis Rous (d.1659), a fellow Christian Platonist and patron of Hartlib, had possession of 'Carew's manuscript of Witches and Spirits', which remained unpublished 'because many things were of privat concernment to that family'. More, it should be noted, had been partially prompted to initiate an in-depth inquiry into witchcraft and related phenomena by a letter from Worthington addressed to him via Hartlib; SUL, HP, 28/2/58B; 18/1/9A–B. It is also worth noting that for a brief period in the late 1650s, Joseph Glanvill acted as chaplain to Rous, who may have stimulated his interest in witchcraft and related subjects.

clouds to drop'.[90] Some time around 1657, Beale's life-long interest in occult and preternatural activity led him finally to put down on paper his personal thoughts and recollections on such topics. He was clearly encouraged to do so by reading the conjectures of his old friend, Lady Ranelagh, whose 'discourse & proposals concerning Dreames' he had recently read.[91] Between 1657 and 1658, as Beale grew ever more dispirited by growing civil and religious unrest, he bombarded his friend Hartlib with lengthy accounts of his own dreams and encounters with the spirit world. A treatise on the 'art of interpreting dreams' was planned, portions of which were lodged with Hartlib for his approval. At the same time, Beale provided countless instances of the divinely inspired acts of prophets and healers, whose dreams and visions encouraged his growing faith in his own ability to foresee the future.[92] Beale's passion for oracular dreams and the like was to a large extent stimulated by his reading of the pansophist Jan Amos Comenius (1592–1670), who supplied him with copies of his own works on the subject, including those relating to the visions of a number of contemporary European prophets. In 1658–9, Beale's reading of Comenius' *Lux in Tenebris* (1657) provoked fevered debate among his friends in the Hartlib circle as to the authenticity of a range of prophetic utterances emanating from three Protestant visionaries in central Europe.[93] Shortly afterwards, prompted by his reading of Comenius' *Visiones Nocturnae* (1659), he entered into correspondence with John Oliver, a fellow minister in Somerset, in which he eagerly discussed a range of new prophetic utterances delivered by the German seer Stephen Mellish.[94] Beale now as-

[90] SUL, HP, 62/7/2A. For a letter to an unnamed correspondent, recounting various providential occurrences in Beale's early life, see ibid. 60/1/1A–4B. In an earlier letter to Hartlib, Beale cited the testimony of Bodin with regard to angelical visitations which he had gleaned from reading Henry More's *Antidote Against Atheism* (London, 1653); ibid. 51/52B.

[91] Ibid. 25/5/1A.

[92] Ibid. 25/19/1A–28B. Interestingly, Beale claimed to be a seventh son, an attribute that in this period was widely believed to confer special powers on the recipient, including the ability to heal; ibid. 25/5/4B. He may even have practised medicine on a small scale among his parishioners in Herefordshire. In 1659 he informed Hartlib that by 'Memorative applications God hath oft-times made mee a preserver of other men's lives', and cited examples to bolster his claims; ibid. 51/75A–B.

[93] Ibid. 52/59B; 31/1/67B, 69B; 51/62B–63A; 33/2/11B–12B. The *Prophecies* of Christopher Kotter, Christiana Poniatova, and Nicholas Drabicius, originally printed in Latin at Prague by Comenius and presented to Frederick of Bohemia, were later translated and published in London in 1664 by Robert Codrington, who dedicated them to Frederick's son, Prince Rupert.

[94] SARS, DD/PH 205, 71–114. The letter to Oliver was undated (71–2), and is followed by extracts from the work of Mellish, as well as others taken from letters written by Comenius to Beale dating from 1656 to 1661 (87–114). As the Vicar of Montacute, Oliver chose to resign his living in 1661; *Cal. Rev.*, 373. A colleague and admirer of Beale's in the late 1650s, it is clear that Oliver's estimation of Beale changed markedly after the Restoration following the latter's decision to conform. Thus Oliver designated Beale 'a woefull timeserver', who 'would say any thing in private that would please his company, any thing in [the] pulpit that would please the times'. He added, that '[o]ut of pretences to moderation he would show mee many papers that pretended to prophesy good to the evangelick party [i.e. nonconformists], & valued them as if they had beene oracles; but both they & hee proving mere windy vapours [he] left them both'; SARS, DD/PH 205, 72. In many respects, the relationship between the two men typifies the difficulties that so many dissenters felt in attempting to forge a common middle ground in religion in the aftermath of the Restoration church settlement. Oliver's own mental turmoil at the prospect of quitting the church in 1661, when he considered a career in medicine, is vividly illustrated by the letter which he wrote to a colleague in the summer of that year; see Bodl., Rawlinson Letters 109, fo. 83r.

serted that of the twenty-nine dreams related by Mellish, twelve were already
fulfilled, and ten were 'just now on the stage'. That left seven, 'all comfortable for
ye protestant churches', which Beale claimed would come to pass by 1663. Convinced by the success of Mellish's prognostications, Beale returned to re-examine
the claims of those made by the three prophets in *Lux in Tenebris*, concluding
that 'the Angelicall visits of Cotter, [and] the Ecstasies of Christina & Drabicius...were not altogether delusions'. The eirenic tone of these prophecies, their
prediction of the destruction of the Catholic Church and conversion of the Turks,
and the fact that they were due to come to pass in 1666, lends credence to the
suggestion that Beale's enthusiastic reception of Greatrakes may have owed much
to his immersion in such writings.[95]

It was during the course of his correspondence with Hartlib on prophetic
dreams and visions that Beale expatiated at length on the existence of witches
and demons, which he saw as the necessary concomitant of a world in which
good angels regularly protected and inspired holy men and seers.[96] In the years
immediately prior to the Restoration, Beale wrestled with a host of arcane issues
relating to the nature and being of spirits, good and bad. Eager to avoid any
imputation of meddling with black magic or necromancy, he nonetheless remained convinced of the providential nature of God's oversight of the sublunary
world, which was most obviously manifest through the regular activities of angels
and demons. In August 1657, he sent a book of prodigies to Hartlib, with a plea
for their proper and careful investigation. A year later, he continued to speculate
as to the nature of good and evil spirits, prompted on this occasion by reading
the work of Henry More and John Worthington on the immortality of the soul.[97]
Beale's growing interest in such matters extended to lengthy discussions on the
efficacy of charms and spells and the Devil's status as the 'prince of the air'. All
such phenomena, in Beale's eyes, provided evidence of the wondrous providence
or guiding hand of God, a project he shared with many in Hartlib's circle, including Robert Boyle, his sister, Lady Ranelagh, and their mutual friend,
Benjamin Worsley. It also provided ammunition in the war against atheism and

---

[95] SARS, DD/PH 205, 71. Beale's interest in these prophecies continued in the early years of the
Restoration. In 1662, in correspondence with his friend and fellow virtuoso John Evelyn, he again
waxed lyrical over the claims of the prophets and the significance of the year 1666, concluding that
'by thousands of proofes I am encouraged to expect that as we beginn to reforme philosophy...So
God is hastning to reforme Theology'; BL, Add. MS 78,683, fos 44r–46v, 55r–v. It was widely
rumoured, of course, that Greatrakes himself was addicted to, or was the victim of, similar 'delusions', it being widely reported in 1665 that he 'now dreames of nothing but converting the Jew
and Turk'; *Conway Letters*, 262–3. Moreover, it was probably no coincidence that Mellish's prophecies were partially translated and published in English in 1663 by another admirer of Greatrakes,
the German iatrochemist, Albertus Otto Faber, as *XII Visions of Stephen Melish a Germane: Being
such as Concern the Affairs now in Agitation between the French King & the Pope* (London, 1663). For
Faber, see p. 84 and n.
[96] See, for example, SUL, HP, 25/5/11B; 25/5/17B, 19B; 25/5/22B–23A.
[97] Ibid. 31/1/35A–50B; 51/21A–28B. In the former, Beale anticipated Greatrakes when he asserted that 'in our sleepe sometimes wee receive advise for the remedyes of diseases, that are not by
humane skill cureable'; ibid. 31/1/47B–48A. Beale's interest in dreams was a lifelong fixation. As late
as October 1670 he affirmed his belief in premonitory dreams, signs, and portents in a letter to Robert
Boyle; Boyle, *Correspondence*, iv, 189–93.

moral degeneracy which men like More, Beale, and Boyle saw as the inevitable product of the collapse of Protestant consensus engendered by almost two decades of religious and political strife.

Like Beale, Robert Boyle and his sister provided Hartlib with a constant flow of communications providing instances of wonderful cures that defied conventional logic as well as accounts of demonic activity. In 1655, for example, Lady Ranelagh was the source for a tale of witchcraft that had apparently been told to Charles I by his physician, the Huguenot, Dr Theodore Mayerne (1573–1655). At the same time, Robert Boyle was reported to be in possession of 'a piece of Carrichter about Witchcraft', which had been translated into English at the behest of Colonel Arthur Hill, an Irish landowner and associate of Benjamin Worsley.[98] It seems highly likely that Boyle and his sister encouraged Beale in his psychic researches, with intermediaries such as Worsley supplying additional evidence. In 1658, for example, Beale longed to 'heare Dr Worseleyes relation of the discontented Woeman that raysd the discontented spirite', while noting in the same letter Lady Ranelagh's cautious remarks on the use of charms in curing the bite of a rabid dog.[99] Although Beale does not cite Robert Boyle directly in his manuscript writings on spirits, demons, and divine prophecy, the latter would surely have approved of Beale's distinctively Baconian approach to the study of prodigies and illustrious providences. In a letter to Hartlib in August 1657, Beale prefaced his account of a volume of prodigies 'aspecting our late troubles' by setting out the rules by which he hoped to progress this work:

> Here I begin with my frequent expostulation. Are all prodigyes, & Signes to bee despised, & neglected? If soe, Howe cam all Historians, inspired, holy & prophane, soe constantly to record them? On the contrary if they ought to be heeded, Where are the interpreters: what care is imployed for them? To trye them, to encourage them, to enable them, to informe them? Where is there Colledge, what discipline appointed, or allowed? Is it a business soe slight That it deserves noe discipline, but must bee left, as it were only to chance?[100]

A month later, he was forced to reflect further on this work in response to the recent initiative of the Presbyterian minister Matthew Poole (d. 1679), who

---

[98] Ibid. 29/5/29A, 36B. Lady Ranelagh may have heard the story told by Dr Mayerne from his widow, Lady Mayerne, who was also a witness to the remarkable feats of Sarah Wight in 1647; Jessey, *The Exceeding Riches of Grace*, 'To the reader'. In 1655, Hartlib also reported the publication of that 'excellent Narration . . . which was before given to Mr Boyle when hee was in France', i.e. the French edition of the *The Devill of Mascon*, published in 1653. 'Carrichter' was Bartholomaeus Carrichter (d.1574), occult philosopher and friend of John Dee, who served as physician to the Emperor Maximilian. The work referred to here is probably Carrichter's *On the Curing of Magical Illnesses* (1551).

[99] SUL, HP, 51/24A–25A. Worsley's account of the 'discontented woman' is probably a reference to the biblical story of the witch of Endor [1 Samuel 28:7–25].

[100] Ibid. 31/1/35A–B. Beale's list of questions is redolent of those prepared by Boyle himself when he set out to investigate Greatrakes' cures in April 1666; see BL, Add. MS 4293, fos 50–3. For discussion of the contemporary debate surrounding the validity of testimonial evidence, see S. Shapin, *A Social History of Truth: Civility and Science in Seventeenth-Century England* (Chicago, 1994).

announced his intention to create a 'Register of Illustrious Providences'.[101] Beale's observations make interesting reading, for not only do they provide further insights into the depth and seriousness of his engagement with supernatural phenomena, but they also demonstrate, once again, how such interests meshed with his wider ecumenical concerns. While agreeing then with the chief thrust of Poole's project—something which he claimed to have pursued in isolation for more than twenty years—Beale had some important reservations or words of caution, most of which related to the need to create as broad a religious consensus as possible in the collection of testimonials. He therefore suggested that in order to avoid the imputation that Poole's design was little more than a 'stratagem . . . to advance a Presbyteriall faction', the organizers should solicit the testimonies of the reverend and learned of all denominations, despite the fact that they might otherwise be of 'diversity of iudgement, in speculations & Questions of discipline'. By softening some words and terms in the original manifesto, Beale thus thought it more likely that 'wee may acquire the Testimony & obtaine the engagement of ye ablest of them whose countenances are clouded against us, either upon the secular quarrel or upon other notional accompt'. Beale even named those opponents whom he wished to draw into the project, referring specifically to Henry Hammond (1605–1660), Ralph Cudworth, and George Lawson (d. 1678).[102] Indeed, he specifically requested that Cudworth and Lawson be approached as they were best qualified 'to debate upon the hidden & deepe inquiryes' and discern 'what are true prodigyes' and how these might be 'distinguished from the Ordinary or necessary operations of nature' so that 'we may arrive to the interpretation of Prodigyes, Visions, & other Signes'. Beale, then, clearly saw the ecumenical potential in such a scheme which he hoped might be an instrument 'to knit us into some association & mutuall correspondence'. Accordingly, he promised at the first opportunity to meet with clerical colleagues in Herefordshire and to 'animate others to consider the works of Gods hand', although he also enjoined Poole to observe due discretion in the publication of such providences, fearing the ill consequences of the

---

[101] Beale's observations on 'Mr Pooles Designe' appear in three anonymous extracts, all dated 23 September 1657. Internal evidence, however, clearly indicates Beale's authorship, as for example, where he refers to his uncle, Sir Walter Pye; CUL, MS Dd.III.64, no. 62, fos 138r–141v. The same collection also contains a copy of Poole's 'Designe for Registring of Illustrious Providences'; ibid. no. 61, fos 136r–137. For what might be a further contribution to the debate by Beale, see CUL, MS Oo.VI.114, fos 23r–26. The cautionary note that it contains about the prophecies reported by men like Henry Pinnell, and the suggestion that a collection of contemporary providential occurrences in England since the beginning of the civil wars 'might very well have equalled the most of those I have read in 'Cotterus, Christina or Drabicius', suggests Beale as the likely author.

[102] Henry Hammond was one of the leading defenders and apologists for old-style Anglicanism during the Interregnum. Richard Baxter nonetheless regretted his passing, his death in 1660 marking 'a very great loss; for his Piety and Wisdom would have hindered much of the Violence which after followed'; *ODNB*, sub Hammond, Henry. George Lawson, a minister in Shropshire, wrote a learned critique of Hobbes' *Leviathan*. A long-term friend and critic of Baxter, at the Restoration he favoured a 'maximal comprehension within a national settlement'. In the context of the current discussion, it may not be without significance that Lawson's close relation, Dr John Carr (d.1675), an eminent Cambridge physician who contributed a poetical encomium to Lawson's *Politica* in 1660, was providing Henry More with confirmatory evidence in the case of the demon drummer of Tedworth in 1663; *ODNB*, sub Lawson, George; *Conway Letters*, 216.

appearance of poorly accredited instances in the public domain.[103] Any reservations that Beale felt for the project were apparently soon overcome. Within a few months he was sending Hartlib details of providential instances collected locally which he specifically requested were for 'Mr Pooles use' alone and 'Not for the Mercuryes'.[104]

Beale's attempt to classify and evaluate prodigious and preternatural phenomena according to Baconian principles in many ways anticipated the work of members of the Royal Society, like Joseph Glanvill, who proposed the adoption of similar strictures governing the rules of evidence in relation to demonic and spectral activity.[105] It also confirms the groundbreaking research of Stuart Clark, who has argued that the study of witchcraft and demonology was not a marginal, unscientific, or irrational pursuit, but constituted an important aspect of the work of early modern natural philosophers. The investigation of preternatural occurrences was serious scientific work. Not only did it help to establish the crucial boundary between the natural and supernatural realms, but by exploring occult causation natural philosophers hoped to uncover new and powerful technologies for the improvement of mankind.[106]

Such aims of course were central to the work of Robert Boyle, who lost few opportunities to encourage trustworthy allies like Beale and Glanvill in this valuable research.[107] But it also posed dangers, none more so than when the task of collecting reliable testimony fell into the hands of untrustworthy witnesses or religious 'fanatics'. On such occasions, it was easy for men like Boyle, and their scientific

---

[103] CUL, MS Dd.III.64, no. 62, fos 139r, 139v, 141r. Beale specifically mentions a clerical colleague, Mr S, as one most likely to further this work in the county. He also cites two examples for Poole's collection, including one prompted by his recent reading of 'a very good sermon' preached by George Hall in London. Hall, a fellow student of King's College, Cambridge, in the 1630s, was, according to Beale, 'converted' following the providential death of Richard Juxon in the College in 1635. Hall, of course, like Beale, was a religious moderate in the 1650s and future supporter of Greatrakes; see pp. 73, 90.

[104] SUL, HP 52/16A–17B. Beale described his informant, Powell, as preacher of the gospel at Munsley in Herefordshire [given in error as Mursley in HP transcript].

[105] Beale may well have attempted to both encourage and shape Glanvill's witchcraft project. In October 1666, for example, he reported to Boyle that Glanvill 'intendeth something Theologically in defence of the Emergent Providencyes for the Season of all ages, & of the guifts of Gods holy spirite for Inventions to the benefit of the Worthy Against Atheists & Scoffers'. Beale promised to supply Glanvill with 'suggestions both Historicall & prudentiall Which he seems to accept of, & professeth conformity'. Although Beale here almost certainly refers to Glanvill's apologetical works on behalf of the Royal Society, it seems highly likely that he also shared his interests in those other providential operations of witches and spirits which Glanvill was publicizing at this time. He may well, however, have been snubbed by Glanvill for in April 1668 Henry Oldenburg was reporting to Boyle that Beale 'utterly disowns to have any power with M[r] Glanvill in his last writings, since he wrote against dogmatizing'; Boyle, *Correspondence*, iii, 260; iv, 64.

[106] Clark, *Thinking With Demons*, especially chapters 16–19.

[107] Michael Hunter has recently suggested that John Beale was the intended dedicatee of the Latin preface to Boyle's 'Strange Reports', a work that was to include discussion of a range of supernatural phenomena, including witches, apparitions, and magic. It nonetheless remained unpublished at the time of Boyle's death (it was originally intended to appear as an appendix to his *Experimenta et Observationes Physicae* of 1691), probably as a result of Boyle's deep-seated fear that it would damage his reputation as a gentleman and a natural philosopher, and so leave him exposed as over-credulous and excessively prone to superstition; Hunter, 'Magic, Science and Reputation', 228–35.

work, to become compromised. A case in point concerns Boyle's contact with the radical Baptist preacher and polemicist, Henry Jessey (1601–1663), who Beale reported in 1659 as corresponding with Boyle and supplying him with a relation concerning the work of the Elizabethan magician, John Dee (1527–1609).[108] Boyle's acquaintance with Jessey probably came about as a result of his sister's involvement in the case of the prophetess Sarah Wight (see pp. 135–6), a *cause célèbre* that continued to attract comment and attention throughout the 1650s. In the early years of the Restoration, however, Jessey's publication of a series of inflammatory and subversive anti-royalist prodigies that achieved wide popular circulation must have prompted Boyle and Beale to reassess his reliability as a witness. Indeed, it was probably Jessey and his radical supporters that Beale had in mind, when he wrote to Boyle in September 1665 with the news of Greatrakes' cures, which he described as 'a convincing evidence of the powerful name of our Lord Jesus, *in a season that need some evidence, that all revelations were not fanatical*'.[109]

Given the claims of dangerous enthusiasts and sectaries such as Jessey to detect the hand of God at work in the trials and tribulations of Anglican ministers and royalist magistrates, it was essential for moderates such as Beale and Boyle to vet thoroughly accounts of prodigies and other preternatural occurrences.[110] This work was by its nature politically sensitive. As Simon Schaffer has commented, the Restoration of the monarchy demanded 'the correct attribution of power to bodies'. Such concerns, of course, were particularly acute in a polity in which recourse to the metaphor of a revived body politic was, as we have seen, replete with real meaning and significance.[111] This was most readily apparent in the revival of the dramatic ceremonial surrounding the royal touch for scrofula. It also featured prominently, however, in the work of those natural philosophers associated with the Royal Society who were called upon to adjudicate the extraordinary cases of

---

[108] SUL, HP, 51/73B.

[109] Boyle, *Correspondence*, ii, 522 [my emphasis]. Beale himself referred to the Sarah Wight case in an undated letter to Hartlib; SUL, HP, 31/1/28B. He did not, however, send Jessey's published account on the reasonable assumption that Lady Ranelagh, a participant in the affair, had in all probability already provided him with a summary of the main events. Although I have found no record of communication between Lady Ranelagh and Hartlib on this subject, the latter was asked by Henry Appelius, John Dury's brother-in-law, to send copies of Jessey's book to his house in Holland in 1648; HP, 45/1/47A–B. For divided reactions in the nonconformist community to Jessey's *Mirabilis Annus* tracts, and discussion of their authorship, see K. V. Thomas, *Religion and the Decline of Magic: Studies in Popular Beliefs in Sixteenth- and Seventeenth-Century England* (London, 1971), 95–6.

[110] The debate surrounding the veracity of these and similar stories, and their political significance, in the middle decades of the seventeenth century is discussed more fully in J. Friedman, *Miracles and the Pulp Press during the English Revolution: The Battle of the Frogs and Fairford's Flies* (London, 1993). For a specific case study, dating from the troubled years of the early Restoration, see A. Warmington, 'Frogs, Toads and the Restoration in a Gloucestershire Village', *Midland History*, 14 (1989), 30–42.

[111] S. Schaffer, 'Regeneration: The Body of Natural Philosophers in Restoration England', in C. Lawrence and S. Shapin (eds), *Science Incarnate: Historical Embodiments of Natural Knowledge* (Chicago, 1998), 83–120 [quote at 84]. In a sermon preached on coronation day in 1661, Henry King, Bishop of Chichester, argued for a close correlation between the outward physical appearance and inner spiritual and moral condition of the individual, citing the case of Richard III as one clearly demarcated by his 'deformed Body and ill aspect'; H. King, *A Sermon Preached at White-hall on the 29th of May* [1661] (London, 1661), 13–15 [quote at 15]; cf. [J. Higham], *A Looking-Glass for Loyalty: or the Subjects Duty to his Soveraign* (London, H. Brome, 1675), 160–2.

men like the blind Dutchman, Jan Vermaasen, who claimed to be able to tell colours by touch, or that of the Cambridge graduate Arthur Coga, whose melancholy was cured by the infusion of the blood of a sheep.[112] In such cases, Boyle and others demanded close examination of the moral character, social status, and general trustworthiness of those who witnessed such phenomena, as well as applying similar strictures to those who were the object of their curiosity and study. In the process, the bodies of men like Greatrakes, his patients, and his interrogators became potential sites of experimentation. Boyle, for example, repeatedly sought to replicate Greatrakes' therapeutic stroking by imitating his actions, or wearing the Irishman's gloves. Others, such as the virtuoso John Wilkins, performed a variety of experiments upon the bodies of Greatrakes' patients, including pricking them with pins in order to verify the stroker's claim that he was able to expel malignant spirits to the body's extremities, where they proved insensitive to pain.[113]

In order to receive the approbation of the natural philosophers, it was equally important for the virtuosi to examine and assess the moral rectitude of prodigious healers like Greatrakes. It was probably for this reason that Beale, who had not previously met Greatrakes but was keen to promote his cures, sought to gain the imprimatur of his friend, Robert Boyle, who shared Beale's vision of a regenerate society. Once again, Greatrakes represented an exemplary figure in the eyes of Beale, a charismatic magistrate and religious moderate whose appearance in the early 1660s signified a coded message of divine disapproval of the religious and political divisions that permeated Restoration Britain. Beale eagerly embraced such thoughts. Like so many of Greatrakes' known associates and admirers, Beale's advocacy of religious moderation and antipathy to coercion in spiritual matters predated the Restoration. Throughout the 1650s, he argued in favour of a comprehensive religious settlement that would guarantee the continued existence

[112] Schaffer, 'Regeneration', 90–4 [Vermaasen], 94–105 [Coga]. Other members of the Royal Society who were known to have shown an interest in Greatrakes' feats included the naturalist John Ray (1627–1705), who refers to reading about 'the Business about great Rakes' in June 1667, as well as, in all probability, the pionering statistician John Graunt; E. Lankaster (ed.), *Memorials of John Ray* (London, 1846), 17; Appendix 2. Interest in Greatrakes in scientific circles continued into the next decade. In 1674, the French cleric and scholar Pierre Daniel Huet (1630–1721) wrote to Oldenburg requesting information about the truth and status of his alleged cures. He was prompted to do so by a recent meeting with the German natural philosopher Gottfried Wilhelm Leibniz (1646–1716), who 'showed me on his return from England a book which he had brought back about the natural faculty of a certain Irishman who cured all kinds of diseases by touch alone'. Oldenburg replied confirming Greatrakes' limited ability to cure tumours and other pains in the body which, like many of his colleagues, he attributed to his extraordinary constitution and 'sanguine temperament'; Oldenburg, *Correspondence*, x, 493; xi, 28.

[113] For a good summary of the various tests and experiments carried out by Boyle, More, and others on Greatrakes in order to establish the precise status of his cures, see Schaffer, 'Regeneration', 105–15. For Wilkins' experiment using pins, see Greatrakes, *Brief Account*, 56–7, 73. Again, there are some interesting parallels here with the tests used by witch-hunters in order to discover those insensitive spots on the body where the Devil's familiars suckled on the witch's blood. If, as Greatrakes believed, the spirits which he drove out from the bodies of his patients were demonic in origin, their insensitivity to physical pain might explain the phenomena described by Wilkins. Similar experiments were performed by Cromwell's son-in-law, Viscount Fauconberg; ibid. 72–3. For a contemporary example of a Wiltshire woman taking such preventative measures against a woman whom she held responsible for her violent fits, see WSA, A1/110, Easter 1664, nos 19, 143.

of a national church free from dogmatism and doctrinal disputes. In various letters to Hartlib and Lady Ranelagh, to whom he seems to have acted as some form of spiritual adviser, he repeatedly argued against ceremonial formalism, and the debates it engendered, on the grounds that it was inimical to the propagation of true faith and godliness. It was no coincidence, he wrote in a letter to Lady Ranelagh probably dating from the late 1650s, that division and dissent first appeared in the Christian church with the advent of persecuting and authoritarian state churches that sought to impose prescribed forms of worship upon their subjects. Significantly for Beale, such disputes had opened the door to Satan, who saw them as an opportunity to introduce all manner of 'Idolatrie, charmes, exorcismes, conjurations, mummeries, nonsense, contradiccion of sense Reason & Spirit', and subsequently constituted a 'stumbling block...& a wedge to teare asunder all the children of the Gospell'.[114]

The identification of religious division and conflict with satanic witchcraft in the context of Beale's wider concerns at this time is intriguing and highly suggestive. Among other things, it may help to provide an explanation as to why the firmest and most outspoken proponents of belief in witchcraft in this period tended to be associated with those individuals and groups who were most active in seeking religious reconciliation and restoring harmony to the body politic. Belief in an active spirit world was reassuring to men like Beale because it helped to provide an explanation for those divisions which threatened to tear apart the fragile unity of the nation. It also provided a solution. By focusing on what he and others saw as an essentially uncontentious realm of theological belief—the existence of spirits, witches, demons, and angels—fellow Protestants were exhorted to put aside their differences and create a new national church that eschewed the twin extremes of sectarian 'enthusiasm' and Roman Catholicism. In this context, it is hardly surprising that providentialism formed such an important element in the thinking of moderate churchmen and their lay allies who pushed for the creation of just such a church in the final years of the Commonwealth and the initial stages of the Restoration.

[114] SUL, HP, 27/16/10A.

6

Epilogue and Conclusions

The Stroaker Graitrix was a sot.
And all his Feat-Tricks are forgot
'A Canto upon the Miraculous Cure of the Kings-evil performed by His Grace,
the D[uke] of M[onmouth]', in *A Choice Collection of Wonderful Miracles,
Ghosts and Visions* (London, 1681), 4.

THE AFTER-LIFE OF A MIRACLE HEALER, 1666–83

Most accounts of Greatrakes have assumed that once he departed England for his native Ireland in late May 1666, he happily retired to the obscurity from whence he had emerged and gave up the practice of stroking which had temporarily brought him to the forefront of public attention. Soon, the concern of the populace would turn to new disasters and problems, most notably the terrible fire that consumed nine-tenths of the city of London in September 1666 as well as the calamitous defeat suffered by the English fleet at the hands of the Dutch in the following year. Consequently, little effort has been made to chart the later life of the Irish stroker. In the first half of this final chapter, I attempt to reconstruct from the scanty fragments of evidence that remain what happened to Greatrakes after 1666 and to trace his vestigial influence, albeit modest, on the life of his community and the wider history of Restoration Britain. Ultimately, of course, Greatrakes' name and reputation as a healer faded from historical view. Occasional attempts to explain away his cures by recourse to a range of naturalistic explanations, including mesmerism, have been advanced, but in most respects the furore surrounding Greatrakes in the early 1660s has been consigned to the dustbin of history, another example of the superstitious and credulous mindset of the pre-modern age. This image of Greatrakes, however, as crank or showman, as I have tried to show, does scant justice to the real impact which he had upon Restoration society. In concluding this biography of the man and his mission to heal the damaged and diseased bodies of his fellow countrymen and women, I suggest that it is possible to attach far greater significance to this episode in the early history of Restoration Britain, even if, in the long term, Greatrakes' failure to convince all of his charismatic powers was to prove symptomatic of a wider failure of those in power in the 1660s to heal the divisions unleashed by two decades of civil war and political and religious conflict.

One point that is clear from the surviving evidence is that Greatrakes continued to stroke the sick and maimed on his return to Ireland, and did so for the rest of his life, despite the declining interest of the Restoration media and those in authority. Various sources testify to his continuing practice in Ireland following his return to his native land in the spring of 1666. In December 1666, Lord Broghill, the son of the Earl of Orrery, reported that Greatrakes had spent four or five days at his father's new house at Charleville in Cork, where he performed 'many cures before my father'.[1] Greatrakes also returned on numerous occasions to England, where he continued to stroke large numbers of men and women in the towns and villages of the west of England. In 1668, for example, prior to his departure to Ireland, he wrote to Robert Boyle from Bristol in the hope of convincing the great natural philosopher of the miraculous origin and nature of his cures. From the tone of this letter it is evident that Boyle was still experiencing doubts about the nature and authenticity of Greatrakes' claims, a symptom perhaps of the typically scrupulous and innate diffidence that he brought to bear in judging all phenomena that were open to public controversy and debate. Greatrakes thus supplied him with new examples of his healing powers, referring to cures he had performed in Bristol, Marlborough, Minehead, and elsewhere. He also alluded to having paid a return visit to Ragley to 'see the most incomparable Lady of the world...for worth, & sufferings my Lady Conway'. Here, he happily records that many of those in the neighbouring town of Alcester, whom he had stroked two years earlier, were still in good health and fully recovered. But despite the public nature of these cures, Greatrakes does not appear to have courted excessive publicity, especially in London, where he 'resolved to doe no thinge'.[2]

Unfortunately, Greatrakes' letter to Boyle provides no further clues as to the specific purpose of his visit to the capital in 1668, nor is it possible to say with any certainty the reason for his subsequent journeys to London in 1672 and 1675. In 1672, Greatrakes' friend and neighbour, Sir Francis Foulke,[3] received a letter from

[1] NLI, MS 4728, 10–11; BL, Stowe MS 747, fo. 113; *HMC Fourth Report, Part 1, Report and Appendix* (London, 1874), 280. The young Broghill was sufficiently convinced on this occasion to exclaim 'I do now believe he can do merickles'. Greatrakes was still performing his cures as late as November 1680 in Dublin; see J. E. Bailey, 'Andrew Marvell and Valentine Greatraks, the Stroker', *Notes and Queries*, 9 (1884), 62–3. However, an acquaintance later recalled that 'his Virtue was much abated' in these years; BL, Add. MS 4291, fo. 151r.

[2] Boyle, *Correspondence*, iv, 98–102. In resuming his acquaintance with Robert Boyle, Greatrakes made a point of offering his services to Lady Ranelagh and the Earl of Orrery, as well as soliciting Boyle's assistance in seeking help for his friend, the Cork Quaker, Colonel Robert Phaire. A reprint of Greatrakes' *Brief Account*, addressed to Boyle, was published by Samuel Dancer at Dublin in the same year, 1668.

[3] For a brief biography of Foulke, a tenant of the Earl of Cork at Camphire, between Youghal and Cappoquin, see T. C. Barnard, 'The Political, Material and Mental Culture of the Cork Settlers, 1649–1700', in P. O'Flanagan and N. G. Buttimer (eds), *Cork: History and Society: Interdisciplinary Essays on the History of an Irish County* (Dublin, 1993), 339. Like Greatrakes, Foulke had been active in the rendition of Munster to Cromwell in 1649, and he subsequently colluded with the Protectorate government, acting as JP for counties Cork and Waterford. As a client of Broghill, he promoted the Restoration and sat as MP for county Cork in the General Convention of 1660. He was pardoned, along with Greatrakes, in 1661, and thereafter sat as MP for Clonmel in the Dublin Parliament. By the late 1660s, like Greatrakes, he was in severe financial straits. He claimed to have spent over £2,000 improving his estates at Camphire, much of which had been lost as a result of the imposition of the Act of Settlement. He sought permission for his case to be heard by a local commission and requested that Greatrakes, among others, might adjudicate his case. His problems were still unresolved by the

him at London in which he referred to current political news, including a report emanating from the court that the King was angry with the Prince of Orange 'for not making himself an absolute King'. In conveying this gossip to the Countess of Orrery, Foulke also alluded to Greatrakes' observation that the Duke of Bucking-ham had become 'perverted in his religion since the time he was at sea with the Duke of York'.[4] Three years later, Greatrakes was again in London, this time acting as a go-between for his old friend, Colonel Robert Phaire, and Phaire's new spir-itual mentor, Lodowick Muggleton.[5] That this was more than just a casual, passing acquaintance on Greatrakes' part is evident from a poem that he wrote in praise of Muggleton, in which it is clear that he shared the self-styled prophet's religious and millennial vision, even if he was 'yett no Beleiver of this Com(m)ission'. This brief eulogy is worth reproducing in its entirety for the light which it sheds on Greatrakes' own highly personal and somewhat unorthodox religious credo:

Great prophet of this Third and last Commission
Seraphick in thy state Divine phisitian
What Tropes can speake thy praise or colours draw
The Luster of thy mind the living Law
And Misterys unfoulded dost thou teach
Which neither men nor Angells yet could reach
The Curtaines thou hast drawne and lett us see
The hidden Misteryes of Eternity
Who the onely true God is thou dost show
And what the Devil was and is thou dost know
And also the Angells nature thou dost tell
And Mans, where Heaven is and also Hell
And what's the soule no Riddle is to thee
Thou great discoverer of Eternity
Great Paul such sublime secrets never taught
Though into the Third heaven hee was caught.[6]

At first sight, Greatrakes' transparent admiration and respect for Muggleton as an inspired and true prophet sits awkwardly with the earlier picture that I have

early 1670s, when he sought the intercession of his patron, the Earl of Orrery. Like Orrery, he was passionately anti-Catholic and increasingly favoured an alliance with the Dutch in the 1670s in their struggle with Louis XIV's France; see NLI, MS 11,961, 317; R. Dunlop (ed.), *Ireland under the Commonwealth: Being a Selection of Documents Relating to the Government of Ireland from 1651 to 1659*, 2 vols (Manchester, 1913), i, 66n–67n; T. C. Barnard, 'Lord Broghill, Vincent Gookin and the Cork Elections of 1659', *English Historical Review*, 88 (1973), 356; *CSP Ireland, 1660–1662*, 318; BL, Stowe MS 744, fos 170v–171r; WSxRO, MS 13,223 (13), (14), (18); Bodl., Carte MSS 59, fo. 615; 67, fo. 72r; 68, fo. 150r.

[4] E. MacLysaght (ed.), *Calendar of the Orrery Papers* (Dublin, 1941), 105–6. Earlier the same year, Foulke, in further letters to the countess, referred to having received a 'tearse of cyder' from Great-rakes. At the same time he recommended a young Irish Protestant brewer, who had previously worked for Greatrakes, to the service of his patron; ibid. 97, 98.

[5] 'Supplement to the Book of Letters, written by John Reeve and Lodowicke Muggleton', appended to *The Works of John Reeve and Lodowick Muggleton*, 3 vols (London, 1832), iii, 11–14. Muggleton mentions meeting Greatrakes on three separate occasions and discussing with him the payment of a token, which was still unpaid at the time of writing, as Greatrakes had now travelled to Devon.

[6] BL, Add. MS 60,220, fo. 18v.

drawn of the charismatic Irishman's religious position. Muggleton belongs—or so we have been led to believe—to the radical underground of the Civil Wars, a representative of that sectarian impulse to 'turn the world upside down'.[7] Unlike the moderate episcopalians and nonconformists who desired a renewal of church unity under a revised Anglican communion, and who were so conspicuous in their support for Greatrakes in the 1660s, Muggleton and his select band of followers lay outside the mainstream and did not seek readmission to the fold. Highly critical of the falseness and hypocrisy of the established church, and its coercive jurisdiction over tender consciences, Muggleton the prophet routinely condemned to everlasting damnation those who opposed his commission. Muggleton would thus appear to represent a strange bed-fellow for the peaceable and moderate Greatrakes. However, as recent analysis of Muggleton and his movement has suggested, this image may be erroneous for there was much in Muggleton's teaching and personality that was likely to have struck a responsive chord in Greatrakes and was consistent with the latter's broad, religious outlook.

According to William Lamont, for example, Muggleton was indulgent toward the practice of occasional conformity, and made little effort to proselytize. As a result, he barely troubled the authorities (he was prosecuted only once after 1660, for blasphemy in 1677), and his followers were likewise left unmolested as they rarely attended regular meetings of worship. Unlike their spiritual cousins, the Quakers, Muggleton's disciples avoided head-on confrontation with the powers-that-be. Muggleton himself, if we believe Lamont, was not therefore the wide-eyed, fanatical prophet of historical legend. On the contrary, he depicts him as a man capable of great empathy and one who refused to judge others of differing religious persuasions. He also expressed considerable respect for the civil authority of the King and his magistrates, as for example in 1663, when he protested to Sir Thomas Twysden that he had 'always been obedient to the civil laws of the land...neither did I ever break any of the King's laws, neither in the old king's time, nor now...neither have I had any meetings at my house, nor have been at any no where else, not since His Majesty's restoration, nor many years before'.[8] It is not difficult to see how such a man might have evoked the admiration of Greatrakes.

Greatrakes' fraternization with men like Muggleton, outwardly peaceable and respectful of royal authority and the magistracy, should not therefore be read as evidence of his own latent, subversive proclivities. Throughout the 1660s and 1670s, Greatrakes entertained Muggletonian and Quaker friends like Colonel Phaire and William Penn (1644–1718), while at the same time retaining the

---

[7] See for example J. E. C. Hill, *The World Turned Upside Down: Radical Ideas During the English Revolution* (London, 1972); Hill, 'John Reeve and the Origins of Muggletonianism', in J. E. C. Hill, B. Reay, and W. Lamont (eds), *The World of the Muggletonians* (London, 1983), 64–110.

[8] W. Lamont, *Puritanism and Historical Controversy* (London, 1996), 33, 37–8; 'A Volume of Spiritual Epistles', in *Works of Reeve and Muggleton*, iii, 93. Like Greatrakes, Muggleton too had deplored the sectarian divisions of the 1640s and 'withdrew into private contemplation and melancholia until 1650'; *ODNB*.

friendship of devout conformists such as Sir Ames Meredith.[9] Although his actions in this respect may have raised eyebrows in England, in post-Restoration Munster such activity would appear to have generated little overt comment or criticism. Greatrakes was after all, like Penn and Phaire, a gentleman, and a Protestant gentleman to boot. Just why such behaviour was widely condoned is apparent in a letter that Greatrakes' patron, the Earl of Orrery, Lord President of Munster, wrote to the young Quaker William Penn in May 1670, following his ill treatment at the hands of the mayor of Cork.[10] In such instances, gentility carried precedence over religious uniformity, particularly where there was no evidence to suggest that the holding of heterodox religious opinions posed a threat to the safety of the state.

We are not in a position to know for certain what attracted Greatrakes to men like Muggleton in the 1670s. Nor is it possible to ascertain whether his friendship with Muggleton, as well as his close relationship with leading Muggletonians in Ireland such as Colonel Phaire and Major John Denison of Dublin,[11] represented a growing antipathy on Greatrakes' part to the doctrinal and ceremonial trappings of established religion. From the time that the first reports of his miraculous gift of healing began to circulate in 1665, there had been rumours of Greatrakes's involvement with the radical fringe in the previous decade. He was also widely reported to be an admirer of the Silesian mystic Jacob Boehme, which, it has been speculated,

---

[9] Penn dined with Greatrakes and Phaire in company with Captain Rous and Captain Wakeham on 28 April 1670. In the previous November, he entertained Colonel Phaire and Greatrakes' close companion and business partner, Sir Ames Meredith; I. Grubb (ed.), *My Irish Journal. 1669–1670 by William Penn* (London, 1952), 26, 51.

[10] Penn visited county Cork in 1669–70, ostensibly to resolve tenancy problems related to his estates there. However, he soon ran into trouble with the authorities on account of his religion. Fortunately for Penn, he was protected from persecution by the intercession of the Earl of Orrery, a family friend, who subsequently wrote to the young Quaker expressing 'much wonder that the Mayor of Corke [Matthew Deane] should give any Gentleman bee hee of what religion or sect soe ever such ill language as you send me word he gave you, for severall sorts of Religion is but variety of opinions, which certainly cannot make any man degenerate from being a Gentleman who was born soe'. Orrery's open-mindedness in religious matters, however, was tempered by his known preference, for reasons of state, for a single Reformed confession: 'I hope to see you write ere long as much in the defence of the Protestant religion, as you have for the profession of the Quaquers'; H. J. Cadbury, 'More Penn Correspondence, Ireland, 1669–1670', *Pennsylvania Magazine of History and Biography*, 73 (1949), 12–13.

[11] In 1699, Denison's daughter, Mary Marshall, recalled Greatrakes' visits twenty years earlier to her father's house in Dublin, where he cured, among countless others, her brother John; BL, Stowe MS 747, fo. 113. For correspondence between Denison and Muggleton, see 'A Volume of Spiritual Epistles', in *Works of Reeve and Muggleton*, iii, 457–63. Denison is also warmly remembered in a letter from Muggleton to the Cork merchant and acolyte, George Gamble, in August 1677; 'Supplement to the Book of Letters', in ibid. iii, 26. Gamble, like his father-in-law Robert Phaire, was a former Quaker. In 1675 he was instructed by his friend, Sir Thomas Southwell, to recoup all rents and arrears owing from Valentine Greatrakes for his lands in Limerick on pain of imprisonment (discussed further on pp. 166–7); BL, Add. MS 21,135, fos 46r–v. Further links between Greatrakes and the Cork Muggletonians are suggested by the payment of a debt for £250 in the stroker's will to Mrs Elizabeth Faggetor or Flaggator of Cork. Her husband, Henry, was another former associate of Phaire, who had converted with him from Quakerism to Muggletonianism some time after 1671. The Cork Quakers subsequently wrote approvingly of the sudden sickness and death that overcame him shortly after his conversion; RCBL, MS 80/B2/2, 285; K. L. Carroll, 'Quakers and Muggletonians in Seventeenth-Century Ireland', in D. Blamires, J. Greenwood, and A. Kerr (eds), *A Quaker Miscellany for Edward H. Milligan* (Manchester, 1985), 51, 54; 'Supplement to the Book of Letters', in *Works of Reeve and Muggleton*, iii, 11.

may have attracted him to the Behmenist Muggleton.[12] On balance, it is highly probable that Greatrakes had encountered such ideas in Ireland in the 1650s. Working alongside men like Phaire and his business partner, the Baptist Jerome Sankey, he must have come into frequent contact with the radical wing of the English Revolution. But his willingness to engage and associate with the spokes-men for that heterodox body of ideas does not of itself testify to an acceptance of their views on Greatrakes' part. He was not alone in this stance and like others he almost certainly withdrew support when radical thinking threatened to mutate into what others perceived as moral degeneracy. Indeed, as early as the mid 1650s, there is evidence, as we have seen, to suggest that Greatrakes was both attracted to specific aspects of contemporary radical thinking, while at the same time repelled by the practical immorality and atheism it often bred.

On 6 June 1655, official depositions reveal that one Lieutenant Valentine Greatrakes certified that in conference with a minister, Thomas Royle, he heard him utter 'divers blasphemous expressions'.[13] Unfortunately, we have no other details of this exchange, or information surrounding the nature of the ideas ex-pressed by Royle. Nor is it possible to ascertain with any certainty why Greatrakes was called upon in 1655 to give evidence against the clerical blasphemer. It is likely, however, that the prosecution of Royle and Greatrakes' deposition reflected the growing swing toward religious conservatism in Irish governing circles that at-tended the imminent displacement of the radical Fleetwood as lord deputy in favour of the more conservative Henry Cromwell in 1655. Greatrakes, along with numerous other army officers in Munster, faced suspicions about his political loy-alty and religious orthodoxy, a product, no doubt, of his close acquaintance and growing friendship with the radical Governor of Cork, Colonel Robert Phaire. Royle, like Greatrakes, had also fallen under the spell of Phaire, who used his political influence in the 1650s to both shelter and foster radical sectarianism in Cork and the surrounding neighbourhood. Royle himself looks suspiciously like a convert to Ranter notions and practices. In addition to blasphemy, he was accused in 1653 of bigamy and adultery. Later that year, it was reported in Ireland that his wife, Margaret Seney, was still married to her first husband, and that she 'was very lately carted in London for some notorious and scandalous misdemeanours'. The couple protested their innocence, but, despite being ordered to return to England,

---

[12] The suggestion is made by Barry Reay in his 'The Muggletonians: An Introductory Survey', in Hill, Reay and Lamont (eds), *The World of the Muggletonians*, 47–8. In addition to hinting darkly at Greatrakes' immorality, swearing and immoderate behaviour in touching women, Samuel Mather depicted the stroker as formerly 'a great Admirer of Boehmen' and 'a wild Behmenist' who had la-boured under 'the Highest Spiritual frenzie'; BL, Sloane MS 1926, fos 4v–5r. For the influence of Boehme on the radical sects of the 1650s, see K. V. Thomas, *Religion and the Decline of Magic: Studies in Popular Beliefs in Sixteenth- and Seventeenth-Century England* (London, 1971), 270–1; N. Smith, *Perfection Proclaimed: Language and Literature in English Radical Religion 1640–1660* (Oxford, 1989), 185–225; B. J. Gibbons, *Gender in Mystical and Occult Thought: Behmenism and Its Development in England* (Cambridge, 1996), 120–42; A. Hessayon, *'Gold Tried in the Fire': The Prophet Theauraujohn Tany and the English Revolution* (Aldershot, 2007), 284–324.

[13] RCBL, GS 2/7/3/20, 24. The accusation of blasphemy probably dates from January 1653, when an associate, Poole, was found not guilty of the same offence by the radical Chief Justice of Munster, John Cook; see p. 66n.

Royle was still under restraint in Cork a year later when he was ordered to leave Ireland before 10 June 'and not to return again...without Licence'.[14]

Greatrakes' admiration for Muggleton and his earlier engagement with radical civil war sectarianism suggests a consistent interest in, or attraction to, religious unorthodoxy. It is even possible that his mission to heal was partly inspired by his immersion in the radical ferment of the 1650s. Greatrakes' colleague and business partner, Jerome Sankey, like other leading Baptists, apparently claimed to exorcize possessed patients by the use of fasting and prayer. In 1660, his inveterate enemy, Sir William Petty, described how Sankey had attempted to cure one Mr Wadman by such methods.[15] The medical etiology employed by Sankey was, as we have seen, remarkably similar to that propounded by Greatrakes in order to explain the efficacy of his stroking in the 1660s. However, as much as Greatrakes may have been influenced by aspects of the radical culture that he encountered in the early 1650s, it does not follow that he was, or remained, a convert to the 'good old cause'. Nor did conformity to the Church of England after 1660 preclude respect for the ideas and beliefs of those who either opted out, or were excluded from, mainstream religious life. In the absence of conclusive evidence, the best we can say of Greatrakes' religious position after 1660, and his later attraction to self-styled prophets like Muggleton, is that it was entirely consistent with a theological outlook that embraced variety and open-mindedness. Although Greatrakes chose to remain within the Anglican fold, he, and others like him, campaigned for a comprehensive religious settlement that licensed peaceable dissent, as long as it did not lead to civil disturbances or subvert established norms of morality. It is worth repeating again that there is no evidence to suggest that he ever broke with communion from the established church after 1660. Prior to his death in 1683, for example, he requested that he should be buried in the parish church of Lismore, and he bequeathed a small legacy to the minister of Affane, Andrew Chaplin, whom he asked to read his funeral sermon.[16] His conformity is further suggested by his marriage to Alice, the

---

[14] Royle's career can be partially traced in CH, Lismore MS 29, 24 January 1653; T. C. Barnard, *Cromwellian Ireland: English Government and Reform in Ireland 1649–1660* (Oxford, 1975), 110n; RCBL, GS 2/7/3/20, 81–4, 89; *HMC Manuscripts of the Earl of Egmont* (London, 1905), i, 523. Phaire, too, was accused of dabbling with Ranterism; National Library of Wales, MS 11440D, fos 131, 133.

[15] W. Petty, *Reflections upon Some Persons and Things in Ireland, by Letters to and from Dr Petty. With Sir Hierome Sankey's Speech in Parliament* (London, 1660), 101–2. Petty was also responsible for exposing the 'fraudulent' cures of the Catholic healer, Father O'Finallty (see p. 62). In both cases, Petty's scepticism was founded upon a profound attachment to naturalistic explanations for such phenomena. Wadman, in Petty's eyes, was suffering from nothing more severe than 'a fit of melancholy', which was ultimately cured by a course of bloodletting. Unfortunately, Petty's response to Greatrakes' therapeutic skills is unrecorded. For relations between Petty, Greatrakes and the latter's brother, William, see pp. 166–8.

[16] RCBL, MS 80/B2/2, 285. Chaplin's first appointment was as vicar of nearby Dungarvan in 1655. He became vicar of Affane in 1662, and also served as prebend and vicar of Seskinan (1662), as well as vicar of Kilmolash (1664). In 1683, Chaplin appeared with Greatrakes' brother, William, as plaintiff in a case (unspecified) in the Court of Chancery in Tipperary; W. H. Rennison, *Succession List of the Bishops, Cathedral and Parochial Clergy of the Dioceses of Waterford and Lismore* (Waterford, 1922), 71, 138, 143, 162 and n., 207; RCBL, GS 2/7/3/20, 188; NAI, MS 4974, *sub* 1663; *Sixth Report of the Deputy Keeper of the Public Records in Ireland* (Dublin, 1874), 57.

daughter of the deceased Bishop of Elphin, Henry Tilson (1576–1655), following the death of his first wife, Ruth, in January 1678.[17] Little is known of Greatrakes' relations with his new in-laws, but on the limited evidence of his will, they would appear to have been cordial. Several of his wife's relations are mentioned in person, including his brother-in-law, Thomas Tilson, who had successfully petitioned the King in 1662 for compensation following the sufferings and losses endured by his father prior to his death in 1655.[18]

A MEETING OF LIKE MINDS: GREATRAKES AND EDMUND BERRY GODFREY

As patchy and inconclusive as the evidence is regarding Greatrakes' specific religious and political beliefs, both before and after 1660, some further light is cast by a series of letters that he received from various friends and acquaintances in London between 1666 and 1672. Original copies of these letters, including thirteen from Sir Edmund Berry Godfrey, are currently deposited in the National Library of Ireland. Oddly, given the celebrity of Godfrey, they have until recently attracted little interest among historians of Restoration Britain. They do, however, contain a wealth of information with regard to the religious and political concerns of the correspondents, as well as testifying to the intense loyalty and devotion that many of his most ardent admirers felt for the charismatic Irish healer. This is especially evident in the letters of Godfrey, the London magistrate, whose alleged murder at the hands of Catholic plotters in 1678 was to spark a major political crisis in Britain (see Fig. 8).[19]

---

[17] Ruth's recent death is alluded to in a letter of James Banfield to Sir Robert Southwell, dated 16 January 1678; BL, Add. MS 38,015, fo. 190r. Hayman mistakenly gives the date of her death as 1675; Rev. S. Hayman, 'Notes on the Family of Greatrakes', *The Antiquary. Quarterly Archaeological Journal and Review*, 4 (1863–4), 90.

[18] RCBL, MS 80/B2/2, 285; Bodl., Carte MS 42, fo. 633. In April 1665, Thomas Tilson was soliciting the Duke of Ormond for a place in the Registry. Ormond had previously assisted Tilson in securing 'imployments in your Graces Court in Tipperary'; Bodl., Carte MS 34, fos 94r–v; see also, ibid. MS 160, f.32v. The family's struggle to gain recompense following their father's death is referred to in a petition of 1656, which mentions the plight of the Bishop's four children, including Alice; RCBL, GS 2/7/3/20, 16. Bishop Tilson, a friend of Strafford and Archbishop Laud, was made Bishop of Elphin in 1639. He fled to England in 1645 and resided in Yorkshire, where he was much reduced financially but continued to preach and bestow the sacraments according to the Anglican liturgy. His daughter, Alice Greatrakes, née Tilson, possessed estates at Meddop Hall in county Wexford.

[19] NLI, MS 4728. The significance of these letters for historians keen to explore the mental world of Godfrey has now been fully discussed and analysed by Alan Marshall. For a general account of the correspondence between Greatrakes and Godfrey, and the close relationship between the two men, see his *The Strange Death of Edmund Godfrey: Plots and Politics in Restoration London* (Stroud, 1999), 36–9. For a more detailed analysis, with which I broadly concur, see A. Marshall, 'The Westminster Magistrate and the Irish Stroker: Sir Edmund Berry Godfrey and Valentine Greatrakes, Some Unpublished Correspondence', *Historical Journal*, 40 (1997), 499–505. The provenance of these letters is something of a mystery. Marshall mistakenly claims that the letter book was donated to the National Library of Ireland in the late nineteenth century by a John B. Dowling of Dublin. In fact, they were purchased from Mr Dowling in 1953. The letters themselves were almost certainly part of a larger batch, now dispersed or lost. All attempts to trace these, including correspondence with Mr Dowling's descendants, have proved unsuccessful. For a complete transcript of the letters, see Appendix 3.

Fig. 8. Playing card depicting the murder of Sir Edmund Berry Godfrey in 1678. Engraving, English school, late seventeenth century. The Bridgeman Art Library. Godfrey's 'murder' at the hands of papist conspirators, and the widely held belief that Catholics, led by James, Duke of York, were seeking to overthrow the Protestant settlement in England, led to a resumption of intense religious and political conflict in England after 1678.

Godfrey first met Greatrakes in London during the Irishman's brief visit to the capital in the spring of 1666. Immediately impressed by his gift and the authenticity of his cures, he subsequently offered Greatrakes refuge from the hordes of sick people who eagerly sought his help and opened his house in Westminster as a makeshift surgery. Following Greatrakes' return to Ireland in May 1666, the two men entered into a voluminous, and often intense, correspondence. Though very different in personality (Godfrey was gloomy and introspective by nature), the two men shared similar religious and political concerns, as is evident from Godfrey's frequent comments, often judgemental, on events in London and at court. They also shared a common interest in entrepreneurial activity. While in London, Greatrakes had used the social networks that he had made while healing as an opportunity to further his own, multifaceted business concerns. Godfrey, a wealthy merchant trading in timber and coal, proved an eager and willing partner.[20] Above all, the common bond that seems to have sealed the two men's friendship was their shared commitment to a providential vision of the world, in which every event, no matter how large or small, formed part of a grandiose divine plan. Godfrey clearly believed that Greatrakes' capacity to heal provided direct evidence of God's perpetual supervision of, and intervention in, the day-to-day lives of men and women. But equally significant in terms of one of the central tenets of this book, Godfrey's faith in the providential success of Greatrakes' cures reflected the London magistrate's wider vision of the Restoration body politic, and his desire to see an end to civil and religious strife. Writing shortly after the great fire that consumed most of the city of London in September 1666, Godfrey thus wrote of his growing fear that the recent troubles in Scotland, and the continuing tumults in England, might once again threaten to unleash civil war upon the three kingdoms:

> I fear the same spirit of devision, have entered into both houses of Parliament which makes an Ill aspect over the whole Nation. I pray God to heal our breaches, & compose the differences amongst us, for that we are almost at our witts ends here, what betwixt the apprehensions of Danger from the Fannaticks at one hand & The Papists on the other, we scarce look upon ourselves in a secure or safe condition on any side, beside the Common enemy abroad watching for an advantage & opportunity to destroy us both.[21]

Elsewhere in Godfrey's correspondence with Greatrakes, his ambivalent attitude to religious dissent and the growing debate on toleration is evident. In February 1667, for example, he refers to the increase in 'Fanatick Meetings about Town... not without some connivance of Authority', and the general expectation that 'Tolleration...will certainly be granted very suddenly'.[22] Reading between the lines, Godfrey, like so many of Greatrakes' supporters and patrons in 1666, would appear to have favoured comprehension over toleration as a solution to the religious divisions of the time. Toleration implied acceptance of a permanent rift in the body politic. Instead, Godfrey, like many nonconformists who faced the full rigour of legal coercion, remained wedded to the notion of a single church that embraced minor doctrinal and ceremonial differences and might include moderate dissenters such as his friend Colonel Owen of Mortlake. Gentlemen like Owen, despite his nonconformist connections (for which, see p. 94 and n), did not fall under the description of 'fanatick' in Godfrey's vocabulary. For others, however, it was a thin and ever-changing dividing line that separated reasonable from unacceptable dissent. Godfrey himself seems to have blown hot and cold on this

---

[20] The mutual business concerns of the two men are referred to throughout their correspondence.

[21] NLI, MS 4728, 6. Interestingly, Godfrey was readily convinced that the great fire, though clearly an act of 'the immediate hand of God', was effected by the 'evill Instruments of men', i.e. Catholic fifth columnists; ibid.

[22] Ibid. 9.

particular issue. His most bitter comments, however, were reserved for those in government circles, who in true Machiavellian fashion manipulated religious divisions as and when it best suited. In January 1672, for example, he reported attempts by the government to placate the nonconformist interest prior to a renewal of war with the Dutch. Godfrey was under no illusions as to what was intended by such political machinations. Once they had 'served their own Turn' and the Dutch were defeated, it would simply be a matter of time before 'a third party of different principles to theirs will be most in Favour'.[23]

Partly in response to policies such as these, Godfrey felt increasingly alienated from the government and the court, and became more and more outspoken and critical in his comments to Greatrakes regarding the nature of royal government. He frequently voiced his disquiet as to the direction of foreign policy, particularly with regard to the pro-French stance of the early 1670s. At the same time, he was becoming alarmed by tales of corruption and the generally effete and morally de-based character of life at the court of Charles II. Whether or not Greatrakes shared these views is unclear, though it seems evident that Godfrey expected that his opin-ions would meet with a sympathetic response from his Irish friend. Greatrakes' extolling of the virtues of a simple country life over that of the corrupt city cer-tainly struck a responsive chord in the cynical Godfrey. In February 1667, for ex-ample, Godfrey was provoked to a lengthy disquisition on the weakness and immorality of women, and the promiscuity of court life, after reading a letter from Greatrakes in which he extolled the virtues of a 'Retired, Innocent and vertuously Industrious, country Life, which ingenious description of yours, put me in mind of Paradice'.[24] Indeed, Godfrey had become so disenchanted with life in London in the late 1660s that he frequently intimated to Greatrakes that he would soon visit his old friend at his country seat in Ireland, and might even retire there for good, though in the event he does not appear to have made the journey.

The appeal of the country way of life over that of the court and city implied, within the context of seventeenth-century political discourse, a measure of support for the political opposition of the day. Reading between the lines—many of the early letters are heavily self-censored[25]—Godfrey was becoming increasingly uneasy with the general tone and direction of government policy, and was particularly concerned by the manner in which the generality of the House of Commons was willing to concede much of that body's authority and independence in return for

---

[23] Ibid. 25. Godfrey's lenient attitude as a JP towards dissent is evident from the complaints levelled against him by various informers in 1676; see TNA, PC 2/65, 249, 296, 335.

[24] NLI, MS 4728, 8; cf. Greatrakes' comment, directed to Lady Ranelagh's physician, Dr Daniel Coxe, that 'might I gaine a £1000 a yeare duringe my life I would neither live in a Citty (to loose the happiness of my innocent Countery life) nor take money from others for that which God had freely bestowed on me'; Boyle, *Correspondence*, iv, 102.

[25] See, for example, Godfrey's admonition to Greatrakes to 'be very carefull of what you write & to whome for that many have sufferd lately for being too free in their intelligences and occurrences, Es-pecially now that letters are soe often broake open, & exposed to the various scanning & Censuring of those to whom they were never writ.'; NLI, MS 4728, 3. A few months later, he reiterated his advice, asking that he 'write spearingly' of personal and public news from Ireland 'for that I shall easily guess at more then will be convenient for you to express'; ibid. 5.

profit and place. During the course of 1671, Godfrey was principally of the view that the hopes of the nation lay with the House of Lords, whose members, he felt, acted with far more integrity and independence than those of the lower chamber. In particular, it was the Lords that had resisted a new excise bill that would have effectively granted the king financial independence for the foreseeable future, a measure that Godfrey believed would have called into doubt the very existence of parliament.[26]

Similar concerns are evident in the letters of lesser known correspondents with Greatrakes dating from April and May 1670. In all these letters, there is an undercurrent of sympathy for the situation of moderate nonconformists like Thomas Manton (d.1677), who was then in prison, as well as support for the Duke of Buckingham, who had recently been restored to royal favour. Buckingham is singled out for praise in one letter for his opposition to the passage of the second Conventicle Act, which, the correspondent assures Greatrakes, is not to be so much feared now that the Lords, prompted by Buckingham, had 'taken away the sting of the said act, and with a little Discretion to be shewn as well in the Nonconformist, as Justice of the Peace, it will not prove so terrible a Law, as prima facie, it appeared to be'.[27] Others, however, were not so readily convinced of the benign nature of the new legislation. Later the same month John Adams reported to Greatrakes that since the passing of the Act, sixty MPs and hundreds of magistrates had resigned their judicial posts 'upon account of their unwillingness, to put in execution the new Act against Conventicles, which they apprehend to be very severe'. A month later, in May 1670, another correspondent informed Greatrakes that the only means by which the Act might be implemented was through the use of the military:

> There are few sober or understanding men left in [the commission of the peace], But such as must act with assistance of the Military Power, who 'tis believd will be encouraged to put affronts & give Blows to some of those that shall be found at those Meetings, on purpose to provoke them to a Resistance... That so the greater advantage may be taken against them.[28]

As a magistrate in Ireland, the ramifications of the new Act would not have been lost on Greatrakes. They were also an immediate concern for his friend, Godfrey, a JP in Westminster, who during the course of the 1660s had shown himself to be broadly sympathetic to the plight of moderate nonconformists. For men of business like Greatrakes and Godfrey, there were also pressing economic reasons for seeking to moderate judicial persecution of dissent. The demands of commerce and economic necessity frequently overrode religious distinctions, and many, Greatrakes and Godfrey included, fully appreciated the negative impact of religious persecution on the free flow of trade. Godfrey's correspondence with his Irish friend is, not surprisingly, replete with references to his own financial concerns and problems, as well as containing frequent offers of assistance to his new-found acquaintance. Among other schemes mentioned by Godfrey, Greatrakes would

---

[26] Ibid. 26–7.   [27] Ibid. 15–17.   [28] Ibid. 19–20, 22.

appear to have formed an embryonic business partnership with Sir William Smith, who was present on numerous occasions to witness Greatrakes' cures in 1666.[29] Greatrakes also sought Godfrey's expert advice on a proposal to export wood from his Irish lands. In time, Godfrey's role as a middle man and facilitator seems to have given way to more active involvement in the day-to-day business affairs of his Irish friend which, by the early 1670s, were once again threatened by a new cash flow crisis. The tone of Godfreys's last two letters suggests that these developments were placing a strain on their friendship. Unfortunately, the loss of the rest of this correspondence makes it impossible to ascertain the degree to which their relationship may have suffered as a result of Greatrakes' financial difficulties.

Though Greatrakes had successfully weathered the threatened storm posed by the Irish Act of Settlement (all his Irish estates were confirmed in 1666, a fact welcomed by Godfrey in a letter of November in that year), various sources suggest that by 1670 he was once again in dire financial straits. With interests in land scattered across various counties of southern and central Ireland, his income from rents and other sources was clearly insufficient to cover the costs of his various investments. As late as 1674, he was still being pressed by the corporation of Exeter to repay in full those debts incurred when he purchased a share in the city's Irish debentures in 1656.[30] Meanwhile, closer to home he was being pursued by a number of irate debtors, including Sir William Petty (1623–1687) and Sir Robert Southwell (1635–1702), who faced consistent obstruction from Greatrakes and his family.[31] For over two years, from 1671 to 1673, Petty attempted to extricate unpaid rents from Greatrakes' brother, William, for properties at Hoarstown in county Wexford. Initial efforts were made by Petty's cousin, Sir John Petty, who reminded William Greatrakes in 1671 that it was now two years since he took out the lease on these lands and that in that time he 'hath not received a farthing rent out of it'. At the same time, he bemoaned his inability to contact William's brother, Valentine, who would appear to have counter-signed the lease (in later correspondence, Petty clearly felt that Valentine was 'properly my Tenant').[32] Matters became more urgent in 1672, when

---

[29] Smith was a leading proponent of Greatrakes' cures, providing testimonials in ten cases that included three of his own servants. Given the date of some of these, he may well have been involved in supervising their publication in Greatrakes' absence. Smith's religious and political position is difficult to determine. He was probably described correctly in 1682 as a trimmer and a time-server, who had veered between support for the King and his enemies in the 1640s and 1650s and who continued to blow hot and cold with regard to the prosecution of nonconformity after 1660; Henning, iii, 445–6.

[30] It is clear from the record in the Chamber Act Book that Greatrakes' prevarication and delaying tactics, which dragged on for years, radically reduced the amount of money that he finally paid to the corporation in 1675. Exeter's rulers, not surprisingly, expressed themselves only too glad to bring an end to this 'long and troublesome business'; see DRO, ECA 11, 203 and *passim*.

[31] Sir Robert Southwell was a distant cousin of Greatrakes. His family had moved to Munster in the early years of the seventeenth century, where his great uncle, Sir Thomas Southwell (d.1626), married Anne Harris (d.1636), a celebrated poet and the daughter of Greatrakes' great grandfather Sir Thomas Harris. Greatrakes later stroked Anne's second husband Colonel Henry Sibthorpe (d.1672) in London in 1666. Sibthorpe was a soldier who had served in Munster before 1627, and later fought for the King in the Civil War. In his will of 1670, he left various bequests to his faithful servant Joan Mulys, who was probably related to another of Greatrakes' patients, Richard Mulys (see pp. 96n.–97n.); J. Klene (ed.), *The Southwell-Sibthorpe Commonplace Book* (Tempe, Arizona, 1997), xix–xx; *ODNB*, sub Johnson, Robert; Greatrakes, *Brief Account*, 72; *CSP Ireland, 1625–1632*, 293; Green, *CPCC*, ii, 1375; TNA, PROB 11/340, fos 369r–370r.

Petty travelled to Ireland with the specific intention of forcing all his tenants who owed him money to pay up in order that he might pay off his English debts. Again, the tone of Sir William's initial contact with his 'cousin', William Greatrakes, was friendly and gently admonitory and he concluded by exchanging pleasantries and wishing his wife to be remembered to him and his spouse. However, the mild tone did not last long. Gentle persuasion soon turned to threats, and in November 1672 Petty tried to put pressure on Valentine to settle the debt. When this failed, Petty resorted to the threat of legal action, though no details of the outcome appear in the surviving documentation.[33] The cause of the protracted dispute with Southwell were the leases on lands in county Limerick that Greatrakes had purchased from his brother-in-law, Sir William Godolphin (1635–1696), in 1668, shortly before the latter's departure for Spain.[34] In his absence, Godolphin had wisely delegated Southwell to act as his deputy, and it was in this capacity that he wrote to Godolphin in July 1670, informing him of Greatrakes' failure to pay the last year's rent.[35] Four years later, Godolphin sold out to Sir Robert, and within a year Greatrakes was once again being pestered by his new landlord for overdue rents. When Greatrakes defaulted, Sir Robert initiated legal proceedings through his attorney, James Banfield of Kinsale, in order to secure repossession of the estates. Under concerted pressure, Greatrakes finally paid his arrears, but within two years the whole cycle of default and threats of repossession was repeated. Protracted legal debate ensued, but Greatrakes refused to budge, claiming that his problems were not of his own making, but were rather caused by obdurate and penurious sub-tenants.[36]

During the early course of these difficulties, it is apparent that Greatrakes was not averse to leaving his business transactions to the care of his first wife, Ruth, who on at least one occasion during her husband's absence entered into a fierce debate with Sir Robert Southwell's attorney at Affane over the issue of the Limerick

---

[32] BL, Add. MS 72,859, fo. 42r. For Petty's relationship with Ireland that went back to the 1650s, see F. Harris, 'Ireland as a Laboratory: The Archive of Sir William Petty', in M. Hunter (ed.), *Archives of the Scientific Revolution: The Formation and Exchange of Ideas in Seventeenth-Century Europe* (Woodbridge, 1998), 73–90.

[33] These protracted negotiations can be followed in BL, Add. MS 72,858, fols 24r, 35v, 41r, 41v, 53v, 97r. Petty was probably related to the Greatrakes' through William Greatrakes' wife, about whom nothing is known.

[34] For a copy of the lease agreement, which stipulated that Greatrakes would pay an annual rent of £240, see BL, Add. MS 21,135, fo. 41. These lands, part of a vast estate expropriated from the Cromwellian financier Samuel Avery (see p. 80n.), are also referred to in Godolphin's will of March 1669, where he bequeathed them to his sister, Ruth Greatrakes, and her children; *HMC House of Lords MSS, 1697–1699* (London, 1905), 123.

[35] BL, Add. MS 34,331, fos 150v, 153r. For Southwell's letter to Greatrakes, requesting immediate payment of the rents for Cornello in county Limerick, see BL, Add. MS 38,015, fo. 126r.

[36] One of Greatrakes' principal debtors was his 'cousin', Barry Drewe, of Ballyduff, county Waterford, who was refusing to pay Greatrakes until an agreement could be reached over the boundaries of his lands at Rushine in county Limerick. For over three years, Banfield attempted to bring the two men together to resolve their differences, but the matter was still unsettled in 1679; see BL, Add. MS 38,015, fos 161r, 164r, 196r, 249r. Drewe was related to Greatrakes via his second marriage to Ruth Nettles of Toureen, the daughter of Greatrakes' sister, Mary; see Appendix 1. Greatrakes also referred in 1677 to an outstanding debt of £170 owed to him by Ensign Thomas Gibbons, who held a sub-tenancy in county Limerick. Gibbons was probably the son of Captain John Gibbons, of Miltown, county Cork, who was pardoned along with Greatrakes in 1661 and held lands in lease from him; see BL, Add. MSS 25,692, fos 34v, 35r [inverted]; 38,015, fo. 179v; *CSP Ireland, 1660–1662*, 317; Bodl., Carte MS 165, fo. 46.

leases. In the event, Greatrakes put forward various proposals and schemes to counter Sir Robert's suggestion that a new lease should be issued, all the while stalling for more time in order to raise the necessary cash. At one stage in the proceedings, it was even suggested by Banfield that Greatrakes was in no position to bargain as he had already entered into a new agreement with Sir Thomas Southwell, a kinsman of Sir Robert, over the lands in question. Ultimately, there is no evidence that any agreement was reached, though it may be significant that no mention is made of the Limerick lands in Greatrakes' will of 1683.[37]

During the course of these exchanges, Sir Robert's attorney noted that one of Greatrakes' stalling tactics involved reference to Sir Edmund Berry Godfrey, who, it was alleged, was enmeshed in Greatrakes' financial and legal transactions as late as May 1677.[38] Ever since the two men had first met in 1666, Greatrakes had been keen to capitalize on Godfrey's business connections in the city of London. From the earliest letters, Godfrey had promised to do all in his powers to promote Greatrakes' various commercial adventures, in particular his interest in the Irish salt works of Sir William Smith.[39] He subsequently acted as Greatrakes' surrogate and agent in London, and may well have invested in some of the Irishman's business ventures. Godfrey's intelligence and connections proved vital, none more so than in providing access to the court of James, Duke of York. In 1671, Greatrakes was anxious to purchase the lease of lands held by the Duke in county Limerick (probably to consolidate his already impressive holdings there), and in order to set the wheels in motion had begun negotiations with the Duke's land agent in Ireland, John Shadwell.[40] Godfrey had met Shadwell in London and reported back to Greatrakes that while reluctant to invest money himself, he would do all in his power to promote his interests with the Duke's commissioners with whom he claimed to have 'a very Good Interest'. Godfrey's intelligence proved decisive. By September he was advising Greatrakes to break all contact with Shadwell, and to transfer his attentions to one Turner, who, Godfrey had it on good authority, was now responsible for conducting the Duke's business in Ireland.[41]

Somewhat surprisingly, Godfrey's most recent biographer has made little of these contacts between Godfrey and the court of the Duke of York, while acknowledging his later friendship with other intimates of the Duke such as John Grove and Edward Coleman. The events surrounding Godfrey's death in 1678, which catapulted the country into a political crisis, remains one of the great unsolved

[37] The protracted dispute over the lands of Cornello can be followed in BL, Add. MS 38,015, fos 161r, 164r, 166r, 168r, 177v–178r, 179r–v, 181, 188, 190r, 196r, 201r, 249r. Some indication of the difficulties created for Irish landowners by the passage of the Irish Cattle Bill is suggested by the fact that one of Greatrakes' proposals was dependant upon the revival of the cattle trade with England; ibid. fo. 179v.

[38] BL, Add. MS 38,015, fo. 179r.

[39] Smith had considerable interests in salt production in Kent that were severely disrupted by the Dutch attack on the Medway in 1667. A number of Smith's servants who were cured by Greatrakes had become ill while working at his Kent salt works; NLI, MS 4728, 2–3, 4; Greatrakes, *Brief Account*, 49–50.

[40] Shadwell was the father of the celebrated opposition playwright, Thomas Shadwell (d.1692). The lands in question were among those previously held by the regicide, Edmund Ludlow, which had been granted to the Duke under the Act of Settlement. For Shadwell's role in this process, see NLI, MS 31, 29–30, 53, 85, 93, 104.

[41] NLI, MS 4728, 28–9, 29, 31, 31–2. Godfrey seems to have been on particularly intimate terms with the Duke's servants, Matthew and Charles Wren.

mysteries of English history. Unfortunately, little is known about Godfrey's state of mind immediately prior to his death, and much that has been written on the subject is highly speculative based as it is on the second hand evidence of witnesses and friends. Even more frustrating, perhaps, is the possibility that further evidence regarding Godfrey's involvement in the Popish Plot scare and his subsequent death did exist, at least until the early years of the eighteenth century, and may have formed part of the original correspondence between Greatrakes and Godfrey that now only survives in fragments. This much is suggested by the fact that these letters are known to have formed part of a much larger collection which, according to one who claimed to know Greatrakes well, contained 'many remarkable things, & the best & truest Secret History in K[ing] Charles II's Reign'. The author of this statement, written in March 1744, was Alexander Phaire, the son of Colonel Robert Phaire, one of Greatrakes' oldest and most intimate friends. In a series of letters to an unnamed correspondent, the aged Phaire gave a detailed, but often flawed, account of the stroker's life and career, which almost certainly suffered from the fact that it was based on childhood reminiscences dating back over sixty years. On the crucial issue of the correspondence, however, there seems little reason to doubt that Phaire had personal sight of this invaluable cache of letters which he claimed numbered 104 in total.[42] Two questions arise: what might they have told us about the Popish Plot and the death of Godfrey; and what role, if any, did Greatrakes play in these unfolding events?

There are grounds for suggesting that Greatrakes may have been implicated, at least tangentially, in these events because of family connections with the entourage of the Duke of York. Central to this hypothesis is the role played by Greatrakes' brother-in-law Sir William Godolphin in the Plot. Godolphin, who converted to Catholicism in 1671, may well have acted as an intermediary in Greatrakes' attempts to secure the leases of the Duke's Irish estates in the 1670s. As a protégé of Lord Arlington, he seems to have pursued an active, if discreet, policy of promoting the interests of his new faith in Ireland and, not surprisingly, was exposed by Titus Oates as a leading conspirator in the Popish Plot. Oates claimed that Godolphin was to be rewarded with the post of Lord Privy Seal following the accession of James.[43] The most intriguing aspect of Oates' evidence, however, concerns his oblique comment to the effect that Godolphin was not simply a papist, but one who had 'perverted a kinsman of his own'.[44] This may well be a reference to none other than Greatrakes' own son, William (d.1686), who had recently matriculated at Trinity College, Dublin. Six years later, in October 1685, he was residing with Sir William in Madrid, and was suitably impressed by the status, dignity and high esteem in which his uncle was held. At the time, Godolphin was preparing to

---

[42] BL, Add. MS 4291, fos 150v–151r.

[43] Henning, ii, 407–8. In January 1676, an anonymous letter was circulating in Ireland claiming that Sir William Godolphin, on the authority of the Lord Lieutenant, was promoting the view that 'it was the kings intentions to allow Saecular Priests to say Masse publickly or to that effect'. The author further claimed that the Earl of Orrery believed that 'Arlington was in the bottome of it'; NLI, MS 33, fo. 248a.

[44] *Journal of the House of Lords*, vol. 13 [1675–81] (London, 1771), 324.

embark for England, where he was hopeful of preferment at the Catholic court of the newly crowned James II. Of his uncle, William Greatrakes admiringly wrote:

> Hee is generally considered as one of the greatest proofes of the ould Proverb that a Prophet is least Esteemed in his own Country, it being certaine that the commendation of his person & ability is universal throughout the greatest Courts of Europe & the services of his Embassy more usefull to the National interests & crown of England then those of many other Ministers have been, his reputation in this Court is to the highest degree... & yet it seemeth that the consideration of him at home doth not in any degree answer his Name abroad, which I think you will attribute in a great part to the misfortunes that have overtaken him in the late extravagant troubles of England, and partly to the Mallice and Emulation of particular men, which may bee more obvious to you there then explainable by mee here.[45]

Whether or not Valentine Greatrakes' eldest son shared his uncle's religious faith is, on the basis of all available evidence, impossible to determine. But the fact that the Irish healer had profited considerably from his contacts, via his wife's well-connected brother, with the court of the Duke of York, and that these may well have paved the way for further acquisitions of land in county Limerick, lends credence to the idea that he was becoming increasingly compromised, religiously at least, by such relations. His friendship with Godfrey, a man known to harbour sympathy for persecuted Catholics as well as Protestant dissenters, may have brought him further into the orbit of court Catholicism and may go some way to explaining the possibility of his son's attraction to Godolphin and his uncle's faith. As for Godfrey, one can only speculate on the contents of the lost letters with Greatrakes, which, if Colonel Phaire's aged son is to be believed, intimated at close links between Godfrey and court circles. In pursuing Greatrakes' interests with the Duke's servants and entourage, he ran the risk of becoming fatally compromised. Outwardly a respectable Protestant magistrate of unblemished character, Godfrey had led something of a secret life as a covert sympathizer and hanger-on at the court of the Catholic heir to the throne in the 1670s. When the security of his position was jeopardized by the exposures and hit-and-miss speculations of Titus Oates in 1678, he was placed in an almost impossible position. Under the circumstances, suicide may have been one of the few options open to one of Greatrakes' most devoted friends.[46]

---

[45] G. D. Burtchaell and T. U. Sadleir (eds), *Alumni Dublinenses: A Register of the Students, Graduates, Professors and Provosts of Trinity College in the University of Dublin, 1593–1860* (Dublin, 1935), 343; BL, Add. MS 28,051, fos 208r–v. William Greatrakes married Mary, the daughter of Jonah Wheeler, of Greenan, county Kilkenny, in December 1683. He died on 27 September 1686. His wife was pregnant at the time of his death, but the child, a son, died shortly after birth; Hayman, 'Notes on the Family of Greatrakes', 93; RCBL, MS 80/B2/2, 285; Appendix 1. William's father-in-law was the son of Jonah Wheeler, Bishop of Ossory.

[46] This is the verdict of Godfrey's most recent biographer, who assembles a mass of supporting, though largely circumstantial, evidence to suggest that Godfrey took his own life; see Marshall, *Strange Death of Edmund Godfrey*, 180–5. Godfrey's deep-seated friendship with Greatrakes, which may, as Marshall implies, have owed something to the London merchant's repressed homosexuality, is also evident in Godfrey's will of 1677 in which he left his Irish friend £10 'for mourning who I am sure will truly weare it for my sake'; TNA, PROB 11/359, fo. 357v.

Greatrakes himself did not long survive his old friend. Details of the last few years of his life are sketchy. From what remains it is none the less evident that he continued to play an important role in the life of his community, both as magistrate and local dignitary. Outwardly at least, Greatrakes' life was respectable and conformist. He also continued to practise his healing gifts, though without the publicity of former years.[47] As late as November 1680, a woman named Osborne recorded observing Greatrakes' stroking at the house of Mrs Denison in Dublin. On the basis of her testimony, he was still capable of drawing large crowds of patients and inquisitive onlookers. His methods had not changed. She reported that he continued to minister to rich and poor alike, and never for financial reward. She also provided an interesting description and character reference, alluding to his wealth (£1,000 a year) and great charity toward the sick. Above all, however, she corroborated earlier depictions of Greatrakes as a religious moderate and conformist, who continued to heal 'not to keep up any Sect or Partty'. He was, she concluded, 'a Church of England Man, but no Bigot', one who appeared to 'vallu any Man for being good, what ever Church he is of'.[48] In 1681, he was serving as a JP in county Tipperary, and one of the last official acts of his life was to sign, along with his son, William, a loyal declaration to the King in the wake of the abortive Rye House Plot in September 1683. Two months later, Greatrakes was dead, buried in all probability at the parish church of Affane, rather than Lismore as he had stipulated in his last will and testament.[49] He was rapidly followed to the grave by his second wife Alice and two sons, William and Edmund (d.1691 or 1692).[50]

---

[47] Greatrakes' powers were also subjected to public disparagement at this time as they became conflated with those of another charismatic healer, the Duke of Monmouth. In 1681, amid growing tension related to the imminent meeting of Parliament at Oxford, Tory propagandists took the opportunity to deride Greatrakes as a 'sot' whose cures were summarily dismissed as 'Feat-Tricks' long forgotten. More importantly, they paled into insignificance alongside those of Monmouth, who was depicted as a cheat or seventh son, 'the Great Mountibank of our sick State'; 'A Canto upon the Miraculous Cure of the King's Evil, performed by his Grace the D of M', in *A Collection of Wonderful Miracles, Ghosts, and Visions* (London, 1681), 4. Harold Weber has convincingly suggested that the attribution of this work to the Whig publisher Harris was almost certainly spurious and represented part of a wider campaign orchestrated by the Tories to bring the cause of the Duke and exclusion into disrepute; H. Weber, *Paper Bullets: Print and Kingship under Charles II* (Lexington: Kentucky, 1996), 77–81.

[48] Bailey, 'Andrew Marvell and Valentine Greatraks, the Stroker', 62–3. The anonymous author refers to Greatrakes' acquaintance with her brother, Osborn. It is tempting to speculate that this was Greatrakes' near neighbour and business partner, Nicholas Osborne, of Cappagh, county Waterford, for whom see page 100n.

[49] Bodl., Carte MS 59, fo. 247; NLI, MS 11,960, 212. By his will, dated 20 November 1683 and proved on 26 April 1684, Greatrakes asked to be interred in the church at Lismore. He left numerous bequests, as well as settling various debts, granting all his lands in England to his eldest son William. The patents for his English estates lay in the hands of his 'trusty friends' Roger Pomeroy of Sandridge and George Newton of Allaleigh of Devon. He also granted a portion of £1,000 to the wife of his younger son, Edmund; RCBL, MS 80/B2/2, 285. For Pomeroy (1629–1708), a landowner, MP for Dartmouth and opponent of exclusion, see Henning, iii, 261–2.

[50] For an abstract of the will of Alice Greatrakes of Meddop Hall, dated 26 March 1684 and proved 26 January 1685, see RCBL, MS 80/B2/2, 285. For William Greatrakes, see above note 45. Valentine's younger son Edmund, described as under twenty-five in his brother's will in 1685, married Anne, the daughter of Thomas Wilcox, a wealthy glass manufacturer from Bristol, on 18 May 1687. He made his will on 30 April 1691 and was dead by 3 June 1692, when it was proved; Bristol Record Office, will of Edmund Greatrakes.

'INHABITING THE BORDERS OF THE SPIRITUAL AND MATERIAL WORLD': GREATRAKES' PLACE IN HISTORY

Valentine Greatrakes was witness to, and often a participant in, some of the most memorable events of the seventeenth century. Forced to flee his native Ireland in the wake of a major uprising of the majority Catholic population, his formative, adolescent years were spent in Devon, a county torn apart by civil war and growing social, religious, and political unrest. Too young to play an active role in these events, he subsequently returned to Ireland where he played a minor, though nonetheless significant, part in the Cromwellian conquest and settlement of his native land. Profiteering from place and patronage, he rapidly resumed his familial claims to land in Munster in the 1650s and was, by the end of the decade, firmly established there as a gentleman landowner and member of the local ruling elite. The Restoration of the monarchy in 1660, however, threatened all these gains. In common with others of his social ilk, he now stood accused of profiteering at the expense of his loyal, Catholic neighbours, and faced the loss of those lands and estates accumulated in the previous decade. While Greatrakes once again weathered this particular storm, he must have been only too aware of the delicate state of the balance of power in Ireland in the early 1660s. Like so many others of his class, Greatrakes was dependent upon a fragile alliance of disparate interest groups and parties—soldiers and adventurers from England, as well as native Irish Protestants—whose ills, I have argued, were the original focus of Greatrakes' divine mission to heal the sick in these years. Recognizing that such complaints were not restricted to the body politic of Ireland, Greatrakes subsequently brought his gift of healing to England where, in 1666, he became the focus of public attention, attracting vast crowds of patients and onlookers, among whom were to be found leading figures in the religious and political establishment of both the capital and country. Greatrakes' appearance in the limelight, however, was brief. Within months, Greatrakes mania had subsided and little more was heard, publicly at least, of the man and his charismatic claims to heal the sick and maimed. His death in 1683 passed largely unnoticed, by which time the British state was once again entering another critical phase in which a resurgent monarchy set out to crush all religious and political dissent in the wake of the Exclusion Crisis and the abortive attempt to assassinate Charles II and his brother and future heir James, Duke of York.

Throughout these tumultuous years, Greatrakes had shown himself, above all else, to be a survivor. Living in an age of flux and uncertainty, he frequently came into contact and forged partnerships with a wide range of people, whose backgrounds and beliefs were very different from his own. To some extent, as I suggest in chapter 2, such alliances were born out of economic necessity, a product of his desire to restore the financial and material interests of his family in the radically altered circumstances of the 1650s. Greatrakes, a loyal Anglican and royalist by upbringing and education, soon established close links with an emerging radical fringe, leaving him open to the charge years later that he was little other than a closet radical himself, or worse an opportunist timeserver or trimmer who 'being of no Religion himself, is indifferent what Religion others should be of'.[51] While there is little doubt that Greatrakes' motives in working closely alongside men such as the Baptist Hierom Sankey were pecuniary in nature, it would be a mistake, I believe, to think of him as acting in an ideological vacuum. Forced by events to reconsider his options, financial and otherwise, men like Greatrakes had little choice but to engage in business and debate with the new men who assumed authority in the 1650s. In the process, some, Greatrakes among them, found common ground and a sense of mutual respect, which in time fostered new attitudes to matters of faith and promised an end to the interminable mud-slinging and name-calling that characterized religious life in this period.

This desire to search for a peaceful, moderate and dogma-free solution to the religious travails of the middle years of the seventeenth century I have here and elsewhere dubbed as eirenicism. The label is, as some have noted, not without its problems. Michael Hunter, for example, has suggested that it creates 'strange bed-fellows', lumping together Anglicans and radical sectaries.[52] My analysis of Great-rakes' most avid admirers does indeed bear out this finding, as there is little doubt that, superficially at least, they represent a diverse collection of individuals from a variety of religious and political backgrounds. On closer inspection, however, it is possible to discern much common ground. The vast majority, for example, were to some extent tainted by the accusation of having collaborated with, or profiteered from, the Cromwellian regime. Most notable, perhaps, is the presence of a large number of Anglican clergymen who were educated and began their careers during the Interregnum. The experience of working alongside 'puritan' tutors and colleagues, and the friendships formed at this time, undoubtedly helped to lay the foundations for what has become known as latitudinarianism, a term which, like so many other religious labels used at this time, has proven problematic for historians. It would be a mistake, however, to jettison the use of terms such as 'eirenic' and 'latitudinarian' altogether in the absence of alternative descriptors. As this case study of Greatrakes suggests, and much recent scholarship confirms, any attempt to understand the religious and political debates of this period by recourse to simple polarities such as victors and defeated, royalists and republicans, or Anglicans and puritans/dissenters, is now largely redundant. The blurring of religious and political distinctions and the permeable and contingent nature of the boundary separating 'Church' and 'Dissent' suggests instead that historians need to proceed with care when attempting to define religious affiliations in this period.[53]

[51] [D. Lloyd], *Wonders No Miracles; or Mr Valentine Greatrates Gift of Healing Examined* (London, 1666), 8.

[52] M. Hunter, 'How Boyle Became a Scientist', in *Robert Boyle 1627–1691. Scrupulosity and Science* (Woodbridge, 2000), 49.

[53] There is now a growing literature on latitudinarianism that empasizes the idea of the movement as one characterized by common attitudes (moral, moderate, and anti-dogmatic) rather than a single, coherent ideology, which in turn reflects the ill-defined nature of religious positions after the Restoration; see for example W. M. Spellman, *The Latitudinarians and the Church of England, 1660–1700* (Athens, GA, 1993), 5; J. Andrews and A. Scull, *Undertaker of the Mind: John Monro and Mad-Doctoring in Eighteenth-Century England* (Berkeley, 2001), 78.

Thinking about religion in this way also makes sense within the context of the recent historical debate surrounding the Restoration of the Stuarts and the period to which it has given its name. In particular, the growing emphasis on 'Restoration' as a long-drawn out process rather than a single event, characterized by uncertainty and instability, calls into question the viability of traditional labels denoting religious affiliation.[54] It is the mere fact that nothing was settled by 1666 that provides the Greatrakes episode with its overwhelming significance. Here, then, was a further opportunity for those dissatisfied with the initial settlement of religious affairs to voice their concerns and propose an alternative blueprint for government in church and state. Rather than seek to impose unity by force and diktat, many, both within and outside the established Church, were eager to appropriate the exemplary Greatrakes as a model citizen or magistrate, whose moderation and morality stood in stark contrast to those, from the King down, who currently oversaw the body politic.[55] In the event, the moment passed, and within a short space of time new ruptures within church and state threatened once again to overwhelm the nation. Most commentators, past and present, now date the beginnings of this crisis to the final years of the 1660s, culminating in the emergence of new partisan divisions and party labels in the aftermath of the Popish Plot and the attempt to exclude the king's brother from the throne.[56] By now, men who had previously worked together in the hope of restoring consensus and unity to the body politic found themselves in opposing camps, a fact readily illustrated by the fate of so many of Greatrakes' former admirers.[57]

[54] See especially the various contributions to *Albion*, 25 (1993), which was devoted entirely to an exploration of these themes and issues. I am particularly struck by Jonathan Scott's insight that we should prefer to see the period after 1660 as 'an ambition, a deeply felt desire, not an accomplished fact', and the Restoration itself as 'a process quickly inaugurated, but tardily and bloodily achieved'; J. Scott, 'Restoration Process: Or, If This Isn't a Party, We're Not having a Good Time', *Albion*, 25 (1993), 637.

[55] In particular, much has been made of the sexual promiscuity of the King and his court, and its role in eroding confidence and belief in the sacrosanct nature of the royal body and Stuart kingship; see especially R. Weil, 'Sometimes a Scepter is only a Scepter: Pornography and Politics in Restoration England', in L. Hunt (ed.), *The Invention of Pornography: Obscenity and the Origins of Modernity, 1500–1800* (New York, 1993), 125–56.

[56] Among those who have sought to date the first major fault lines in the Restoration settlement to the period from about 1667–70: R. Ashcraft, *Revolutionary Politics and Locke's Two Treatises of Government* (Princeton, 1986); G. S. De Krey, 'The First Restoration Crisis: Conscience and Coercion in London, 1667–73', *Albion*, 25 (1993), 565–80; D. Hirst, 'Samuel Parker, Andrew Marvell, and Political Culture, 1667–73', in D. Hirst and R. Strier (eds), *Writing and Political Engagement in Seventeenth-Century England* (Cambridge, 1999), 145–64. Likewise, Richard Baxter dated the defection of the dissenters' former allies among the ranks of the Anglican clergy to the period after the Great Fire, when 'a great part of those that were called Latitudinarians began to change their temper, and to contract some malignity against those that were much more Religious than themselves'; R. Baxter, *Reliquiae Baxterianae* (London, 1696), iii, 19.

[57] Among those who gravitated towards dissent and the Whigs: Thomas Alured, Richard Bland, William Boreman, Edward Cooksey, Daniel Coxe, William Denton, Andrew Marvell, Alexander Merreal, John Patrick, William Popple, John Starkey. For those who moved in the other direction, favouring a hardline in defence of Church and King: John Beale, Sir Thomas Bludworth, Simon Patrick, Sir George Waterman. Others, such as John Cressett, who would appear to have entered the service of James, Duke of York, some time in the 1670s, may have done so in the hope that he would facilitate the grant of a general toleration to dissenters.

Hindsight, of course, is a wonderful attribute, but one which historians adopt at their peril. It is now clear that by the end of the seventeenth century, Britain was evolving into a pluralist society that guaranteed the right of its citizens to peaceable dissent and a limited freedom to worship outside the constraints of the established Church. It is equally apparent that this was not the aim of those, including the vast majority of Greatrakes' supporters and probably Greatrakes himself, who were critical of the restored government of Charles II in the inaugural years of his reign. While much clearly remains to be done in order to elucidate how the process of restoration played out in the years after 1660, the story of Greatrakes the healer does provide some tantalizing clues as well as suggest future lines of enquiry. One such avenue relates to the role played by body politics in this period. As this and other studies suggest, there is much to be learned from a study of the way in which early modern bodies were utilized as a vehicle for social, religious and political comment. The case of the anorexic maid, Martha Taylor, for example, which excited a great deal of interest in the press in 1668, provides an illuminating and well-documented example of the way in which a medical condition might be appropriated for partisan political ends.[58] Medicine and its practitioners, as I argue elsewhere, were becoming increasingly politicized in this period, a product in part of the Civil Wars, but also a by-product of the early modern preoccupation with the idea of the body politic itself and its role as a heuristic device. The current consensus of scholars suggests that such analogical forms of thinking were dealt a terminal blow with the execution of Charles I. However, the Greatrakes affair and other examples from the post-Restoration period suggest otherwise, and ought to prompt further investigation into this most obdurate and popular of early modern conceits.[59]

The original idea of the body politic, based as it was upon a neoplatonic understanding of the 'magical' operation of correspondence in the cosmos, was firmly rooted in a providentialist worldview that incorporated belief in a range of spiritual, preternatural and supernatural phenomena. Greatrakes himself was only too conscious of the fact that in the words of one of his admirers, Henry More, he and his contemporaries inhabited 'the borders of the spiritual and material world'.[60] And like More and others, he was fully aware of the way in which the boundaries that separated these two worlds had become, in his own lifetime, the subject of

---

[58] See especially S. Schaffer, 'Piety, Physic and Prodigious Abstinence', in O. P. Grell and A. Cunningham (eds), Religio Medici: *Medicine and Religion in Seventeenth-Century England* (Aldershot, 1996), 171–203.

[59] Among those who have suggested an end date of around 1649 for the body politic as an explanatory and not just metaphorical conceit, see K. Sharpe, *Politics and Ideas in Early Stuart England* (London, 1989), 28–31; R. Zaller, 'Breaking the Vessels: the Desacralization of Monarchy in Early Modern England', *Sixteenth Century Journal*, 29 (1998), 757–78. Much of this writing seems to be predicated on a somewhat outmoded belief in the inherently radical nature of puritanism as first proposed by Michael Walzer. In line with much recent work on the nature of seventeenth-century puritanism, I argue here and elsewhere for the continuing attraction of such analogical systems of thought for conservative-minded Puritans both before, during and after the Civil Wars; see my *Medicine and the Politics of Healing in Seventeenth-Century Britain* (forthcoming).

[60] H. More, *An Antidote Against Atheism* (London, 1653), 155.

intense debate. He can hardly have been surprised, therefore, by the interest that his cures stimulated in learned circles, providing as they did much vital data for natural philosophers in their quest to understand better the place of spirit in the material world. Moreover, 'boundary work' of this kind was, of necessity, political in character, shaped as it was by the need to refute what many saw as the growing threat of atheism as expounded by various wits and scoffers in the coffee houses and taverns of the capital and elsewhere.[61] This much has largely been acknowledged by those historians, mostly historians of science, who have commented on the Greatrakes affair and related phenomena. However, it remains the case that there is more to be learned about the state of science in Britain in this period, and its relationship to wider religious and political concerns, from episodes such as these. One cause of continuing concern is the use of reified labels that often fail to acknowledge the eclectic and often convoluted nature of early modern natural philosophy. Others have sought to perpetuate the notion of a consistent scientific approach in the work of the early members of the Royal Society. The problem is compounded by those who, in the words of Allison Coudert, have sought to posit a 'clear-cut correlation between the mechanical philosophy and occultism or a straightforward correlation between specific scientific theories and corresponding religious and political beliefs'.[62] One unfortunate by-product of such thinking has seen the Royal Society co-opted as an agent of the state, particularly in relation to its role in 'naturalizing' prodigies in the interest of 'Anglican orthodoxy' and social stability.[63]

Like religion, science too in this period poses real problems in terms of the nomenclature which historians are required to adopt in defining individuals and their respective approaches to the natural world. Increasingly, historians of science have become more cautious in this respect, preferring contemporary labels such as 'natural philosophy' or 'natural theology' in order to describe the work of early modern

[61] For the importance of the sociological concept of 'boundary work' in Restoration science, see for example J. Henry, 'The Fragmentation of Renaissance Occultism and the Decline of Magic', *History of Science*, 46 (2008), 6. To a large extent, Henry echoes the pioneering work of Stuart Clark and his claim that early modern investigation of phenomena such as witchcraft and the preternatural owed much to Baconian notions of the 'prerogative instance'; S. Clark, *Thinking With Demons: The Idea of Witchcraft in Early Modern Europe* (Oxford, 1997), especially Chapters 16 and 17.

[62] A. Coudert, 'Henry More and Witchcraft', in S. Hutton (ed.), *Henry More (1614–1687): Tercentenary Studies* (Dordrecht, 1989), 117–18.

[63] See for example W. E. Burns, *An Age of Wonders: Prodigies, Politics and Providence in England 1657–1727* (Manchester, 2002). While there is much to admire in Burns' approach, especially his emphasis on the role of political factors in the decline of the prodigious, I remain unconvinced by his somewhat over-simplistic approach to religious and political differences in the period, as well as his over-reliance on the evidence of individuals such as the Cambridge theologian John Spencer (1630–1693). Here and elsewhere, Burns has characterized Spencer as a latitudinarian; Burns, '"Our Lot is Fallen into an Age of Wonders": John Spencer and the Controversy over Prodigies in the Early Restoration', *Albion*, 27 (1995), 237–52. Aside from his residence at Cambridge, I have found no compelling evidence to suggest that he shared the views of his latitudinarian colleagues there. For a more nuanced assessment of Spencer, and the approach of natural philosophers to prodigies in this period, see C. Carter, '"A Constant Prodigy?". Empirical Views of an Unordinary Nature', *The Seventeenth Century*, 23 (2008), 266–89.

'scientists'. The use of the former term has proven particularly helpful in that it accurately reflects the extent to which most natural philosophers of the period became engaged in scientific work because of its ability to shed light on the divine origins of the universe and the prevailing relationship between God, humankind and nature. Natural theology, on the other hand, is best understood as a species of natural philosophy, one which proved attractive to a number of scholars and divines during the Restoration, especially those who inclined towards a peaceable and moderate settlement of religious affairs. The latitudinarian roots of natural theology have often been noted.[64] Less evident in the scholarly literature, however, is due acknowledgement of the breadth of the intellectual concerns of those who espoused this particular brand of 'natural religion' which, as this study of Greatrakes suggests, incorporated a profound interest in, and desire to investigate, manifestations of the wondrous, prodigious and supernatural. Here, I have suggested that exponents of natural theology such as Boyle and the Cambridge Platonists were attracted to Greatrakes, not out of necessity or embarrassment as some have claimed, but rather to seek confirmation of the rational foundations of their faith through divine revelation.[65]

The prominent role played by latitudinarians, especially clergymen of that ilk, in the exposure and promotion of a wide range of preternatural or spiritual phenomena, including witchcraft, requires a case study in its own right. Crucially, the investigation of such matters also provided an opportunity for moderate men on both sides of the religious divide to establish ecumenical links as is evident from the numerous examples of interdenominational cooperation exhibited by those who both witnessed and publicized such events. As I hope to show elsewhere, these develop-

---

[64] See for example J. Gascoigne, *Cambridge in the Age of the Enlightenment: Science, Religion and Politics from the Restoration to the French Revolution* (Cambridge, 1989), 63–6; J. Twigg, *The University of Cambridge and the English Revolution 1625–1688* (Woodbridge, 1990), 255–6. Despite noting difficulties in using the term 'latitudinarian', Gascoigne is surely right to argue that it provides a 'key to understanding the religious mentality' of the age. He also has some wise words to say about the mutable nature of the term, and the fact that it went through numerous incarnations, being constantly reshaped by changes in the wider social, religious and political environment of late seventeenth-century England; ibid. 4–5.

[65] E. Duffy, 'Valentine Greatrakes, the Irish Stroker: Miracle, Science and Orthodoxy in Restoration England', in K. Robbins (ed.), *Religion and Humanism* (Oxford, 1981), 257, 263, 269. It goes without saying that I cannot concur with Duffy's conclusion that the latitudinarians' version of rational Christianity 'had no real place for a Protestant thaumaturge'; ibid. 269. More recently, Scott Mandelbrote has attempted to depict two strands of thought in the 'natural theology' tradition, the one represented by Robert Boyle and John Wilkins, and the other by the Cambridge Platonists. At the heart of their differences he locates a much greater respect for regularity and disdain for the wondrous in the works of the former, while stressing the excessive credulity of the latter with regard to the presence of spirit and spiritual phenomena such as witchcraft in the sublunary world; S. Mandelbrote, 'The Uses of Natural Theology in Seventeenth-Century England', *Science in Context*, 20 (2007), 451–80. To what extent such fissures were present in 1666, when Boyle and Wilkins were engaged with Greatrakes, is a moot point. Wilkins, it should be noted, had also been attracted to Tedworth a few years earlier in order to investigate the case of the Demon Drummer. In addition, he was on close personal terms with many of the Cambridge Platonists, friendships that were formed during his brief tenure as Master of Trinity College, Cambridge, in 1659–60, when he was instrumental in establishing a club devoted to the pursuit of a moderate settlement of religion in the chambers of 'the great trimmer and latitudinarian' Hezekiah Burton at Magdalene College. It is tempting to speculate that Wilkins protégé and fellow admirer of Greatrakes, Clement Sankey, a former fellow of Magdalene, was another member. For Burton, and his interest in witchcraft, see p. 139n.

ments were deep rooted, probably originating in the universities and county 'associations' of the 1650s, and continued to proliferate for decades after the Restoration. They are evident, for example, in the celebrated trial of the Lowestoft witches in 1662, in which the judge Matthew Hale (1609–1676) and natural philosopher and physician Sir Thomas Browne (1605–1682), both eminent spokesmen for the latitudinarian cause, played a prominent role.[66] They can also be found at work in many of the pamphlets and treatises published in these years aimed at convincing an atheistic age of the reality of witches, demons and spirits. The popular and exhaustive compendia of the moderate Anglican clerics Nathaniel Wanley (d.1680) and William Turner (1653–1701) provide striking examples of the genre that clearly owed much to the well-established links that both men had forged with their dissenting colleagues.[67] Similar cooperation was also evident in a series of widely publicized miracle healings that took place among various congregations of dissenters in London in the 1690s.[68] While there is little doubt that the enthusiasm of moderate divines for such cases did eventually flag by the end of the century, it would be a grave mistake to assume, as some have suggested, that interest in spirits and witches was essentially marginalized in this period as the special preserve of a minority of deluded 'enthusiasts'.

In conclusion, I think it is possible to argue that the appearance of Greatrakes as miracle healer in the early years of the Restoration provides a number of important clues as to the often convoluted process whereby his contemporaries were forced to

[66] P. Elmer, 'Towards a Politics of Witchcraft in Early Modern England', in S. Clark (ed.), *Languages of Witchcraft: Narrative, Ideology and Meaning in Early Modern Culture* (Basingstoke, 2001), 114. Hale, a close friend of Richard Baxter, was himself actively engaged in 'research' aimed at exploring the boundary between the material and spiritual realms. His belief in witchcraft, and prominent role as a 'credulous' judge in various witch trials, constituted an important aspect of his thought and was entirely consonant with his eirenic approach to the religious divisions of his day; *ODNB*; A. Cromartie, *Sir Matthew Hale, 1609–1676: Law, Religion and Natural Philosophy* (Cambridge,1995). For an interesting, if somewhat flawed, attempt to explain Browne's role in the Lowestoft trial as a manifestation of his fixation with the relationship between matter and spirit, see K. Killeen, *Biblical Scholarship, Science and Politics in Early Modern England: Thomas Browne and the Thorny Place of Knowledge* (Farnham, 2009), 109–54.

[67] N. Wanley, *The Wonders of the Little World, or, A General History of Man* (London, 1678); W. Turner, *A Compleat History of the Most Remarkable Providences, Both of Judgment and Mercy, Which have Hapned in this Present Age* (London, 1697). Wanley, a product of Interregnum Cambridge and associate of Henry More and Richard Baxter, was widely read with a strong interest in all branches of natural philosophy, especially medicine and anatomy. He was appointed vicar of Holy Trinity, Coventry, in 1662 on the ejection of his friend, the Presbyterian John Bryan (d.1676), whose funeral sermon he preached; *ODNB*; *Cal. Rev.*, 83–4; TNA, PROB 11/367, f.63r. Turner was vicar of Walberton in Sussex from 1680 until his death in 1701. Much admired in dissenting circles, many of Turner's examples of divine prodigies were drawn from nonconformist sources. He was particularly indebted to his great friend and 'peace maker', Philip Henry (1631–1696), in whose nonconformist household Turner had resided in the late 1660s when he served as tutor to Henry's sons. The work itself was dedicated to John Williams (d. 1709), Bishop of Chichester, a pro-exclusionist Whig and Boyle Lecturer in 1695–6, who favoured religious comprehension; *ODNB*, sub Turner, William [which errs in stating that *A Compleat History* was dedicated to John Hall] and Williams, John; [P. Henry], *The Life of the Rev. Philip Henry, A.M. . . . Corrected and Enlarged by J. B. Williams* (London, 1825), 123, 231–2.

[68] J. Shaw, *Miracles in Enlightenment England* (New Haven, 2006), 119–43. I fully concur with Shaw's view that the cures of these women were widely seen as a commentary upon the sinful state of the nation in which eirenic or ecumenical concerns were uppermost in the minds of many of those, dissenters and conformists, who promoted and wrote about the same. I hope to discuss these themes more fully, particularly the role of medical men in authenticating these cures, in a series of future publications.

confront and engage with a world that was undergoing major social, political and intellectual change. Greatrakes himself, as we have seen, was a man whose life straddled two distinct worlds. Born just over a decade before the Civil Wars that would throw all former certainties into turmoil, he, like so many of his contemporaries, yearned for a return to stability and unity and the reestablishment of a society underpinned by order and harmony. Many, Greatrakes included, believed the key to success lay in a reaffirmation of belief in a providential deity, whose care for humankind was manifest on a daily basis. Faith in such a worldview, however, was clearly being eroded in the wake of the religious and political upheavals of the middle decades of the seventeenth century. By the time of Greatrakes' death in 1683, a growing number of his contemporaries were beginning to question the age-old verities that presupposed a constant and active God, including the concept of a single, unified and hierarchical body politic that mirrored the state of government in both heaven and hell.[69] Until fairly recently, most historians of this period have tended to assume that the transition from a unitary state, in which there was a single ruling polity, ecclesiastical and civil, to a pluralistic society was, if not smooth, then leastways ineluctable and predictable. Today, such assumptions no longer hold sway, as historians have become increasingly aware of the contingent and uneven nature of religious, political and intellectual change in the period after 1660. Critically, as this study suggests, we are also becoming more conscious of the interrelated nature of these changes as the old barriers that demarcated political history from intellectual history, or the history of ideas from events, are slowly dismantled.[70] In the last resort, I would therefore suggest that Greatrakes is best understood as a consummate purveyor of what David Lederer has recently described as 'spiritual physic',[71] that is, one who subscribed to a worldview in which the physical wellbeing of individuals and communities was inextricably linked to broader moral, social and political factors. Such thinking retained its appeal for many long after Greatrakes' death as the case of the 'Bavarian Greatrakes', Johann Joseph Gassner (1727–1779) strongly suggests. Gassner's biographer Erik Midelfort has recently proposed that we ought to see the Bavarian exorcist and healer as 'a vehicle . . . to explore the awkward and ungainly transition to secular modernity'

---

[69] A memorable feature of so much of the literature of this period is the emphasis that contemporaries placed upon the idea of hell and demonic rule as an exemplary form of government that exhibited order and hierarchy. It is implicit in Glanvill's allusion to the Devil 'as a name for a Body Politick' (see p. 111) and is consistently reflected in the concerns of Greatrakes, his supporters and many others in this period. I hope to expand on this theme more fully at a later date.

[70] In part, this work is intended as a contribution to what Tim Harris has described as 'a social history of politics' in Restoration Britain. In later work, I hope to expand on this theme, and Mark Knights' related observation regarding the impact of natural philosophy and medicine upon political developments and debate in this period; T. Harris, *Restoration: Charles II and His Kingdoms 1660–1685* (London, 2005), 12–14; M. Knights, *Representation and Misrepresentation in Later Stuart Britain* (Oxford, 2005), 57–62.

[71] D. Lederer, *Madness, Religion and the State in Early Modern Europe: A Bavarian Beacon* (Cambridge, 2006). In this sense, Greatrakes shared much in common with those other practitioners of spiritual physic in Restoration England, the nonconformists, many of whom combined medical practice with ministerial and pastoral duties. I discuss this aspect of the Restoration medical scene more fully in my *Medicine and the Politics of Healing in Early Modern Britain* (forthcoming).

in Enlightenment Germany.[72] In a similar spirit, I would like to propose that the life and career of Greatrakes the stroker can play a similar role in exposing the complex route to modernity in late seventeenth-century Britain, one that takes full cognizance of a wide spectrum of cultural beliefs and practices, no matter how outmoded or irrelevant they may appear from the perspective of the present day.

[72] H. C. E. Midelfort, *Exorcism and Enlightenment: Johann Joseph Gassner and the Demons of Eighteenth-Century Germany* (New Haven, 2005), 7.

APPENDIX 1

The family tree of Valentine Greatrakes

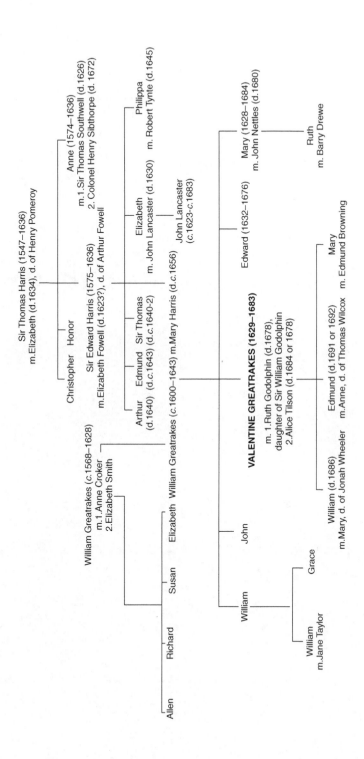

APPENDIX 2

A biographical index of those either cured by Greatrakes or who testified, witnessed or commented upon his cures

Fuller biographical entries, with sources, are provided in the main body of the text for those whose names are asterisked.

*Thomas Alured (d. 1708). Alured witnessed the cures of **Anthony Nicholson** and **Dorothy Pocock**, 10 April 1666; Greatrakes, *Brief Account*, 83–5.

*Jeremiah Astel. In a letter to an unnamed Oxford Fellow, dated 10 March 1666, Astel approved Greatrakes' cures of various unnamed patients, including children, as well as commenting positively upon his moderation, morality, and compassion. He had intended to forward a separate account to his friends **Robert Boyle** and Dr Edmund Dickinson (1624–1707), but due to lack of time asked the receipient to pass on the attached letter to the two men; Greatrakes, *Brief Account*, 91–4.

Benjamin and Edward Barcock. Son and father, respectively, they provided a certificate, dated 1 April 1666, confirming that they had been stroked and successfully cured by Greatrakes. Benjamin, aged about twenty, was treated for a range of complaints, including griping of the guts and fits. His father, a tallow chandler, aged about fifty, suffered from deafness. Both men lived in the parish of St Benet Fink, London. In addition to Edmund Barcock's own testimonial, the cures of the two men were attested by **Benjamin Whichcote** and **Ralph Cudworth**; *Brief Account*, 66–7; LMA, GB 0074 P69/BEN 1.

[Mrs] Bateman. According to Greatrakes, she was 'a neighbour's wife, who lived nigh Tallowbridge', and was cured of an ague in 1665; Greatrakes, *Brief Account*, 25. She was almost certainly the wife of Stephen Bateman (p. 60n.), a long-standing friend and business partner of the stroker.

*Lionel Beacher. Beacher was the author or part-author of *Wonders If Not Miracles* (London, 1665), the first published account of Greatrakes' cures. Two variant copies of the letter written by Beacher, and cited therein, dated 18 May 1665, survive in the library of the Royal Society. One was appended by **John Beale** in a letter addressed to **Robert Boyle**, dated 7 September 1665. Beale himself had received the same from **Thomas Sydenham** and surmised that it was a copy made by his old associate **Benjamin Worsley**, whose handwriting he knew well; Boyle, *Correspondence*, ii, 522; RS, EL/B1/106; EL/M1/36.

*John Beale (1608–1683). Beale reported Greatrakes' cures to **Robert Boyle** in a letter dated 7 September 1665; Boyle, *Correspondence*, ii, 522.

Thomas Belasyse, Viscount Fauconberg (1628 or 1629–1700). According to the testimony of the physician **James Fairclough**, Fauconberg was present at the cure of **John Jacomb**. There, he performed an experiment which involved pricking with a pin those parts of Jacomb's body that went numb following Greatrakes' stroking. Fauconberg was the son-in-law of Oliver Cromwell, who, despite his royalist inclinations, served the governments of the Interregnum in various capacities, but later welcomed the Restoration; Greatrakes, *Brief Account*, 72–3; *ODNB*.

Colonel [John] Birch (1615–1691). According to Greatrakes, Birch was an eye-witness to those at Worcester who collapsed in his presence (presumably as victims of diabolical possession) in February 1666; Greatrakes, *Brief Account*, 33. Of Weobley, Herefordshire, Birch invested heavily in bishop's lands in Bristol and Herefordshire in 1650 and 1651. His religious and political position fits no obvious pattern, but he consistently advocated moderation in religious affairs throughout the 1650s and 1660. In the Convention Parliament of 1660, he argued that the Anglican liturgy was not established by law. Active in the Cavalier Parliament, Clarendon instructed Bishop **Herbert Croft** to renew Birch's leases of church lands without the resumption of an entry fine. He supported occasional conformity and opposed over-rigorous use of the church courts to prosecute nonconformists. He was nonetheless a regular attender of the established church. Birch was clearly a religious moderate, keen to broker a broad-based religious settlement that was inclusive rather than exclusive. In October 1660, for example, he acted as an intermediary between Clarendon and Richard Baxter, imploring the latter to accept the bishopric of Hereford. Further evidence of his disaffection with the Restoration settlement is provided by Samuel Pepys who recorded a conversation with him in 1670, in which Birch predicted the imminent fall of the bishops and royal support for a broad policy of toleration that would include Catholics. Birch sat as an MP for various constituencies covering the whole of the period from 1646 to 1691. In that capacity, he sought to bring in a bill to repeal the Irish Cattle Act in 1677; *ODNB*; Henning, i, 653–60; Bodl., Rawlinson MS B 239, nos 493, 501, 602, 618, 635; Baxter, *Reliquiae Baxterianae*, ii, 281; Latham and Matthews, *Diary of Samuel Pepys*, ix, 44–6.

Richard Birch. He attested to the cure of **Peter Noyes**, 10 May 1666; Greatrakes, *Brief Account*, 87–8. Identity uncertain. He may be the same as the Richard Burch, 'sectarist' and Yeoman Warder of the Tower of London, who petitioned for the lease of sequestrated tithes in Monmouthshire and Breconshire in 1652; Green, *CPCC*, iii, 1712–3; *CSPD, 1660–1661*, 104.

Richard Bland (d. 1692). A nonconformist merchant from Hoxton in Shoreditch, Bland attested to the cure of **Mary Surman** or **Sermon** at the house of **Colonel John Owen** at Mortlake, 20 May 1666; Greatrakes, *Brief Account*, 91; LMA, HMD /x/ 158–61, 166, 167.

*Sir Thomas Bludworth (1620–1682). Bludworth, Lord Mayor of London at the time of Greatrakes' visit to the capital, played host to the stroker in early March 1666. Among those cured at his house was **John Doe**. He was also present as a witness to cures performed elsewhere in London; Greatrakes, *Brief Account*, 54–5; *Great Cures and Strange Miracles Performed by Mr. Valentine Gertrux*, 3.

Lewis Bonivent. Aged twenty-seven, she suffered from lameness in all parts following childbirth. She was subsequently examined by **Robert Boyle** and two physicians, **William Denton** and **James Fairclough**, who declared her fully recovered, 26 April 1666; Greatrakes, *Brief Account*, 43–4.

Mr Boreman. Boreman was the recipient of a letter written by his friend, **Edmund Squibb**, and dated 20 April 1666, in which the latter recounted his own cure and that of others at the hands of Greatrakes at the house of Lady Verney; Greatrakes, *Brief Account*, 77–8. Identification uncertain. However, it is tempting to speculate that this may be William Boreman, physician, witch-hunter, and member of the Behmenist circle of John Pordage and the early Philadelphians, whose preoccupations closely mirror those of Greatrakes; Defoe, *A System of Magick*, 13–16, 209–32.

*Michael Boyle (1609 or 1610–1702). As Archbishop of Dublin, Boyle interviewed Greatrakes in July 1665 and concluded that his cures were largely fraudulent and only supported by those 'who were on the same side with him in the last wars'; *Conway Letters*, 262; BL, Add. MS 4182, fos 29v–30r.

*Robert Boyle (1627–1691). According to Henry More, Boyle, one of the leading natural philosophers of his age, claimed to have witnessed at least sixty cures performed by Greatrakes. Greatrakes himself dedicated his *Brief Account* to Boyle, who carried out a wide range of tests and experiments on him in an attempt to explain the origin and cause of his gift of healing. He also penned a lengthy reply to the published letter of Henry Stubbe, mischievously addressed to Boyle, in which he made it clear that Stubbe had overstepped the mark in exposing him to potential embarrassment; *Conway Letters*, 273; BL, Add. MS 4293, fos 50–2; Add. MS 4376, 1–15.

*Joseph Boyse (1660–1728). At Boyse's request, Mary Marshall of Dublin sent him a letter in May 1699 providing an account of the various cures performed by Greatrakes among her family some twenty years earlier. Boyse forwarded the letter to his friend Ralph Thoresby, a member of the Royal Society, and it was subsequently published in that Society's journal the following year; BL, Stowe MS 747, fo.113; *Philosophical Transactions*, 21 (1700), 332–4.

Edwin Brewns or Browne (d. 1668). Brewns or Browne attested to the cure of Dorothy Wardant at Mortlake, 9 April 1666; Greatrakes, *Brief Account*, 56. He was a London merchant and common councilman, who also owned property at Mortlake. Brewns served as a parish official there from 1659 until 1665. His will, made at the height of the onset of plague in August 1665, refers to the 'calamitous tymes which God hath most iustly sent amongst us for our ill returnes of mercys received'. Browne's politics are not known. His two executors (son-in-law William Rawstorne and brother-in-law and neighbour John Buckworth) were later prominent in the Tory leadership of London. His brother Samuel, on the other hand, was married to a daughter of Thomas Papillon, future leader of the London Whigs; Woodhead, *Rulers of London, 1660–1689*, 39; SHC, 2397/3/1; 2414/4/2; TNA, PROB 11/327, fos 360v–362r.

*[Henry] Bromley (d. 1667). Of Upton-on-Severn, Worcestershire, Henry Bromley was the brother of Thomas (below) and suffered miserably from the after-effects of a severe quartane ague. Greatrakes ministered to him for five to six days at Ragley Hall in February 1666; Stubbe, *Miraculous Conformist*, 29. He is not to be confused with Henry Bromley (1632–1670), of Holt Castle, Worcestershire, who sat as MP for the county in 1660.

*Thomas Bromley (1630–1691). Brother of Henry (above). He attested to the cure of John Hawkins of Thatcham, Berkshire, 14 April 1666; Greatrakes, *Brief Account*, 80–1.

*Sir Roger Burgoyne (1618–1677). On 12 February 1666, Burgoyne wrote to Sir Ralph Verney in anticipation of the arrival of Greatrakes in London, describing him as 'one who opens the eyes of those that have been blind many years and cures cancers in the breast, which he seldom fails in'; *HMC Seventh Report*, 464.

Captain Burroughs. The son of one Captain Burroughs was cured by Greatrakes at the Charterhouse Yard in 1666; *Great Cures and Strange Miracles*, 3.

Thomas Burt. A day labourer of Radclive, Buckinghamsire, and servant of Sir William Smith, he suffered from an ague contracted while working at his master's saltworks in Kent. Smith procured the services of Greatrakes through the assistance of his friend Edmund Godfrey, and subsequently certified him as cured at his house in Lincoln's Inn Fields, 6 March 1666; Greatrakes, *Brief Account*, 49–50.

William But or Buts. A servant of Sir William Smith, he was cured by Greatrakes of an ague contracted while working at his master's saltworks in Kent; Greatrakes, *Brief Account*, 50, 69.

Mr Carrington. A scrivener, living near Charing Cross, Carrington had been lame for many years prior to being cured at the hands of Greatrakes in the home of Lady Ranelagh and at the behest of her neighbour Thomas Sydenham in 1666; BL, Add. MS 4293, fo.53. He was still alive in 1670; TNA, PROB 11/333, fos 458v–459r.

Christian Cavendish, Countess of Devonshire (1595–1675). Her home at Roehampton, just outside London, was the site of numerous cures performed by Greatrakes in 1666. Many of these were carried out on the Dowager Countess' servants and employees and were witnessed, among others, by **Walter Stonehouse**, Gentleman of the Horse, and **Richard Mulys**, the Countess' auditor, as attested 30 April 1666; Greatrakes, *Brief Account*, 65–6. She was a committed royalist, her house at Roehampton serving as a refuge for plotters throughout the 1650s. After the Restoration, her fortunes revived and her home became a flourishing centre of learning and political intrigue; *ODNB*.

Henry Chapman. Chapman was stroked by Greatrakes at Minehead, Somerset, in June 1668. Greatrakes reported that he was still well in September of the same year, when he was described as a neighbour of **Samuel Crockford**; Boyle, *Correspondence*, iv, 101.

Richard Chiswell. According to **Samuel Jeake the elder** of Rye in Sussex, Greatrakes failed to cure Chiswell of a sciatica by his normal methods and resorted instead to a surgical operation which Jeake claimed killed his unfortunate patient; ESxRO, FRE MS 4223, fo. 198r.

*[Richard] Christmas (1615–1679).** A Bristol merchant and prominent figure in Presbyterian circles in the city, he witnessed several of Greatrakes' cures in Bristol in the summer of 1668; Boyle, *Correspondence*, iv, 100.

George Claire. Claire's son, aged six, was cured by Greatrakes of an impostume or abscess in the bowels, as attested by two physicians, **James Fairclough** and **Albertus Otto Faber**, 19 April 1666. George Claire was described as a grocer living in Grace Church Street, London, at the time of the cure of his son; Greatrakes, *Brief Account*, 76–7.

Anthony Combs. Of Jerusalem Alley, Grace Church Street, London, he was cured by Greatrakes of an ulcerated leg, 16 April 1666. Combs himself confirmed the cure in a letter addressed to **Sir Nathaniel Hobart**, dated 24 April 1666. The cure was also witnessed by **Richard Hals**, **Sir William Smith**, and **Dr James Fairclough**; Greatrakes, *Brief Account*, 79–80.

*Lady Anne Conway (1631–1679).** The debilitating headaches suffered by Lady Anne provided the original reason for Greatrakes to visit England in 1666. Although he failed in her case, he subsequently used her home as a base from which to heal countless others in the neighbourhood; *Conway Letters, passim*.

*Edward Conway, Earl of Conway (c.1623–1683).** Although Greatrakes failed to alleviate the migraines suffered by his wife (above), the Earl was nonetheless convinced that he had cured many others, including the son of a prebend of Gloucester. However, he did not believe that the stroker's cures were miraculous, ascribing them instead to 'a sanative virtue and a natural efficiency' inherent in the Irish healer's constitution; *Conway Letters*, 268.

*Edward Cooksey (d. 1693).** Cooksey was Mayor of Worcester in early 1666, when he invited Greatrakes to visit the city to perform his cures. He also witnessed the effect of Greatrakes' presence on those suffering from the falling sickness; Greatrakes, *Brief Account*, 33.

*Daniel Coxe (1640–1730).** Coxe, a royal physician, attested to the cure of **Anne Field**, 12 April 1666. He also corresponded with **Robert Boyle** on the subject of Greatrakes' cures in March 1666, having observed him in action at various locations in London; Greatrakes, *Brief Account*, 46–7; Boyle, *Correspondence*, iii, 82–90.

*Captain John Cressett (d. 1707).** Cressett was a first-hand witness to the cure of **Grace Knight**, the daughter of alderman **William Knight**. He also wrote a letter in support of the stroker, dated 5 May 1666, in which he defended Greatrakes from the allegation of one of his detractors that he was a common swearer. **David Lloyd**, the author of that rumour, had earlier penned a very different account of a botched cure performed by the Irishman at the house of Captain Cressett on one of the inmates of the Charterhouse in March 1666; Greatrakes, *Brief Account*, 7–8, 54; [Lloyd], *Wonders No Miracles*, 23.

Samuel Crockford (d. 1696). According to Greatrakes, Crockford was willing to send testimonials to **Robert Boyle**, certifying cures performed at his house in Minehead in 1668, as well as testifying to the cure of one of his sons in Ireland three years previously; Boyle, *Correspondence*, iv, 100–1. Crockford was a merchant who would appear to have removed from Youghal to Minehead in Somerset some time in the mid 1660s. He was made a freeman of the former in 1647, where he owned various properties and his name also appears on a subsidy roll in 1662 as a gentleman living at Balligagin in county Waterford. His local links may account for his being chosen to act as a go-between in collecting Greatrakes' longstanding debt to the corporation of Exeter in 1670. In 1672–3, he served as a churchwarden in Minehead and was later appointed as executor to the Restoration vicar of the town, Nicholas Prowse. He may also have retained some form of connection with the household of the Earl of Orrery, acting occasionally as the Earl's agent in England after the Restoration; Caulfield, *Council Book of Youghal*, 266, 291; NLI, MS 6255, undated, 1652–3?; Walton, 'Subsidy Roll', 69; DRO, ECA 11, 203; Hancock, *Minehead*, 56, 123–125, 282–283, 321; WSxRO, Orrery MS 13,222 (5); TNA, PROB 11/434, fos 34r–35r.

*****Herbert Croft (1603–1691)**. Croft, the Bishop of Hereford, was reported to have said that Greatrakes' cures were 'to his owne certaine knowledge, beyond all the power of nature'; Thompson, *Correspondence of the Family of Hatton*, i, 49.

Charles Cudworth (d. 1684). He was cured by Greatrakes as certified by his father, Ralph Cudworth (below), 18 April 1666; Greatrakes, *Brief Account*, 60; *Conway Letters*, 273.

*****Ralph Cudworth (1617–1688)**. Cudworth witnessed numerous cures at the hands of Greatrakes, including his young son **Charles** (above), **Elizabeth Thomas**, **Robert Toples**, and **Benjamin** and **Edmund Barcock**. With his friend and colleague, **Benjamin Whichcote**, he also accompanied Greatrakes on a visit to remonstrate with his detractor **David Lloyd**, who had accused the stroker in print of acting dishonestly and immorally; Greatrakes, *Brief Account*, 9, 60, 64, 66–7.

*****Sir Abraham Cullen (1624–1668)**. With William Rushout, Cullen witnessed the cures of **William Jones** and **Dorothy Wardant**, as certified, 9 April 1666; Greatrakes, *Brief Account*, 55–6.

Sarah Dancer. She was cured by Greatrakes in 1665; Oldenburg, *Correspondence*, ii, 496. She was the daughter of Sir Adam Loftus and wife of Sir Thomas Dancer (for whom, see p. 96 and n.).

Jane Deane. Of Swallowfield, Berkshire, she was aged about eighteen when she was cured by Greatrakes at the house of **Sir William Smith** in Lincoln's Inn Fields in April 1666. Her cure was witnessed by **John Wilkins**; Greatrakes, *Brief Account*, 67–8.

John De Bruy. According to the testimonial of **Sir John Godolphin**, De Bruy witnessed the cure of **Anne Robinson** on 21 April 1666; Greatrakes, *Brief Account*, 52–3.

Mrs Dee. According to **Mary Marshall**, Mrs Dee was 'my Uncle Pope's daughter', and was cured by Greatrakes at Dublin (date unknown); BL, Stowe MS 747, fo. 113. She may have been related to Captain or Major Robert Dee, Lord Mayor of Dublin in 1660, when he was active in promoting the Restoration; Bodl., Carte MSS 59, fo. 617; 68, fo.200.

*****Sir John Denham (1614 or 1615–1669)**. As early as 20 February 1666, it was being reported from inside Charles II's court that the King intended to invite Greatrakes to

London in order to 'offer him Sir John Denham to worke his wonders upon'. Eleven days later, the King sent for Greatrakes to cure Denham. By April, however, it was being reported that the courtier Denham was now 'stark mad, which is occasioned (as is said by some) by the rough striking of Greatrakes upon his limbs'; Bodl., Carte MS 46, fo. 257v; *CSP Ireland, 1666–1669*, 52; *HMC Sixth Report*, 339. Other rumours suggested that Denham's madness had been brought on by the knowledge of his young wife's affair with the Duke of York.

*John Denison. According to Denison's daughter, **Mary Marshall**, her brother John was cured by Greatrakes at their father's house in Dublin (date unknown). Other sources suggest that Greatrakes was still treating large numbers of patients in Dublin at the house of Mrs Denison in 1680; BL, Stowe MS 747, fo. 113; *Notes and Queries*, 9 (1884), 62.

*William Denton (1605–1691). Denton, who served as physician in ordinary to both Charles I and Charles II, attested to the cure of **Anne Kelly**, **Lewis Bonivent**, and **Eleanor Dickinson**, 26 April 1666; Greatrakes, *Brief Account*, 43–4, 45.

Monsieur De Son (Du Son or D'Esson). De Son was cured of severe back ache by Greatrakes in the chambers of Prince Rupert in 1666; Oldenburg, *Correspondence*, iii, 59. De Son was a French engraver, inventor, and projector. In 1653, Samuel Hartlib reported that he 'hath beene formerly in England a man of a thousand Mechanical Inventions'. At the time he was living in Holland, where he was supposed to be about to launch a new vessel without sails that, it was claimed, would be 'the bane of the English fleet'. By 1664, he was back in England, where he worked primarily on lenses, watches, and a new carriage for Charles II. His chief patron was **Sir Robert Moray**. A number of his papers were published in the *Philosophical Transactions* of the Royal Society. He apparently held no fear of the plague, frequenting, it was claimed, infected houses with impunity; Keblusek, 'Keeping it Secret', 37–56; SUL, HP, 28/2/60A; Thurloe, *State Papers*, i, 541; Oldenburg, *Correspondence*, ii, 478n and *passim*.

[Robert] Devonshire. A surgeon from Minehead in Somerset, Devonshire was willing to testify to cures performed by Greatrakes in the town in 1668; Boyle, *Correspondence*, iv, 101. Devonshire was licensed to practise surgery in the diocese of Bath and Wells, 19 September 1662. He was probably related to Christopher Devonshire, a prominent merchant and Quaker in Minehead. Christopher, who helped to draw up an inventory of Robert's goods in late 1684, was himself described as a 'loving friend' of the Earl of Orrery and may have acted as one of his bankers in England; SARS, D\D/Bs/39, sub 19 September 1662; DD\SP/1684/173; Hancock, *Minehead*, 23, 86–7; Morland, *Somersetshire Quarterly Meeting of the Society of Friends, 1668–1699*, 270; NLI, MS 33, fo. 218.

Eleanor Dickinson. A widow of Clerkenwell, she was aged about forty-five when she was cured by Greatrakes of a dropsy in the presence of **Robert Boyle** and the physicians **William Denton** and **James Fairclough**. Her cure was also attested by **Albertus Otto Faber** and **Thomas Pooley**, 16 April 1666; Greatrakes, *Brief Account*, 44–6.

Mary Dimmack. A servant of **Sir William Smith**, she was cured of a cancerous 'sore leg' by Greatrakes in 1666; Greatrakes, *Brief Account*, 51.

*John Doe. The son of Sir Charles Doe (d. 1671?), a London alderman and goldsmith (for whom, see p. 99 and n.), John Doe was cured of violent headaches by the stroking of Greatrakes at the house of **Sir Thomas Bludworth**, Lord Mayor, in early March 1666, as recounted by Doe in a letter to **Dr James Fairclough**, dated 9 May 1666; Greatrakes, *Brief Account*, 54–5.

Walter Dolle the elder and younger. Walter Dolle the younger, aged about nineteen, was treated by Greatrakes for a paralysis on his right side at the house of **Edmund Godfrey** in early March 1666. He later supplied a testimonial, dated 25 April 1666, which was countersigned by his father Walter, a goldbeater at the Hand and Hammer, Pye Corner, London, as well as **Robert Boyle, Dr James Fairclough,** and **William Yates.** His cure was also independently verified by the clergyman **Simon Patrick.** Dolle the younger was at the time serving an apprenticeship with the celebrated engraver **William Faithorn.** In 1674, he was said by Robert Hooke to be experimenting with the use of mezzotints; Greatrakes, *Brief Account*, 47–8, 61–2; *ODNB*.

John Dugdale. Dugdale attested the cure of **William Floyd,** who was suffering from the king's evil, in 1666; Greatrakes, *Brief Account*, 81–2. Identity uncertain. He may have been John (1628–1700), the son of Sir William Dugdale (d. 1686), Garter King of Arms, a minor courtier resident in St James' Palace in 1666; *ODNB*, sub Dugdale William.

*George Evans (1631–1702). Evans, a clergyman, attested to the cures of **Robert Furnace, Elizabeth Sharp,** and **Robert Toples,** 3 April 1666; Greatrakes, *Brief Account*, 63–4.

*Albertus Otto Faber (1612–1684). Faber, a chemical physician, attested to the cures of five of Greatrakes' patients in London, viz. **Eleanor Dickinson, Anne Robinson, Sarah Tuffly,** the young son of **George Claire,** and **John Harrison;** Greatrakes, *Brief Account*, 46, 52–3, 76, 76–7, 89.

James Fairclough (d. 1685). Fairclough, a London physician, was one of Greatrakes' most dedicated admirers, attesting to the cures of no less than twenty-eight of his patients; Greatrakes, *Brief Account*, 43–9, 51–2, 52–3, 54, 68–74, 76–8, 79–80, 83–6. Unfortunately, relatively little is known about Fairclough. Educated at Caius College, Cambridge in the 1650s, he was granted an MD in 1661. A native of Upholland, Lancashire, he owned land in Cambridgeshire and London. In the early 1670s, he provided testimonials for three fellow practitioners, one of whom, unusually, was a Quaker, Griffith Owen (d. 1717). He died in the chambers of his son at the Middle Temple in February 1685; Venn, ii, 116; Inderwick, *Calendar of the Inner Temple Records*, iii, 454; TNA, PROB 11/379, fos 148v–150r.

William Faithorne (1616–1691). Faithorne witnessed the cures of **Mary Glover** and **Margaret Westley** in 1666. His apprentice **Walter Dolle the younger** was also stroked by the Irishman; Greatrakes, *Brief Account*, 47–8, 61, 90. Faithorne was one of the most celebrated engravers of his day who was responsible for the portrait of Greatrakes on the frontispiece to his *Brief Account* as well as for the images of many other notable Restoration figures, including **Robert Boyle.** An inveterate royalist, he fought for Charles I in the Civil War, was taken prisoner, and subsequently banished. He returned to England in the early 1650s, and by the middle of the decade was producing engraved images of Cromwell for the new regime; *ODNB*; Hunter, *Boyle: Between God and Science*, 140–1.

Jane Farrington. According to **Dr James Fairclough,** she was cured by Greatrakes of a palsy; Greatrakes, *Brief Account*, 73.

John Felton (c.1633–1667). On 6 February 1666, Felton wrote to **William Sancroft** (1617–1693), recounting in some detail Greatrakes' successes while he lodged at Ragley Hall. Felton's informant was **Ezekiel Foxcroft;** BL, Harleian MS 3785, fos 111r–v. Felton was educated at Caius College, Cambridge, in the 1650s, proceeding BD in 1662, and died there in 1667; Venn, ii, 129.

Anne Field. Aged about twenty-eight and the wife of Thomas Field, a pastry cook in Wood Street, London, she was cured of headaches and blindness by Greatrakes. Her testimonial, witnessed by **Robert Boyle** and three physicians, **James Fairclough, Thomas Williams,** and **Daniel Coxe,** was dated 12 April 1666; Greatrakes, *Brief Account*, 46–7.

*John Flamsteed (1646–1719). As a young man, Flamsteed, the future astronomer royal, was stroked on two occasions by Greatrakes, once at Affane in 1665, and again at Worcester in February 1666; Baily, *Account of the Reverend John Flamsteed*, 12, 16, 21.

William Floyd. Floyd, the son of Gabriel Floyd of Longstock, Hampshire, was stroked for the king's evil by Greatrakes at London in the spring of 1666. Among those present to witness and authenticate the cure were his father Gabriel, **John Pinckney**, the ejected minister at Longstock, **George Weldon** and **John Dugdale**; Greatrakes, *Brief Account*, 81–2.

Samuel Foster (*c*.1621–1681). On 19 February 1666, Foster wrote to **William Sancroft** enclosing an account of Greatrakes' cures with a request for any further information that Sancroft might have regarding 'his Miracles'; BL, Harleian MS 3785, fo. 109. Foster was a Suffolk clergyman, who had been educated at Caius College, Cambridge, in the 1640s and served as Fellow from 1644 to 1650. In his will, made in 1680, he expressed a staunch devotion to the established church, requesting that his children should not marry any who did not conform to its liturgy and practices. However, specific bequests suggest that he may have sympathized with latitudinarian elements within the Church. He gave a copy of **Simon Patrick**'s *The Christian Sacrifice* (1671) to a clerical cousin, as well as bequeathing an edition of the works of the 'conformable' Puritan Samuel Hieron (d. 1617) to another relative; Venn, ii, 163; TNA, PROB 11/366, fos 181r–182v.

*****Ezekiel Foxcroft** (1629–1674). Foxcroft's account of Greatrakes' cures performed in the neighbourhood of Ragley and at Worcester were reproduced in **Henry Stubbe**'s *Miraculous Conformist*, 32–44. In addition to witnessing the cure of **Nathaniel Stepping** in London, he provided **John Felton** with a relation of the stroker's cures; Greatrakes, *Brief Account*, 83; BL, Harleian MS 3785, fo. 111.

*****Peter Fullwood** (d. 1705). In all probability, the 'Mr Fullwood' who was present with **Henry More** and **Ezekiel Foxcroft** when they witnessed Greatrakes' cures in and around Ragley in February 1666; BL, Harleian MS 3785, fo. 111. Peter Fullwood was the son of the apothecary-cum-physician Gervase Fullwood (*c*.1597–1677), who had taken an active part on the side of Parliament in the Civil War, sitting as a county commissioner in Huntingdonshire as well as serving as a member of the Eastern Association. Peter, along with his brother and fellow physician, William (d. 1685), were students at their father's alma mater, St Catharine's College, Cambridge, the latter proceeding MD in 1659. Peter did not obtain his MD until 1668, though he was licensed to practise medicine by the university in 1662. In November 1665, **Robert Boyle** agreed to assist the younger brother in his medical studies and related interests at the request of **Henry More**; Venn, ii, 186; Poynter and Bishop, *A Seventeenth-Century Doctor and His Patients*, xiii, 108; CUL, Grace Book H, 49; Bedells, *Visitation of Huntingdon 1684*, 58, 76–7; Boyle, *Correspondence*, ii, 589–90; Cooper, *Annals of Cambridge*, iii, 352; Kingston, *East Anglia in the Civil War*, 386.

Margery Furnace (d. 1669). Wife of Robert (below), she was cured of an ague by Greatrakes in 1666; Greatrakes, *Brief Account*, 71.

Robert Furnace. Husband of Margery (above), Robert Furnace, variously described as a 'metalman' and 'noted tinker' of Clerkenwell, was cured of lameness by Greatrakes' stroking in April 1666 in the presence of, among others, **Robert Boyle** and **Dr James Fairclough**. Boyle is reported to have experimented with the use of Greatrakes' glove in attempting to alleviate Furnace's condition; Greatrakes, *Brief Account*, 48–9, 63, 71; BL, Add. MS 4293, fo. 52.

Thomas Gambon. Aged seventy-one, Gambon, who lived within six miles of Minehead in Somerset, was said to have been cured of a crippling condition in Ireland in 1665. Three years later, he travelled to Minehead to thank the stroker in person for his assistance; Boyle, *Correspondence*, iv, 101. Gambon may have had Irish connections. In 1662, Connor and William Gambon of Ballinity in Waterford, were listed on the county's subsidy roll; Walton, 'Subsidy Roll of County Waterford, 1662', 77.

*Joseph Glanvill (1636–1680). Although there is no firm evidence that Glanvill was a first-hand witness to Greatrakes' stroking, he later gave wide credence in print to the view that his cures were 'above the common methods of Art and Nature'. In order to substantiate these claims, he cited the authority of his friend **George Rust** and other, unnamed members of the Royal Society. In addition, he refers to having discussed the case of the witch of Youghal with Greatrakes at Ragley. Elsewhere, Glanvill took **Henry Stubbe** to task for coopting Greatrakes' cures in order to undermine some of the fundamental principles of the Christian faith; Glanvill, *Saducismus Triumphatus*, ii, 90–4, 189; *idem, Praefatory Answer to Mr Henry Stubbe*, 60–1.

Mary Glover. Of Aylesbury, Buckinghamshire, Glover was deaf and partially blind. She had previously sought help from a range of practitioners, finally securing relief at the hands of Greatrakes in 1666. Her cure was witnessed by **John Owen**, **Matthew Porter**, **John Grone**, and **William Faithorn**; Greatrakes, *Brief Account*, 90.

*Sir Edmund Berry Godfrey (1621–1678). Godfrey's house in London was the venue for a number of Greatrakes' cures in the spring of 1666. In July 1667, Godfrey told his Irish friend that he was his 'Constant Assertor and Admirer', and that he would be 'glad on all occasions to Testifie the Truth thereof to the World, indispight of all Lyers and Gainsayers'; Greatrakes, *Brief Account*, 40, 48, 50; NLI, MS 4728, 10.

Sir John Godolphin (1636–1679). Greatrakes' brother-in-law Godolphin attested the cure of **Anne Robinson** in April 1666; Greatrakes, *Brief Account*, 52–3.

Thomas Gookin. According to Greatrakes, Gookin, a merchant from Kinsale, witnessed several hundred of his cures in 1668, and was willing to provide testimonials to **Robert Boyle**; Boyle, *Correspondence*, iv, 102. Gookin was the son of Sir Vincent Gookin (d. 1638), and thus half-brother to Vincent Gookin (d. 1659), the Cromwellian MP for Bandon and Kinsale, and Robert Gookin(d. 1666 or 1667), who played a vital role in promoting the Cromwellian seizure of Munster in 1649. Both men profited from the land settlement of the 1650s, the latter protecting his interests after the Restoration by conveying his lands on a long lease to Roger Boyle, Earl of Orrery. Thomas likewise engaged in business with Orrery and like many other Munster planters retained property interests in the west country of England. In June 1663, one Thomas Gookin, esquire, of Lincoln's Inn was involved in a mortgage transaction with Dorothy Seymour, the daughter of Sir Edward Seymour, deceased, of Berry Pomeroy, Devon. Like his brothers, Thomas was also on intimate terms with the Penns. In June 1666, Thomas dined with Colonel Robert Phaire and the young Quaker, William Penn. He later served as 'sovereign' or chief magistrate of Clonakilty, county Cork, in 1674 and 1692; *Analecta Hibernica*, 15 (1944), 212; Grubb, *My Irish Journal*, 25, 74n; Derbyshire Record Office, D 547M/T26.

Captain [John] Graunt (1620–1674). In 1668, Captain Graunt and his wife, of Bristol, were travelling companions with Greatrakes in the west country, where they were witness to many of his cures; Boyle, *Correspondence*, iv, 99–100. He may be the same as Captain John Grant, who wrote to Sir Robert Harley from Salisbury in March 1668, asking him to use his influence to assist with problems relating to the collection of the hearth tax in Wiltshire. If so, then he was almost certainly John Graunt (1620–1674), the celebrated statistician and close friend of Sir William Petty, who mentions him frequently in his correspondence. Graunt, an influential figure in the city of London, held the rank of captain in the trained bands. According to his friend John Aubrey, he had been brought up as a Puritan, but later in life became interested in Socinianism and, much to the disgust of Petty, ultimately converted to Catholicism. Greatrakes refers to Captain Graunt as residing in Bristol; however, he may have been a temporary resident, using the city as a base while he performed his office as collector of the hearth tax in the west of England; *HMC Fourteenth Report*, 307; BL, Add. MS 72,858, fos 24, 25v; *ODNB*, sub Graunt, John.

John Grone. Grone witnessed the cures of **Mary Glover** and **Margaret Westley** in 1666; Greatrakes, *Brief Account*, 90.

*George Hall (1613–1668). Although not present, as far as is known, at any of Greatrakes' cures, Hall, then Bishop of Chester, was in correspondence with Greatrakes in August 1665. In an extant letter written by the stroker to Hall, dated 19 August 1665, Greatrakes thanked the Bishop for his encouragement and support, and went on to explain the nature and origin of his miraculous gift. Hall provided a further character reference for Greatrakes in a letter dated 27 April 1666, extracts from which were later published in an attempt to expose **David Lloyd** as a fraud and a liar; Bodl., B.15.8 Linc; Greatrakes, *Brief Account*, 7.

Henry Hall (1637–1700). While dining with Hall on 2 May 1666, Greatrakes stroked the son of **Sir Bulstrode Whitelocke**; Spalding, *Diary of Bulstrode Whitelocke*, 704. Henry Hall was the son of Bartholomew Hall (d. 1677) of Henley-on-Thames, attorney general of the duchy of Lancaster in 1649. Henry later served as a Commissioner for the Peace and High Sheriff of his native Oxfordshire. His brother Bartholomew married a niece of the Independent clergyman Dr John Owen (1616–1683); Spalding, *Contemporaries of Bulstrode Whitelocke*, 111; Squibb, *Visitations of Oxfordshire 1669 and 1675*, 3–4; TNA, PROB 11/456, fos 249r–v.

Richard Hals. Hals attested the cure of Anthony Combs in April 1666; Greatrakes, *Brief Account*, 79–80.

Mrs Haly. Described by **Mary Marshall** as 'my oposit neighbour', she claimed that her uncle **Charles Lemon** had been cured by Greatrakes at Dublin (date unknown); BL, Stowe MS 747, fo. 113.

Susan Hamilton, Lady Glanawly (d. 1687). 'Lady Glanaly' was cured by Greatrakes of a headache, the pain going out 'at her fingers', at an unknown date but before the death of her first husband in 1678; *Notes and Queries*, 9 (1884), 62–3. Susan Balfour of Pitcullo was the third wife of Hugh Hamilton, first Lord Hamilton and Baron Glanawly, a Scottish-born soldier who was created an Irish peer by Charles II in 1661. He settled at Ballygawley in Tyrone in 1662, and later served as an Irish Privy Councillor as well as a Captain of Horse. After her husband's death, Susan married Henry Mervyn and died at Dublin on 11 December 1687; *ODNB*, sub Hamilton, Hugh; Bodl., Carte MS 163, fo. 52.

John Harrison. Aged thirty-one and living in Southwark, Harrison was stroked by Greatrakes on several occasions culminating in his cure from the king's evil on Easter Monday 1666. Harrison's certificate, which was authenticated by **Albertus Otto Faber** and **George Weldon**, was proffered in an attempt to dispel the false allegations of the stroker's detractors who, he believed, acted out of fear that 'their Dagon of Profit must fall hereby'; Greatrakes, *Brief Account*, 88–9. Possibly related to Mrs Harrison (below).

Mrs Harrison. In August 1666, **Edmund Godfrey**, a kinsman of the Harrisons, wrote a letter to Greatrakes in which he referred to his 'long Patient', Mrs Harrison, who now [has] better thoughts of your actings'. Cured of a wen and a general scrofulous condition by Greatrakes earlier that year, she feared a year later that it may have risen again; NLI, MS 4728, 3, 12–13. She was probably Jane, the wife of James Harrison, a relative of Godfrey's brother-in-law, Edmund Harrison (1591–1667), the Royal Embroiderer; Marshall, *Strange Death of Edmund Godfrey*, 15, 21.

*Henry Hatsell (d. 1667). In the first published account of Greatrakes' cures, confirmation of their authenticity and miraculous status was provided, among others, by 'Captain Haslell [sic] of Plymouth', who had received an account of the same from his son in Ireland in 1665; *Wonders If No Miracles*, 4. Hatsell's informant was probably his eldest son Henry

(1641–1714), who later became a judge and Baron of the Exchequer. He was a zealous Whig and regular correspondent with the radical exclusionist MP for Plympton, George Treby (1644–1700), who defended the 'seditious' printer **John Starkey** in 1677; *ODNB*; Derbyshire Record Office, D 239 M/O.

John Hawkins. Of Thatcham, Berkshire, he was aged about twenty-five in April 1666, when he was cured by Greatrakes of a sciatica in his hip in the presence of **John Patrick** and **Thomas Bromley**; Greatrakes, *Brief Account*, 80–1. He was the son of Peter Hawkins (d. 1680) of Thatcham and later served as churchwarden in the town in 1688. His brother Richard (1636–1692) was a wealthy London wine cooper and prominent Whig supporter; Berkshire Record Office, D/A/81/120; Barfield, *Thatcham*, i, 186; Woodhead, *Rulers of London*, 86.

John Hawtrey (1645–1715 or 1716). Of Burnham, Buckinghamshire, Hawtrey was cured by Greatrakes of the king's evil in 1666, as attested by **Robert Boyle** and **Dr James Fairclough**; Greatrakes, *Brief Account*, 49. He was the son of Edward Hawtrey (1600–1669), Vicar of Burnham, who was ejected from his living in 1650, but restored at the Restoration. At the time of his cure, John was a student at King's College, Cambridge. He later pursued a clerical career. His sister Mary married fellow clergyman Samuel Edlin (1637–1698), a close friend of **Clement Sankey**; *Wal. Rev.*, 74; Venn, ii, 338; PROB 11/331, fos 269r–v.

John Hayes. Described as 'servant to Dr Worley' (i.e. **Dr Benjamin Worsley**), Hayes' cure at the hands of Greatrakes was described in a letter written by **Dr James Fairclough** to **Sir William Smith**, dated 5 May 1666; Greatrakes, *Brief Account*, 71.

Sir John Hinton (d.1682). Hinton, a royal physician, was present at York House to witness Greatrakes' attempt to 'dispossess' a young girl. Hinton's verdict on the truth or otherwise of such claims is unrecorded; Greatrakes, *Brief Account*, 33. A staunch episcopalian and loyal servant of the Stuarts, Hinton suffered a great deal for his devotion to the royal cause in the 1640s and 1650s; *ODNB*.

*Sir Nathaniel Hobart (1600–1674). Hobart, alongside his son-in-law **Sir William Smith**, supplied a certificate, dated 24 April 1666, attesting to the cures of **Joseph Warden**, **William Levell**, and **Francis Steele**. He also observed the cure of **Anthony Combs**; Greatrakes, *Brief Account*, 51–2, 79–80. Nathaniel was the youngest son of Sir Henry Hobart (d. 1625) and married Anne Leeke, a cousin of the Buckinghamshire Verneys. Anne was remembered in the will of Dame Ursula Verney in 1666, the executor of which was **Edmund Squibb**. Hobart died on 19 February 1674 and was buried two days later in the church of the Middle Temple, London; *HMC Seventh Report*, 458; Thurloe, *State Papers*, iii, 410; Verney and Verney, *Memoirs of the Verney Family*, ii, 190 and *passim*; TNA, PROB 11/326, fo. 116r; 11/377, fos 132Ar–v; Inderwick, *Calendar of the Inner Temple Records*, iii, 450.

Benjamin Huskins. According to **Dr James Fairclough**, Huskins, a gunner in the Tower of London, was healed by Greatrakes in 1666; Greatrakes, *Brief Account*, 71.

Mary Jackson. Jackson, of Wood Street, London, was cured of an impostume above her eye, as witnessed by **Benjamin Whichcote**, in 1666; Greatrakes, *Brief Account*, 64.

John Jacomb. According to **Dr James Fairclough**, Jacomb, of George Alley, Southwark, who suffered from 'exquisite and continual pains', was healed by Greatrakes' stroking in 1666. **Thomas Belasyse, Viscount Fauconberg**, applied the pricking test to the numb parts of Jacomb's body; Greatrakes, *Brief Account*, 72–3.

*Samuel Jeake the elder (1623–1690). In the course of a lengthy correspondence with fellow dissenter **Thomas Morris**, Jeake poured scorn on Greatrakes' healing claims, citing the example of a local man, **Richard Chiswell**, whom he implied had died as a result of the stroker's surgical incompetence; ESxRO, FRE 4223, fos 153–202. Jeake was a prominent merchant in the port town of Rye in Sussex. During the 1650s, he held the post of town clerk, a role he combined with lay preaching. He was deprived of his office after the Restoration, but continued to play a leading role as defender of the interests of the town's sizeable dissenting community. He was also something of an intellectual, possessing an important library that included a copy of Greatrakes' *Brief Account*; *ODNB*; Hunter *et al.*, *A Radical's Books*.

*Katherine Jones, Viscountess Ranelagh (1615–1691)**. Greatrakes conducted various 'experiments' at the home of Lady Ranelagh in Pall Mall in 1666 during the course of which he cured both her servants and one of her daughters. He also cured, among others, her brother-in-law, **Charles Rich**; BL, Add. MS 4293, fos 50–1, 53v; Greatrakes, *Brief Account*, 32, 35; Boyle, *Correspondence*, iii, 86. Lady Ranelagh's Puritan credentials were renowned in Restoration London. In August 1661 she became the object of government scrutiny and suspicion when her house was used for Presbyterian worship. Two years later, she interceded on behalf of some of those accused in the Dublin plot, and by 1676 she was attending the meetings of Richard Baxter. She would appear to have been highly sympathetic to the plight of the nonconformists after 1660 and supported various schemes aimed at encouraging cross-denominational links and greater religious unity in Protestant circles; *ODNB*; *CSPD, 1661–1662*, 71; Lynch, 'The Incomparable Lady Ranelagh', 25–33; Connolly, 'Manuscript Treatise', 170–3; Connolly, 'A Proselytising Protestant Commonwealth', 244–64.

William Jones. The son of Walter Jones of Mortlake, he was treated by Greatrakes at the house of **John Owen** in 1666. His cure was witnessed by Owen, **Sir Abraham Cullen**, **William Rushout**, and **Richard Mulys**; Greatrakes, *Brief Account*, 55–6, 66.

Hester Jordan. Of Bitterly, Shropshire, Jordan was aged twenty-two, when she was cured by Greatrakes of a dumbness at Worcester in February 1666; Stubbe, *Miraculous Conformist*, 41–2. She was probably the daughter of Thomas Jordan of Bitterly, whose son, also Thomas, matriculated at Oxford in 1666, proceeding BA in 1670; Foster, ii, 834.

Anne Kelly. Of Old Windsor, Berkshire, she was aged twenty-one and had been suffering from a dead palsy on the right side of her body for over fourteen years, when she was stroked by Greatrakes in April 1666. She was subsequently examined by **Robert Boyle**, **Dr Fairclough**, **Dr Denton**, and **Sir William Smith**. Greatrakes later met her again on board a ship travelling from Bristol to Minehead in 1668 when he described her as the 'young woman which Doctor Wilkin's brought me', and upon whom the experiment with the pin was tried; Greatrakes, *Brief Account*, 43; Boyle, *Correspondence*, iv, 101.

Thomas Kenian. Described as a gentleman, he attested to the cure of **Sarah Tuffly**, 19 April 1666; Greatrakes, *Brief Account*, 76.

Grace Knight. Grace was the nine-year old daughter of alderman **William Knight** (below). She was cured of a 'flux of rheum' in her eye by the application of Greatrakes' rubbing and spittle in 1666. In addition to her father, her cure was witnessed by **Dr Fairclough** and **John Cressett**; Greatrakes, *Brief Account*, 54.

*William Knight (d. 1683)**. He attested to the cure of his daughter, Grace (above); Greatrakes, *Brief Account*, 54.

*Captain John Lancaster (*c.*1623–*c.*1684)**. Lancaster, who was Greatrakes' cousin, was one of the first to affirm the truth of Greatrakes' claims in print. In the summer of 1665, he affirmed that his cures had been attested by 'many men of note in Ireland'; *Wonders If Not Miracles*, 4.

Thomas Langham. Langham was cured of severe headaches by Greatrakes' stroking in Prince Rupert's chambers in March 1666; Greatrakes, *Brief Account*, 85.

Mr Lawrence. A merchant of Youghal, Greatrakes claimed in a letter written to **Robert Boyle** in 1668 that Lawrence was willing to testify to hundreds of cures that he had witnessed first-hand in that year; Boyle, *Correspondence*, iv, 102. He was perhaps Thomas Lawrence, who paid a rate in Youghal in 1670; Caulfield, *Council Book of Youghal*, 331.

Mr Lee. A 'worthy citizen' of London, who was cured by Greatrakes in 1666; *Great Cures and Strange Miracles*, 5.

Charles Lemon. Described as 'secretary to the commissioners in Dublin', he was cured, according to **Mary Marshall**, at an unknown date by Greatrakes. She described Lemon as the uncle of **Mrs Haly**; BL, Stowe MS 747, fo. 113. Elsewhere, he is referred to as 'Clerke to the Commissioners at the Board'. He may be the man of the same name, an ensign, who petitioned Ormond for a commission in the Irish army. One Charles Lemmon proceeded MA from Trinity College, Dublin, on 26 January 1661. He may be the same as Charles Lemon, 'gentleman', tenant for a plot of land on Oxmantowne Green, Dublin, in 1665. He was listed as an inhabitant of St George's Lane in the parish of St Andrews, Dublin, in 1659. The man cured by Greatrakes was probably related to Sir William Lemon (d. 1667), Treasurer at War, MP, and member of the Committee for Compounding during the Commonwealth whose Irish lands (in Meath) were confirmed by the Act of Settlement. He was instrumental in passing letters between **Lady Ranelagh** and her brother, **Robert Boyle**, in 1665; Bodl., Carte MS 154, fo. 22r; *HMC Ormonde MSS*, 830; Burtchaell and Sadleir, *Alumni Dublinenses*, 494; Gilbert, *Calendar of Ancient Records of Dublin*, iv, 332; Pender, *Census of Ireland, 1659*, 363; *Calendar of Treasury Books*, i, 199; *Fifteenth Report*, 177; JRL, Irish MS 125, fo. 40v; Boyle, *Correspondence*, ii, 582.

William Levell. A cook at the Cock in Leadenhall Street, London, he was aged twenty-four and suffering from acute pain in his hip and knee when he was sent out of St Bartholomew's Hospital to Greatrakes for cure. His case was attested by **Sir William Smith** and **Sir Nathaniel Hobart**, 24 April 1666; Greatrakes, *Brief Account*, 51–2.

Mrs Lile. Lile was a friend of **Mary Marshall** in Dublin, who was cured by Greatrakes (date unknown); BL, Stowe MS 747, fo. 113.

*David Lloyd (1635–1692)**. Lloyd, reader at the Charterhouse, was the author of the anonymously published *Wonders No Miracles* (1666), an uncompromising attack on the veracity of Greatrakes' cures, as well as his religious, political, and moral standing. His authorship was revealed by Greatrakes in his *Brief Account*.

[John] Love. In an early manuscript life of the Earl of Orrery (no longer extant), one Mr Love, the author, was reputed to have said of Greatrakes that 'he could not remove his Pectoral and Rheumatic Pains; but that after he had unjustly ridiculed him, he was witness to his curing the Falling Sickness beyond Credit'; Sir James Ware, *Works*, ii, 198. Love was almost certainly the same as the John Love who wrote to Orrery's brother, **Robert Boyle**, in 1688 from his home at Torbehy, near Mitchelstown, county Cork. There, he refers to the fact that he has 'for the last seven years of his life' been given bread by the Earl in return for which he hoped to fulfil a commission to translate a recent history of the Waldensians published at Leiden in 1669. The work in question was Jean Léger's two-volume *Histoire Generale des Eglises Evangeliques des Vallees de Piémont, ou Vaudoises*. In the same year, one John Love published a treatise on the art of surveying and mathematics which he dedicated to Robert Boyle and on the frontispiece to which he described himself as one of the 'meanest' of Boyle's 'servants'; Boyle, *Correspondence*, vi, 249–50; Love, *Geodæsia*.

Sir Charles Lyttleton (1629–1716). In March 1666, Lyttleton wrote to Sir Christopher Hatton informing him that Greatrakes 'grows in that esteeme among us that I heard the B[isho]p of Hereford [i.e. **Herbert Croft**] yesterday say he had done thinges, to his owne certaine knowledge, beyond all the power of nature, though, if you will read my friend Mr Stubbs [i.e. **Henry Stubbe**] upon him, you may thinke he may be mistaken, and yet enough to make it wonderfull what he does'; Thompson, *Correspondence of the Family of Hatton*, i,

49. Of Hagley Hall, Worcestershire, Lyttelton was a die-hard royalist. He later served as Lieutenant-Governor of Jamaica from 1662 to 1664 where he presumably made the acquaintance of the physician Henry Stubbe; Henning, ii, 783; *CSP Colonial: America and West Indies, 1661–1668*, 243.

*Mrs [Mary] Mackworth (d. 1679). The widow of the parliamentarian soldier Humphrey Mackworth (1603–1654) (for whom, see p. 100 and n.), she was cured by Greatrakes of a breast cancer at Affane in December 1665; *Conway Letters*, 267.

Margaret Macshane. Of Ballnakelly, Lismore, Macshane, a tenant of the Earl of Cork, was a long-term sufferer from the king's evil and was one of the first to be cured of the disease by Greatrakes at his house at Affane, in the presence of Dr Anthony, 'a famous physician, then at my House'; Greatrakes, *Brief Account*, 23–4; Bodl., B.15.8 Linc.

William Maher. Maher was the son of William Maher (or Lem Maghur) of Salterbridge, near Lismore, a tenant of the Earl of Cork. A sufferer from the king's evil, he was Greatrakes' first success sometime around 1662 or 1663. It is probably his image that adorns the frontispiece to Greatrakes' *Brief Account*; ibid. 22–3; Bodl., B.15.8 Linc; RS, EL/M1/36.

*Thomas Mall (d. 1672 or 1673). Mall, a nonconformist minister from Devon, visited Ireland in 1665 to witness Greatrakes' cures at first hand and may thus have acted, along with his associate Henry Hatsell, as one of the informants who supplied information on Greatrakes to the anonymous publisher of *Wonders If Not Miracles* (1665). A letter of Mall's to a friend, Thomas Georges, and dated 28 July 1665 from Youghal, was copied by John Beale and forwarded to Robert Boyle in September 1665; Boyle, *Correspondence*, ii, 522; RS, EL/M1/36.

[Sir] John Mandeville. His ploughman in county Tipperary was cured of a sciatica by Greatrakes in 1665; *The Newes*, 13 July 1665.

Margaret Manning. A servant of Lady Ranelagh, she was stroked by Greatrakes at her mistress' house in Pall Mall and before Robert Boyle in April 1666; BL, Add. MS 4293, fo. 50.

Mary Marshall. Marshall was the daughter of John Denison of Dublin. In May 1699, she wrote to the Presbyterian minister Joseph Boyse of Dublin, then visiting Yorkshire, giving, at his request, an account of several cures performed by Greatrakes at the house of her father in Dublin some twenty or more years earlier. Her letter was subsequently sent to Boyse's friend, Ralph Thoresby, who forwarded it to John Evelyn. A year later, it was published by the Royal Society; BL, Stowe MS 747, fo. 113; *Philosophical Transactions*, 21 (1700), 332–4.

*Andrew Marvell (1621–1678). In April 1666, Marvell witnessed, along with his cousin Thomas Alured and nephew William Popple, the cures of Anthony Nicholson and Dorothy Pocock; Greatrakes, *Brief Account*, 83–5.

John Massam. A stationer of Bread Street, London, he witnessed, alongside his brother Thomas (below), the cure of their sister Mary Sermon or Surman at the house of their cousin John Owen at Mortlake in 1666; Greatrakes, *Brief Account*, 91.

Thomas Massam (d. 1675). A scrivener, of St Bartholomew's, London, he witnessed, alongside his brother John (above), the cure of their sister Mary Sermon or Surman at the house of their cousin John Owen at Mortlake in 1666; Greatrakes, *Brief Account*, 91. Massam was a prominent figure in the London Scriveners' Company, serving as steward in 1659, assistant in 1665, and warden in 1673 and 1674. He was also politically active, being elected as a common councilman for Farringdon Without (St Sepulchre's) in 1675. Massam was a wealthy scrivener, who owned land in Middlesex and Hertfordshire, as well as renting lands to Bulstrode Whitelocke in Berkshire and Buckinghamshire. In the will of his cousin and business partner Colonel John Owen, bequests were made to Thomas and Mary

Massam, 'the children of my cousin Thomas Massam'; Bodl., Rawlinson D 51; Woodhead, *Rulers of London*, 113; TNA, PROB 11/347, fos 277v–279v; 11/359, fos 177v–179v; C 10/489/96.

Captain John Maurice (d. 1671). In a letter to **Robert Boyle** in 1668, Greatrakes claimed that Maurice, described as the collector of Minehead, was willing to corroborate cures performed by him in the town in that year; Boyle, *Correspondence*, iv, 101. Maurice was a government agent in Minehead after the Restoration. Between 1666 and 1671, he corresponded regularly with Secretary Williamson and others, providing a constant flow of information with regard to naval affairs, as well as local religious and political news; Hancock, *Minehead*, 284–5; *CSPD, 1665–1671, passim*; TNA, PROB 11/337, fo. 166v.

*Sir Ames Meredith (1617–1669). Although Meredith's name does not appear on any list of those who attested to Greatrakes' cures, he undoubtedly assisted the healer, both as a friend and collaborator, in promoting his claims to heal the sick by stroking in 1665–6. According to **Henry Stubbe**, he shared a chamber with Greatrakes at Ragley Hall in February 1666, and in the previous year he was responsible for introducing Greatrakes to his brother-in-law, **George Hall**, Bishop of Chester; Stubbe, *Miraculous Conformist*, 11.

*Alexander Merreal (c.1635–1707). A stationer of Bread Street, London, Merreal witnessed the cure of **Mary Sermon** or **Surman** at the Mortlake home of **John Owen** in 1666; Greatrakes, *Brief Account*, 91; Plomer, *Dictionary of Printers and Booksellers 1641–1667*, 127; *idem, Dictionary of Printers and Booksellers 1668–1725*, 204.

Joan Merrick. Of Minehead, she was cured by Greatrakes of a tympany in 1666, and remained in good health in 1668; Boyle, *Correspondence*, iv, 102.

Anne Meyerne. Of Ludgate Hill, Meyerne attested to the cure of her two daughters, **Mary Smith** and **Anne Waring**; Greatrakes, *Brief Account*, 85–6. She was the wife of the merchant John Christopher Meyerne (d. 1679); TNA, PROB 11/360, fos 111r–v.

Sir Robert Moray (d. 1673). In October 1665, news of Greatrakes' cures 'amongst his country people' had reached Moray, but, he wrote to **Henry Oldenburg**, 'I believe nothing of the whole matter as yet'. On 9 April 1666, Moray wrote to **Henry Slingsby**, a colleague at the Royal Society, describing the King's sceptical and negative reaction to Greatrakes' cures. Moray himself remained non-committal, claiming that while 'printed books talk things of him, I have not yet taken the pains to read [them]'; Oldenburg, *Correspondence*, ii, 561; *HMC Sixth Report*, 339. Moray, a soldier by profession, was a leading Scottish Presbyterian and supporter of the Stuarts, who helped to promote the Restoration of Charles II in 1660. Keenly interested in all branches of natural philosophy, he was one of the founder members of the Royal Society. In particular, he shared Charles II's passion for chemistry, assisting the King in experiments in the new laboratory constructed at Whitehall after 1668. He would appear to have developed an early passion for chemical medicine while living in exile at Maastricht in the late 1650s. Moray was a consistent advocate throughout the 1660s of an eirenic approach to the religious problems of the day, and used his influence at court to promote moderation towards dissenters. He was also addicted to 'portents and prophecies', though his final verdict on Greatrakes does not survive; *ODNB*; Stevenson, *Letters of Sir Robert Moray*; Harris, 'Lady Sophia's Visions', 129–55.

*Henry More (1614–1687). More was present at Ragley in early 1666 when Greatrakes attempted to cure his great friend and correspondent, **Lady Anne Conway**. He later discussed the cures with **Robert Boyle** who confided to him that he had been a spectator 'of at least 60 performances of his'. More concluded in a letter to Lady Conway that Boyle was likely to do Greatrakes 'more creditt then any body'. At the same time he alluded to the 'reall good' which Charles, the son of **Ralph Cudworth**, had received at the hands of the Irishman; *Conway Letters*, 273 and *passim*; BL, Harleian MS 3785, fo. 111; More, 'Scholia on Enthusiasmus Triumphatus', appended to his *A Collection of Several Philosophical Writings*, 51–3.

*Sir Anthony Morgan (1621 or 1622–1668). Morgan was present in the shop of the stationer, John Starkey, when Edmund Squibb claimed to have witnessed Greatrakes cure two unidentified persons of the 'Phthysick' in April 1666; Greatrakes, *Brief Account*, 77–8.

*Thomas Morris. In November 1666, Morris entered into a correspondence with his friend and business partner Samuel Jeake the elder in which the two men debated the nature of a true church. One sure proof was the ability to perform miracles, Morris citing a number of contemporary examples of the practice, including that of Greatrakes, 'one of the Church of England'. He went on to describe how two acquaintances had sought relief at the stroker's hands, one a young maid suffering with the king's evil, the other a gentlewoman with 'sore eyes'. The former recovered completely, while the latter 'received no benefit at all'. Morris, a Baptist, was sufficiently impressed to reconsider, albeit briefly, rejoining the Anglican fold; ESxRO, FRE 4223, fos. 172r, 198r, and *passim*. Morris had previously engaged in religious controversy in 1655, when he published a defence of Baptist practices in a debate with Benjamin Morley and Robert Everard; Hunter and Gregory, *Diary of Samuel Jeake*, 65n, 166; Morris, *A Messenger Sent*.

*Richard Mulys. Mulys claimed to have witnessed several cures by Greatrakes at the house of his employer, Christian Cavendish, Countess of Devonshire, as well as others at the Mortlake home of John Owen, including that of William Jones; Greatrakes, *Brief Account*, 66.

Anthony Nicholson (1601–1667). Nicholson was relieved of chronic pains throughout his body by Greatrakes' stroking on the advice of Benjamin Whichcote and George Rust. His cure was performed in the presence of Andrew Marvell, Thomas Alured, Thomas Pooley, William Popple, and Dr James Fairclough; Greatrakes, *Brief Account*, 83–4. Anthony Nicholson, father and son, were Cambridge booksellers. The father, who was almost certainly Greatrakes' patient (he claimed to have been suffering for over twenty-three years), was probably born in Cambridge in 1601, dying there in April 1667. His name was appended to three works, all theological, published in Cambridge between 1648 and 1652, including one by the Cambridge Platonist and 'voice of moderation', Nathaniel Culverwell (1619–1651). His son, Anthony (d. 1680), was a bookbinder at the Six Bells in Cambridge from 1667 until his death in 1680. Nicholson the elder and his wife would appear to have been intimate friends with the royalist minister, Humphrey Babington (d. 1692), who was ejected as a Fellow of Trinity College, Cambridge, in 1650 for refusing the Engagement; Plomer, *Dictionary of Printers and Booksellers 1641–1667*, 137; idem, *Dictionary of Printers and Booksellers 1668–1725*, 218; Gray and Palmer, *Abstracts from Wills*, 104–7; Bodl., Tanner MS 54, fo. 98; *ODNB*, sub Culverwell, Nathaniel.

William Nicholson (1591–1672). In a letter of 9 February 1666, Lord Conway wrote to Sir George Rawdon announcing that 'this morning the Bishop of Gloucester [William Nicholson] recommended to me a prebend's son in his diocese, to be brought to [Greatrakes] for a leprosy from head to foot, which hath been judg'd incurable above ten years, and in my chamber he cured him perfectly'. According to Henry Stubbe in his account of the same incident, the boy was said to be fourteen years old; *Conway Letters*, 268; Stubbe, *Miraculous Conformist*, 28.

Captain [John] Norris (d. 1668). Norris was the royal excise collector at Minehead in the 1660s. Greatrakes was visiting Captain Norris' house in 1668 when one of his old patients, Thomas Gambon, visited him to confirm his continuing good health; Boyle, *Correspondence*, iv, 101. A royalist in the Civil War, Norris was at Oxford when Charles I surrendered in 1646. He subsequently compounded on 5 December 1646. In all probability, he is the the same man as the Captain John Norris of Limerick, who in 1655 petitioned the Irish board as the 'agent for the Marchants of Bristoll'. In the same year he was granted a licence to 'export' 500 Irish Catholics to America. Norris' will was witnessed, among others, by **Samuel Crockford**; Hancock, *Minehead*, 278; Green, *CPCC*, ii, 1592; NLI, MS 11,961, 268–73, 274; BL, Egerton MS 212, 30; TNA, PROB 11/330, fos 18v–20r.

Mrs Anne Norton. 'My Lady Nortons daughter of Lee (nigh Bristol)' sent for Greatrakes in the summer of 1668 to staunch the bleeding from the mouth of her sister, Anne. Greatrakes was rewarded with wine and cider; Boyle, *Correspondence*, iv, 100. Greatrakes may have erred in refering to his patient as Anne. According to the will of Sir George Norton (d. 1668) of Abbot's Leigh, near Bristol, who died shortly before Greatrakes' visit, he and his wife Ellen (d. 1677) had only two daughters, Ellen and Grace. Sir George was a staunch royalist who sheltered the future Charles II at Abbot's Leigh in the aftermath of the battle of Worcester. Despite the family's earlier loyalty, Ellen, who married William Trenchard (1640–1710) in 1668, and Sir George's second son, Edward (1654–1702), became deeply involved in the various plots against Charles II and fled into exile in the Netherlands. The Nortons would appear to have possessed Irish connections and may have lived there in the 1650s. In 1659 George Norton, esquire, Grace Norton, and Anne Norton, 'gent[lewomen]' were listed as inhabitants of the parish of Killurth in county Cork. In 1672 Sir George's son and heir, also George (d. 1715), married Frances Freke, an educated young woman, who, like Anne Conway, harboured literary aspirations. Her aunt, Elizabeth Freke, married an Irish cousin and lived in county Cork. A frequent visitor to Abbot's Leigh, she kept a diary (1671–1714), but no mention is made of Greatrakes; TNA, PROB 11/326, fos 266r–v; *ODNB*, sub Norton, Frances, and Norton, Edward; *JCHAS*, 16 (1910), 152; Pender, *Census of Ireland, 1659*, 235; Anselment, *Remembrances of Elizabeth Freke*.

*****Peter Noyes (d. 1666)**. Noyes, a gentleman of Shinfield in Berkshire, originally sought medical advice from Dr Thomas Willis at Oxford, but following the failure of various physicians there to cure him of the king's evil, Willis advised Noyes to go to London and seek cure at the hands of Greatrakes. Noyes' cure was attested by **Richard Birch**, **Jasper Walker**, **Thomas White**, **Stephen Parkes**, and **Edward Phipps**, 10 May 1666; Greatrakes, *Brief Account*, 87–8.

Winifred Noyes. The wife of Peter Noyes (above), 'with tears and perswasive arguments', she persuaded Greatrakes to stroke her husband, and subsequently signed the published testimonial of his cure; Greatrakes, *Brief Account*, 87–8. Following the death of her husband in 1666, she married George Gosnold, a gentleman from Beaconsfield in Buckinghamshire, in February 1671; Foster, *London Marriage Licences, 1521–1869*, 570.

Henry Oldenburg (*c.*1619–1677). Oldenburg, secretary to the Royal Society, was initially sceptical of Greatrakes' claims, reporting the views of one of his correspondents, **John Beale**, that the stroker had formerly used charms and studied magic, and that he now attempted to recover the blind and raise the dead. He seems to have shifted position somewhat by March 1666, when he wrote to **Robert Boyle**, declaring that Greatrakes did achieve some success by friction, 'insinuating (perhaps) some salubrious steams or spirits of his owne, into sickly people's bodies'. Some of his evidence was based on conversations with **Mr De Son**. In 1674, Oldenburg confirmed this naturalistic view of Greatrakes' methods when, in response to a query from a European correspondent, Pierre Daniel Huet (1630–1721), he suggested that the Irishman's cures 'did not… extend beyond tumours and pains in the body, which he chased out by a strong friction'; Oldenburg, *Correspondence*, ii, 496, 512–13, 556; iii, 59; x, 493; xi, 28; *ODNB*.

Osborne family. Various members of the Osborne family witnessed Greatrakes' cures in Dublin at the house of the wife of **John Denison** in 1680; *Notes and Queries*, 9 (1884), 61–3.

*****Captain or Colonel John Owen (d. 1679).** Owen, a London grocer and stationer, witnessed numerous cures by Greatrakes in 1666, including many at his home in the Surrey parish of Mortlake. Those cured included **William Jones, Dorothy Wardant, Mary Glover, Margaret Westley,** and **Richard Whitall.** In a letter to **Robert Boyle,** he also gave details of his own cure at the hands of Greatrakes and was clearly an enthusiastic promoter of the stroker's cause; Greatrakes, *Brief Account*, 55–6, 74–5, 86–7, 90.

Stephen Parkes (d. 1675). Parkes attested to the cure of **Peter Noyes** in 1666; Greatrakes, *Brief Account*, 88. Parkes was probably the dissenter and scrivener of that name, of All Hallows, Bread Street, London, who subscribed £250 to the crown in 1670. He died in 1675. A number of Greatrakes' supporters emanated from this part of London, including fellow scrivener **Thomas Massam,** who witnessed the will of Parkes' father Edward (d. 1651) in 1651; De Krey, *London and the Restoration*, 409; TNA, PROB 11/349, fos 190v–191v, 273r–v; 11/215, fos 72r–73v.

*****John Patrick (1632–1695).** Patrick, the brother of fellow clergyman Simon (below), attested to the cure of **John Hawkins** in April 1666; Greatrakes, *Brief Account*, 80.

*****Simon Patrick (1626–1707).** The clergyman Patrick attested to numerous cures wrought by Greatrakes in London in April 1666, including those of a servant of **William Faithorn** (probably **Walter Dolle**), the wife of **Samuel Smith** of Newbury, and an unnamed artist. He also provided a glowing testimonial of Greatrakes' religious and political conformity; Greatrakes, *Brief Account*, 61–3.

*****Colonel Robert Phaire (1618 or 1619–1682).** A close friend and neighbour of Greatrakes, Phaire was frequently stroked by him for various complaints, including fever and ague, as were other members of his family; Greatrakes, *Brief Account*, 27; BL, Add. MS 4291, fos 150v, 151r–v.

Edward Phipps. Phipps attested to the cure of **Peter Noyes** in London in May 1666; Greatrakes, *Brief Account*, 88.

*****Henry Pierce (c.1624–1680).** Rector of Shaw-cum-Donnington, Berkshire, Pierce attested to the cure of **Nathaniel Stepping,** 10 May 1666; Greatrakes, *Brief Account*, 83.

Pierson. Pierson was a Dublin smith whose two daughters were cured of the king's evil by Greatrakes, date uncertain. According to **Mary Marshall,** one of the women was still alive and living in Dublin in 1699; BL, Stowe MS 747, fo. 113.

*****John Pinckney (c.1619–1680).** Pinckney, a nonconformist minister from Hampshire, attested to the cure of one of his former parishioners, **William Floyd,** who suffered from the king's evil, on 31 March 1666; Greatrakes, *Brief Account*, 81–2.

*****Captain John Pley (d. c.1679).** Pley was named, along with **John Lancaster** and **Henry Hatsell,** as a witness to the veracity of claims emanating from Ireland in 1665 that emphasized the miraculous powers of Greatrakes' stroking; *Wonders If Not Miracles*, 4.

Dorothy Pocock. Dorothy, the wife of John Pocock of Chieveley in Berkshire, was described as aged forty-five when she was stroked for a tumour by Greatrakes in London, the cure being attested by **Andrew Marvell, Thomas Alured, Thomas Pooley,** and **Dr James Fairclough** on 10 April 1666; Greatrakes, *Brief Account*, 84–5.

Thomas Pooley. Pooley, who was described in one affidavit as MA, attested to the cures of **Eleanor Dickinson, Anthony Nicholson,** and **Dorothy Pocock** in April 1666; Greatrakes, *Brief Account*, 45–6, 83–4, 84–5.

*****William Popple (1638–1708).** Along with his uncle **Andrew Marvell** and **Thomas Alured,** Popple attested to the cure of **Anthony Nicholson** in London in 1666; Greatrakes, *Brief Account*, 83–4.

Matthew Porter. Porter, a Londoner, attested to the cures of **Mary Glover** and **Margaret Westley** in 1666; Greatrakes, *Brief Account*, 90. Given the place of Margaret Westley's residence, Porter was probably the same as the Matthew Porter, laceman, who died and was buried in the parish of Christ Church, London, on 18 August 1693. In his will, he left numerous bequests of godly, devotional works by authors such as William Perkins and William Gouge. It also refers to his wife Margaret (possibly Greatrakes' patient), whom he describes as 'a very weakly woman [who] cannot struggle with the world'. There is no record, however, of their marriage in the extant parish registers; Littledale, *Registers of Christ Church, Newgate*, 310; TNA, PROB 11/416, fos 89r–90r.

Thomas Porter. Described by **Henry Stubbe** as his 'very worthy and good friend', Greatrakes cured him of pains in his legs after a second course of stroking in Worcestershire in February 1666; Stubbe, *Miraculous Conformist*, A2v–A3r.

*Sir George Rawdon (1604–1684). According to Greatrakes, the two men met at Ragley Hall in 1668 where Rawdon had witnessed various cures and was now willing to provide testimonials of the stroker's healing powers; Boyle, *Correspondence*, iv, 102. Rawdon was the brother-in-law, agent, and private secretary of **Edward Conway, Viscount Conway**, and was employed by him in 1665 to act as an intermediary in negotiations to bring Greatrakes to Ragley in order to cure his wife, **Lady Anne Conway**. A leading figure in the Government of Ulster, he represented Carlingford in the Irish Parliament of 1661. Rawdon was appointed a Privy Councillor as well as a commissioner to execute the proposed land settlement of Ireland in the 1660s. He was rewarded with a baronetcy in May 1665. Rawdon was critical of the Ulster or 'Scottish' Presbyterians and a warm friend to the Anglican church; *ODNB*; *Conway Letters*; Berwick, *Rawdon Papers*; Bailie, 'Sir George Rawdon', 2–9.

Mrs Frances Read. Read, of Pall Mall, was cured of persistent headaches by Greatrakes in March 1666, as witnessed by **George Weldon** and **Sir William Smith**. She also claimed to have been present on numerous other occasions when the Irishman performed his cures; Greatrakes, *Brief Account*, 82–3.

*Mrs Reynolds. Described as a shopkeeper's wife from Alcester, Warwickshire, she was cured by Greatrakes at Worcester on 1 February 1666; Stubbe, *Miraculous Conformist*, 32. She was almost certainly the wife of John Reynolds (d. 1671), a mercer and prominent dissenter in Alcester (for whom, see p. 79 and n.).

Charles Rich, fourth Earl of Warwick (1616–1673). According to **Daniel Coxe**, Rich, who suffered terribly from the gout, was 'considerably relieved' on being stroked by Greatrakes at the house of his sister-in-law, **Lady Ranelagh**, some time in February or March 1666; Boyle, *Correspondence*, iii, 86. Charles Rich was the second son of the parliamentarian Robert Rich, second Earl of Warwick (d. 1658), and succeeded to the earldom on the death of his elder brother in 1659. A figure of some standing in Essex (he served as *custos rotulorum* from 1660 until his death in 1673), he is perhaps better known today as the husband of the Puritan diarist Mary Rich, née Boyle (1624–1678), sister to **Lady Ranelagh** and **Robert Boyle**. From her base at Leez Priory in Essex, the ancestral home of the Rich family, she devoted her life to local godly and charitable causes, providing much-needed support for local dissenting ministers after the Restoration; *ODNB*, Rich, née Boyle, Mary.

Anne Robinson. According to **Sir John Godolphin**, Anne Robinson, servant to Major Wilmott of Aldersgate Street, London, was successfully stroked by Greatrakes on 21 April 1666 in the presence of Godolphin, **Drs Faber** and **Fairclough**, **George Weldon**, **Edward Sleigh**, and **John de Bruy**; Greatrakes, *Brief Account*, 52–3.

Anne Rose. According to **Dr Fairclough** in a letter to **Sir William Smith**, Anne Rose, a widow in the Minories, who had been troubled with headaches for twenty years, was healed by Greatrakes in 1666; Greatrakes, *Brief Account*, 71–2.

Thomas Rugge (d. 1670). Rugge, a Londoner, kept a diurnal or diary covering the years 1659 until his death in 1670. On 9 April 1666 he reported the enormous interest in Great-rakes' mission to London, alluding to claims that he cured the deaf and lame. He himself concluded that though he did not cure everyone who came to him for relief, certainly 'som hee did'; BL, Add. MS 10,117, fo. 157v. Rugge was a barber by trade and lived in the wealthy parish of Covent Garden. A staunch royalist and loyal Anglican, he kept a diary in the form of a compendium of newsletters and observations; *ODNB*.

*William Rushout (d. 1671). Rushout attested to the cures of **William Jones** and **Dorothy Wardant** at Mortlake, 9 April 1666; Greatrakes, *Brief Account*, 55–6, 56.

Russell. In July 1667, **Edmund Godfrey** referred to one Russell, who had recently received relief from Greatrakes at Affane; NLI, MS 4728, 10.

*George Rust (*c.*1628–1670). One of Greatrakes' main clerical supporters, Rust claimed to have witnessed around one thousand of the Irishman's cures at Ragley over a period of about a month, specifically referring to his treatment of an old woman at Alcester. Along with his friend and colleague, **Benjamin Whichcote**, he also advised the Cambridge bookseller **Anthony Nicholson** to seek relief at the hands of Greatrakes. In addition, he provided a glowing testimonial of Greatrakes' religious and political conformity which was included not only in Greatrakes' autobiography but also in Glanvill's work on witchcraft; Greatrakes, *Brief Account*, 60–1, 83–4; Glanvill, *Saducismus Triumphatus*, i, 90–2.

Richard Salter (d. 1705). In 1676, Salter wrote to the ecclesiastical historian, **John Strype**, referring to Greatrakes' cures and the cool response at Cambridge to Glanvill's published defence of them. Salter himself seems to have remained neutral with regard to the argument over the true nature and origin of the stroker's methods; CUL, Add. MS 1, no. 26. Salter, a Fellow of Jesus College, Cambridge, was serving as rector of King's Lynn in 1676; Venn, iv, 9.

William Sancroft (1617–1693). In February 1666, Sancroft, the future Archbishop of Canterbury but then Dean of York and St Paul's, was the recipient of two letters from **John Felton** and **Samuel Foster**, both former Fellows of Caius College, Cambridge, recounting the success of Greatrakes' cures at Ragley Hall; BL, Harleian MS 3785, fos 109, 111r–v; *ODNB*.

*[Clement] Sankey (d. 1707). One Mr C. Sankey attested, along with **John Wilkins**, to various cures performed by Greatrakes on three separate occasions in London in April 1666; Greatrakes, *Brief Account*, 56–7.

Mrs Serillen. She was the daughter-in-law of one Mr Hartlie, and was cured by Greatrakes of the king's evil at Dublin (date unknown); BL, Stowe MS 747, fo. 113.

Mary Sermon or Surman. The wife of William Sermon (Surman), physician, of St John's Court, Cow Lane next to Smithfield, Mary was cured by Greatrakes at the house of **John Owen** at Mortlake in May 1666. The cure was witnessed by her brothers **Thomas** and **John Massam**, as well as **Richard Bland** and **Alexander Merreal**; Greatrakes, *Brief Account*, 91. William Sermon (1629–1680) was an empiric, who established a lucrative practice following his cure of George Monck, Duke of Albermarle (1608–1670), in 1669. He was subsequently appointed physician-in-ordinary to Charles II and was granted a Cambridge MD in 1670. He was seemingly absent in Bristol, treating plague victims there, during the time of Greatrakes' visit to London; *ODNB*.

Elizabeth Sharp. Of Dowgate, Thames Street, she was cured by Greatrakes of a chronic lameness in one leg in the presence of **Sir William Smith**, **Thomas Windham**, and **George Evans** on 3 April 1666; Greatrakes, *Brief Account*, 64.

Anne Shelley. According to **Dr Fairclough**, Shelley was cured by Greatrakes of a palsy in 1666; Greatrakes, *Brief Account*, 73.

*Nathaniel Sibley (*c.*1644–1688). In a letter, dated 5 May 1666, addressed to **John Owen**, Sibley, aged twenty-four, of Coleman Street, London, described how he had been cured of a 'tissick' or 'cough of the lungs' by Greatrakes at the house of **Sir George Waterman**; Greatrakes, *Brief Account*, 75–6.

*Colonel Henry Sibthorpe (*c.*1588–1672). According to **Dr James Fairclough**, Sibthorpe, aged about seventy-eight, was cured by Greatrakes of deafness in 1666; Greatrakes, *Brief Account*, 72.

Ed[ward] Sleigh (d. 1675 or 1676). According to the testimony of **Sir John Godolphin**, one 'Ed. Sleigh' witnessed the cure of **Anne Robinson** on 21 April 1666; Greatrakes, *Brief Account*, 52–3. Identity uncertain, but in all probability Edward Sleigh (d. 1675 or 1676), a barrister, of Gray's Inn. Sleigh was the son of Sir Samuel Sleigh (d. 1679) of Derbyshire, who sat as an MP for Essex in 1654–5 and Derbyshire in 1656–8. He was briefly a student at Christ's College, Cambridge, before entering Gray's Inn on 20 November 1655. He was called to the Bar in 1664. Sleigh may have been attracted to Greatrakes through the influence of 'the worthy and most obliging' Dr **Henry More**, to whom he left a small bequest in his will of 1675. Sleigh would appear to have been well connected to scholarly circles in London and Cambridge. Among those to receive books and legacies in his will were various of his contemporaries at Christ's, such as the moderate churchman Dr William Owtram (d. 1679) and 'worthy friend' Thomas Burnett (d. 1715), a protégé of **Ralph Cudworth**. Others mentioned include the Whig lawyer and colleague at Gray's Inn, Thomas Hunt (1611–1683) and the ejected minister and natural philosopher Samuel Ogden (*c.*1628–1697) of Derby. He seems to have been widely read, leaving a copy of Hobbes' *Leviathan* to his former tutor, Dr Owtram, as well as a three volume edition of the works of **Henry More** to his sister. His brother Samuel (d. 1675), a contemporary at Christ's and Gray's Inn, was married to the daughter of Archibald Palmer of Wanlip, Leicestershire, a leading figure in dissenting circles in that county; Venn, iv, 90; Foster (ed.), *Register of Admissions to Gray's Inn*, 275; TNA, PROB 11/351, fos 329r–330r.

Henry Slingsby (1619 or 1620–1690). In April 1666, Slingsby was the recipient of numerous letters, most of which were highly sceptical with regard to Greatrakes' cures, especially that of the 'distracted' courtier **Sir John Denham**; *HMC Sixth Report*, 339. Slingsby was the second son of Sir William Slingsby (d. 1634) of Yorkshire. He was appointed Deputy Master of the Royal Mint in 1660, and served as Master from 1667 to 1680, when he was suspended for irregularities (he was finally dismissed in 1686). He was also an original Fellow of the Royal Society, but was expelled in 1675 for non-payment of his dues. An acquaintance of Pepys, who described him in 1665 as 'a very ingenious person', he was later befriended by John Evelyn who shared Slingsby's interest in antiquities and music. His relative and namesake, Sir Henry Slingsby, was executed for plotting against Cromwell in 1658; *ODNB*.

Mary Smith. Mary was the wife of Arthur Smith, a mercer, living at the Lion within Ludgate. She was aged twenty-three when she was cured by Greatrakes of head pains in 1666 in the presence of **Dr Fairclough**. Mary, along with her mother, **Anne Meyerne**, signed a testimonial, dated 1 May 1666; Greatrakes, *Brief Account*, 85–6. Mary was the daughter of John Christopher Meyerne (d. 1679), gentleman, of St Mary le Bow, London; TNA, PROB 11/360, fos 111r–v.

Samuel Smith, wife of. On 14 April 1666, **Simon Patrick** attested to the cure of Mrs Smith, the wife of Samuel Smith of Newbury, Berkshire, who had suffered from back and hip pains for over seven years; Greatrakes, *Brief Account*, 62.

W. Smith. A surgeon, he attested to the cure of **Sarah Tuffly**, 19 April 1666; Greatrakes, *Brief Account*, 76. Identity uncertain, though he may be William Smith, who was appointed surgeon in ordinary supernumerary to Charles II, 20 October 1666; TNA, LC3/26, fo. 144.

*Sir William Smith (1617–1697). Smith was one of Greatrakes' chief admirers, extolling his therapeutic skills on numerous occasions. He witnessed and attested to the cures of **Anne Kelly, Thomas Burt, William But, Mary Dimmack, Joseph Warden, William Levell, Francis Steele, Robert Furnace, Elizabeth Sharp**, and **Francis Read**. Burt, But, and Dimmack were all 'servants' or employees of Sir William; Greatrakes, *Brief Account*, 43, 49–51, 51–2, 63–4, 82–3.

*Arthur Squibb. Describing himself as MA of Oxford, Squibb attested, with his uncle, Edmund (below) and others, to the cures of two unnamed persons of the 'Phthysick' at the shop of **John Starkey** in London in April 1666; Greatrakes, *Brief Account*, 77–8; Burtchaell and Sadleir, *Alumni Dublinenses*, 772.

*Edmund Squibb. In a letter to a friend **Mr Boreman**, Squibb claimed to have been cured of severe head pain by the stroking of Greatrakes, who also cured a servant of his of a similar ailment, both in March 1666. He further verified the cure of two people at the shop of **John Starkey**, stationer, in London in April 1666. Among those present on this occasion was his nephew, **Arthur Squibb** (above); Greatrakes, *Brief Account*, 77–8.

*Sir Thomas Stanley (d. 1667). In July 1667, **Edmund Godfrey** referred to a recent letter from Greatrakes in which he had alluded to 'a straing Cure wrought on one at Sir Thomas Stanleys house [in county Waterford], and withall the attestation of the manner and proceeding therein, under the hand of Sir Thomas Himself'; NLI, MS 4728, 10–11.

John Starkey (d. 1691). Starkey was the printer and publisher of Greatrakes' autobiographical *Brief Account* who arranged with the author for the various testimonials to be collected prior to publication and his own departure for Ireland in May 1666. Clearly more than just a disinterested publisher, Starkey's shop at the Mitre, near Middle Temple Gate, in Fleet Street, was the scene on at least one occasion of Greatrakes' demonstration of his gift of healing; Greatrakes, *Brief Account*, 77–8, 95–6. A London bookseller, Starkey was later to play a very prominent role as an activist in Whig circles and was frequently prosecuted for the same. Following the Rye House Plot he sought refuge in Holland. In addition to publishing 'old political classics', he was also responsible for printing large numbers of medical and alchemical works; *ODNB*; Knights, 'John Starkey and Ideological Networks', 125–44.

Francis Steele. Aged sixty-three, Steele was sent to Greatrakes by Dr John Micklethwaite of St Bartholomew's Hospital, his subsequent cure being attested by **Sir William Smith, Sir Nathaniel Hobart**, and **Dr Fairclough**, 24 April 1666; Greatrakes, *Brief Account*, 52.

Nathaniel Stepping. Stepping, a market gardener from Hogsden [Haggerston], near Shoreditch, was treated by Greatrakes for a swollen and painful knee. The cure was attested by **Henry Pierce, Ezekiel Foxcroft** and **Dr Fairclough**; Greatrakes, *Brief Account*, 83.

Walter Stonehouse. Stonehouse described himself as gentleman of the horse to the **Countess of Devonshire** in attesting to 'several very wonderful Cures' wrought by Greatrakes on various unnamed servants and others in the Countess' employ, dated 30 April 1666; Greatrakes, *Brief Account*, 65. A demy or scholar of Magdalen College, Oxford, Stonehouse proceeded BA in 1647 and MA in 1660. He was the son of the celebrated botanist Walter Stonehouse (d. 1655), rector of Darfield in Yorkshire. One of his sisters, Anna (d. 1691), married the Anglican clergyman and patristic scholar, William Cave (1637–1713), who was appointed Vicar of Islington, Middlesex, in 1662; Foster, iii, 1429; *ODNB*, sub Cave, William.

[Mrs] Storey. Storey was the landlady of **Robert Boyle**. In 1666 her young son was cured by Greatrakes at the house of her neighbour, **Lady Ranelagh**, in Pall Mall; BL, Add. MS

4293, fo. 53v. She was the wife of Abraham Story or Storey, a stone mason or master builder, who frequently acted as the recipient of letters addressed to **Robert Boyle** and **Henry Oldenburg** from May 1660 onwards. A speculator, he was certainly heavily involved in the construction of numerous large buildings for wealthy patrons in Westminster, and was friendly, among others, with the Boyles and Robert Hooke. He retired to Richmond, Surrey, and died there in 1696, his wife having predeceased him; Maddison, *Life of Robert Boyle*, 133; Oldenburg, *Correspondence*, ii, 255; Boyle, *Correspondence*, i, 411 and n, and *passim*; BL, Add. MS 22,063, no. 173; Henderson, 'Unpublished Material', 137, 139–40; TNA, PROB 11/431, fos 95r–97r.

John Strype (1643–1737). Strype was the recipient of a letter from **Richard Salter** in 1676, who was responding to a request for further information regarding the nature of Greatrakes' cures; CUL, Add. MS 1, no. 26. Strype, the son of a Dutch immigrant silk merchant, was a moderate Anglican clergyman and noted ecclesiastical historian who came from a family with pronounced nonconformist sympathies. His brother-in-law was the Presbyterian minister John Johnson. His mother was reported to have sheltered nonconformist ministers in her house in London during the plague. Nonetheless, Strype conformed at the Restoration and was educated at Cambridge, where he proceeded BA in 1666 and MA in 1669. He subsequently held various minor preferments before becoming Vicar of Low Leyton, Essex, in 1674; *ODNB*; Morrison, 'John Strype', 21–8.

***Henry Stubbe (1632–1676).** Stubbe was an infamous controversialist and pamphleteer whose *Miraculous Conformist* (1666) provides invaluable information with regard to the nature and reception of Greatrakes' cures in the vicinity of Ragley Hall and Worcester in February 1666. Further insights into the problematic nature of Stubbe's motives in publishing this work can be found in Robert Boyle's correspondence of 1666; BL, Add. MS 4228, fos 106–111; BL, Add. MS 4376, fos 1–15; Boyle, *Correspondence*, iii, 93–107.

***Thomas Sydenham (1624–1686).** The celebrated physician Dr Sydenham seems to have acted from an early stage as an active proselytizer on Greatrakes' behalf. In September 1665, he was threatening to overwhelm **Henry Oldenburg** and the Royal Society 'with clear evidences of such wonders'. In the same month, he supplied **John Beale** with the testimonials of **Lionel Beacher** and **Thomas Mall**, thus suggesting that he was acting informally as Greatrakes' agent in his native south-west. In addition, when Greatrakes visited London in 1666, Sydenham was among those who presented individuals for cure, including **Mr Carrington**, the scrivener, at the home of his next-door neighbour **Lady Ranelagh**; Oldenburg, *Correspondence*, ii, 522; BL, Add. MS 4293, fo. 53.

Colonel [Richard] Talbot (1630–1691). Colonel Talbot was present at York House in 1666 when Greatrakes claimed to have performed a 'dispossession' on a young woman; Greatrakes, *Brief Account*, 33. During the 1660s, Colonel Richard Talbot acted as a servant of the Duke of York and was frequently sent to his native Ireland by his patron in order to promote the Catholic interest there and to search out lands 'not disposed to Souldiers or Adventurers'. Among those who were apparently concealing their entitlements was **Benjamin Worsley**. In the process, Talbot acquired on behalf of the Duke the title to Kendrick's Lot, lands which had previously been disputed by the Prendergast family and Greatrakes. Talbot's own possessions in Ireland were exempted from the provisions of the Act of Settlement by order of the Privy Council in 1665. In 1679, following widespread fears of an anti-Catholic backlash in the wake of the Popish Plot revelations, Talbot fled England with the collusion of his Catholic physician, Edmund Meara (d. 1681). He returned at the accession of James II, when he was given the job of remodelling the army in Ireland and was rewarded with the title of Earl of Tyrconnell. William King described him as 'more hated than any other Man by the Protestants'; *Calendar of Treasury Books*, i, 411; *CSPD*,

1664–65, 128, 492; *CSPD, 1669–70*, 313; Bodl., Carte MS 60, fo. 460; King's Inns Library, Dublin, Standish Prendergast, Viscount Gort, *The Prendergasts of Newcastle*, 113; *CSP Ireland, Sept 1669–Dec 1670, Addenda 1625–1670*, 313; TNA, PC 2/58, 185; 2/68, 174; King, *State of the Protestants of Ireland*, 53.

Elizabeth Thomas. Of Petty France, Westminster, she was cured by Greatrakes of severe head and back pain, in the presence of **Benjamin Whichcote** and **Ralph Cudworth**, on 3 April 1666; Greatrakes, *Brief Account*, 64. She was possibly the same as the Elizabeth Thomas, who served as a nurse in the parish of St Margaret's, Westminster, during the plague of 1665; Westminster City Library, St Margaret's, Westminster, Churchwardens' Accounts, WL/E/47, week ending 17 July 1665.

*Ralph Thoresby (1658–1725). In 1700, Thoresby forwarded a letter to the diarist John Evelyn (1620–1706) recalling a series of cures performed by Greatrakes on various members of the family of **Mary Marshall** more than twenty years earlier. The original letter was almost certainly communicated to Thoresby by his friend **Joseph Boyse**, to whom Marshall had first written in May 1699; *Philosophical Transactions*, 21 (1700), 332–4; BL, Stowe MS 747, fo. 113.

George Tipping. On 1 March 1666, Tipping, of Bowden, Cheshire, was examined by the officers of the Board of Greencloth, presumably for breaching security in the vicinity of the court. He claimed in his defence to have come to London to be cured by 'Mr Gratterick' of 'dimness of sight and lameness'; *CSPD, 1666–1667*, 543 [catalogued in error as 1 March 1667]. At his interrogation, Tipping added that he was normally employed to look after his father's cattle. While in London, he claimed to have purchased a pistol from a gunsmith in the Strand for self-protection, and to have found lodgings in Tuttle Street. He would appear to have possessed a letter of introduction to Greatrakes signed by the latter's kinswoman, Anne Meredith.

Sir John Topham (d. 1698). Some time around 1680, Topham was cured by Greatrakes of 'a great sore at his breast', despite the fact that initially 'he had no faith in Mr Gratricks'; *Notes and Queries*, 9 (1884), 63. Topham was a revenue inspector in Ireland and is frequently mentioned in the official papers of the time. Made an honorary doctor of laws, he later became Vicar General of Dublin as well as Judge Advocate General of Ireland. He was knighted in 1678 and was elected MP for Newtown Limavady in 1692; Bodl., Carte MSS.

Robert Toples. Of Ellastone, Staffordshire, Topless was cured of the king's evil by Greatrakes in 1666. The cure was attested by **Ralph Cudworth**, **Benjamin Whichcote**, and **George Evans**; Greatrakes, *Brief Account*, 64.

Sarah Tuffly. Tuffly was the servant of John Pryde, living at Red Cross near Essex Gate in the Strand. She was cured by Greatrakes in 1666 in the presence of **Thomas Kenian**, **W. Smith**, and **Drs Faber** and **Fairclough**; Greatrakes, *Brief Account*, 76.

*Margaret and Susan Vicaridge. At Worcester in February 1666, Greatrakes attempted the cure of several children of one Mrs Bickeridge (or Vicaridge) of Tewkesbury in Gloucestershire. All would appear to have suffered from convulsions or falling sickness, including Margaret and Susan. With regard to the latter, the stroker claimed that 'some Evill Spirit [was] gotten into the Body of the Child'; Stubbe, *Miraculous Conformist*, 32–4.

Jasper Walker. Walker attested the cure of **Peter Noyes**, 10 May 1666; Greatrakes, *Brief Account*, 88.

Mrs Walling. A schoolmistress dwelling on the Malvern Hills, she was stroked by Greatrakes on consecutive days at Worcester in February 1666, according to the account of **Ezekiel Foxcroft**. Suffering from fits of the falling sickness, Greatrakes pronounced her 'possessed with a Devil', a diagnosis which seemingly did not accord with his godly patient who put her symptoms down to a bout of wind; Stubbe, *Miraculous Conformist*, 40–1.

*George Walsh (*c.*1621–1692). Walsh reported Greatrakes' failure to cure Sir John Denham to his cousin Henry Slingsby in a letter dated 17 April 1666; *HMC Sixth Report*, 339.

*John Ward (1629–1681). In his diary, Ward, Vicar of Stratford-upon-Avon, made numerous references to the method of cure used by Greatrakes and to conversations with him. Ward presumably met the stroker during his stay at Ragley in 1666; D'Arcy Power, 'Transcript of the Diary of John Ward', iii, 606, 609, 629–30, 631; Folger Shakespeare Library, Washington, MS Va 294, fos 23r, 24v, 36v, 37r.

Dorothy Wardant. Wardant was cured by Greatrakes of various chronic pains and an ague according to the testmonials of Sir Abraham Cullen, William Rushout, John Owen, and Edwin Brewns, dated 9 April 1666; Greatrakes, *Brief Account*, 56.

Joseph Warden. Aged forty-five and an able seaman serving aboard the 'Royal Charles', Warden was sent to Greatrakes for cure by Dr Micklethwaite of St Bartholomew's Hospital. On expressing his great frustration at not being able to fight the Dutch, he was rapidly healed of his various ailments and vowed to return to the fray. His cure was attested by Sir William Smith, Sir Nathaniel Hobart, and Dr Fairclough; Greatrakes, *Brief Account*, 51–2, 70.

Mrs Anne Waring. Waring was the daughter of Anne Meyerne, and sister of Mary Smith. She was treated for a sore breast by Greatrakes in 1666, the cure witnessed by her grateful mother; Greatrakes, *Brief Account*, 86.

Mr Warner. Of Bristol, Warner testified to cures undertaken by Greatrakes in the city in 1668; Boyle, *Correspondence*, iv, 100.

Sir George Waterman (d. 1682). In a letter to John Owen, Nathaniel Sibley described how he was cured by Greatrakes at the home of Sir George Waterman in London in 1666; Greatrakes, *Brief Account*, 75–6. An ironmonger and merchant, Waterman was elected as a common councilman for Dowgate in 1654 and 1660–62, and alderman for Bridge Within, 1664–1682. In 1665 he would appear to have been a business partner of Charles Doe. He was knighted on 10 June 1665, serving as Sheriff, 1664–65, and was chosen as Lord Mayor in 1671–72. From 1644 to 1677 he lived in a house in Thames Street. In a loyalist survey of the politics of London's leading figures in 1672, he was described as 'for a while guided by Sr John Lawrence who Ledd him astray, but he begins to hearken now to the Court of Aldermen' (Lawrence was the brother-in-law of Sir Abraham Cullen). He was subsequently described as a 'Tory, earlier in the faction', and may have defected to that interest under the influence of his son-in-law Sir William Russell, a leading figure in Tory circles in the capital; Woodhead, *Rulers of London*, 172; Beaven, *Aldermen of the City of London*, i, 60; ii, 96; TNA, C 10/96/106; BL, Stowe MS 186; TNA, PROB 11/372, fos 76r–v.

Colonel George Weldon (d. 1679). Numerous of Greatrakes' patients were cured at Weldon's lodgings in York Buildings in the Strand, including Anne Robinson, William Floyd, Francis Read, and John Harrison. Weldon himself received relief for a 'fit of the stone' from Greatrakes' stroking; Greatrakes, *Brief Account*, 52–3, 53–4, 68, 81–2, 82–3, 89. Colonel George Weldon was the son of the Kentish Parliamentarian Sir Anthony Weldon (1583–1648). A resident of the affluent parish of St Paul's Covent Garden, he was an intimate friend and acquaintance of Sir Edmund Berry Godfrey, and subsequently gave evidence to the enquiry called to examine Godfrey's death in 1678. According to Weldon's account, Godfrey spent the evening before his death at Weldon's house where he had met Edmund Coleman, Jesuit servant to the Duke of York. He deposed that the two men had read over several papers, presumably Oates' depositions in the Popish Plot. Weldon's

Catholic sympathies are further suggested by the conversion of his son Ralph (1674–1713) to Roman Catholicism during the reign of James II. As a Benedictine monk, he later wrote a manuscript life of the King; *ODNB*, sub Weldon, Sir Anthony; *HMC Eleventh Report*, 48; Knight, *Killing of Justice Godfrey*, 253–254; Bodl., Ashmole MS 851, 240; *ODNB*, sub Weldon, Ralph; NLI, MS 4728, 4, 12, 32.

Margaret Westley. Westley, of the parish of Christ Church, London, claimed that she had been cured of blindness in one eye by Greatrakes' ministrations in 1666. Her cure was witnessed by **John Owen, Matthew Porter, John Grone,** and **William Faithorn**; Greatrakes, *Brief Account*, 90.

*Benjamin Whichcote (1609–1683). Whichcote was a celebrated Cambridge scholar and Platonist who witnessed the cures of various sufferers at Ragley, Alcester and London in 1666. Among those attested by Whichcote were **Elizabeth Thomas, Robert Toples, Mary Jackson,** and **Benjamin** and **Edmund Barcock**. He also provided a glowing testimonial of Greatrakes' moderate and conformable religious disposition and refers to the Irish stroker's help in curing him of a chronic condition; Greatrakes, *Brief Account*, 58–9, 64, 66–7.

Richard Whitall. In a letter of 4 May 1666 to **Colonel John Owen**, Whitall, of Tower Wharf, London, described his cure at the hands of Greatrakes at Worcester in February of that year. He went on to list numerous other 'miraculous cures' performed by Greatrakes at Worcester, including those suffering from the falling sickness, gout, wens, 'the Blind and the lame'. Owen subsequently testified that Whitall was given further relief at his house at Mortlake later that year; Greatrakes, *Brief Account*, 86–7. In 1664, Whitall, along with his partner Matthew Crouch, was facing the loss of certain estates at Tower Wharf following the appeal of Frances Clement, the daughter of Sir John Sedley, to Charles II. Clement petitioned the King for restitution to these lands which were once in the possession of her father-in-law, the regicide judge, Gregory Clement. One Colonel Richard Withall was described at the Restoration as late Commander of the House, Gardens and Park at Eltham. Whitall may also have possessed links with the city of Worcester, where he was first healed by the stroker. In 1647, one Richard Whatall was appointed constable of All Saints ward in the city, whilst ten years later, a man of the same name was leasing land from the borough; *CSPD, 1660–61*, 237; *CSP Ireland, 1663–65*, 513; Bond, *Chamber Order Book of Worcester*, 435; WRO, Shelf A 14, fo. 30v.

Grace White. According to **Dr Fairclough**, White, who was suffering from an inveterate palsy in the leg, was cured by Greatrakes in 1666; Greatrakes, *Brief Account*, 73–4.

Thomas White. White witnessed the cure of **Peter Noyes** in 1666; Greatrakes, *Brief Account*, 88.

Dr Whitecock. Dr Whitecock was present in the chambers of **Robert Boyle** when **Mr Carrington** was cured by Greatrakes on 10 April 1666; BL, Add. MS 4293, fo. 53v.

*Sir Bulstrode Whitelocke (1605–1675). Between 2 and 9 May 1666, Greatrakes stroked Whitelocke's seven year old son, Stephen (1659–1688 or 1689), on three separate occasions. On the first, Greatrakes claimed that he would be able to do little good for the boy because there was a dislocation of the hip joint; Spalding, *Diary*, 704.

Major [Thomas] Wilde. Major Wilde was present at Worcester in February 1666 when he witnessed the effect of Greatrakes' stroking on those suffering from the falling sickness; Greatrakes, *Brief Account*, 33. Wilde had a reputation as a violent persecutor of nonconformists in Worcestershire in the early 1660s. He was also assiduous in rounding up plotters and other suspicious and 'ill-affected' men at this time. His zeal would appear to have got the better of him in 1667, when some prominent local dissenters initiated a counter-action against him for false arrest; Nickalls, *Journal of George Fox*, 515; *CSPD, 1664–65*, 330–1, 366; *CSPD, 1665–1666*, 230; TNA, PC 2/59, 424–5.

*Captain [William] Wildey (d. 1679). In late March 1666, Greatrakes visited Wildey's house at Stepney, where he cured the wife of a neighbour, **Richard Wolrich**; Greatrakes, *Brief Account*, 79.

*John Wilkins (1614–1672). Wilkins was present on numerous occasions when Greatrakes effected his cures. He subsequently provided testimonials, including one attesting to the cure of **Jane Deane**. He also tried the experiment of pricking the numbed parts of Greatrakes' patients with a pin at the house of **Dr Fairclough**; Greatrakes, *Brief Account*, 56–7, 67–8, 73.

William Willett (*c*.1616–*c*.1679). According to Greatrakes, Willett was willing to corroborate his successful cure of several people in the city of Bristol in 1668; Boyle, *Correspondence*, iv, 100. Willett, a merchant adventurer, briefly served as sheriff of Bristol between June and September of 1668. In the following year, he was living in the parish of Christ Church, Bristol; McGrath, *Merchants and Merchandise*, 237n; Beaven, *Bristol Lists*, 314; Bristol Record Office, P/XCh/Ch/7; TNA, PROB 11/366, fos 267v–268r.

*Thomas Williams (*c*.1621–1712). Williams attested to the cure of **Anne Field**, 12 April 1666; Greatrakes, *Brief Account*, 46–7.

Thomas Windham. Windham certified the cures of **Robert Furnace** and **Elizabeth Sharp** in 1666; Greatrakes, *Brief Account*, 63–4.

*Richard Withie. Withie was a Worcester attorney with whom Greatrakes lodged in February 1666; Stubbe, *Miraculous Conformist*, 32; WRO, Shelf A 10, Box 3, iii.

Richard Wolrich, wife of. Wolrich, of Ratcliffe, Middlesex, was a surgeon who provided a testimonial for the cure of his wife's various pains at the hands of the stroker in a letter addressed to Greatrakes, 16 April 1666; Greatrakes, *Brief Account*, 78–9. She was probably the aunt of **John Cressett**. She appears in Edward Cressett's will as 'my sister Woolridge', with two children, Thomas and Mary. Dorothy Woolrich, widow, of St Martins in the Fields, died in 1679. In her will, witnessed by Elizabeth Cressett (probably the daughter of John), she mentions her son Thomas, a clergyman in Kent, and daughter Mary Swan, widow. Dorothy also witnessed the will of Mary Cressett (d. 1669), widow of Edward and mother of John. Her husband's testimonial letter mentions her first meeting with the stroker at the house of a neighbour, **Captain Wildey**, with subsequent sessions at Lincoln's Inn Fields, where John Cressett hosted Greatrakes; TNA, PROB 11/312, fos 289v–291v; 11/361, fos 335v–336r; 11/331, fo. 115r.

*Benjamin Worsley (1618–1678). According to **Dr Fairclough**, **John Hayes**, 'servant to Dr Worley', was cured by Greatrakes in London in 1666. A year earlier, Benjamin Worsley had transcribed a copy of **Lionel Beacher**'s account of Greatrakes' cures in Ireland which reached **Robert Boyle** *via* **Thomas Sydenham** and **John Beale**; Greatrakes, *Brief Account*, 78–9; Boyle, *Correspondence*, ii, 522.

William Yates. Yates attested to the cure of **Walter Dolle the younger** in April 1666; Greatrakes, *Brief Account*, 47–8.

APPENDIX 3

Letters addressed to Valentine Greatrakes, 1666–1672

These letters form MS 4728 in the National Library of Ireland, Dublin, and were probably part of a larger correspondence that was extant in the early eighteenth century. It was originally purchased by the Library in December 1953 from John B. Dowling of Dublin. All attempts to trace the provenance of these letters has failed to uncover further clues as to the whereabouts of the remainder of the correspondence, alluded to by Alexander Phaire, the youngest son of Greatrakes' great friend, Colonel Robert Phaire, in 1744.

The manuscript is paginated and in a late seventeenth- or early eighteenth-century hand. The letters are presumably copies of the originals but there is no clue as to the identity of the amanuensis. In attempting to transcribe the letters in chronological order, the copyist misdated letters no. 5 (as 12 February 1667) and no. 16 (as 27 January 1671). These have now been reordered to create a correct chronology, using new style dating throughout.

On the fly leaf at the front of the manuscript is a note that reads: 'These from my worthy friend Valentine—Sir I have wrote to your Brother twice and received no answer'.

Pasted in to the back of the volume is a note in modern handwriting, which reads:

'Enclosed are the Greatrakes Letters With many thanks Acting on Mr A [Lany?]'s suggestion I sent some extracts to the *English Historical Review* but they were not accepted. I am now trying another magazine & if successful will let you know. A.P.'

A.P. was almost certainly the same as the A. Peter, who owned the letters in 1903. In that year, he wrote to *Notes and Queries* [9th ser., 11, p.248] requesting information regarding several of Greatrakes' correspondents.

This transcription is reproduced here with the kind permission of the Board of the National Library of Ireland.

1. EDMUND GODFREY TO GREATRAKES, 30 MAY 1666 [1–2]

30 May 1666. These for his honoured Friend Valentine Greatracks Esqier at the Right honourable Lord Conways at Ragley.

Honoured friend

If you had seen in what place & with what difficulty I found Conveniency of pen & paper, being on this Thursday past eleven of the Clock, & Fast day, you would value my letter at a higher rate, & make the reception thereof more acceptable unto you then either I may deserve or hope for; But looking upon this as a Iust punishment on my remissness of waiting on you, at the time of your going out of Town which extraordinary occasions of Business unseasonably pressing on me; And to much confidence in of your not Setting out, in such a Storm, made me Somewhat presume on; However having missed of my expected Content & desires in the one, I could not be wanting to you & my Self in the other: But to express my sencibleness of such neglect, & withall herein to enclose such letters as I received in your behalf, since I had the honour of receiving the last farewell visit from you, the which may possibly be of more Concernment to you, than all the respects or Service which I have yet been able to pay or express, since your being in these parts. And I do hartily wish, that your particular kindness unto me, by your longer than was design'd residence in these parts, may not have given you too Iust occation to repent of the Ill hour of our acquaintance, which Crime I shall endeavour to expiate by your advancing your Interest what I am able in all here, wherein your self or I may be concern'd; In order whereunto, I have this morning at large discoursed your Concerns with Sir W.Smith,[1] who gives me all assurance of harty respects & kindness for you, The like from Mr Lane;[2] And I do verily believe you will find their performances answerable to their promises: But if they should fail in either (which unworthy Opinion I dare not entertain of them) You may be confident of my Solicitations & dayly importunitys in your behalf; which shall be as earnestly, &, I hope, as effectually prosecuted, as if my All, & more then my Self lay at Stake upon the Score of that Success.

This being the present occation of the trouble hereof; And the desire of the expressions of the Griefe & harty affection & Sympathy which I bear in the parting and apprehended loss of so dear a friend, as I assure you, your Self is, & the memory of you ever shall be unto me; I conclude with the unfeyned desires that the blessing of God Allmighty go along with you, in all your wayes & undertakings & subscribe my Self what Really I am

Your affectionate Faithfull & Respectfull Servant. Edm: Godfrey.

30 May 1666. At the Crown at St Giles waiting the passing by of the Carryer, where at another time & on an other occation I should be asham'd to be seen.

P.S. I had once the honour to be Schoolfellow & Fellow Boarder at Mr Lambert Osbolstones Schoolmaster of Westminster Schoole,[3] with the Right honourable Lord Conwey, at whose house I hope these will find you, Pray if you see occasion, & that he hath any remembrance of my name. Let my most humble Respects & service be here with accompany'd unto him, which it may be for your sake (if not for my own) may find acceptance at his hands. The like over & over to Good Sir Amos Meredith[4] at your meeting, & your most happy second self tho unknown to me. *Vale, vale, valias diu iusq[ue] ad Redeundum in t[erram] videndum, aut in Aeternum.*[5]

E.Godfrey.

Commit thy way unto the Lord & he will bring thy desire to pass in the mean time never despair of his mercys nor distrust his Providence.

Etiam et in Monte Providebit Deus.[6]

---

[1] Sir William Smith, who witnessed a number of Greatrakes' cures in 1666.

[2] Probably Richard Lane, appointed groom of the King's bedchamber, 2 February 1661; TNA, LC3/24, fo. 3. In 1665, Smith and Charles Sydenham conveyed the right to construct salt works in Ireland to Lane and Edward Cooke of Chiswick (see below note 7); SARS, DD\Whb/39, 2779–80.

[3] Lambert Osbaldestone (1594–1659), puritan schoolteacher and opponent of Laud; see *ODNB* and Marshall, *The Strange Death of Edmund Godfrey*, 8–9.

[4] Sir Ames Meredith, the constant companion and business partner of Greatrakes.

[5] 'Farewell, farewell, stay well until we meet again in earth or in heaven'.

[6] 'While in the wilderness, God will provide'; a paraphrase of Genesis 22:8 recounting the story of Abraham and Isaac and the burning bush.

2. EDMUND GODFREY TO GREATRAKES,
14 AUGUST 1666 [2–4]

14 Aug[ust] 1666. To Valentine Greatracks Esq. in Dublin.
My Worthy Good Friend.

Yours I received from Chester bearing date 22 of June for which I most hartily thank you: as also for another without date or place, but conceive twas writ in Dublin, by reason of some passages therein, which I had long since answered, had I not been dayly in expectation of Sir William Smith's coming to Town, whereby to have given him an account of your Relation of his Salt affair in Ireland; & of your expected trust & Commission in that place in order to the better carrying on of his Service, then I find it hath yet been don, or that his business hath been mannag'd either with care or good Conduct. But so it is that his being in Kent & Bucks hath denyed me the opportunity of Conference with him, on that Subject; So that I fear I shall not be able to give you any Satisfactory answer thereunto untill his next coming to town, which will not be yet this three weeks. In the mean while I would wish you to advise with Collonell Cook,[7] & upon consultation had with him & Mr Lane[8] (who I doubt not is with you before this time) to endeavour the redress of what inconveniencys you meet with in the way wherein his Concerns ought to be carryd through; especially to rectifie what is don amiss, with as little charge, alteration, or Noise as needs must; I shall not need to say any more to you, *Verbum Sapienti Sat est;*[9] However I think it is Very requisite that you should have a Sufficient authority, either from them there or Sir William here to warrant your proceedings, & give you all possible Power & Countenance therein, whereof pray be pleased to give me further Intimation, in your next, & withall on what terms you act, for I assure you no man is more faithfully Sollicitous of your Content & happiness then my self, who do earnestly desire your well being and with my soul to be instrumental therein, if possible. I am very glad Colonell Cook hath been so friendly & civill unto you, God continue the same, & raise you up more such Instruments, which I question not but in his good time he will do, Remembring his promiss of committing thy way unto the Lord, & he will bring thy matter to pass. I thank you for the particular account you give me of the state of affairs in Ireland, which I am sorry to hear of, & should be glad to hold a Correspondence with you particularly as to a continued information thereof, and perhaps no man may have more Itching ears after news than my self, yet out of the respect & affection that I bear you, and as I desire your happiness, I wish you to be very carefull of what you write & to whome for that many have sufferd lately for being too free in their intelligences and occurrences, Especially now that letters are soe often broake open, & exposd to the various scanning & Censuring of those to whom they were never writ. Pray get your business to be dispatched first at the Court of Claymes, & then 'twill be true enough to Speak truth; In the mean time, remember your old Grammer verse *Quid de quoq viro, et cui dicas saepe caveto.*[10] All your friends of my Family & Relations blessed be God are

---

[7] Colonel Edward Cooke (d.1684), of Chiswick, Middlesex. In 1668, he wrote to the Duke of Ormond proposing that the latter should take into his service Richard Mulys, a friend and associate of Edmund Godfrey, who, like Godfrey, testified to Greatrakes' cures in 1666; Bodl., Carte MS 215, fo. 506. Cooke was an old acquaintance of Mulys, as both men had previously been in the employ of the dowager countess of Devonshire. Cooke, who accompanied Ormond to Ireland in 1662, was a commissioner in the Irish Court of Claims; *HMC Fifteenth Report*, 158–73. He was also a partner with Sir William Smith in his Irish salt works scheme, which is probably alluded to here.

[8] See note 2.

[9] 'A word to the wise is sufficient'.

[10] 'Take care what you say of any man'; Horace, *Epistles* 1.18.6.

well, & speak their respects & harty Service unto you, Especially your long Patient Mrs Harrison,[11] who now hath better thoughts of your actings, she being quite cured of her Wen, which you took off from her side, & the wound quite well, Since which time her Scorbutick distemper wherewith she was sorely oppress'd is broak out into an Itch & Scabbied humour to her great refreshment of Spirit, whereof she is now allmost quite well, & clean cur'd (as we say) by the use of Epsom water and it could otherwise be expected, butt that so long a Settled Scrophulous Indisposition, & that had so long made the Wen a Receipt of its Corruption, should find some other vent, when that was check'd & taken away. I hope you doe continue an Intercourse of respectfull Intelligence & advise with the Lord Conaway for that I would not be any means, that you should neglect him, or be wanting in all due respects to him & when ever it shall please God to send him to Town I shall not fail to wait upon his Lordship, as much & more on your behalf than my own. Your last to me Speak nothing of honest Sir Amos Meredith who I hope is well with you, & has as much of your friendship as ever; Pray speak him with my hearty Service & Respects & the like to your good & vertuous Lady, tho unknown, whose health & happyness together with a prosperous condition to your self and yours is faithfully desired, & dayly pray'd for by Dear Sir

Your truely affectionate & faithfull Friend. Edm. Godfrey.

Green Lane, neer York House, 14 August 66.

Be sure you keep your word in holding a Correspondence with me, for that I assure you that every thing that comes, but in your name is extraordinary wellcome & most acceptable to. EG.

3. EDMUND GODFREY TO GREATRAKES, 22 NOVEMBER 1666 [4–6]

22 November 1666 My worthy good Friend

Yours bearing date the 10° of October last I received most Gladly, although my slow return of answer thereunto speaks the Ioy I had at ye Receipt of the same and I assure you shall ever be continued in the Respects that I have for you or any thing that comes from you. But that which did much retard my answer thereunto was the common & confident Report, (& that Believe'd by your very Friends) That you were dead, Madam Owen[12] her self being verily perswaded of the truth, thereof neither could we be convinc'd of ye Contrary untill I had received advice from your Brother Sir John Godolphin,[13] whereat I was exceedingly overjoy'd, The like were many more of your good Friends here (being no small number, whose good wishes & respectfull services do accompany this unto you): I have not been wanting in the observance of your desires, to speak your respectfull service to all your acquaintance here & particularly to Sir William Smith[14] & his Lady, Madam Owen Collonell Weldon[15] & his Lady &c. I perceive that Sir William Smith's Salt Work here in Kent hath not been so well

---

[11] Possibly Jane Harrison, a sister of Godfrey's, or one of her husband's relations. Jane Godfrey married James Harrison, who became a business partner with Edmund Godfrey in the 1650s. Edmund later employed his nephew, Godfrey Harrison, in his thriving woodmongers' business, a relationship that was to cause him much grief in future years.

[12] The wife of Colonel John Owen, at whose Mortlake residence Greatrakes had performed cures earlier in 1666.

[13] Greatrakes' brother-in-law.

[14] See note 1.

[15] Colonel George Weldon, for whom see Appendix 2.

manag'd this year, as to produce him proffit or any great content thereon; whereof he being conscious, was not overforward for you or my self to go down, & be an eyewitness of the great miscarriages therein, as I perceive you have since been in Ireland of the same kind; but he hath now concluded with Mr Sydenham[16] his Partner upon taking sole management thereof into the hands of his own Instruments for the year ensuing, whereby he doth promiss himself much better conduct, & a return answerable; I hope the like of that in Ireland whereof now & then pray favour me with a word of advice; as also what may farther occurr in relation to your own Conserns, or the Publick there; But of them write spearingly, for that I shall easily guess at more then will be convenient for you to express. The like you may do by what I write from hence: I do heartily Congratulate the good return you have received of the well wishes & prayers of your Friends here, in that successful entertainment you found, with the Committee of Claymes: And that it hath pleased God so to dispose of your affairs there, as that you can truely say, your Lott is fallen in a fair Grownd, and a Good thing is your Heretage, and that you enjoy your own with so much content & thankfulness, as I perceive you do; which I pray God continue to you and increase upon you, tho' God knows how long we have yet to enjoy our selves or any thing that we have here; For I can see nothing but apprehentions of new fears & troubles, especially when I do not find, that good use made of our deliverance out of former Dangers & Judgments, wherein I am bound to take notice, & return you thanks for your particular concern for me in my pres-ervation from the late fury of Fire, wherein my Estate did suffer very considerably, Notwith-standing that through Gods mercy & Goodness my own Habitation was preserv'd: And I took that personall hurt on that occation, by being over forward in helping to suppress ye same by the fall of a piece of timber on my Back, that will stick by me while I live, unless by Gods blessing on the help of your hand I may find Cure of that Bruise. I hope your seasonable return in the nick of time, as I perceive you did, and God Almighty's providence so ordering the disposall of your affairs at the Court of Claymes & elsewhere in all your Concernes; for which blessed be his holy name who is wiser & better to us in all things then we can be to our selves, will rather be an incouragment to you to take an other turn into England, whereby you may yet be an Instrument here, once again of much good & Gods glory, & I hope by what hath befaln you since, & God hath brought to pass for you by means of new rais'd Friends, & formerly unknown unto you, you will have noe cause to repent of your last being here. Things look here with an evill face in Refference to new troubles like to arise out of Scotland, & we our selves much devided here in England, & I fear the same spirit of devision, hath entered into both houses of Parliament which makes an Ill aspect over the whole Nation: I pray God to heal our breaches, & compose the differ-ences amongst us, for that we are almost at our witts ends here, what betwixt the apprehen-tions of Danger from the Fannaticks on one hand & The Papists on the other, we scarce look upon ourselves in a secure or safe condition on any side, beside the Common enemy abroad watching for an advantage & opportunity to destroy us both, And tho it is out of all dispute, that there was much of the Immediate hand of God in Consuming of the Citty by fire, and so ordering the fierceness of the horrible storm, & Tempest to continue all that while, as there was also in the preservation of that now standing & remaining part, Being chiefly saved & preserv'd, by an allaying & shifting of the wind, yet it is out of all dispute confest & discover'd by Severall fires since in other Places, & letters, intercepted hinting the same, that evill Instruments of men were employed, in the execution of that Wrathe and Iudgment of God, which he hath most Iustly brought upon us: Dear Sir you may perceive

---

[16] For Charles Sydenham, see note 2.

by this how unlimmitted my affections are, & how large a Subject a Friend is to write upon or unto, I have only room enough present my service to your virtuous Lady & Sir Amos Meredith, & to assure you that I am & ever shall be

Your faithfull Friend & Servant. Edm. Godfrey.

4. EDMUND GODFREY TO GREATRAKES, 2 JULY 1667 [10–13]

Sir

Yours of the 12 of May last I received most Gladly, being brought by one Russell,[17] who had sometime waited on you at your house at Affane, & there (throw Gods Blessing) received much benefit & help in his limbs by your stroaking, whereat I was very much rejoyc'd & ever shall be at the hearing of any thing that may tend to the advancement of Gods Glory, & your own Credit and commendation; The man blessed be God continues in perfect health, & the use of his limbs, all his Pains, Aches, numness &c being quite taken away, by the help of your hand. You make mention of a straing Cure wrought on one at Sir Thomas Stanleys house,[18] & withall the attestation of the manner & proceeding therein, under the hand of Sir Thomas Himself, A Copie whereof would be most acceptable to me, & no disservice to your self; of whose worth & of God Almighty's peculiar blessing on you in the Gift of Healing, I am a Constant Assertor & Admirer; and shall be glad on all occasions to Testifie the Truth thereof to the World, indispight of all Lyers & Gainsayers. Pray oblidge me with the Continuance of a correspondence, & Intercourse of Letters as often as you can, especially of all such remarkable passages; and as to any other Publick Concerns, writ little of them unless it be that which you need not care who reads it. I confess I have small reason to expect this favour at your hands, because I have not kept touch, nor been so punctuall with you in answering your Letters, as I ought to have been, especially of your last, which with all others from you I keep carefully by me amongst my choicest Reserves, But the contents and desires therein, not being such as I could at all give you any incouragement therein to proceed, was the occation of my silence which (as you may remember) was to have had some imployment under Mr Gauden[19] the Victualler, or to have sent over a quantity of Pipe staves to neither of which I can give you Incouragment by reason of the Hazzard of the Seas, and badness of pay here, it being an easyer matter for any man to make his Condition worse & Impaire his Estate by having to do with any publick undertaking here, then to amend & improve himself thereby, unless it be in knowledg of his Folly, by too much experience to his Loss. I am advisd by this Bearer Russell of the Pleasantness of your seat at Affane, & the happyness of your condition in the enjoyment of your Self & yours there; all which your own letter & the expressions therein so full of content & Gratious Frame of Spirit, do abundantly witness, to your great Commendations, & truely give me leave to use freedom with you, I think you are happyer than you (it may be) deserve, then your self can attain to, For that I think the foundations of the Earth are like to be shaken, & God Almighty will reduce us to our primitive condition of humility & poverty and I hope, amendment of lives & manners before he removes his Iudgments from us; The

---

[17] Unidentified.

[18] Greatrakes' old friend and acquaintance, Sir Thomas Stanley, for whom see pp. 56–7.

[19] Denis Gauden (c.1600–1688), navy victualler, was frequently mentioned by Pepys in his diary. An alderman of the city of London, he was knighted in 1667 while serving as sheriff (1667–8). He possessed a large house at Clapham, but was eventually bankrupted through the navy's failure to pay its debts.

apprehention whereof together with the Relation of your sweet & retir'd manner of enjoying yourself, & the desire of having your Company, hath almost tempted me to become a retir'd man, & wait upon you in Ireland, where I have some small Concern of my own, & Friends to live upon. Sir Amos Meredith[20] & my self have had many discourses on this subject Since I had the happiness of seeing you; we have often remembered you as I doubt not he will acquaint you at larg at his next meeting you (if in the mean time he do not write you on that subject). In the Interim I cannot but take notice of your remembrance of me & thoughts of kindness for me, which you are pleas'd to Signifie, in willing me to send unto you the name of some Friend or Correspondent of mine at Bristoll, to whome you intend to send over a token of your Love & Product of your Fishery in Ireland to me; which if you are resolvd on, I shall recommend the [...][21] of your token of kindness to one Mr James Bridger[22] Merchant in Bristoll, who is as well known there as any man in the City, & will take care to see the same carefully convey'd to me here. I have duely observ'd & perform'd all your Commands Services & Respects as are severally due to all your Friends, as you have given me in charge in your last, Who all rejoyce at the tidings of your welfare, & hartily desire the Continuance thereof, with all other additions requisite to Happiness, which are all comprizd in Content & Serenity of Mind & Spirit.

Major Weldens lady[23] hath lately been delivered of another lusty Boy whereof they both do not a little bragg; I had much adoe to escape being a Godfather there, as Sir Amos can inform you & with what difficulty I resisted those Sollicitations & importunitys.

My self & Family, blessed be God, continue in health, & in the same condition of affectionate Respects & Service for your self as ever; especially your Quondam Patient Mrs Harrison,[24] who hath been much frightened with the apprehention of her wen's rising again, But thanks be to God it hath hitherto prov'd nothing but Fansy, & I hope will never be more. I shall now quite tire you out with reading my severall impertinencyes, only give me leave to add one necessary line more, for the tender of my most affectionate Respects & Services to your Second Self whom for your sake, I am bound to honnour & respect, being very well assur'd, that having the happiness of your Converse & Company, she cannot be a most excellent improv'd Creature & Christian, whereof I do really believe I shall be an eye witness, as of all other your enjoyments at Affane, before I dye. In the mean time be assur'd of the reallity & constancy of the true Friendship and Service of him that doth heartily love & honour you, & will never forget to express & subscribe himself Dear Sir

Your affectionate faithfull Friend & servant. Edm.Godfrey.

Greens Lane neer York House. 2 July 1667.

5. EDMUND GODFREY TO GREATRAKES, 12 FEBRUARY 1668 [6-10]

Yours bearing date Christmas eve I received tho allmost a month in coming, & I do assure you with as much Ioy & Satisfaction to me as if I had received some great Favor from the hands of my Prince; so greatfull & well pleasing is your memory to me, & any thing that

---

[20] See note 4.

[21] Word illegible.

[22] James Bridger, merchant, of Bristol, was the son of Samuel Bridger (1584–1650), a gentleman from Dursley in Gloucestershire. His brother and fellow merchant Joseph (1628–1686) emigrated to Virginia in 1652, and was later joined there by James.

[23] See note 15.   [24] See note 11.

comes from you, that immediately I do apprehend the thoughts of enjoying your self therein, from whome I can no more be divorsed in affection, by distance of place or time then the Loadstone can loose its influence & power on ye Iron by reason of Remoteness or discontinuance of usage of its Faculty.

As for the Salmon you were pleased to send for Mr Owen[25] & my self to Bristoll, I heartily thank you for your kindness therein intended to me, but I never heard any thing thereof, except in this your last letter, nor I fear Ever shall, nor Mr Owen who is your Faithfull friend & Servant as allso his Lady, & upon all occasions both of them are ready to express the same in an extraordinary manner. He hath lately had no small trouble to get off from holding the Sherriff of London, Notwithstanding that he had a very great loss in the late Fire, But at length after he had held Alderman 6 months he was admitted to fine for Sheriffe at a very high rate, I think little less than 1000 li.[26] My self allso was hardly put to it to be excusd from that office, to prevent which, I was constraind to put off my trade & employment with all my stock of Debts to my nephew Godfrey Harrison,[27] (who is now upon his marriage), By which means I do intend, God willing, to disengage my self from my great Incumbring Employments, whereby I hope if God permit to have leesure & opportunity of coming & seeing you in Ireland, within less than two years time. It may be by this time twelve month or soon after, where we will lay our heads together to consider what proffit may be raised out of that Country trade, which I perswade myselfe may turn to account if rightly mannagd.

As for the Acts Against Irish Cattle[28] I am confident it will not continue to be put into force two years to an end, & we in England shall be at the greatest Loss by reason of the said Act, which will undoubtedly occasion the suspending of Execution thereof If not the totall repealing of the same before many years. I shall be Glad to see that good effect of the Act against Transporting of Irish Cattle as that your Nobles & Gentry would turn Merchants, or Betake themselves to any Industrious Ingenuity. It were a great Reformation here to see them affected with Civility, or Sobriety, nothing but an act of pure Necessity will put us upon those Courses—*Magister Artis Ingeniiq Lagitor Venter.*[29] And to speak truth nothing spoyles these Nations but Ease & Plenty.

I wish that Sir William Smiths Salt Works for his sake as well as my own, may turn to better account then as yet they have don, For that I fear he hath run out much mony thereon, And the Dutch Fleet, when it came into the River, pulld upp all their Pans & spoild most of their utensills.[30]

As to your Woods you write of I fear it will not Quit cost to bring the Timber over hither, unless in Clove-board or Pipestaves which methinks should be a better Commodity, if directly transported from Ireland into Spain, or to our Islands & plantations beyond seas, Oaken timber being now sold here at London at cheaper rates than it was before the Fire viz 45 or 46 per load at most.

I am mightily pleas'd with you [sic] Heavenly expressions of the Contententment [sic] which you find, & enjoy in your Retired, Innocent and vertuously Industrious, country

---

[25] Colonel John Owen.

[26] For Owen's travails in 1667, see p. 94 and n.

[27] See note 11.

[28] The Act forbidding the importation of Irish cattle into England threatened ruin to many Irish farmers as well as those western ports on the mainland that traded across the Irish Sea. The Bill had a stormy passage through Parliament and did not finally pass into the statute book until February 1667.

[29] 'The stomach is the teacher of art and the source of wit' [i.e. necessity is the mother of invention]; Persius, *Satires*, Prologue 10.

[30] The bold attack of the Dutch on the English fleet moored in the Medway estuary in June 1667 was widely seen as a disaster and further eroded confidence in the government of Charles II.

Life, which ingenious description of yours, put me in mind of Paradice, & our first Parents therein being in a state of Innocency Before the temptation of the Forbidden Fruits; and the Devill in Woman had prevaild on them to Deboachery; But that you should yet find & enjoy such a Woman, & a Wife & a mother of children, is a Miracle of Miracles, next to that of the Virgin Mary, and seems to represent a new Creation unto me. For certainly the originall stock of Grace & vertue is long since decayd & lost in that Sex, But if you alone have got a Phenix or a Susanna in your Garden, 'twill be your wisdome to keep her always there, at least wise in her Country Innocency & enjoyments. *Sabina qualis*,[31] If you would have her to your self or expect she should long continue so, and let not the discourses of London & Whitehall enter into her ears or affect her fancy and believe me 'tis a bold Adventure in you to acquaint any man herewith, especially one in my condition, who certainly design a visit unto you if God permit. You do half stagger me whither I should continue my resolution, for fear of comming away from you worse thought of than when I shall come unto you first. A woman, a Wife, & a Mother of many Children, Vertuous, Wise, & Good, & That Back'd with Scripture to confirm it, 'Tis more strange than the Hermaphrodite here in Town,[32] being the Prodigy of the Times, who hath gained greater Reputation and more followers, than the late Stroaker, or all the Fanatick Meetings about Town, which do dayly increase, not without some connivance of Athority [sic] (If not Tolleration) which 'tis believ'd will certainly be granted very suddenly.

I have so much to write to you that I know not where to end, unless it be in the confirmation of my Resolution of seeing you very suddenly with Gods leave, which I propose to do, (& to enlarge these discourses, and many more, *ore tenus*,[33] & also to see & Reverence that Saint your Wife, to whose Shrine pray let my Service and Selfe be honoured in sacrifice) you may as well be assur'd of, as of the real Respects & sincere affections of Dear Sir

Your most affectionally united Friend & Servant next to the Relation of a Wife.

Edm.Godfrey

P.S.

I must take leave to enlarge a little more as not knowing where to end, Remembring *Scriptus et a tergo nec dum Finitus Orestes*.[34] Your Ladys Brother, Sir John Godolphin,[35] hath some times enquired of his sisters health & your own, of me, & the way & manner of conveying a letter unto you, which he hath promised to doe under covert of my Paquet, But as yet I never received any from him.

Mr Harrison & his wife, my nephew Godfrey Harrison[36] & All Friends here, blessed be God continue as you left them, & desires the Tender of their Respective Services & best affections unto you.

---

[31] 'Like the Sabine women'; Horace, *Epodes* 2.41. The passage refers to the ideal wife, who stays at home to look after the children and faithfully await the homecoming of her husband.

[32] An account of the hermaphrodite was published by Thomas Allen (d. 1685) in the *Philosophical Transactions* of the Royal Society in 1668; ii, 624–5. Oldenburg informed Boyle that he had accompanied Allen to visit and examine the hermaphrodite in London in December 1667; Oldenburg, *Correspondence*, iv, p. 78.

[33] 'by word of mouth' or 'verbally'. The phrase was a legal term used to describe oral testimony or evidence only.

[34] Godfrey alludes here to the passage in Juvenal, *Satires*, 1.6, which refers to the tragedy of Orestes 'that fills every space on the page, but still has not come to an end'.

[35] See note 13.

[36] See note 11.

Here was on Shrove Tuesday last at night a very Grand Mask & Play acted, By the Lady Castlemain[37] & most of the Court Ladys in their own Persons, wherein was shewn all the Glory at once of the English Court in dyamonds & Jewells 'tis believ'd to above the vallue of a million of mony. They having sent every where into the Citty & Country to but borrow & procure the same, such Ambition there was of outvying one another therein, that the sparkling of the brightest starrs, in a frosty night may be accounted as counterfeit & dull in comparison of them; whereunto all Ambassadors in Town were sollemnly Invited.

Last week Sir John Trevor[38] was knighted and set forward on his Journey to France, to give the King thereof an account of the late defensive league enter'd into by the English, Dutch, Spaniard Swede & Emperor against his most Christian Majesty.

6. EDMUND GODFREY TO GREATRAKES, 6 FEBRUARY 1669 [13–14]

Most worthy Honourd & Good Friend

Yours bearing date the 8° of January I received since the writing of my last unto you, which I assure was more welcome unto me, than ever the most kind letter from an Amoroso to his Mistress or *sic è contra* from her to him There being such an establishd rooted & flourishing Friendship in my heart & soul towards you beyond that of the Love of Women, That it is out of the Power of all time or chance, change of air, Company or Countrys, to make any Change or alteration therein, orsomuch as to shake the least Root or Fibre thereof; And it is not the least satisfaction to me that I find the same Resentments & Passions in your Mind & thoughts, towards me; which Good Opinion and kind Condescention of yours I shall alwayes endeavour to cherrish & observe (tho I must alwayes come short of that) And no more be guilty of doing any willful Act that may endanger the Forfeiture thereof, than I shall of doing Injury to my own Soul. I shall not fail to be mindfull of the severall Contents of your said Letter, as well for your Interest therein like to be Comprehended as my own, only give me leave to time the Matter & manner thereof as prudently as I can; I do assure you there shall be no neglect of either on my part. As to what concerns Ireland here, it is now confidently reported and generally believ'd by the most knowing, that the Duke of Ormond[39] will be layd aside, & that whosoever shall supply his room, whither Titular Lieutenant & Commissioner either under the Kings Majesty, or his deputy, That Lord Orrery[40] will certainly be the chief Instrument if not Conductor of that Affaire. And a good interest in him, will be more advantageous to him that can obteyn the same, then in any Man besides either in England or Ireland in refference to the Concerns of that Place; therefore besure to stand firm on that Bottom, and you cannot Miscary.

[37] Between 1661 and 1665, Barbara Villiers, Countess of Castlemaine (1641–1709), bore Charles four children and exerted a powerful political influence at the court throughout the 1660s.

[38] Sir John Trevor (1624–1672) was an old Cromwellian who attached himself to the rising star of Henry Bennet during the 1660s. He sat as MP for Great Bedwyn between 1663 and 1672 and was appointed a privy councillor in 1668. He also served as envoy extraordinary to the court of France in 1663 and 1668. Trevor was coldly received on the latter occasion, when he was instructed to conclude a peace. His own inclinations, however, lay in another direction as it was widely known that he was pro-Dutch and favoured the Triple Alliance in Europe; Henning, iii, 602–4.

[39] James Butler, first Duke of Ormond (1610–1688), Lord Lieutenant of Ireland, 1662–1669, 1677–1685.

[40] Greatrakes' patron, Roger Boyle, first Earl of Orrery (1621–1679). In the event, Ormond was removed in 1669 and succeeded as Lord Lieutenant by Lord Robartes.

You do not know how soon your kind offer may be accepted of by me in relation to your Frank & Friendly invitation of me into Ireland And the sooner because I find it comes accompany'd with your Wives Commission, which uses to be Paramount to that of the Mans here in England in refference to Domestick affaires. The Commands of the Bed & Board properly belonging to that Sex; and that man that dares be overactive in house Government without the Goodwomans Consent, many times ends his Government Passively.

My most humble service to your sweet Consort & Sharer in your Dominion & happiness, who I hope with your self will pardon my freedome and accept of the sincere Respects and affectionate Service of him, who is Incapable of expressing how much he is

Your most obliged Friend & humble Servant. Ed: Godfrey.

Greens Lane 6° February 68 [i.e. 1669].

P.S.

The thankfull acknowledgment of my self and Nephew are herewith presented for your Care and kindness in the affair of Quarter Master Whitroe,[41] with farther trouble and Instractions [sic] therein to you.

7. ELLIS LOCKIER[42] TO GREATRAKES, 2 APRIL 1670 [15–18]

My dear & worthy Good Friend

Were it not that I have an Indefatigable and endless affection & service for you, I should be wearyd out and totally discouragd from writing or sending any more to you, after so many unsuccessful Letters, without answer or acceptance, However this may assure you of the pleasure & happyness that I am with you, by communication of words & lines, which I fear never attain the honour of your eyes or hands. But supposing that some luckyer Mercury may be the Conveyancer hereof take as followes.

Your Lord Bartlett[43] sets forward on Easter Tuesday towards you and designes his first stage at St Albans, where the Farmers of the Irish Excise and Revenue design to treat him nobly both at Supper, Breakfast next day, and a Banquet to be carryed in his followers Coaches, They reckon to spend 300 li in defraying all expences on himself & Company in that place. I hope he may prove a good Governor being a very Civill & oblidging Person, and I think his opinion is for Tolleration in point of Religion, on all sides. He is one in whom I perswade my self to have a good Interest, especially in one of his Secretarys, and others relating to him, whereof I do intend to make tryall at my coming there. Lord Angier[44] the new Vice-Treasurer cannot set out till the week after that who does also profess great

[41] Probably Jason Whitroe, listed as quartermaster to the Irish regiment of Colonel Daniel Redman in May 1661; *Mercurius Publicus*, 30 May to 6 June 1661.

[42] Unidentified. Possibly an alias employed by Godfrey.

[43] John Berkeley, first Baron Berkeley of Stratton (1607–1678), served as Lord Lieutenant of Ireland from 1670 to 1672. He was deeply unpopular with the Protestant interest for his sympathetic handling of, and tolerant attitude toward, the native Catholic population.

[44] Francis Aungier, third Baron Aungier of Longford (c.1632–1700), was elected MP, with Roger Boyle, Earl of Orrery, for Arundel in 1661. His political future, however, lay in Ireland, where he was a client of Ormond. He was rewarded for his loyalty to the crown with several grants of forfeited Irish land. He succeeded Sir George Carteret as Vice Treasurer in Ireland in 1670 and served in that office until 1673. According to Marvell, he bought the post, worth £5,000 a year, for £11,000. His frequent absences from Ireland drew complaints from Lord Robartes, the new Lord Deputy; Henning, iii, 613–15; Margoliouth, *Poems and Letters of Marvell*, ii, 311.

favour and friendship for me, I hope I shall not be necessitated to relye thereon. D.B.[45] is got up again, & pretty well recovered, of which he gives good Testimony, by his diligent attendance at the Lords house very often this Parliament & many times at Court where he hath got a considerable interest in his Majesty as well as other favorites there, notwithstanding the late affront put upon him by the Lady Castlemain[46], in getting Hampton Court from him as also knocking off one of the Padlockes, by the Dukes order hung on one of the Padlock course Gates, and sending the same to be particularly put into his own hands as a Present from her Ladyshipp which he wishd to be return'd back again to her, by the Servant that brought it (to be hangd upon his Ladys—if twere possible to keep her honest).

He doth vex and cross the Bishopps very hartily in the house of Lords insomuch, as what with his Interest and the assistance of others of the Temporall Lords the Bill against Conventicles[47] sent up thither from the house of Commons had never passd if the King had not gon thether forenoon and afternoon, and Continued amongst them 5 or 6 hours together at a time to further the same, both by Countenance & Speeches what he was able; and yet at last there is a proviso brought in by the Lord Chamberlain against which the house of Commons have excepted, & cannot convince the Lords of altering the same neither by Conferrence nor free Conferrence and unless the King be willing to have his own Prerogative waved all the Powers & penaltys mention'd in the said Act, or any other Act of Parliament relating to Religion, or spirituall power & Jurisdiction are fully & absolutly vested in the King by that Proviso, which enables him to dispense with this Act, or any other law made already relating to Religion; And a great many wise men believe that the King will not have his Prerogative in that point till he sees how kindly the Bishopps will use him, in their Courts, in a little Concern of his own, after the Lord Ross's act[48] is pass'd, to allow him to marry again during the life of his former Wife, from whom he is now divorc'd by the Bishopps Courts and labours to procure an act of Parliament (which he will certainly obteyn) to make lawfull his second marriage, notwithstanding his first wife be living: The King & all the Courtiers are zealous for the Lord Ross. The Queen Duke of York and all their conjoin'd interest oppose it what they Can (tho in vain). And tis believed that the Bishopps Court will hereafter dash upon that Rock, (it may be) to pieces; however if the King should be prevaild on to have the proviso of his prerogative rejected, in the Lords Bill against Conventicles The Lords have very much taken away the sting of the said act, and with a little Discretion to be shewn as well in the Nonconformist, as Justice of the Peace, it will not prove so terrible a Law, as prima facie, it appeard to be. 'Tis believ'd the houses will sit now all the holy days, that they may make an end for the Court to attend the feasting at Windsor, on St Georges Day, for the solemnizing whereof great preparations are making. The houses of Parliament did adjourn from Thursday to Saturday, & not sit on Good fryday, but 'tis believe'd that Easther Monday & Tuisday, will not be so religiously observ'd, unless it be by passing bill on those days against Religion. The King, Duke of Monmouth, Duke of Bucks, Lord Lautherdall, Lord Buckhurst, Baptist May & your new Lord Lieutenant suppd together at his

[45] George Villiers, second Duke of Buckingham (1628–1687).

[46] See note 29.

[47] Buckingham was sympathetic to the dissenters' cause, and frequently intervened on their behalf in the deliberations of the Privy Council and Parliament.

[48] On 11 April 1670, John Manners, first Duke of Rutland (1638–1711), obtained a private Act of Parliament enabling him to re-marry following the divorce from his first wife, Lady Anne Pierrepoint. The political implications of the Act are envisaged in the following passage, where Lockier hints at the support of the King in this matter, interested as he was in the theoretical possibility of divorcing his own wife.

house at St James on Monday night last all sitting at the same table & were very merry.[49] Dr Manton,[50] the quondam Minister of Covent Garden, was lately sent to the Gatehouse by Sir John Bennet and Sir Edmund Windham two justices of the Peace,[51] upon the act made at Oxford,[52] in the Plague Year 1665 where he is to continue six months without Bayl. Duke of Albemarle[53] does not yet ly in State, unless it be in Heaven, which many doubt & few believe, yet the Court begin to think he can do it there at an easier rate than I fear the King can procure it for him on earth. Faith of trusting to & with Courtiers being as much wanting here as mony & Good Consciences. The noyse of the Lord Ross's bill passing in Parliament has so affected & affrighted the Good Women of this town, that 'tis hop'd twill make them better wives then otherwise they would have been, as apprehending themselves to be bound thereby to the Good behaviour, so that a man may now venter on Matrimony with less fear & Danger than heretofore. They are like to hinder the Citty of London above 150,000 li per annum in trade by making all the Ground, next the waterside, whereof are now Dyers houses and trades used, as also Timber Merchants, Wood mongers Brewers and many other beneficiall trades to the Citty, They must all Quit the same by act of Parliament[54] & have all their wharfes and Ground taken from them and many of them, the houses which they have built, pulld down to take away the said Ground viz 40 foot in some places, in others above 100 besides what they mean to take more out of the Thames, to make an open key parade & way for coaches to goe from Whitehall to the Tower and when 'twas argued at the Committee, that this would undo the Citty, & make those trades go over to Southwark, Lymehouse St Katherines & Wapping, it was answerd by some of said Committee, that all the Inhabitants of those places were the Kings subjects, and deserv'd to be enrichd by having a trade brought them, as well as the Citty of London. The Court Party together with those whose necessitys force them to yield to anything, so they may continue their Priviledges of Parliament are most prevalent there, & carry all before them. I cannot think of more But to ask your Pardon for troubling you with so much, assureing you that no man hath more & greater Respects & affectionate service for your self and yours than

Your Faithfull Friend & humble Servant. Ellis Lockier.

[49] John Maitland, second Earl and first Duke of Lauderdale (1616–1682); Charles Sackville, Lord Buckhurst (1643–1706); Baptist May (1628–1697). May was a Groom of the Bedchamber, 1662–5, and Keeper of the Privy Purse, 1665–85. He attended the Duke of York in exile in the 1650s, and later had the confidence of the King, despite his known aversion to France, popery, and arbitrary government. As one of Lady Castlemaine's 'wicked crew', he helped to engineer the downfall of Clarendon. He was returned as MP for Midhurst in January 1670 with the aim of introducing a bill, modelled on the precedent set by Lord Roos' divorce case, to enable the King to divorce Catherine of Braganza. Following the King's change of heart, May was rewarded with the office of keeper of Windsor Great Park; Henning, ii, 35–6.

[50] Thomas Manton (1620–77) was one of the leading figures in the Restoration nonconformist movement, who, with Richard Baxter, was involved in high level discussions with the government aimed at securing a broader-based or more 'comprehensive' settlement of the religious question.

[51] Sir John Bennet (1616–1695) was the brother of Sir Henry Bennet, and sat on the bench as a JP for Middlesex and Westminster. Sir Edmund Wyndham (c.1600–1681) was a staunch Anglican and hardline opponent of dissent. He served as JP for Westminster, Middlesex and Surrey; Henning, i, 623–5; iii, 773–5.

[52] The Five Mile Act (1665), which forbade ejected ministers from living within five miles of their former parishes.

[53] George Monck, Duke of Albemarle (1608–1670), the architect of the Restoration. The state funeral of Monck, who died on 3 January 1670, and was not buried until 30 April, was delayed due to the Government's financial plight.

[54] The 'Act for the rebuilding of the city of London, uniting of Parishes and rebuilding of the Cathedral and Parochial Churches within the said City' (22 Ch.II c.11) extended the powers of the original Act of 1666.

Pray spake my sincere Respects & humble Tenders to your Lady with 1000 thanks for your great kindness to my Relations, whereof I shall make me happy to wait on you, in the long vacation whereof I intend to take the beginning, that I may have the longer enjoyment of your good Company, & see as much of your Country as I can in that time.

London 2d Aprill 1670.

8. JOHN ADAMS[55] TO GREATRAKES, 26 APRIL 1670 [19–20]

Sir

I question not but you have Received 2 of mine since I had the last from you, which gives account of the Success of tryall concerning Titles of Lands. Your great paines & care therein, hath been already acknowledgd as they must also now again, & so often as any occasion presents of Remembering your kindness; I second my former Iudgment in this also, That if the said Verdict be not to be retriev'd, by a new Tryall, we must endeavour to Compound with & buy out the Interest of that Drunken Levite from whom we thought our selves long since secure, as well by the Confirmation of our Title in our Grant out of the Court of Claymes as upon former tryalls with him in the Exchequer at Dublin, But of this we shall be advisd by you when it shall please God to make us happy by meeting, in the mean time to hold fair with that Bacchus's Priest and to sound him a little what he would take for his Int'rest which if it may be procur'd on reasonable terms, we shall never trouble ourselves with any new Tryalls, in the mean time the Continuance of your Favour is desired, towards the Recovery of Arrears in the Tenants hands, and as much disswading, or hindring (as fairly may be) of the Tenants from paying any Rent, to that spirituall Monster of that part of the Lands which by this late tryall, he pretends to be his. The rest that I shall trouble you with is what passes for News here.

The King its believ'd will return from Newmarket on Thursday next When changes are expected, of which place it may be said, as of Affrica of old, *Semper apportar aliquid Novi.*[56] The Duke of Albemarles Interment and Solemnitys are *ex voce Populi,*[57] design'd for Saturday next. But I do not conceive they can be ready for it untill the Middle of next Week. Madam the Dutchess of Orleance[58] is provided for at Dover castle against the middle of May, but some will have it to be the 24 Ditto before her arrivall. Doctor Manton[59] continues

---

[55] In all probability, John Adams of Mullingar, an associate of Lord Wharton, who was involved in a prolonged legal battle in the 1660s with Ridgley Hatfield, a Dublin alderman, over an entitlement to land in Ireland. It is this affair that is presumably alluded to in the first part of the letter to Greatrakes; see Bodl., Carte MS 228, fos 21–2, 26v, 37r. In February 1667, Adams sought legal advice from Samuel Bull, Greatrakes' attorney in the Court of Claims; ibid. MS 117, fo. 261.

[56] 'Always producing something new'; Pliny the Elder, *Natural History*, 17.8.42.

[57] 'Out of the mouth of the people'; i.e. by popular acclaim.

[58] Henriette Anne, duchess of Orléans (1644–1670) was the youngest child of Charles I and Henrietta Maria. Married to the younger brother of the French king, Louis XIV, she acted as a go-between in the protracted negotiations between her brother Charles II and Louis that culminated in the signing of the secret Treaty of Dover in 1670. She died shortly after returning to France.

[59] See note 50.

still in the Lady Broughton's lodgings[60] being an appartment of the Gatehouse, where he is handsomly accomodated and dayly visited and Relievd by Divers great Persons of honour & Quality, to the much improving & bettering of his Condition and estate, more than when he was at Liberty. Divers Parliament Men to the number of 60, besides severall others (not of the Parliament) almost out of Number have been with the Lord Keeper to put them selves out of the Commission of the Peace, upon account of their unwillingness, to put in execution the new Act against Conventicles, which they apprehend to be very severe, amongst the rest are Sir Thomas Leigh, Sir Richard Piggot Sir Richard Ingoldesby, Esquier Price all Parliament Men of Bucks,[61] *cum multis aliis*[62] of other Countys; others do threaten, again, as vigorously to execute the said Law, and the Fanaticks as obstinately to oppose the same by non Complyance, but submitting to any Penaltys or Punishment to meet as frequently & boldly as ever, time & experience must shew which side will be weary first & lay down their Bucklers; All that lean any thing that way are lately put out of the Militia Commission & Lieutenancy of the City of London, viz. Sir John Frederick, Sir Thomas Allen, Sir John Laurance, Sir William Turner, Sir William Bolton, Sir William Hooker, &c.[63] The Atturney Generall[64] is now certainly on his Last Leggs, (if he be at all able to make use of them); & cannot possibly get up May hill, The Sollicitor is voted for that Employ, but who shall succeed him is yet uncertain, some talk of the Speaker, tis believd that Lord Keeper will suddenly lay himself aside, or be layd aside by others: tis generally believed that the Lord Roberts[65] shall keep his place of Privy Seale & be gratifyed here least he make some bustle at Council, or otherwise in the house of Lords, at next Parliament, which will certainly meet in October again. Earl of Anglesye[66] is received into Grace & favour again, and of the Privy Council as formerly which he hath obteynd by opposing the Bill against Conventicles, in the house of Lords where the King being frequently present, was pleasd to say, that he never heard any man spake more reason & better in all his life, & that he was too hard for the Bishops, put them all together. Not else But due Respects to all as due

From Sir

Your Loving friend & Servant John Adams. 26° Aprill 1670.

[60] Mary, Lady Broughton (d.1695), was the widow of Sir Edward Broughton (d.1665). She inherited the post of Keeper of the Gatehouse at Westminster following her husband's death from wounds received at the battle of Lowestoft. She may have held nonconformist sympathies since she had previously been married to the Cromwellian Keeper of the Gatehouse, Aquila Wyke (d.1659). She was eventually removed from the post after she was found guilty of extortion and hard usage of prisoners in 1672.

[61] Thomas Lee (1635–1691) and Richard Ingoldsby (1617–1685), who was Lee's stepfather, sat as MPs for Aylesbury in the Cavalier Parliament; Henning, ii, 718–23, 633–4. Neither Piggot or Price are listed in Henning. The reference to Piggot may be an error for Sir Richard Temple (1634–1697), elected MP for Buckingham in 1661. Like Lee and Ingoldsby, Temple was hostile to the Second Conventicle Act; ibid. iii, 539.

[62] 'with many others'.

[63] Sir John Frederick (1601–1685), MP for Dartmouth 1660 and London 1663–1679. Initially supportive of the Restoration, his loyalty was subsequently called into question. Sir Thomas Allen (d.1690), Sir John Lawrence (d.1692), Sir William Turner (1615–1693), Sir William Bolton (d.1680?) and Sir William Hooke (1612–1697) were all prominent members of the corporation of London, former sheriffs and lord mayors, who were either sympathetic to, or supportive of, nonconformity.

[64] Sir Geoffrey Palmer (1598–1670) was succeeded as Attorney General by Sir Heneage Finch.

[65] John Robartes, second Baron of Truro (1606–1685). A Presbyterian during the Civil War, he outwardly conformed after the Restoration, despite lingering doubts about his continuing Presbyterian sympathies.

[66] Arthur Annesley, first Earl of Anglesey (1614–1686). For all but a brief period, Anglesey proved himself a die-hard supporter of nonconformity in Restoration England, despite his own outward conformity to the Anglican church.

9. SAMSON TRUELOCK[67] TO GREATRAKES, 14 MAY 1670 [21–4]

My worthy Good Friend

Yours of the 19th of Aprill came safe to hand, And all the kind offers therein mention'd are as friendly & kindly by me resented, as I am sure they are therein expressd & intended accordingly: In exchange whereof I will return my self unto you, with the saying of the Poet. *Nil mihi rescribas, tu tamen ipse veni.*[68] And shall not fayl to observe your advice & directions, in the manner of my Conveyance, But shall not be ready for that Work, untill after Trinity Term; so that amongst all the tediousnesses of the Long Vacation, You may expect the additionall Inconveniency of my Company also. I shall against that time (God willing) observe all the rest of your Commands, as well relating to your Lady as your self, from whome I hope I shall be made happy, in the mean while by frequent intercourse of Letters, of which I am sure none have formerly miscarryed, by your address of them to Durham Yard, by which directions, they would certainly come safe to my hands; But for the future, since I have left that place, you may please to direct them to me at the Wood Wharfe in Greens Lane neer York house, in the Strand, as formerly. Your said Letter makes mention of 400 li or 500 li you desire to borrow on good & clear title of English Security of England, But you mention not where the land lyes, nor how any man may see your Evidences & title thereof, whereby to give satisfaction to the lender. But of that we shall discourse more at large, when I come there; and doubt not but to accommodate you at my Return on good terms. In the mean while you may please to make use of what mony you can receive of Rents there according to former power given you, & I question not to receive other considerable summs at my coming to Dublin, & elswhere in that Country. Pray be pleasd to Inform your Self (& me also by letter) where my Lord of Ardglass lives, my Lord Angiers, Sir George Hamilton,[69] with all which I have something to do in mony matters, besides Mr Cook Merchant in Dublin,[70] & therefore I question whether it will not be my best & readyest way to come first to Dublin, & take some order in my concerns there first besides that I must wait on my Lord Lieutenant & my very good Friend Mr Froud[71] one of his Secretarys but in these things I must be advisd by you, & expect a word or two thereof by your next. The news here is (which will prove stale before it comes to you) that the Duke of Monmouth was lately made privy Councillor, as also Lord Anglesy restored unto Grace and Favour & Great Opinion of the King, for his well speaking in the Act against Conventicles, Notwithstanding the King passd the said Act. Whereof no body yet can tell what will be the consequence: I find the Solders like to be the only Justices to put it in execution, for that what of those that have put themselves out & what have since been put out by a Second purging of the Commission of the Peace. There are few sober or understanding men left in, But such as must act with assistance of the Millitary Power, who 'tis believd will be encour-

---

[67] Unidentified. Given the reference to Edmund Godfrey's address in Green Lane, this may be another alias employed by the London magistrate.

[68] 'Don't reply, but come yourself'; Ovid, *Heroides*, 1.2.

[69] Thomas Cromwell, third Earl of Ardglass (1653–1682). He was married to Honora Boyle, the daughter of Michael Boyle, archbishop of Dublin. For Angier, see note 44. Sir George Hamilton (c.1608–1679), a convert to Roman Catholicism, was the Duke of Ormond's brother-in-law. A loyal royalist in Ireland during the 1640s, he was restored to all his former lands after the Restoration.

[70] Unidentified.

[71] Philip Frowde (1645–1715 or 1716), the son of Sir Philip Frowde (d.1674), corresponded with Ormond's secretary Sir George Lane in 1665 and 1666. He later served as secretary to Lord Berkeley, Lord Lieutenant from 1670 to 1672; Bodl., Carte MS 34, fos 519, 585.

aged to put affronts & give Blows to some of those that shall be found at those Meetings, on purpose to provoke them to a Resistance or striking again That so the greater advantage may be taken against them, But I do not find but that they are all peaceably minded to suffer any injury without resisting only they will continue their Meetings, to do which the Quakers have begun. And when they were prevented in London by the Soldiers from meeting at their Place appointed, They continued Preaching in the Streets, doe what the Soldiers could; & the Lord Mayor[72] also who was very civill to them: In order to this; there are Soldiers laid, both Horse & Foot in every Quarter of the Citty & Southwark also—The King went & din'd with Lady Castlemain,[73] at his return from Newmarket, & spent much time there before he went to see the Queen; Also when Duke of Albemarle was buryed, (which was a poor, pittyfull Sneaking shew) there not being one Gentleman mourner in a long Cloake, to attend the Ceremony, except those that were Close Mourners, by the Kings Command, but all like loose Ruffenly fellows or Pickpocketts in dirty Shirts, & open foul linnen, & in Quirpoe[74]). The King appointed a Place to be made for the Queen to see the said shew out of the Banquetting house Window, but himself went to the Lady Castlemains lodgings to see it & stood there, with her whereupon the Queen left the Banquetting house Window, & went to the Duke of Ormonds lodging & there satt with them to see the said shew. I doubt not but you have already heard what pranks were playd at Newmarkett.

The Attorney Generall is dead,[75] & the Sollicitor succeeds him & Sir Edward Turner[76] Speaker of the house of Commons is made Sollicitor, & Sir Edward Thurland[77] is Sollicitor to the Duke of York, in Sir Edward Turners Roome. We have lately had four houses in Covent Garden fallen down to the Ground suddenly, without hurting any body, but all the Goods therein spoild; two of them were in one of the Piazza's wherein lived Sir John Coradon,[78] the late Queen Mothers Phisitian & the other Sir John Bastiman[79] President for the King of Swedeland. The other two houses were towards Bridgett street, behind the former. Here hath been great Preparations for St Georges Feast to be held at Windsor-Castle, on the 5 and 6th of May, & warrants issued out against the said day. But because the Prince of Orange is not come over, who is intended to be installed at the said Feast, the said meeting is put of untill his Coming. We are all next week for Dover Castle to meet Madame the Kings Sister[80] there, who accompanys the King of France into Flanders, & upon his return back again to Calais hath obteynd leave from the King of France to come to Dover for 4 or 5 dayes, where our King & Court do intend to treat her & all her Company very Highly. 'Tis believd the mayn end of her coming (besides Mistresses & Pleasures) is to try if she can prevaile with our King to relinquish the Dutch Interest, & Adhaere to the French in his

[72] Sir Samuel Starling, Lord Mayor of London 1669–1670. Known as a persecutor of dissenters, he nonetheless was known to have befriended ejected ministers such as Zachary Crofton.
[73] See note 29.
[74] *Quirpoe, querpo or cuerpo*: not wearing a cloak so as to show the shape of the body.
[75] See note 64.
[76] Sir Edward Turnor (*c.*1617–1676) was MP for Hertford and Speaker of the House of Commons from 1661 to 1671. He served in various offices of state: Attorney General to the Duke of York, 1660–70; Solicitor General, 1670–1; and Chief Baron of the Exchequer, 1671–6. Although a staunch Anglican, he probably favoured some form of limited toleration; Henning, iii, 613–15.
[77] Edward Thurland (1607–1683), MP for Reigate, 1661–73. A dependant of the Duke of York, he served as solicitor-general to the Duke from 1660 to 1670, and attorney-general, 1670–3; Henning, iii, 562–3.
[78] Sir John Colladon (d. 1675) had in fact served various members of the royal household since 1640. A Huguenot and protégé of the royal physician, Sir Theodore Mayerne, he was at the time of this letter personal physician to Queen Catherine.
[79] Unidentified.   [80] See note 58.

designs in Flanders: 'Tis confidently reported here amongst wise men, that the Lord Bartlett[81] hath writ very honourable things to the King, of the Lord Roberts[82] transactions in Ireland, & that he will be well received when ever he comes over; The Lord Roscommon[83] (who is his Privado) was lately over here & in private with the King at Newmarkett, after he had first been with the Duke of Buckingham here, & the next day went away again from the King with letters to Lord Roberts in Ireland according to the tenure whereof 'tis believd Lord Roberts will govern himself either for coming to London or going to Truro in Cornwall. Duke of Bucks is very great again with the King, himself, Lord Lotherdale [i.e. Lauderdale], & Secretary Trevers are the Ruling Caball, when they please to enlarge, Lord Orrery, Lord Ashley, Bishopp of Chester, & Sir Robert Murray, are added.[84] To this neither Subject's time, nor Paper, will suffer Inlargment. Only let me trespass so far on all with your Patience & Goodness to boot, as to subscribe my self

The most Faithfully loving of your Intimate Friends
London 14th May 1670. Samson Truelock.

10. [EDMUND GODFREY] TO GREATRAKES, 24 APRIL 1671 [25–8]

24 April 1671

Youres of the 27 March last, I received whereby am advisd of your welfare as also of mine Safe coming to your hands—I shall not fail to observe your order & directions in Refference to Mr Hynde,[85] whereof you may in due time receive a satisfactory account. Since my last, the Dutchess of York[86] is dead & Buried, betwixt Protestant & Papist, No body knows what, so let her lye. Here are various reports of wives for [the] Duke [of] York. Tho for my part I do not think him so much in hast in that design neither do I believe do his Physitians advise so, for that I know somewhat of that concerns, There is a fresh young Lady lodgd for him at Richmond in the house of a friend of mine,[87] with 2 Matrons or spies alwayes to tend upon her, & out of one of their Companys she never stirrs, nor hath any access to her without them perhaps to try if a sound issue may be begotten before we do overhastily adventure on Matrimony. 'Tis confidently reported & believed here that the Lord Fairfax[88]

---

[81] i.e. Berkeley; see note 43.   [82] See note 65.

[83] Wentworth Dillon, fourth Earl of Roscommon (1637–1685), was a loyal royalist, poet and friend of Orrery, to whom he was related by marriage. He later turned down the offer of administrative posts in the Irish government in favour of soldiering.

[84] Anthony Ashley Cooper, first Baron Ashley (later Earl of Shaftesbury) (1621–1683). For John Wilkins, Bishop of Chester, and Sir Robert Moray, see Appendix 2.

[85] Dr Samuel Hinde. In 1671, Hinde, of Dublin, described his life in a letter to the King as 'an Iliad of Sufferings, for the service of both their Majesties'; *CSPD, 1671*, 465.

[86] Anne Hyde, Duchess of York (1637–1671), was the eldest daughter of the disgraced Earl of Clarendon. She died on 31 March and was buried in Westminster Abbey on 5 April 1671.

[87] Possibly William Church of Richmond, Surrey, who, after Godfrey's death, described how in 1677 the melancholic magistrate was wont to shun the company of his own kind and to pass the time with footmen and the keepers of the bowling green at Richmond; Marshall, *Strange Death of Edmund Godfrey*, 154–5.

[88] Thomas Fairfax, third Lord Fairfax of Cameron (1612–1671). His daughter, Mary (d. 1704), married George Villiers, second Duke of Buckingham, in 1657. Godfrey alludes here to her husband's affair with the Countess of Shrewsbury, one of the greatest scandals, among many, of Charles II's reign. In 1668 Buckingham had killed Francis, the eleventh Earl of Shrewsbury (c.1623–1668) in a duel caused by his affair with the Earl's wife. He was subsequently pardoned by the King and moved the Countess into one of his London residences.

hath written a letter of reproof to his Daughter [the] Duchess [of] Buckingham for being
to easy & forward in complyance with [the] Duke [of] Buckingham in refference to the
transactions betwixt him & [the] Countess [of] Shrewsbury & that he hath sent for her
down into Yorkshier, whereat the fore mentiond will not be sorry. Mr Mountague[89] the
late Ambassador in France is newly come over hether, Some say want of supply of monys
is a great cause of his return, but undoubtedly 'twas much his wiser Course to come
hither, than to stay at Paris, especially if the King of France stay most part of this Summer
about Flanders, as 'tis expected he will, & then it will be nearer to go to him from hence
then Paris. Sunday night last went from hence the Lord Bellasis[90] and others to comple-
ment the King of France at Dunkirk: & on Wednesday next goes over the Duke [of]
Buckingham to beget a Right understanding betwixt the two Crowns, If that work be
now to be don. I hope these will be as right on apprehention of the true Interest betwixt
England & Holland, whereof many do make a great Question. But this Good hath been
don for England, by the King of France's coming into Flanders that he hath sent hither
for Supplys of provisions to be sent over in our ships, whereof great plenty hath already
been sent & more every day going. Insomuch as all manner of Corn is very much risen
in price both in Kent, Sussex & Essex, & 'tis believed will have a good influence all the
Nation over, They carry over fat Oxen, Calves, & other live Provisions, every day. We
have much alarm'd the Common People here, by sending of 1200 foot & 3 troops of
horse to Guard the sea coasts which I think signifies little besides terrifying the People
who have the same apprehetions of Danger ('tho on farr less cause) as when the Dutch
burnt our Ships at Chattham,[91] only it opens every ordinary mans mouth against us, for
having no fleet at Sea this Summer; But to spake differently there is neither need of one
nor Danger of the other, For that the French do come to Flanders without any manner
of Fleet at Sea, not having Shipps enough to attend them there, so as to bring his ordinary Provisions, upon which account he hath passed a Compliment on our King by his
Envoy, That he did this to avoyd all occation of making us Jealous of him, Not fearing
any want of provisions where he hath so good a Neighbour & plentifull Country to be-
friend him, as the King of England & all his Dominions. Here hath lately been a great
Dispute & many Conferences between the Lords & Commons concerning a Bill of New
Impositions, or General Excise,[92] which the Lords would in no wise consent to, And
hereupon on Satturday last in the afternoon the King went to the House of Lords & there
passed 18 publick Bills & 14 private ones & so prorogued them to the 16th of Aprill next
year. And in the opinion of most wise men the Lords have gaind a great point of the
Commons, in this action, 1st in easing the people of a generall Excise, which the Commons had granted to be laid on them; Next in shewing to the Court, & house of Commons, That they can check their proceedings notwithstanding the powerfull Interposition

[89] Ralph Montagu (1638–1709) was Equerry to the Duchess of York, 1662–5, and Master of the
Horse to the Queen, Catherine of Braganza, 1665–78. He also served as Ambassador to France,
1669–72 and again in 1676–8. A client of Arlington, he was nonetheless ignorant of the negotiations
surrounding the secret clauses inserted in the Treaty of Dover. Following his election to Parliament in
1678, he became a supporter of exclusion; Henning, iii, 86–9.

[90] John Belasyse, first Baron Belasyse of Worlaby (d. 1689). A Roman Catholic, he was later imprisoned in the Tower on the evidence of Titus Oates. He subsequently served as first Lord of the Treasury
under James II.

[91] In 1667; see note 35.

[92] For discussion of the various arguments between the Commons and Lords over the Excise Bill,
see for example Spurr, *England in the 1670s*, 18–20.

of Preferments Profitable Places, Ready & mony, or Pensions, into the Bargain; many believe that This Parliament will not meet, to sett again, They having much lost their Reputation with the People; Besides the Lords understand what Gratifications have passd to make them so free & liberall of the publick Purse; And thereupon 'tis believ'd will disputes most Bills that shall come from them hereafter. The Bill against Popery as well as that against Fanaticks, are both laid aside together, by the Lords & with the Bill of Generall excise will fall to the Ground & Signify nothing. There is a good moderate Bill passt, for Settling of Maintenance for the Ministers in London where the Citty was burnt Down;[93] Tho the Clergy would fain have had much higher, But I think now 'tis Indifferently well for all Partys. Next there is another very good Bill passd, sessing of all houses within the 4 next parishes, towards satisfying the Loss & Dammage of him whose house shall be blown up or demolished to prevent the farther spreading, & increase of Fire.[94] The Act of Grace & Generall Pardon, was not offerd, as was widely intended at Breaking up of Sessions, by reason they did not agree upon the Generall Excise, which the Commons had granted for 9 yeares, & would certainly have been made perpetuall to the King & his Heires, for ever, By the next Parliament. And then these very Commons that had granted it, might have been most deservedly kickd out of Dores, For that the King would then have had no need of them. If this Act of Indemnitie had Passt, Sir Thomas Sandis, O Bryan & Reeves[95] were by name mentioned for Pardon, notwithstanding they were condemned by the same sessions of Parliament A thing never heard before & contrary to Parliamentary proceedings; only the Kings Judges & the Earl of Clarendon were Ioyn'd together in the said Bill to be exempt from pardon. I thank you for taking care with your Friend Mr H for clearing the remaining foot of account For that nither my Nephew nor my self can possibly come over this year; And if you please let that remainder be paid & cleard to me & not to him, it being my own particular Concern; for other accounts that are or may be betwixt your self and my nephew, I do not intermeddle in. This being sufficiently Impertinent, & more tedious, to you to read than me to write, it is time that I give you ease & Release from so long a Bondage by subscribing my self. Most worthy honoured Sir

  Your Faithfull Friend & humble Servant
  Allways Wives & Relations
  are understood to be presented with
  Respectfull Salutes & service
  Tho, not at all times mention'd at large.

---

[93] 'An Act for the Better Settlement of the Maintenance of the Parsons, Vicars, and Curates in the Parishes of the City of London Burnt by the Late Dreadful Fire there'; 22 & 23 Ch.II.c.15.

[94] 'An Act for the Determination of Differences touching Houses Burnt or Demolished within Four Years since the Late Dreadful Fire in London'; 22 & 23 Ch.II.c.16.

[95] Godfrey alludes here to an infamous attack perpetrated by Sir Thomas Sandys, Captain O'Brien and Miles Reeves of the Duke of Monmouth's troops upon Sir John Coventry (c.1636–1685) in December 1670, when he was violently assaulted in the street. Sandys had been made Lieutenant and Major of the King's troop of Guards in October 1670. In February 1671, a newsletter reported that Sir Thomas Sandys and Captain O'Brien were at the Hague 'attending the progress of the proceedings against them here'; *CSPD, 1671*, 106. The two men had presumably fled the country while they anxiously awaited their fate. Godfrey's indignation was shared by the general populace and many of Coventry's fellow MPs in Parliament. In January 1671 an Act, commonly known as the Coventry Act, was passed 'to prevent malicious maiming and wounding'; 22 & 23 Charles II.c.1; Grey, *Debates of the House of Commons*, i, 333–49.

11. E[DMUND] G[ODFREY] TO GREATRAKES,
3 JUNE 1671 [28–9]

3 June 1671

Sir

I have sent two unto you Since I had the honour of receiving any from you. In my last I complain'd of very great unkindness from G[odfrey] H[arrison] not without just Cause, Tho I hope I shall now come of better than I could then expect; However my design in advising you of his Actions, was to make You wary, & carefull of not being deceived by him. For that I have a hearty Love & respect for you, as for an honest Man & True Friend, which I praefer before a Brother much more beyond the relation of an unworthy kinsman, Therefore *Praemonitus, Praemonitus*;[96] It is now your own Fault if you rely on him too much & be deceived either in point of kindness or Confidence. Since my last I have met with one Mr Shadwell of Ireland[97] who came to me in your Name, to desire the advance of 20 li towards the charges of carrying on some business, & obteyning a Lease of certain Lands from [the] Duke [of] York for you, he shewd me also your letter to him, on that account, which does only order the Lease to be left with me & speaks your Intention of Gratitude besides payment of all charges to him, at his Return into Ireland; But gives him no Commission to me, Nor me any order to pay any mony to him, which could not come so unseasonably to me at any time as now, by reason of my Neph-ews ill usage of me, (whereof I have already inform'd you) who keep all my Estate he can possibly from me on account of that Difference & therefore I have not the command of Mony as formerly, Tho, as free a heart to serve you as ever, & hope I shall never have Cause to change my affectionate Resolutions, & Iudgment in that point. My last to you spoke of my desires of a Receipt of the 18 li & which I received of Mr Hynde of Staple Inn[98] for your use, he having desired my said Receipt over to his Brother in the Country (since deceasd) and the last enclosd in mine from you under your hand & seal, himself keeps; Therefore I ought to receive such an other acknowledgment from you, as may Justifie me in the receiving & disposing of the said mony by your direction, & for your use, For that you know it was towards 30 li by me paid on a Bill of Exchange by your ap-pointment whereof, there still remains due to me 12 li, which Inconvenient time, I ques-tion not but you will remitt me; And a Receipt or acknowledgment as forementiond, For me to keep by me for my own Iustification. The shortness of time & hast of the Post, will not suffer me to trouble you with news, only to assure you that I am & shall be to Your-self & Yours A very Faithfull Friend & Servant whilst

E[dmund] G[odfrey].

---

[96] 'Warning, warning'.

[97] John Shadwell (d. 1684), father of the Poet Laureate Thomas Shadwell (*c*.1640–1692). A royalist in the Civil War, John Shadwell, who trained as a lawyer, removed to Ireland after the Restoration. In 1662, he served as Attorney General of the province of Connaught. Three years later, in 1665, he was active in the Court of Claims on behalf of his master, the Duke of York, in seeking to retrieve lands once held by the regicide Edmund Ludlow. In 1666, he wrote to the Lord Lieutenant, Ormond, begging for his support in the forthcoming election to the recorder-ship of the town of Galway. He was subsequently appointed to the post; Bodl., Carte MS 145, fo. 28; NLI, MS 31, 29–30, 53, 85, 93, 104; *HMC Ormonde Manuscripts*, 243–4; *CSPD, 1671*, 498.

[98] See note 85.

12. [EDMUND GODFREY] TO GREATRAKES,
17 JUNE 1671 [29–30]

17 June 1671

My very Dear & worthy Good Friend

Yours of the 7 Currant I received tho was out of Town at its arrivall here; I take notice of the contents thereof, & shall Faithfully observe the same; Tho, Mr Shadwell[99] hath been pressing me for mony above this Fortnight before the passing of the Lease, Whereunto I was fain to reply no order in the Case, He pretends great want thereof before the seals can be affixt, & insisted much on 20 li. The Lease I see approv'd of under the hand of some of the Dukes Commissioners, amongst whom I have a very Good Interest. I shall examine the particulars of the lands according to your Instructions in your last letter contained, & in other things obey your Commands & directions. I was at your brother Sir John's Lodgings, But his out of Town, with the Court, however I will endeavour to find out your uncle Dr Godolphin,[100] and Question not to effect the same either by enquiry of them about Bloomsbury or at Exceter House, whereof I shall God willing give you a farther account by the next post. What passeth here at present for News, is, That [the] Duke [of] Buckingham gets ground & advantage every day of Lord Arlington[101] They being the two Potent interfering favorites; Castlemain supports the latter and Nell Gwyn[102] takes part with the Former. And I will assure you it is a Measuring cast, which of the she Rulers hath the best Interest. Lord Ashley[103] is of Nell Gwyns party & a Great Admirer of her Power more than her Parts, tho both highly considerable. Common fame hath already made him Lord Treasurer here, Who undoubtedly hath the best quallifications for that employ; Sir T.Cliff[104] is under some cloud of unkindness, for advising the Parliament to be prorogued for a twelve Month, & his Council not so much cry'd up, as formerly: All the Judges have been advisd withall, whether the Parliament may not be calld to meet again, before the said Time (as well to sweeten them By continuance of Priviledges, as to facilitate the Work of obteyning an other Land tax or Grant of a Generall Excise). For that this tax in Masquerade doth come far short of Expectations 8 or 9 of the Judges (as I am inform'd) have given the opinion in the Negative against the Parliaments meeting before the time whereunto they are prorogued; The other 3 or 4 at most are affirmative, & for their Meeting. John Ashburnam[105] of the bedchamber is Dead, & so is Serjeant Fountayn.[106] A young Lady one Ramsden of the North[107] whose Friends

---

[99] See note 97.   [100] Sir John Godolphin. See note 13.

[101] Henry Bennet, first Earl of Arlington (1618–1685), trusted adviser to the King.

[102] For Castlemaine, see note 29. Much of the popularity of Nell Gwyn (1651–1687) resided in her Protestantism. By this date, however, both women were losing out in the affections of the King to Louise de Kéroualle, Duchess of Portsmouth (1649–1734), who was sent to Charles' court to act as an agent for the French and Catholic interest.

[103] See note 84.

[104] Sir Thomas Clifford (1630–1673) was one of the rising stars in Charles' government and one of the main architects of the royal indulgence of 1672, which allowed freedom of worship to Roman Catholics and Protestant dissenters.

[105] John Ashburnham (*c.*1603–1671) sat as MP for Sussex, 1661–7. An old royalist, he had served Charles I as Groom of the Bedchamber, 1628–42 and as Treasurer of War, 1642–6. In 1661, he was reappointed to the former position under Charles II; *ODNB*.

[106] John Fountaine (1600–1671) served as a circuit judge during the Interregnum. A friend of fellow jurist Sir Matthew Hale, he shared the latter's nonconformist sympathies and was responsible for introducing Hale to Richard Baxter in 1667; *ODNB*.

[107] Possibly a relation of the Ramsdens of Longley Hall and Byram, Yorkshire. Sir John Ramsden (1594–1646) fought for the King in the Civil War and died a prisoner at Newark. His son William (1625–1679) succeeded him and was knighted in 1663.

would have given her 4000 li Portion, & of a very honorable Family, being very handsome and brought to Court, was there debocht, whom her Friends cast of on that account & being afterwards neglected by the Court, stabb'd herself & dyed on Thursday Morning last, leaving it first under her hand in a letter to her Mother, That nobody had known her but our Master.[108] The King of France & most of the Princes of Germany have resolvd to bring under their Yoke all the Hanse towns There And to make themselves absolute Masters over all the Reipublicks, & Towns & Cittys there, & afterwards of Holland if they can, 'Tis believed that Brunswick must surrender to them in ten day or on a fortnight at Farthest, The next they fall upon will be Callen,[109] & so to the Rest, Lubeck, Stoad,[110] & all other Imperiall Cittys which are become free, as Hamborough Dantzick &c. And the Emperour would fain assist the Hans Towns if he knew how, for that the King of France hath sent to have his eldest son chosen King of the Romans, which thing being once don he must succeed as Emperour, And no doubt but Care will be taken that the present Emperour's life be not over long. The King of France hath sent a Menaceing Message to the Pope that if he shall hinder his son's Election, he will permit the Great Turk to overan all Italy & Germany. Here is a generally believ'd Report, That our Jamacians have taken St Domingo, in Hispaniola, & fortified themselves there with intent to keep it. Not else from

Your faithfull Friend to serve you [unsigned].

13. [EDMUND GODFREY] TO GREATRAKES, 27 JUNE 1671 [31]

27 June 1671
Mr Valentine Greatracks
My worthy Friend

Since my last to you, which advisd of the Difficulty of finding out Doctor Godolphin's house, by reason of Sir Johns being out of Town,[111] however with much enquiry I found out his habitation, being private & very convenient, where I left your letter, I have since had the opportunity of waiting on him, where I found Sir Amos Meredith[112] his Lady or Sister I know not which, Where we remembred yourself & Lady. But as to the 15 li you write of, it cannot be obteyn'd, He having laid out all his mony in building, & therefore desires to be excus'd. I have seen the Counterpart of the Dukes lease to you in Mr Shadwells hands, wherein are conteyned many more parcells of lands then are expressd in your Letter, he is very pressing for 15 li to pay fees to the Secretary, and other Officers, which certainly I could not have deny'd any Man That should as the same on your account had not my hands been so strictly bound up, before by my Nephew, Against whom I have now depending three sutes in Chancery, besides what I have at Common Law. Mr Shadwell pretends it not safe for him to part with the Duke of Yorks lease out of his hands to any man before he see you seale the Counterpart, which methinks has somewhat of reason in it. I shall be ready to receive your further Commands therein, & in what else I may be Serviceable to you, To whom I professe an unalterable Kindness & Friendship whilst I am

Your faithfull Friend & Servant
My Respectfull Salutes & service
to your Good Lady.

---

[108] i.e. King Charles II.   [109] i.e. Cologne.
[110] i.e. Stade, near Hamburg, in Lower Saxony, a port and member of the Hanseatic League.
[111] See note 13.   [112] See note 4.

234 *Miraculous Conformist*

14. [EDMUND GODFREY] TO GREATRAKES, 20 SEPTEMBER 1671 [31–2]

20 September 1671

Sir

Mr Hynd[113] is not yet come out of Devon & will not be here till Term. I have been some time out of Town since my receipt of your last, bearing date 9th August, & therefore have not writ you since that time. I hope you have not paid any bill of exchange to Mr Shadwell as I understand he did intend to draw upon your in Ireland For that I do now perceive by his own mouth that his Interest is not great with the Duke [of] York or his Commissioners or other servants belonging to him; And that Mathew Ren[114] the Dukes Secretary is his professd Enemy. I have also got out of him by discourse that one Turner[115] hath got the making of the Dukes leases from him. And that the Lord [...][116] & Charles Ren, ye Secretarys Brother,[117] divide those proffetts & perquisits between them, & altogether exclude him & Neither do I believe he will long continue in any relation to that employment under the Duke, or if they cannot be so soon quit of him, his Interest there will be very little, so that having no Power Favor nor Salery he will soon be weary thereof. The said Mr Turner (as I am informd) is gon over to Ireland a month since & I presume hath your lease with him, amongst others to be deliver'd there; from whome you will receive the same, without any obligation to Mr Shadwell unless for promoting of the same, Therefore I conceive your Gratuity will be expected there, And best laid out for your Advantage, so that if you have not already paid Mr Shadwell his bill of 16 li I would not wish you to be too forward therein, Pray make no words of this advice which I hope will not come too late, & as soon as you can inform me of the receipt hereof, & if Mr Turner hath been with you in Ireland, and of all Things else relating to Your Concerns wherein I may render you any service here The which no man shall more cheerfully & faithfully perform that your most Intire hearty friend & Servant &c.

Major Weldon[118] is Quite blown up & gon aside

his Wife lodgeth in Covent Garden

however they do very honestly to their Children

as far as their Estate will go.

15. [EDMUND GODFREY] TO GREATRAKES, 3 OCTOBER 1671 [32–3]

3 October [1671]

My most Honourd & Faithfully Good Friend

I have lately received two from you being much of the same tenor concerning the lease of Molagh abby lands,[119] wherein I shall endeavour to serve you to the utmost of my

---

[113] See note 85.

[114] Matthew Wren (1629–72) was the son of Bishop Matthew Wren and cousin of the famous scientist and architect, Sir Christopher Wren. He sat as MP for Mitchell, 1661–72. He served first as secretary to Clarendon from 1660–67, and then as secretary to the Earl's son-in-law, the Duke of York, from 1667 until his death in 1672. He was depicted by Marvell as 'bloated Wren' and a parasitical presence on the Government benches in the Commons; Henning, iii, 762–3.

[115] Unidentified.   [116] Word illegible.

[117] Charles Wren (d. 1681), brother of Matthew.   [118] See note 15.

[119] The lands of Mullough Abbey were in county Tipperary and formed part of Alderman Kendrick's lot. Greatrakes paid the quit rent on these lands in 1664. At the time, he was presumably

Power, & doubt not in some kind of answering your Expectations therein, If your business be not don to your hands, by a shorter way & means, whereof I doubt not but you
by this time advisd By Mr Turner his having been with you in Ireland, who as I am informd by Mr Shadwells own mouth, hath got his Employment of making of leases from
him, & doth afterwards carry them over into Ireland, & with his own hands delivers
them to the partys concernd, and is to transact all other things there at the same time on
the Dukes Behalfe, whither he is now gon some six week since. Therefore you cannot but
have heard of him there, who I believe hath carryed your lease with him. He wants of all
Mr Shadwells Imployment, And he acquainted me himself that Mat[thew] Ren the
Dukes Secretary, hath no kindness for him, But that Mr Charles Ren the Dukes Secretarys Brother, & this Mr Turner divide the proffitts & perquisits of his place betwixt them
So that he is now a *non Significat*, of all which I have formerly advisd you. This hath made
me backward in observing Bill of exchange on Mr Bingham,[120] whereof I perceive you did
also advise Mr Shadwell, who hath been with me to be fingering the mony. But I told him
the Bill would signifie nothing, untill Mr Hynds comming to Town, who would not
come out of Devonshire till the end of Michaellmas Term, & that this Bill was by you
signd on presumption that Mr Hynde was already come to town; Mr Shadwell sayes he
shall go for Ireland within this Fortnight, Tho I believe the hopes of this mony would yet
tempt him to stay A month longer; But he shall have none for that he cannot serve you.
As soon as the King & Duke comes to town from Newmarkett & Suffolk and Norfolk
Progress, which they have lately gon, & the Queen also, I will not be unmindfull of your
concern with Mr Ren; but I do strongly perswade my self that you will effect the same
yourself with Mr Turner while he is Ireland, But if that should fail you I will lay my self
out *pro ultimate virium*,[121] with Sir Allen Broderick[122] and others of the Dukes Commissioners & Agents here, to serve you: But one thing I take very unkindly that you should
so much distrust my Friendship or willingness of serving you That I would not be free or
forward therein, without the hope or encouragement of a Reward or Bribe held forth
unto me, from your self. And tho I must acknowledge mony to be very short with me at
present, & any honest gain would be welcome unto me being a worse man in my Estate
by 4000 li then when I had last the honour to see you; yet I am not of the Opinion, That
all offers of gain, ought to be embracd from all persons. That I should either sell my
Gentility, Generosity, or the worth of my Friend for mony, or Farme out any favour that
I were capable of doing him for a price: I remember the saying of a young Roman Gentleman taken in Battle, being of Good Countenance & parts, was offerd an honourable
service under his Conquerour his Reply was—*Non sum sic natus, ut Sordide Servirem, aut*

leasing them from the descendants of John Kendrick. However, they were subsequently forfeited to
the Duke of York as part of the Restoration land settlement in Ireland whereby the Duke was
granted 'deficiencies' to make up for the land that should have been granted to him from regicides
who had subsequently been pardoned; BL, Add. MS 25,692, fos 3, 4v; King's Inns Library, Dublin,
S. Prendergast, Viscount Gort, *The Prendergasts of Newcastle Co. Tipperary, A.D.1169–1760*,
112–13.

[120] Unidentified.

[121] 'for the best of men'.

[122] Sir Allen Broderick (1623–1680) sat as MP for Orford in the Cavalier Parliament. His younger
brother, St John, was a Cromwellian officer in Ireland. Allen, however, had served as a Sealed Knot
conspirator in the 1650s and was subsequently knighted after the Restoration for his services to the
Crown. He was appointed Surveyor-General in Ireland, 1660–7, and acted as a Commissioner for the
Irish land settlement, 1663–9. He also sat as MP for Dungarvan, 1661–5. A follower of the Duke of
York until at least 1671, he may have had some part in the alleged mishandling of the Duke's Irish
estates in 1668, part of which had been purchased from Broderick; Henning, i, 721–4.

Adularer, aut quovis aliis modoq[ue] deditus, et Disengenue vivirem,[123] My charitable Minds, & Good Intentions must suffer under what I have lost & been defrauded of, But pray let these things dwell & dye with you, & go no farther. As to your extraordinary kind & friendly proffer of coming to live with you, with that Frankness of your expressions therein, I do assure you they have made a deep impression in me And have given me the greatest comfort I have met withall since my unhappy Afflictions. And if God spare me health & ability of Body, I will yet come & see that bad Country, where so good a man lives, & dares continue his friendship and kindness to one in adversity, & distress as well as prosperity & plenty.

Your old friend Sir Edmund Godfrey is turn'd a great Courtier again, & having kis'd the Kings hand, hath been very kindly received at Whitehall, & there Courted into an acceptance of all his Commissions again, ever since Aprill last; If he wo'd be throw paced, he might be some body amongst them, But I fear he hath a foolish & Narrow Conscience, And that spoyles him and all that use it, My paper bids me break off, & say you must believe more than I can write or speak how faithfully I am

Yours

Respects & Service to Wives (being second selves)

are always understood, Tho not Exprest

You cannot be ignorant of the strange Turns & Changes we have had of late in Refference to the Farmers of the Customs & proroguing the Parliament for above 12 months & more are dayly expected at Court. The ruling Favorite is [the] Duke [of] Buckingham. Castlemain, Arlington & that party go down the Wind, Tis believd this Parliament will never meet again to sett & do any thing; in the mean time, we have a great Confidence in France. If not help of Mony else the Parliament must meet soone.

16. [EDMUND GODFREY] TO GREATRAKES, 27 JANUARY 1672 [24–25]

27 January 1671 [i.e. 1672]

My Dearest Good Friend

Since my last to you which I think bore date 16th Instant I have met with my nephew[124] (tho' at distance enough betwixt our selves) who still perseveres in his unnaturall unkindness to me. God turn his heart & forgive him; But on a full discourse of the Concerns betwixt you in pursuance of your Commission Given me, I acquainted him with the contents of your former letter & withall added my own particular knowledge, of your great disappointment in raising mony on your Estate in the West,[125] & withall related your great pains & charge in his Service; To which he replyd that he did not desire to put you to any charge or expence in his service or that you should take any paines in long Journeys, much less to undergoe any loss of your horses, or other Dammage by his service; But when ever you are in Cash, to return him the remainder of his mony; That you would make your Discount of paines, Charge or Loss by any Service don him, out of what you have Received for him his Answer being the same in refference to the 10 li mention'd in your said letter as layd at the Assizes of Limerick; He desires the Return may be made as soon as may stand with your convenience which I thought could not be don till about Midsummer, at which time

---

[123] 'I wasn't born thus in order to live a life of servility, or to flatter others, or to live shamefully or ignobly'.

[124] Godfrey Harrison; see note 11.

[125] Presumably Greatrakes' inheritance in county Limerick.

I perceive he designs to be in Ireland or soon after. The stoppage of all payments on assignments out of the Exchequer is now stale news. We are now altogether taken up, in making great preparations for a war at Sea, in order whereunto we are like to fit out a great & formidable Navy against Spring; I wish a good cause accompany them with Gods blessing, & success answerable may attend them. Most of the Court Gallantry & Young Gentlemen of the Nation, are like to be engagd in the Service, either by Sea or Land, the Duke of York going out in person as Admirall, and the Duke of Monmouth goes Generall of the land forces, which with what are already employd in France, (as is Reckon'd) will make up betwixt 7 & 8 thousand men at least. The young Gallantry of the times are much affected with this Expedition both by Sea & Land, and greatly possessed with the Love of Grinning Honour to be obteyned thereby. You will soon hear of an other Lieutenant of your Kingdom of Ireland viz The Earl of Essex being Lord Capell.[126] We talk here also of the Marquis of Worcester to be made Lord President of Wales, in lieu of the Earl of Cherberry there, who is like to be layd aside.[127] Desborough, Kelsy & White,[128] the Lieutenant of the Tower in Olivers time, are late come over, with security of Non-imprisonment, most of them having kissed the Kings hand; And one Gosfrett that came with them at whose house they lodged at Amsterdam.[129] Much seeming kindness is at present offer'd unto the Fanaticks; not without design that they may rest quiet, under the Transactions now on foot; But God knowes what shall become of them, after once they have served their own Turn By their means, &, that the Dutch & others are subdued and brought to obedience; 'Tis believed a third Party of different Principles to theirs will be most in Favour. Not else from your affectionate Friend & Servant.

Thursday night being the 25 Instant betwixt nine & ten of the clock broke out a terrible Fire in the Kings play house in Covent Garden, Whereby more than 40 houses are all burn't down & blown up, being all new built & strong brick houses, by which means & the Wind laying about eleven of the clock the fire was extinguishd which would else have endangerd all that end out of Town. The loss susteynd thereby of houses & Goods is Computed at 50,000d pounds, And the great aggrivation thereof to the people is that it began at the house of Good Exercise. Vale.

[126] Arthur Capel, first Earl of Essex (1632–1683), served as Lord Lieutenant of Ireland from 1672 to 1677.

[127] Henry Somerset, third Marquess of Worcester (1629–1700), was appointed Lord President of the Council of the Marches in 1672. He was widely suspected of holding crypto-Catholic beliefs and supporting local papists. He replaced Edward Herbert, third Baron Herbert of Cherbury (1630–1678), whose family seat was at Montgomery.

[128] John Disbrowe (1608–1680) and Thomas Kelsey were Cromwellian loyalists and former Major Generals, who were both suspected of plotting against the restored regime. Disbrowe, Cromwell's brother-in-law, was arrested in May 1660 and disqualified for life from holding public office. Briefly imprisoned in the Tower of London, he escaped to Holland, where he was involved in renewed plotting. He returned to England in 1665, was again imprisoned and on his release in 1667 settled in Hackney. There is no record of his having returned to Holland. Kelsey fled to the Low Countries in 1660, and like Disbrowe was ordered to return to England in 1665. He delayed his return until November 1671 and was finally pardoned in February 1672. White was presumably Major Thomas White, another inveterate plotter. The Government's willingness to treat with these men was part of a wider plan designed to reconcile nonconformists prior to the onset of war with the Dutch.

[129] George Gosfright was a merchant and former associate of the Baptist William Kiffin, who had been engaged in 1668 in exporting factious books to England from his base in Holland; Greaves, *Enemies Under His Feet*, 199; *CSPD, 1667–1668*, 282. An old republican, Gosfright had been made an officer in the militia of London in July 1659; *Weekly Post*, 26 July–2 August 1659. He was almost certainly on close terms with John Disbrowe. In 1668 the latter's son, Samuel, dedicated his Leiden MD thesis, among others, to Gosfright, then a merchant in Rotterdam; Innes Smith, 68.

Bibliography

1. MANUSCRIPTS

Allen Library, Dublin
Jennings MSS, J2/Box 263: miscellaneous extracts from Commonwealth papers and council orders, formerly in the PRO, Dublin, and now destroyed.

Berkshire Record Office, Reading
D/A1/81/120: will of Peter Hawkins of Thatcham, proved 11 October 1680.
D/A2/c 132: Archdeaconry of Berkshire, churchwardens' presentments, Shinfield.

Bodleian Library, Oxford
Additional MSS C 303, 304a, 305, 308: correspondence and papers of Archbishop Gilbert Sheldon.
Carte MSS, vols 31–36, 42–46, 48–51, 59–60, 66–68, 75, 79, 103, 118, 144–145, 154–156, 159–60, 165, 214–215, 219, 221, 228, 243, 494, 530, 634.
Clarendon MSS 29, 75: state papers of Edward Hyde, Earl of Clarendon.
Rawlinson Letters 50, 51, 109: correspondence of Philip, Lord Wharton and associates.
Rawlinson MS A 110: list of payments authorised by Parliament for victualling and equipping the army in Ireland, 1640s.
Rawlinson MS B 239: register of the sale of bishops' lands, 1651.
Rawlinson MS C 372: Thomas Bromley, 'A Discourse of Visions & Other Dispensations called Extraordinary'.
Rawlinson MS D 51: Scriveners' Company London, subscriptions to oath and notes on assistants, 1628–78.
Tanner MSS 31, 45: papers of Thomas Tanner.
V.15.8 Linc.: 'A Copy of Mr. Valentine Greataricks Letter to the Bishop of Chester Touchinge his Cures by Stroakinge' [1665].

Bristol Record Office, Bristol
04447/1: Bristol Quarter Sessions Book, 1653–71.
04447/2: Bristol Quarter Sessions Book, 1672–81.
EP/V/3: Churchwardens' presentments, St James', Bristol, 1637–77.
P/XCh/Ch/7: agreement, Bristol charities, 1669.
Will of Edmund Greatrakes, 30 April 1691.

British Library, London
Additional MS 4182: collection of newsletters, 1665–1746.
Additional MS 4291: miscellaneous letters, collected by Thomas Birch, including extracts of letters from Alexander Phaire on Valentine Greatrakes, 1744.
Additional MS 4293: miscellaneous letters, collected by Thomas Birch.
Additional MS 4460: manuscripts of Ralph Thoresby in the ownership of Thomas Birch, including transcript of the life of John Shawe and extracts from the day books of Dr Henry Sampson.

Additional MS 4765: account of quit rents in the county of Waterford, *c.*1661, extracted from the collection of Jeremiah Milles made in 1747.

Additional MS 4820: Irish funeral certificates, seventeenth century.

Additional MS 10,117: diurnal of Thomas Rugge, 1661–72.

Additional MS 11,314: letters and papers relating to Devon and Cornwall, 1604–82.

Additional MS 21,099: Bulstrode Whitlocke, 'The King's Right to Graunt Indulgence in Matters of Religion'.

Additional MS 21,135: papers of Sir Robert Southwell.

Additional MS 23,217: correspondence addresed to Anne, Viscountess Conway, 1671–9.

Additional MS 25,287: letter book of Lord Broghill, governor of Youghal, 1644–9.

Additional MS 25,692: account book of Valentine Greatrakes, 1663–79.

Additional MS 28,051: correspondence of the Osbourne family, Dukes of Leeds.

Additional MS 32,553: letters to Thomas Hobbes, 1656–75.

Additional MS 34,331: papers of Sir Robert Southwell.

Additional MS 38,015: correspondence of Sir Robert Southwell, 1659–97.

Additional MS 60,220: collection of poems on and by Muggletonians.

Additional MS 72,858: correspondence of Sir William Petty, 1672–5.

Additional MS 72,859: letter book of Sir John Petty, 28 March–15 August 1671.

Additional MS 78,311–78,312: correspondence of John Beale with John Evelyn.

Additional MS 78,683: collection of holograph letters in possession of John Evelyn.

Additional MSS 5063–5103: records of the Fire Court, 1660s.

Althrop MS B4: correspondence of Richard Boyle, second Earl of Cork, Robert Boyle, and Katherine Jones née Boyle, Lady Ranelagh.

Althrop MS B6: letter book of Richard Boyle, second Earl of Cork, and his wife.

Egerton MS 80: letter book of Richard Boyle, first Earl of Cork and other members of his family, seventeenth century, taken from originals in the Royal Irish Academy, Dublin.

Egerton MS 212: extracts from the Commonwealth Council Books, formerly held in Dublin Castle, and now destroyed.

Egerton MSS 1761–1762: transcripts of original records relating to the government of Ireland, 1650–7.

Harleian MS 697: Act Book of the Council of Munster, *c.*1599–1649.

Harleian MS 3785: correspondence of William Sancroft, 1665–89.

Lansdowne MSS 821–823: correspondence of Henry Cromwell, 1654–9.

Sloane MS 1926: [Samuel Mather], 'A Detection of the Imposture of Mr V.G. his pretended gift of Healing'.

Sloane MS 2569: Thomas Bromley, 'A Sermon from Mount Olivet'.

Sloane MS 4227: Rev. Thomas Morrice, 'Memoirs of the Most Remarkabale Passages in the Life and Death of…Roger Earl of Orrery'.

Stowe MS 186: Account of the aldermen, 1672.

Stowe MS 744: miscellaneous original letters, 1640–67.

Stowe MS 747: miscellaneous original letters, 1691–1702.

Cambridge University Library, Cambridge

Additional MS 19: correspondence of Simon Patrick.

Additional MS 20: 'Life of Symon Patrick'.

Additional MS 77: commonplace book of John Patrick.

Dd.III.63–64: Baker MSS.

Mm.I.45: Baker MSS, miscellaneous papers.

Oo.VI.114: Anon., 'Considerations concerning Mr Poole's design', 3 February 1658 [fos 23r-26].

Chatsworth House, Derbyshire
Cavendish MS 78, vol.2: letter book of the first Earl of Cork, 1634–42.
Lismore MS 29: diary of Richard Boyle, second Earl of Cork, 1650–9.
Lismore MS 30: diary of Richard Boyle, second Earl of Cork, 1659–66.
Lismore Papers, vols 1–24: papers of Richard Boyle, first Earl of Cork, *c.*1600–43.
Lismore Papers, vols 30–33: correspondence of Richard Boyle, second Earl of Cork, 1658–63.

Christ's College Library, Cambridge
MS 21: letters to Henry More.

Cornwall Record Office, Truro
G 652/1–2: will of Sir William Godolphin, 15 October 1663; proved 23 December 1663.

Corporation of London Record Office
SF 158–202: Quarter Sessions Files, city of London, 1661–70.

Derbyshire Record Office, Derby
D 239 M/O: papers of Sir George Treby.

Devon Record Office, Exeter
1392 M/L 1644/15, 36: Seymour papers.
DD 62919–62920, 63020: Dartmouth subsidy papers and borough accounts.
ECA 10: Exeter City Archives, Chamber Act Book, 1652–63.
ECA 11: Exeter City Archives, Chamber Act Book, 1663–84.
MF 2: Cornworthy parish registers, 1653–99.
MFC 46/8: Cornworthy parish register, 1565–1653.
PR 1508 M Devon/V 29: Courtenay of Powderham MSS, Account Book of Lady Elizabeth Ameredith, guardian of Sir William Courtenay, 1638–48.
PR/A 338: Principal Registry papers, documents relating to the contested will of George Hall and his wife Gertrude, undated.
PR/A 821: Principal Registry papers, will of John Lancaster, 7 March 1684.

East Sussex Record Office, Lewes
FRE MS 4223: correspondence between Samuel Jeake the elder of Rye and Samuel Morris of London, fos 153–202.

Essex Record Office, Chelmsford
D/AEW27/285: will of Nathaniel Sibley, 3 March 1688.

Gloucestershire Record Office, Gloucester
D 3549/6/2/4: 'Apparitions, miracles, prophecies and witchcraft, 1698–1705' [papers of John Sharp, archbishop of Canterbury].
Smyth of Nibley papers, vols 15 and 16.

John Rylands Library, Manchester
Irish MS 125: transcripts of documents relating to the Irish Court of Claims, Ireland, 1666–8.

King's Inns Library, Dublin
Prendergast Papers, vols 1, 2 and 5: transcripts of papers relating to Cromwellian Ireland.
S. Prendergast, Viscount Gort, 'The Prendergasts of Newcastle, co. Tipperary, AD 1169–1760' (undated ms).

London Metropolitan Archives, London
GB 0074 P69/BEN 1: parish registers of St Benet Fink, 1538–1984.

National Archives, Kew, London
C 6/111/56: Chancery depositions,1651–2.
C 7/216/48: Chancery depositions, 1670s.
C 10/15/78: Chancery depositions, John Lancaster v. John Perrott and Richard Leigh of Cornworthy, 1652.
C 10/96/106: Chancery depositions, Hugh Lambert and Edward Adams, v. George Waterman, Charles Doe and John Marshall, 1665.
LC 3/24–27: papers of the Lord Chamberlain's office.
LS 3/2, 252: Lord Steward's papers.
PC 2/51, 56–71: minutes of the meetings of Privy Council, 1639–40, 1662–87.
PROB 4, 8 and 11: administrations and wills proved in the prerogative court of Canterbury.
SP 24: state papers of the Interregnum, 1649–60.
SP 29: state papers of the reign of Charles II, 1660–85.

National Archives of Ireland, Dublin
MS 4974: Caulfield MSS: extracts from Commonwealth records formerly in PRO., Dublin.

National Library of Ireland, Dublin
MS 31: hearings before the Irish Court of Claims, 1665.
MS 32–33: correspondence of Roger Boyle, Earl of Orrery and his wife, 1660–89.
MS 816: warrants from commissioners of the Court of Claims, 1660s.
MS 4728: copy book of letters addressed to Valentine Greatrakes, 1666–72.
MS 4908: Clonmel assize records, 1663–84.
MS 6239, 6240, 6247, 6248, 6249, 6254, 6255, 6256, 6259: rental books of the earls of Cork, 1637, 1639–41, 1641, 1642, 1649, 1653, 1657–8, 1658.
MS 6900: 'Booke of Receiptes & Disbursements…1641' of first Earl of Cork.
MS 8143: estate papers of the second earl of Cork.
MS 11,959: orders in council, 1651–5 [transcripts from records of the Commonwealth formerly held in the PRO, Dublin, and destroyed in 1922].
MS 11,960: petitions to the council, mainly loyal petitions in the wake of the Exclusion Crisis.
MS 11,961: answers to petitions, 1655–6.

North Devon Record Office, Barnstaple
W.H.Rogers, 'Notes on Bideford', 3 vols [extracts from J. Ingle Dredge's transcripts of the Bideford parish registers].

Representative Church Body Library, Dublin
GS 2/7/3/20: notes relating to ministers of the gospel appointed by the Commonwealth government in Ireland, abstracted by the Rev. St John D. Seymour from original documents, since destroyed, in the PRO, Dublin.
MS 80/B2/2: will abstracts taken from the papers of W. H. Welply.

Royal College of Physicians Library, London
Annals, vol. 3 [1608–47].

Royal Society, London
EL/B1 and M1: Early Letters.
RB 37/1/5: trial of Florence Newton for witchcraft at Cork assizes, 1661.
RB 3/3/14: Robert Boyle's questionnaire regarding Greatrakes and his cures.

Sheffield University Library
H[artlib] P[apers]: papers of Samuel Hartlib, *c.*1600–62 [available on CD-ROM].

Somerset Archive and Record Service, Taunton
DD\PH/205: Phelips of Montacute manuscripts.
DD\Bs/39: diocese of Bath and Wells, subscription book, 1660–69.
DD\SP/1684/173: inventory of Robert Devonshire, surgeon, of Minehead, 1684.

Surrey History Centre, Woking
2397/3/1: Mortlake churchwardens' accounts and vestry book, 1652–1709.
2414/4/2: Mortlake vestry minute book, 1653–96.
QR/2/5: Quarter Sessions Rolls, 1673–8, 1684, 1685.

Trinity College, Dublin
MSS 820, 821, 825: depositions taken of atrocities committed against Protestant settlers in Ireland after October 1641.

Wellcome Library, London
MSS 6170–6176: D'Arcy Power, 'Transcript of the Diary of John Ward, 1648–1679', 5 vols. Originally in the ownership of the Medical Society of London.

West Country Studies Library, Exeter
Olive M. Moger, transcripts of Devon wills, 1600–1800, 22 vols.

West Sussex Record Office, Chichester
MSS 13,221–13,225: correspondence of Roger Boyle, Earl of Orrery, 1659–83.

Wiltshire and Swindon Archives, Chippenham
A1/110: Wiltshire Quarter Sessions Great Rolls, seventeenth century.
D1/39/2/13: Act Book, diocese of Salisbury, 1662–80.
D5/9/2: peculiar of dean of Salisbury, subscription book, 1674–1731.
D5/21/1/39: citations, deanery of Salisbury, 1688–90.

Worcestershire Record Office, Worcester
712 BA 3965: Bishop Skinner's diocesan book.

794.011/BA 2513/20: Act Book of the Diocese of Worcester, 1668–72.
795.02/BA 2302/1,2, 8, 26,33: miscellaneous documents, consistory court of Worcester.
QS 100/97–215: Worcestershire Quarter Sessions records, 1660–1715.
Shelf A 10, Box 3, vol 3: Worcester Chamberlain's Accounts, 1640–69.
Shelf A 14: Worcester Chamber Order Book, 1650–76.

2. PRINTED PRIMARY SOURCES (PRE-1800)

A., T., *ΧΕΙΡΕΞΟΚΗ. The Excellency or Handy-work of the Royal Hand* (London, 1665).
Anglia Rediviva: A Poem on His Majesties Most Joyfull Reception into England (London, 1660).
Atkins, J., *The Naval Surgeon; or, Practical System of Surgery* (London, 1742).
Bartholomew, W., *The Strong Man Ejected by a Stronger than He. In a Sermon Preached at Gloucester* [15 May 1660] (London, 1660).
Baxter, R., *Poetical Fragments Heart-Imployment with God and It Self* (London, 1681).
—— *The Certainty of the Worlds of Spirits* (London, 1691).
—— *Reliquiae Baxterianae or Mr. Richard Baxters Narrative of the Most Memorable Passages of his Life and Times Faithfully Publish'd . . . by Matthew Sylvester* (London, 1696).
—— *The Practical Works of Richard Baxter, 4 vols* (London, 1707).
Bayfield, R., *Tractatus de Tumoribus Praeter Naturam. Or A Treatise of Preternatural Tumors* (London, 1662).
Beckett, W., *A Free and Impartial Enquiry into the Antiquity and Efficacy of Touching for the Cure of the King's Evil* (London, 1722).
Besse, J., *A Collection of the Sufferings of the People Called Quakers . . . from 1650, to . . . 1689*, 2 vols (London, 1753).
Birch, T. (ed.), *A Collection of the State Papers of John Thurloe, Esq.*, 7 vols (London, 1742).
Bird, J., *Ostenta Carolina: or the Late Calamities of England with the Authors of Them. The Great Happiness and Happy Government of K.Charles II Ensuing, Miraculously Foreshewn by the Finger of God in Two Wonderful Diseases, the Rekets and Kings-Evil* (London, 1661).
Boate, G., *Irelands Naturall History* (London, 1652).
Bramhall, T., *A Sermon Preached at Dublin* [23 April 1661] (Dublin, 1661).
Burton, H., *A Divine Tragedie Lately Acted, or A Collection of Sundry Memorable Examples of Gods Judgements upon Sabbath-Breakers* ([London], 1636).
Calamy, E., *An Abridgement of Mr Baxter's History of His Life and Times. With an Account of the Ministers, &c who were Ejected after the Restauration of King Charles II*, 2 vols (London, 1713).
—— *A Continuation of the Account of the Ministers . . . Ejected and Silenced*, 2 vols (London, 1727).
Catalogus Librorum . . . Doctoris Benjaminis Worsley (London, 1678).
A Choice Collection of Wonderful Miracles, Ghosts and Visions (London, 1681).
Coker, M., *A Propheticall Revelation Given from God Himself unto Matthew Coker of Lincoln's Inne* (London, 1654).
—— *A Short and Plain Narrative of Matthew Coker* (London, 1654).
—— *A Whip of Small Cords, to Scourge Antichrist* (London, 1654).
C[ollop], J[ohn], *Itur Satyricum: In Loyall Stanzas* (London, 1660).
Creed, W., *Judah's Return to their Allegiance: And David's Returne to his Crowne and Kingdom* (London, 1660).

Crosby, T., *The History of the English Baptists, from the Reformation to the Beginning of the Reign of George I*, 4 vols (London, 1738–40).

[Denton, W.], *Horae Subseciviae. Or a Treatise Shewing the Original Grounds, Reasons and Provocations Necessitating our Sanguinary Laws Against Papists* (London, 1664).

—— *Jus Caesaris et Ecclesiae Vere Dictae. Or A Treatise of Independency, Presbytery, the Power of Kings, and of the Church... Wherein the Use of Liturgies, Toleration, Connivance, Conventicles... are Debated* (London, 1681).

—— *Jus Regiminis: Being a Justification of Defensive Arms in General and Consequently of our Late Revolutions and Transactions to be the Just Right of the Kingdom* (London, 1689).

The Devil of Deptford (London, 1699).

Di Capua, L., *The Uncertainty of the Art of Physick... made English by J[ohn] L[ancaster] Gent* (London, 1684).

[Digby, J.], *Miracles Not Ceas'd* (London, 1663).

—— *The Reconciler of Religions: Or, a Brief Decider of all Controversies in Matters of Faith* (London?, 1663).

Diurnall Occurrences in Parliament (London, 1642).

Douch, J., *Englands Jubilee: Or, Her Happy Return from Captivity: In a Sermon, Preached at St Botolphs Aldersgate, London* (London, 1660).

Douglas, J., *The Criterion or Miracles Examined with a View to Expose the Pretensions of Pagans and Papists* (London, 1757).

Duncombe, G. [alias Cimelgus Bonde], *Scutum Regale The Royal Buckler, or, Vox Legis, a Lecture to Traytors, who Most Wickedly Murthered Charles the I* (London, 1660).

Eachard, L., *The History of England... Vol. 3 From the Restoration of Charles the Second, to the Conclusion of the Reign of King James the Second* (London, 1718).

Eedes, R., *Great Britains Resurrection. Or England's Complacencie in Her Royal Soveraign King Charles the Second. A Sermon Preached... at Gloucester, June 5 1660* (London, 1660).

Faber, A. O., *A Remonstrance in Reference to the Act, to Prevent and Suppress Seditious Conventicles* (London, 1664).

—— *De Auro Potabili Medicinali, ad Potentissimum Principem, Carolum II* (London, 1677).

Fell, J., *A Sermon Preached Before the House of Peers on December 22 1680. Being the Day of Solemn Humiliation* (Oxford, 1680).

Fowler, E., *The Principles and Practices, of Certain Moderate Divines of the Church of England* (London, 1670).

—— *A Sermon Preached Before the House of Lords* [16 April 1696] *... Being a Day of Publick Thanksgiving... for the Most Happy Discovery and Disappointment of a Horrid Design to Assassinate His Sacred Majesty, and for Our Deliverance from a French Invasion* (London, 1696).

Gauden, J., *ΚΑΚΟΥΡΓΟΙ sive Medicastri: Slight Healings of Publique Hurts Set Forth in a Sermon* [29 February 1659/60] (London, 1660).

[Gell, R.], *ΕΙΡΗΝΙΚΟΝ: or, a Treatise of Peace Between the Two Visible Divided Parties* (London, 1660).

[Gething, R.], *Articles Exhibited to the Honourable House of Commons Assembled in Parliament, Against the Lord Inchiquine Lord President of Munster... Together with a Full and Cleare Answer* (London, 1647).

Getsius, J. D., *Tears Shed in the Behalf of His Dear Mother the Church of England, and Her Sad Distractions* (Oxford, 1658).

Gibbs, J., *Good and Bad Newes from Ireland: In a Letter of Credit from Youghall* (London, 1642).

Glanvill, J., *Plus Ultra; or the Progress and Advancement of Knowledge Since the Days of Aristotle* (London, 1668).

—— *A Praefatory Answer to Mr Henry Stubbe* (London, 1671).

—— *Saducismus Triumphatus: Or, Full and Plain Evidence Concerning Witches and Apparitions* (London, 1681).

Gostelow, W., *Charls Stuart and Oliver Cromwell United, or, Glad Tidings of Peace to all Christendom* (London?, 1655).

The Great Cures and Strange Miracles Performed by Mr. Valentine Gertrux (London, J. Thomas, 1666).

Greatrakes, V., *A Brief Account of Mr. Valentine Greatrak's, and Divers of the Strange Cures by Him Lately Performed. Written by Himself in a Letter Addressed to the Honourable Robert Boyle Esq.* (London, 1666).

Griffith, M., *The Fear of God and the King. Press'd in a Sermon* [25 March 1660] (London, 1660).

—— *The Catholique Doctor and his Spiritual Catholicon to Cure Our Sinfull Soules* [26 May 1661] (London, 1661).

—— *Christian Concord: Or, S. Pauls Parallel between the Body Natural and Mystical. Exemplified in a Sermon* [13 January 1661] (London, 1661).

—— *The Spiritual Antidote to Cure our Sinful Souls Deliver'd in a Sermon* (London, 1662).

Hall, G., *Gods Appearing for the Tribe of Levi: Improved in a Sermon Preached at St. Pauls, Nov. 8 to the Sons of Ministers, then Solemnly Assembled* (London, 1655).

—— *A Fast Sermon, Preached to the Lords...on the Solemn Humiliation for the Continuing Pestilence* [3 October 1666] (London, 1666).

Hall, J., *Select Observations on English Bodies...Englished by James Cooke, To which is now Added Directions for Drinking of the Bath-Water, and Ars Cosmetica, or Beautifying Art: By H.Stubbs Physician at Warwick* (London, 1679).

Hallywell, H., *A Private Letter of Satisfaction to a Friend* (1667).

—— *Melampronoea: Or A Discourse of the Polity and Kingdom of Darkness. Together with a Solution of the Chiefest Objections Brought Against the Being of Witches* (London, 1681).

Hardy, N., *Faith's Victory over Nature, or, the Unparallel'd President of an Unnaturally Religious Father* (London, 1648).

Haworth, S., *A Description of the Duke's Bagnio, and of the Mineral Bath and New Spaw Thereunto Belonging with an Account of the Use of Sweating, Rubbing, Bathing, and the Medicinal Vertues of the Spaw* (London, 1683).

Hibbert, H., *Regina Dierum: Or, The Joyful Day in a Sermon* [29 May 1661] (London, 1661).

[Higham, J.], *A Looking-Glass for Loyalty: or the Subjects Duty to his Soveraign* (London, 1675).

[Hill, A.], *Familiar Letters which Passed between Abraham Hill, Esq. and Several Eminent and Ingenious Persons of the Last Century* (London, 1767).

The Intelligencer (London, 1665–6).

Iter Boreale. Attempting Somthing upon the Successful and Matchless March of the Lord General George Monck, from Scotland, to London...Printed on St. Georges Day, Being the 23d of April, 1660 (London, 1660).

Jessey, H., *The Exceeding Riches of Grace Advanced* (London, 1647).

King, H., *A Sermon Preached at White-hall on the 29th of May* [1661] (London, 1661).

—— *A Sermon Preached the 30th of January at White-Hall 1664* [i.e.1665] (London, 1665).

King, J., *A Sermon on the 30th of January* (London, 1661).

King, W., *The State of the Protestants of Ireland under the Late King James's Government* (London, 1691).

Kingdomes Intelligencer (London, 1661).

Kingston, R., *Pillulae Pestilentiales: or a Spiritual Receipt for Cure of the Plague. Delivered in a Sermon Preach'd in St Paul's Church London, in the Mid'st of Our Late Sore Visitation* (London, 1665).

[Lloyd, D.], *Wonders No Miracles: Or, Mr. Valentine Greatrates Gift of Healing Examined...in a Letter to a Reverend Divine* (London, 1666).

Love, J., *Geodæsia: Or, The Art of Surveying and Measuring of Land* (London, 1688).

Lyngue, J., *Davids Deliverance: Or A Sermon Preached at the Sessions Holden at Maidstone...being the Day of the Coronation of King Charles the II* (London, 1661).

Lysons, D., *The Environs of London*, 4 vols (London, 1792–6).

M., B., *A Letter from a Person of Quality in the Parliaments Army, in Munster, in Ireland, to an Honourable member of the House of Commons* (London, 1647).

Mather, I., *An Essay for the Recording of Illustrious Providences* (Boston, MA, 1684).

Meggott, R., *The New-Cured Criple's Caveat: Or, England's Duty for the Miraculous Mercy of the King's and Kingdome's Restauration* [19 May 1662] (London, 1662).

[Mellish, S.], *XII Visions of Stephen Melish a Germane: Being such as Concern the Affairs now in Agitation between the French King & the Pope...Translated by Albertus Otto Faber* (London, 1663).

Mercurius Publicus (London, 1661).

A Mirror: Wherein the Rumpers and Fanaticks...may see their Deformity...Sent in a Letter by a Friend, to a Votary and Follower of that Faction (London, 1660).

More, H., *An Antidote Against Atheism* (London, 1653).

—— *A Collection of Several Philosophical Writings of Dr Henry More* (London, 1712).

Morrice, Rev. T., *A Collection of the State Letters of the Right Honourable Roger Boyle* (London, 1742).

Morris, T., *A Messenger Sent to Remove Some Mistakes: or a Desirous Instrument of Truth, Unity, Peace and Love in the Church of Christ* (London, 1655).

The Newes (London, 1655).

O'Dowde, T., *The Poor Man's Physician... The Third Edition* (London, 1665).

Ogilby, J., *The Entertainment of His Most Excellent Majestie Charles II, in His Passage Through the City of London to His Coronation* (London, 1662).

Oldmixon, J., *The History of England During the Reigns of the Royal House of Stuart, wherein the Errors of Late Histories are Discover'd and Corrected* (London, 1730).

P., J., *The Loyal Subject's Hearty Wishes to King Charles the Second* (London, 1660?).

Patrick, J., *A Century of Select Psalms* (London, 1679).

[Patrick, S.], *A Brief Account of the New Sect of Latitude-Men Together with Some Reflections upon the New Philosophy* (London, 1662).

Perreaud, F., *The Devill of Mascon, or, A True Relation of the Chiefe Things which an Unclean Spirit did, and said at Mascon in Burgundy in the House of Mr Francis Pereaud* (Oxford, 1658).

[Perrinchief, R.], *The Royal Martyr: Or, The Life and Death of Charles I* (London, 1676).

Peters, H., *Mr Peters Message Delivered in Both Houses...with the Narration of the Taking of Dartmouth* (London, 1646).

Petty, W., *Reflections upon Some Persons and Things in Ireland, by Letters to and from Dr.Petty. With Sir Hierome Sankey's Speech in Parliament* (London, 1660).

Pitt, M., *An Account of one Ann Jefferies... In a Letter from Moses Pitt to the Right Reverend Father in God Dr Edward Fowler, Lord Bishop of Gloucester* (London, 1696).

Reeve, Thomas, *A Dead Man Speaking or the Famous Memory of King Charles I. Delivered in a Sermon upon the 30th of Ian. Last, in the Parish Church of Waltham Abbey* (London, 1661).

—— *England's Backwardness or a Lingring Party in Bringing Back a Lawful King Delivered in a Sermon at Waltham Abbey Church in the County of Essex, at a Solemne Fast* (London, 1661).

—— *England's Beauty in Seeing King Charles the Second Restored to Majesty* (London, 1661).

—— *The Man of Valour, or the Puissance of Englands Great Champion. Delivered in Three Sermons, in the Parish Church of Waltham Abbey, Upon Duke Albemarle's Coming Up to London, and Declaring for a Free Parliament* (London, 1661).

Report of Dr Benjamin Franklin, and Other Commissioners, Charged by the King of France, with the Examination of the Animal Magnetism, as Now Practised at Paris... Translated from the French (London, 1785).

Riland, J., *Elias the Second his Coming to Restore All Things: Or Gods Way of Reforming by Restoring... In Two Sermons* (Oxford, 1662).

Rosencreutz, C., *The Hermetic Romance, or The Chymical Wedding, Wriiten in High Dutch... Translated by E. Foxcroft* (London, 1690).

Rub for Rub: or, an Answer to a Physicians Pamphlet, Styled, the Stroker Stroked (London?, 1666).

Rust, G., *A Discourse of the Use of Reason*, trans. H. Hallywell (London, 1683).

—— *The Remains of that Reverend and Learned Prelate, Dr George Rust... Collected and Published by Henry Hallywell* (London, 1686).

Saint-Evremond, C., *The Works of Mr de St. Evremont*, 2 vols (London, 1700).

Salmon, T., *Modern History: or the Present State of All Nations*, 31 vols (London, 1724–38).

S[ancroft], W., *A Sermon Preached at St Peter's Westminster on the First Sunday in Advent* (London, 1660).

Short, A., *God Save the King: Or, A Sermon Preach'd at Lyme Regis May 18 1660 at the Solemn Proclamation of His Most Excellent Majesty Charles II* (London, 1660).

Sicklemore, J., *To All the Inhabitants of the Town of Youghal who are Under the Teaching of James Wood* (1657).

Smalbroke, R., *A Vindication of the Miracles of Our Blessed Saviour: In which Mr Woolston's Discourses on Them are Particularly Examin'd*, 2 vols (London, 1728).

Smith, C., *The Antient and Present State of the County and City of Waterford* (Dublin, 1746).

Some Reflections on Mr. Wood's Sermon on St. Matthew 7.20. Preached at Bideford-Meeting in Devon, Novemb.5.1688... In Vindication of the Church of England from the Imputations laid upon it by that Author (London, 1690).

Starkey, G., *Royal and Other Innocent Bloud Crying Aloud to Heaven for Due Vengeance* (London, 1660).

—— *Liquor Alchahest, or, a Discourse of that Immortal Dissolvent of Paracelsus and Helmont... Published by J. A. Pyrophlius* (London, 1675).

Stow, J., *The Survey of London*, ed. J. Strype, 2 vols (London, 1720).

Stubbe, H., *The Miraculous Conformist: Or, An Account of Severall Marvailous Cures Performed by... Mr. Valentine Greatarick* (Oxford, 1666).

Sykes, A. A., *A Brief Discourse Concerning the Credibility of Miracles and Revelation* (London, 1742).

Tremaine, Sir J., and Rice, J., *Placita Coronae, or Pleas of the Crown* (London, 1723).

Turner, W., *A Compleat History of the Most Remarkable Providences, Both of Judgment and Mercy, Which have Hapned in this Present Age* (London, 1697).

Walker, R., *Memoirs of Medicine: Including a Sketch of Medical History, from the Earliest Accounts to the Eighteenth Century* (London, 1799).

Walsh, P., *The History & Vindication of the Loyal Formulary, or Irish Remonstrance, So Graciously Received by his Majesty, Anno 1661, Against all Calumnies and Censures in Several Treatises* (Dublin?, 1674).

Wanley, N., *The Wonders of the Little World, or, A General History of Man* (London, 1678).

Ware, Sir J., *The Whole Works of Sir James Ware Concerning Ireland*, ed. W. Harris, 2 vols (Dublin, 1764).

Webster, J., *The Displaying of Supposed Witchcraft* (London, 1677).

Weidenfeld, J. S., *Four Books... Concerning the Secrets of the Adepts* (London, 1685).

Willan, E., *Beatitas Britanniae: Or, King Charles the Second, Englands Beatitude, as Preached to the Incorporation of the Honour of Eye, in the County of Suffolk, March 31 1661 Being the Lords Day before the Election of Their Burgesses, and the Week before the Choice of Knights for the County* (London, 1661).

Wonders If Not Miracles or a Relation of the Wonderful Performances of Valentine Gertrux of Affance near Youghall in Ireland (London, 1665).

Wood, A., *Athenae Oxonienses*, 2 vols (London, 1691–2).

Wood, J., *A Sermon Preach'd at Biddeford, in the County of Devon on the Fifth of November, 1688* (London, 1689).

Woolston, T., *A Discourse on the Miracles of Our Saviour, in View of the Present Controversy Between Infidels and Apostates* (London, 1727).

3. PRINTED PRIMARY SOURCES (POST-1800)

Anderson, J. E. (ed.), *Mortlake Parish Vestry Minute Book, 1578–1652* (Richmond, 1914).

Anderson, R. C., *List of English Naval Captains, 1642–1660* (London, 1964).

Anselment, R. A. (ed)., *The Remembrances of Elizabeth Freke 1671–1714* (Camden Society, 5th ser., 18; Cambridge, 2001).

Baildon, W. P. (ed.), *The Records of the Honourable Society of Lincoln's Inn: Admissions and Chapel Registers 1420–1799*, 2 vols (London, 1896).

Baily, F. (ed.), *An Account of the Revd John Flamsteed, the First Astronomer Royal* (London, 1835).

Beaven, A. B. (ed.), *The Aldermen of the City of London*, 2 vols (London, 1908–13).

Bedells, J. (ed.), *The Visitation of the County of Huntingdon 1684... Corrected by Hon. Janet Gent and Thomas Woodcock* (Harleian Society, 13; London, 2000).

Berwick, E. (ed.), *The Rawdon Papers* (London, 1819).

Bloom, J. H., and James, R. R., *Medical Practitioners in the Diocese of London... 1529 to 1725* (Cambridge, 1935).

Bond, S. M. (ed.), *The Chamber Order Book of Worcester, 1602–1650* (Worcestershire Historical Society, 8; Birmingham, 1974).

Brockett, A. (ed.), *The Exeter Assembly: The Minutes of the Assemblies of the United Brethren of Devon and Cornwall, 1691–1717, as Transcribed by the Reverend Isaac Gilling* (Devon & Cornwall Records Society, 6; Torquay, 1963).

Burtchaell, G. D., and Sadleir, T. U. (eds), *Alumni Dublinensis: A Register of the Students, Graduates, Professors and Provosts of Trinity College in the University of Dublin, 1593–1860* (Dublin, 1935).

Cadbury, H. J. (ed.), *George Fox's Book of Miracles* (Cambridge, 1948).

Calendar of State Papers, Adventurers, 1642–1659.

Calendar of State Papers, Colonial. America and West Indies, 1661–1668.

Calendar of State Papers, Domestic, 1631–1691.

Calendar of State Papers, Ireland, 1647–1660; 1660–62; 1663–65; 1666–69; 1669–70, with Addenda 1625–70.

Calendar of Treasury Books [1660–1689], 8 vols (London, 1904–23).

Caulfield, R. (ed), *The Council Book of the Corporation of Youghal* (Guildford, 1878).

Clark, A. (ed.), *The Life and Times of Anthony Wood, Antiquary, at Oxford, 1632–1695*, 5 vols (Oxford Historical Society; Oxford, 1891–1900).

Cockin, M. S., and Gould, D. (eds), *Mortlake Parish Register, 1599–1678* (Barnes History Society; Barnes, 1958).

Cooke, W. H. (ed.), *Students Admitted to the Inner Temple, 1571–1625* (London, 1868).

Cooper, C. H., *Annals of Cambridge*, 5 vols (Cambridge, 1842–53).

Crossley, J. (ed.), *The Diary and Correspondence of Dr. John Worthington*, 3 vols (Chetham Society, 13, 36, 114; Manchester, 1847–86).

Defoe, D., *A System of Magick; or, A History of the Black Art* (London, 1727), ed. P. Elmer (London, 2005).

Dennett, J. (ed.), *Beverley Borough Records 1575–1821* (Yorkshire Archaeological Society, 84; Wakefield, 1932).

Dunlop, R. (ed.), *Ireland under the Commonwealth. Being a Selection of Documents Relating to the Government of Ireland from 1651 to 1659*, 2 vols (Manchester, 1913).

Fifteenth Report of the Irish Record Commission Respecting the Public Records in Ireland (Dublin, 1825).

Firth, C. H., and Rait, R. S.(eds), *Acts and Ordinances of the Interregnum, 1642–1660*, 3 vols (London, 1911).

Foster, J. (ed.), *London Marriage Licences, 1521–1869* (London, 1887).

—— (ed.), *The Register of Admissions to Grays Inn, 1521–1889* (London, 1889).

—— (ed.), *Alumni Oxonienses: The Members of the University of Oxford, 1500–1714*, 3 vols (Oxford & London, 1891–2).

Gilbert, J. T. (ed.), *Calendar of Ancient Records of Dublin*, 19 vols (Dublin, 1889–1944).

Gray, G. J., and Palmer, W. M. (eds), *Abstracts from the Wills and Testamentary Documents of Printers, Binders, and Stationers of Cambridge, from 1504 to 1699* (London, 1915).

Green, M. A. E. (ed.), *Calendar of the Proceedings of the Committee for Compounding, &c, 1643–1660*, 5 vols (London, 1889–92).

Grosart, Rev. A. B. (ed.), *The Lismore Papers*, 1st ser., 5 vols (1886).

Grubb, I. (ed.), *My Irish Journal 1669–1670 by William Penn* (London, 1952).

Hall, A.R. and M. B. (eds), *The Correspondence of Henry Oldenburg*, 13 vols (Madison, Milwaukee, London and Philadelphia, 1965–86).

Hasler, P. W. (ed.), *The History of Parliament: The House of Commons, 1558–1603*, 3 vols (London, 1981).

Hayden, R. (ed.), *The Records of a Church of Christ in Bristol, 1640–1687* (Bristol Record Society, 27; Bristol, 1974).

Henning, B. (ed.), *The History of Parliament: The House of Commons, 1660–1690*, 3 vols (London, 1983).

[Henry, P.], *The Life of the Rev. Philip Henry, A. M.... Corrected and Enlarged by J. B. Williams* (London, 1825).

Hessels, J. H. (ed.), *Ecclesiae Londino-Batavae Archivum*, 3 vols (Cambridge, 1887–97).

Historical Manuscripts Commission. Calendar of the Carew Manuscripts, 6 vols (London, 1873).

Historical Manuscripts Commission. Fourth Report, Part 1, Report and Appendix (London, 1874).

Historical Manuscripts Commission. Sixth Report, Part 1, Report and Appendix (London, 1877).

Historical Manuscripts Commission. Seventh Report, Part 1, Report and Appendix (London, 1879).

Historical Manuscripts Commission. Eleventh Report, Appendix, Part II. The Manuscripts of the House of Lords 1678–1688 (London, 1887).

Historical Manuscripts Commission. Thirteenth Report, Appendix, Part 1: MSS of the Duke of Portland, vol.1 (London, 1891).

Historical Manuscripts Commission. Fourteenth Report, Appendix, Part III. MSS of the Duke of Portland, vol.3 (London, 1894).

Historical Manuscripts Commission. Fifteenth Report, Appendix, Part VII. The MSS of The Duke of Somerset, the Marquis of Ailesbury, and the Rev.T. H. G. Puleston, Bart (London, 1898).

Historical Manuscripts Commission. Report on the Manuscripts of F. W. Leyborne-Popham (London, 1899).

Historical Manuscripts Commission. Calendar of the Manuscripts of the Marquess of Ormonde, K. P. Preserved at Kilkenny Castle (London, 1904).

Historical Manuscripts Commission. Report on the Manuscripts of the Earl of Egmont (London, 1905).

Historical Manuscripts Commission. Reports. House of Lords MSS 1697–1699 (London, 1905).

Historical Manuscripts Commission. Report on the Records of the City of Exeter (London, 1916).

Hogan, J. (ed.), *Letters and Papers Relating to the Irish Rebellion between 1642 and 1646* (Dublin, 1936).

Horn, J. M., and Smith, D. M. (eds), *Fasti Ecclesiae Anglicanae 1541–1857. Vol.4 York Diocese* (London, 1975).

Hosmer, J. K. (ed.), *Winthrop's Journal History of New England, 1630–1649*, 2 vols (New York, 1966).

Hunter, J. (ed.), *The Diary of Ralph Thoresby, F. R .S.*, 2 vols (London, 1830).

Hunter, M., Clericuzio, A., and Principe, L. M. (eds), *The Correspondence of Robert Boyle*, 6 vols (London, 2001).

Hunter, M., and Davis, E. B. (eds), *The Works of Robert Boyle*, 14 vols (London, 1999–2000).

Hunter, M., and Gregory, A. (eds), *An Astrological Diary of the Seventeenth Century: Samuel Jeake of Rye 1652–1699* (Oxford, 1988).

Hunter, M., Mandelbrote, G., Ovenden, R., and Smith, N. (eds), *A Radical's Books: The Library Catalogue of Samuel Jeake of Rye, 1623–90* (Woodbridge, 1999).

Inderwick, F. (ed.), *A Calendar of the Inner Temple Records*, 3 vols (London, 1896–1901).

Innes Smith, R. W., *English-Speaking Students of Medicine at the University of Leyden* (Edinburgh, 1932).

Jackson, C. (ed.), *The Diary of Abraham de la Pryme, the Yorkshire Antiquary* (Surtees Soc., 54; Durham, 1869).

Jeaffreson, J. C. (ed.), *Middlesex County Records*, 4 vols (London, 1886–92).

Journals of the House of Commons, vols 2 [1640–1643], 6 [1648–1651], 7 [1651–1660] 9 [1667–1687] (London, 1802).

Keeble, N. H., and Nuttall, G. F. (eds), *Calendar of the Correspondence of Richard Baxter*, 2 vols (Oxford, 1991).

Kenyon, J. P., *The Stuart Constitution 1603–1688* (Cambridge, 1966).

Klene, J. (ed.), *The Southwell-Sibthorpe Commonplace Book: Folger MS V.b.198* (Tempe, Arizona, 1997).

Lankaster, E. (ed.), *Memorials of John Ray* (London, 1846).

Latham, R., and Matthews, W. (eds), *The Diary of Samuel Pepys*, 11 vols (London, 1970–83).

Littledale, W. A. (ed.), *The Registers of Christ Church, Newgate, 1583 to 1754* (Harleian Soc., 21; London, 1895).

McGrath, P. (ed.), *Merchants and Merchandise in Seventeenth-Century Bristol* (Bristol Record Society, 19; Bristol, 1955).

MacLysaght, E. (ed.), *Calendar of the Orrery Papers* (Dublin, 1941).

—— 'Commonwealth State Accounts Ireland 1650–1656', *Analacta Hibernica*, 15 (1944), 227–321.

Margoliouth, H. M. (ed.), *The Poems and Letters of Andrew Marvell*, 2 vols (Oxford, 1952–67).

Matthews, A. G. (ed.), *Calamy Revised: Being a Revision of Edmund Calamy's Account of the Ministers and Others Ejected and Silenced, 1660–2* (Oxford, 1934; reissued 1988).

—— (ed.), *Walker Revised Being a Revision of John Walker's Sufferings of the Clergy During the Grand Rebellion 1642–1660* (Oxford, 1948).

Moore Smith, G. C. (ed.), 'Extracts from the Papers of Thomas Woodcock (*ob.* 1695)', in *Camden Miscellany 11* (Camden Society, 3rd ser., 13; London, 1907), 51–89.

Morland, S. C. (ed.), *The Somersetshire Quarterly Meeting of the Society of Friends, 1668–1699* (Somerset Record Society, 75; Woking, 1978).

Munk, W. (ed.), *The Roll of the Royal College of Physicians*, 3 vols (London, 1878).

Nickalls, J. L. (ed.), *The Journal of George Fox* (Cambridge, 1952).

Nicolson, M. H. (ed.), *Conway Letters: the Correspondence of Anne, Viscountess Conway, Henry More, and Their Friends, 1642–1684* (New Haven, 1930; revised ed. S. Hutton, Oxford, 1992).

Oxford Dictionary of National Biography, 60 vols (Oxford, 2004).

Peacock, E. (ed.), *The Army Lists of the Roundheads and Cavaliers, Containing the Names of the Officers in the Royal and Parliamentary Armies of 1642* (London, 1874).

Pender, S. (ed.), *A Census of Ireland, Circa 1659* (Dublin, 1939).

—— *Council Books of the Corporation of Waterford, 1662–1670* (Dublin, 1964).

Plomer, H. R, *A Dictionary of the Printers and Booksellers who were at Work in England, Scotland and Ireland from 1641 to 1667* (London, 1907).

—— *A Dictionary of the Printers and Booksellers who were at Work in England, Scotland and Ireland from 1668 to 1725* (Oxford, 1922).

Powell, D. L. (ed.), *Surrey Quarter Sessions Records. Order Book and Sessions Rolls 1666–1668* (Kingston upon Thames, 1951).

Powell, D. L., and Jenkinson, H. (eds), *Surrey Quarter Sessions Records. The Order Books and the Sessions Rolls, Easter 1663-Epiphany 1666* (Surrey Records Society, 16; Frome and London, 1938).

Poynter, F. N. L., and Bishop, W. J. (eds), *A Seventeenth-Century Doctor and His Patients: John Symcotts, 1592?-1662* (Bedfordshire Historical Records Society, 31; Bedford, 1951).

Rylands, W. H. (ed.), *The Four Visitations of Berkshire, 1532, 1566, 1623 and 1665–6*, 2 vols (Harleian Society, 56, 57; London, 1907–8).

Sharpe, C. K. (ed.), *The Secret and True History of the Church of Scotland, From the Restoration to the Year 1678 by the Rev.Mr.James Kirkton* (Edinburgh, 1817).

Sixth Report of the Deputy Keeper of the Public Records in Ireland (Dublin, 1874).

Spalding, R. (ed), *The Diary of Bulstrode Whitelocke, 1605–1675* (Oxford, 1990).

Squibb, G. D. (ed.), *The Visitations of Oxfordshire 1669 and 1675* (Harleian Society, new ser., 12; London, 1993).

Stevenson, D. (ed.), *Letters of Sir Robert Moray to the Earl of Kincardine, 1657–73* (Aldershot, 2007).

Sturgess, H. A. C. (ed.), *Register of Admissions to the Honourable Society of the Middle Temple, from the Fifteenth Century to the Year 1944*, 3 vols (London, 1949).

Taylor, Rev. A. (ed.), *The Works of Simon Patrick, D.D.*, 9 vols (Oxford, 1858).

Thompson, E. M. (ed.), *The Correspondence of the Family of Hatton*, 2 vols (Camden Soc., 22; London, 1878).

Turner, G. L. (ed.), *Original Records of Early Non-Conformity*, 3 vols (London, 1911–14).

Venn, J., and Venn, J. A. (eds), *Alumni Cantabrigienses…from the Earliest Times to 1751*, 4 vols (Cambridge, 1922).

Verney, F. P., and Verney, M. M. (eds), *Memoirs of the Verney Family*, 4 vols (London, 1892–9).

Vivian, J. L. (ed.), *The Visitations of Cornwall… 1530, 1573, and 1620* (Exeter, 1887).

—— *The Visitations of the County of Devon… 1531, 1564, and 1620* (Exeter, 1895).

Willis-Bund, J. W. (ed.), *Diary of Henry Townsend of Elmley Lovett, 1640–1663*, 2 vols (Worcestershire Historical Society; London, 1915–20).

Woodhead, J. R., *The Rulers of London 1660–1689: A Biographical Record of the Aldermen and Common Councilmen of the City of London* (London, 1965).

The Works of John Reeve and Lodowick Muggleton, 3 vols (London, 1832).

4. PRINTED SECONDARY WORKS

Anderson, J. E., *A History of the Parish of Mortlake* (London, 1886).

Andrews, J., and Scull, A., *Undertaker of the Mind: John Monro and Mad-Doctoring in Eighteenth-Century England* (Berkeley, Los Angeles, and London, 2001).

Appleyard, O. B., 'A Seventeenth-Century Healer, Valentine Greatrakes, 1628–1683', *Practitioner*, 182 (1959), 342–6.

Arnold, L. J., 'Valentine Greatrakes, A Seventeenth-Century "Touch Doctor" ', *Eire-Ireland*, 11 (1976), 3–12.

—— *The Restoration Land Settlement in County Dublin, 1660–1688* (Dublin, 1993).

Ashcraft, R., *Revolutionary Politics and Locke's Two Treatises of Government* (Princeton, 1986).

Auden, J. E., 'Sir Jerome Zankey (or Sankey) of Balderton Hall, co. Salop, and of Coolmore, co. Tipperary', *Transactions of the Shropshire Archaeological Society*, 50 (1940), 171–8.

Aylmer, G., *The State's Servants: The Civil Service of the English Republic 1649–1660* (London, 1973).

——'Collective Mentalities in Mid Seventeenth-Century England: IV. Cross Currents: Neutrals, Trimmers and Others', *Transactions of the Royal Historical Society*, 39 (1989), 1–22.

Bailey, J. E., 'Andrew Marvell and Valentine Greatraks, the Stroker', *Notes and Queries*, 9 (1884), 61–3.

Bailie, W. D., 'Sir George Rawdon: One of the Horns against the Kirk in the Seventeenth Century', *Bulletin of the Presbyterian History Society of Dublin*, 13 (1984), 2–9.

Barfield, S., *Thatcham, Berks, and its Manors*, 2 vols (Oxford and London, 1901).

Barnard, T. C., 'Lord Broghill, Vincent Gookin and the Cork Elections of 1659', *English Historical Review*, 88 (1973), 352–65.

—— *Cromwellian Ireland: English Government and Reform in Ireland 1649–1660* (Oxford, 1975).

——'Crises of Identity among Irish Protestants 1641–1685', *Past and Present*, 127 (1990), 39–83.

——'The Political, Material and Mental Culture of the Cork Settlers, 1649–1700', in P. O'Flanagan and N. G. Buttimer (eds), *Cork: History and Society: Interdisciplinary Essays on the History of an Irish County* (Dublin, 1993), 309–65.

——'The Hartlib Circle and the Cult and Culture of Improvement in Ireland', in M. Greengrass, M. Leslie and T. Railor (eds), *Samuel Hartlib and Universal Reformation: Studies in Intellectual Communication* (Cambridge, 1994), 281–97.

——'Protestantism, Ethnicity and Irish Identities, 1660–1760', in T. Clayton and I. McBride (eds), *Protestantism and National Identity: Britain and Ireland, c.1650-c.1850* (Cambridge, 1998), 206–35.

Barnwell, H. T., 'Saint-Evremond: A French Political Exile in Seventeenth-Century London', *Proceedings of the Huguenot Society of London*, 18 (1952), 449–63.

Bate, F., *The Declaration of Indulgence 1672: A Study in the Rise of Organised Dissent* (London, 1908).

Beaven, A. B., *Bristol Lists: Municipal and Miscellaneous* (Bristol, 1899).

Beaver, D. C., *Parish Communities and Religious Conflict in the Vale of Gloucester, 1590–1690* (Cambridge, MA, and London, 1998).

Bell, W. G., *The Great Plague in London in 1665* (London, 1924; revised ed., London, 1951).

Bennett, G., *The History of Bandon, and the Principal Towns in the West Riding of County Cork. Enlarged Edition* (Cork, 1879).

Berry, H. F., 'Justices of the Peace for the County of Cork', *Journal of the Cork Historical and Archaeological Society*, 3 (1897), 58–65.

——'The Old Youghal Family of Stout', *Journal of the Cork Historical and Archaeological Society*, 23 (1917), 19–29.

Birken, W. J., 'The Dissenting Tradition in English Medicine of the Seventeenth and Eighteenth Centuries', *Medical History*, 39 (1995), 197–218.

Bloch, M., *The Royal Touch: Sacred Monarchy and Scrofula in England and France*, trans. J. E. Anderson (London, 1973).

Bottigheimer, K. S., *English Money and Irish Land: The Adventurers in the Cromwellian Settlement of Ireland* (Oxford, 1971).

——'The Restoration Land Settlement in Ireland: a Structural View', *Irish Historical Studies*, 18 (1972), 1–21.

—'Kingdom and Colony: Ireland in the Westward Enterprise 1536–1660', in K. R. Andrews, N. P. Canny and P. E. H. Hair (eds), *The Westward Enterprise: English Activities in Ireland, the Atlantic, and America 1480–1650* (Liverpool, 1978), 45–64.

Bradshaw, B., and Morrill, J. (eds), *The British Problem, c.1534–1707: State Formation in the Atlantic Archipelago* (Basingstoke, 1996).

Brammall, K. M., 'Monstrous Metamorphosis: Nature, Morality and the Rhetoric of Monstrosity in Tudor England', *Sixteenth Century Journal*, 27 (1996), 3–21.

Breathnach, C. S., 'Robert Boyle's Approach to the Ministrations of Valentine Greatrakes', *History of Psychiatry*, 10 (1999), 87–109.

Buckley, J., 'Selections from a General Account Book of Valentine Greatrakes. AD 1663–1679', *Journal of the Waterford and South-East Ireland Archaeological Society*, 11 (1908), 211–24.

Burdon, P., 'Marvell and his Kindred: The Family Network in the Later Years.1 The Alureds', *Notes and Queries*, 31 (1984), 379–85.

Burke, W. P., *History of Clonmel* (Waterford, 1907).

Burns, W. E., ' "Our Lot is Fallen into an Age of Wonders": John Spencer and the Controversy over Prodigies in the Early Restoration', *Albion*, 27 (1995), 237–52.

—*An Age of Wonders: Prodigies, Politics and Providence in England 1657–1727* (Manchester, 2002).

Cadbury, H. J., 'More Penn Correspondence, Ireland, 1669–1670', *Pennsylvania Magazine of History and Biography*, 73 (1949), 9–15.

Camden, V. J., 'Attending to Sarah Wight: Little Wonder of God's Wonders', *Bunyan Studies*, 11 (2003–4), 94–131.

Canny, N., *The Upstart Earl: A Study of the Social and Mental World of Richard Boyle, First Earl of Cork 1566–1643* (Cambridge, 1982).

Capp, B. S., *The Fifth Monarchy Men: A Study in Seventeenth-Century Millenarianism* (London, 1972).

—*Cromwell's Navy: the Fleet and the English Revolution, 1648–1660* (Oxford, 1992).

Carlino, A., *Books of the Body: Anatomical Ritual and Renaissance Learning*, trans. J. and A. C. Tedeschi (Chicago, 1999).

Carroll, K. L., 'From Bond Slave to Governor: The Strange Career of Charles Bayly (1632?-1680), *Journal of the Friends Historical Society*, 52 (1968), 19–38.

—'Quakers and Muggletonians in Seventeenth-Century Ireland', in D. Blamires, J. Greenwood and A. Kerr (eds), *A Quaker Miscellany for Edward H. Milligan* (Manchester, 1985), 49–57.

Carter, C., ' "A Constant Prodigy?". Empirical Views of an Unordinary Nature', *The Seventeenth Century*, 23 (2008), 266–89.

Champion, J. A. I., *The Pillars of Priestcraft Shaken: The Church of England and Its Enemies, 1660–1730* (Cambridge, 1992).

Clark, S., *Thinking With Demons: The Idea of Witchcraft in Early Modern Europe* (Oxford, 1997).

Clarke, A., *Prelude to Restoration in Ireland: The End of the Commonwealth, 1659–1660* (Cambridge, 1999).

Connolly, R., 'A Manuscript Treatise by Viscountess Ranelagh', *Notes and Queries*, 53 (2006), 170–3.

—'A Proselytising Protestant Commonwealth: The Religious and Political Ideals of Katherine Jones, Viscountess Ranelagh (1614–91)', *The Seventeenth Century*, 23 (2008), 244–64.

Coudert, A., 'Henry More and Witchcraft', in S. Hutton (ed.), *Henry More (1614–1687): Tercentenary Studies* (Dordrecht, 1989), 115–36.

Crawfurd, R., *The King's Evil* (Oxford, 1911).

Cressy, D., 'Monstrous Births and Credible Reports', in Cressy, *Travesties and Transgressions in Tudor and Stuart England: Tales of Discord and Dissension* (Oxford, 2000), 29–50.

—— 'Lamentable, Strange and Wonderful: Headless Monsters in the English Revolution', in L. L. Knoppers and J. B. Landes (eds), *Monstrous Bodies/Political Monstrosities in Early Modern Europe* (Ithaca, NY, 2004), 40–63.

Crocker, R., *Henry More, 1614–1687: A Biography of the Cambridge Platonist* (Dordrecht, 2003).

—— 'A "Sanative Contagion": Henry More on Faith Healing', in M. Pelling and S. Mandelbrote (eds), *The Practice of Reform in Health, Medicine and Science, 1500–2000. Essays for Charles Webster* (Aldershot, 2005), 107–23.

Cromartie, A., *Sir Matthew Hale, 1609–1676: Law, Religion and Natural Philosophy* (Cambridge, 1995).

Dailey, B. R., 'The Visitation of Sarah Wight: Holy Carnival and the Revolution of the Saints in Civil War London', *Church History*, 55 (1986), 438–55.

De Krey, G. S., 'The First Restoration Crisis: Conscience and Coercion in London, 1667–73', *Albion*, 25 (1993), 565–80.

—— *London and the Restoration 1659–1683* (Cambridge, 2005).

—— *Restoration and Revolution in Britain: A Political History of the Era of Charles II and the Glorious Revolution* (Basingstoke, 2007).

Dennehy, C. A. (ed.), *Restoration Ireland: Always Settling and Never Settled* (Aldershot, 2008).

Dewhurst, K., *Dr. Thomas Sydenham (1624–1689). His Life and Original Writings* (London, 1966).

Duffy, E., 'Valentine Greatrakes, the Irish Stroker: Miracle, Science and Orthodoxy in Restoration England', in K. Robbins (ed.), *Religion and Humanism* (Oxford, 1981), 251–73.

Edie, C. A., 'The Irish Cattle Bills: A Study in Restoration Politics', *Transactions of the American Philosophical Society*, 60 (1970).

—— 'The Public Face of Royal Ritual: Sermons, Medals and Civic Ceremony in Later Stuart Coronations', *Huntington Library Quarterly*, 53 (1990), 311–36.

Elmer, P., '"Saints or Sorcerers": Quakerism, Demonology and the Decline of Witchcraft in Seventeenth-Century England', in J. Barry, M. Hester and G. Roberts (eds), *Witchcraft in Early Modern Europe: Studies in Culture and Belief* (Cambridge, 1996), 145–79.

—— 'Towards a Politics of Witchcraft in Early Modern England', in S. Clark (ed.), *Languages of Witchcraft: Narrative, Ideology and Meaning in Early Modern Culture* (Basingstoke, 2001), 101–18.

Farr, D., *John Lambert, Parliamentary Soldier and Cromwellian Major-General, 1619–1684* (Woodbridge, 2003).

Farrow, W. J., *The Great Civil War in Shropshire (1642–49)* (Shrewsbury, 1926).

Faulkner, A., 'Father O'Finaghty's Miracles', *Irish Ecclesiastical Record*, 104 (1965), 349–62.

Ferrari, G., 'Public Anatomy Lessons and the Carnival: the Anatomy Theatre of Bologna', *Past and Present*, 117 (1987), 50–106.

Fitzpatrick, T., *Waterford During the Civil War (1641–1653)* (Waterford, 1912).

Frank Jnr, R. G., 'The John Ward Diaries: Mirror of Seventeenth-Century Science and Medicine', *Journal of the History of Medicine and Allied Sciences*, 29 (1974), 147–79.

Friedman, J., *Miracles and the Pulp Press during the English Revolution: the Battle of the Frogs and Fairford's Flies* (London, 1993).

Furdell, E. L., *The Royal Doctors 1585–1714: Medical Personnel at the Tudor and Stuart Courts* (Rochester, NY, 2001).

Gascoigne, J., *Cambridge in the Age of the Enlightenment: Science, Religion and Politics from the Restoration to the French Revolution* (Cambridge, 1989).

Gaskill, M., 'Reporting Murder: Fiction in the Archives in Early Modern England', *Social History*, 23 (1998), 1–30.

Geertz, C., 'Thick Description: Towards an Interpretative Theory of Culture', in Geertz, *The Interpretation of Cultures* (New York, 1973), 3–30.

Gibson, M., *Possession, Puritanism and Print: Darrell, Harsnett, Shakespeare and the Elizabethan Exorcism Controversy* (London, 2006).

Gillespie, R., 'Small Towns in Early Modern Ireland', in P. Clark (ed.), *Small Towns in Early Modern Europe* (Cambridge, 1995), 148–65.

—— *Devoted People: Belief and Religion in Early Modern Ireland* (Manchester, 1997).

Gowers, I., 'Corrections and Additions to *Walker Revised* as Relevant to Devon Entries. Part 2', *Devon and Cornwall Notes and Queries*, 37 (1993), 137–45.

Gowing, L., *Common Bodies: Women, Touch and Power in Seventeenth-Century England* (New Haven, 2003).

Greaves, R. L., *Deliver Us From Evil: The Radical Underground in Britain, 1660–1663* (New York, 1986).

—— *Enemies Under His Feet: Radicals and Nonconformists in Britain, 1664–1677* (Stanford, CA, 1990).

Greengrass, M., Leslie, M., and Raylor, T. (eds), *Samuel Hartlib and Universal Reformation: Studies in Intellectual Communication* (Cambridge, 1994).

Grell, O. P., 'From Persecution to Toleration: The Decline of the Anglo-Dutch Communities in England, 1648–1702', in O. P. Grell, J. I. Israel and N. Tyacke (eds), *From Persecution to Toleration: The Glorious Revolution and Religion in England* (Oxford, 1991), 97–127.

Hall, A. R., *Henry More: Magic, Religion and Experiment* (Oxford, 1990).

Hancock, F., *Minehead in the County of Somerset. A History of the Parish, the Manor, and the Port* (Taunton, 1903).

Harley, D., 'Provincial Midwives in England: Lancashire and Cheshire, 1660–1760', in H. Marland (ed.), *The Art of Midwifery: Early Modern Midwives in Europe* (London, 1993), 27–48.

Harris, F., 'Ireland as a Laboratory: The Archive of Sir William Petty', in M. Hunter (ed.), *Archives of the Scientific Revolution: The Formation and Exchange of Ideas in Seventeenth-Century Europe* (Woodbridge, 1998), 73–90.

—— 'Lady Sophia's Visions: Sir Robert Moray, the Earl of Lauderdale and the Restoration Government of Scotland', *The Seventeenth Century*, 24 (2009), 129–55.

Harris, Rev. S. G., 'John Tucker, Parish Clerk of Cornworthy and Antiquary', *Transactions of the Devonshire Association*, 25 (1893), 470–81.

Harris, T., *Restoration: Charles II and His Kingdoms 1660–1685* (London, 2005).

Harrison, L. A. B., 'A Vanished Berkshire Family', *The Berkshire, Buckinghamshire and Oxfordshire Archaeological Journal*, 37 (1933), 93–106.

Hayman, Rev. S., 'Notes on the Family of Greatrakes', *The Reliquary. Quarterly Archaeological Journal and Review*, 4 (1863–4), 81–96, 220–36.

—— 'Notes on the Family of Greatrakes: Addenda et Corrigenda', *The Reliquary. Quarterly Archaeological Journal and Review*, 5 (1864–5), 94–104.

Heal, A., *The London Goldsmiths, 1200–1800* (London, Cambridge, 1935).

Heath, J. B., *Some Account of the Worshipful Company of Grocers of the City of London* (London, 1829).

Henderson, F., 'Unpublished Material from the Memorandum Book of Robert Hooke, Guildhall Library MS 1758', *Notes and Records of the Royal Society*, 61 (2007), 129–75.

Henry, J., 'The Fragmentation of Renaissance Occultism and the Decline of Magic', *History of Science*, 46 (2008), 1–48.

Hill, J. E. C., *The World Turned Upside Down: Radical Ideas During the English Revolution* (London, 1972).

——— 'John Reeve and the Origins of Muggletonianism', in J. E. C. Hill, B. Reay and W. Lamont (eds), *The World of the Muggletonians* (London, 1983), 64–110.

Hirst, D., 'Samuel Parker, Andrew Marvell, and Political Culture, 1667–73', in D. Hirst and R. Strier (eds), *Writing and Political Engagement in Seventeenth-Century England* (Cambridge, 1999), 145–64.

Hunter, M., 'Alchemy, Magic and Moralism in the Thought of Robert Boyle', *British Journal for the History of Science*, 23 (1990), 387–410.

——— 'Casuistry in Action: Robert Boyle's Confessional Interviews with Gilbert Burnet and Edward Stillingfleet, 1691', *Journal of Ecclesiastical History*, 44 (1993), 80–98.

——— *The Royal Society and Its Fellows, 1660–1700: The Morphology of an Early Scientific Institution* (2nd ed., Oxford, 1994).

——— 'How Boyle Became a Scientist', *History of Science*, 33 (1995), 59–103.

——— 'Introduction. Fifteen Essays and a New Theory of Intellectual Change', in Hunter, *Science and the Shape of Orthodoxy: Intellectual Change in Late Seventeenth- Century Britain* (Woodbridge, 1995), 1–18.

——— 'Science and Astrology in Seventeenth-Century England: An Unpublished Polemic by John Flamsteed', in Hunter, *Science and the Shape of Orthodoxy: Intellectual Change in Late Seventeenth-Century Britain* (Woodbridge, 1995), 245–85.

——— 'Boyle Versus the Galenists: A Suppressed Critique of Seventeenth-Century Medical Practice and Its Significance', in Hunter, *Robert Boyle (1627–1691). Scrupulosity and Science* (Woodbridge, 2000), 157–201.

——— 'The Conscience of Robert Boyle: Functionalism, "Dysfunctionalism" and the Task of Historical Understanding', in Hunter, *Robert Boyle (1627–1691). Scrupulosity and Science* (Woodbridge, 2000), 58–71.

——— 'Magic, Science and Reputation: Robert Boyle, the Royal Society and the Occult in the Late Seventeenth Century', in Hunter, *Robert Boyle (1627–1691). Scrupulosity and Science* (Woodbridge, 2000), 223–50.

——— *The Occult Laboratory: Magic, Science and Second Sight in Late Seventeenth-Century Scotland* (Woodbridge, 2001).

——— 'Robert Boyle, Narcissus Marsh and the Anglo-Irish Intellectual Scene in the Late Seventeenth Century', in M. McCarthy and A. Simmons (eds), *The Making of Marsh's Library: Learning, Politics and Religion in Ireland, 1650–1750* (Dublin, 2004), 51–75.

——— 'New Light on the "Drummer of Tedworth": Conflicting Narratives of Witchcraft in Restoration England', *Historical Research*, 78 (2005), 311–37.

——— *Boyle: Between God and Science* (New Haven, 2009).

Hunter, R. A., and Macalpine, I., 'Valentine Greatrakes and "Divers of the Strange Cures by Him Lately Performed" on Patients from St Bartholomew's Hospital in 1666', *St Bartholomew's Hospital Journal*, 60 (1956), 361–8.

Hutton, R., *The Restoration: A Political and Religious History of England and Wales 1658–1667* (Oxford, 1985).

Hutton, S., 'Of Physic and Philosophy: Anne Conway, F.M.van Helmont and Seventeenth-Century Medicine', in O. P. Grell and A. Cunningham (eds), *Religio Medici: Medicine and Religion in Seventeenth-Century England* (Aldershot, 1996), 228–46.

—— *Anne Conway: A Woman Philosopher* (Cambridge, 2004).

Jacob, J. R., 'Boyle's Circle in the Protectorate: Revelation, Politics and the Millennium', *Journal of the History of Ideas*, 38 (1977), 131–40.

—— *Robert Boyle and the English Revolution* (New York, 1977).

—— *Henry Stubbe, Radical Protestantism and the Early Enlightenment* (Cambridge, 1983).

Jenkins, J. E., 'Arguing about Nothing: Henry More and Robert Boyle on the Theological Implications of the Void', in M. J. Osler (ed.), *Rethinking the Scientific Revolution* (Cambridge, 2000), 153–79.

Jenner, M. S. R., 'Review Essay: Body, Image, Text in Early Modern Europe', *Social History of Medicine*, 12 (1999), 143–54.

—— 'The Roasting of the Rump: Scatology and the Body Politic in Restoration England', *Past and Present*, 177 (2002), 84–120.

Kaplan, B. B., 'Greatrakes the Stroker: The Interpretation of His Contemporaries', *Isis*, 73 (1982), 178–85.

Keblusek, M., 'Keeping it Secret: the Identity and Status of an Early Modern Inventor', *History of Science*, 43 (2005), 37–56.

Keeble, N. H., *The Restoration: England in the 1660s* (Oxford, 2002).

Kenyon, J. P., 'Andrew Marvell: Life and Times', in R. Brett (ed.), *Andrew Marvell: Essays on the Tercentenary of his Death* (Oxford, 1979), 1–35.

Killeen, K., *Biblical Scholarship, Science and Politics in Early Modern England: Thomas Browne and the Thorny Place of Knowledge* (Farnham, 2009).

Kingston, A., *East Anglia and the Great Civil War: The Rising of Cromwell's Ironsides in the Associated Counties of Cambridge, Huntingdon, Lincoln, Norfolk, Suffolk, Essex, and Hertford* (London, 1897).

Knight, S., *The Killing of Justice Godfrey* (London, 1986).

Knights, M., 'Petitioning and the Political Theorists: John Locke, Algernon Sidney and London's "Monster" Petition of 1680', *Past and Present*, 138 (1993), 94–111.

—— *Representation and Misrepresentation in Later Stuart Britain* (Oxford, 2005).

—— 'John Starkey and Ideological Networks in Late-Seventeenth Century England', in J. Raymond (ed.), *New Networks in Seventeenth Century Britain and Europe* (London, 2006), 125–44.

Lamont, W., *Puritanism and Historical Controversy* (London, 1996).

Laver, A. B., 'Miracles No Wonder! The Mesmeric Phenomena and Organic Cures of Valentine Greatrakes', *Journal of the History of Medicine and Allied Sciences*, 33 (1978), 35–46.

Lederer, D., *Madness, Religion and the State in Early Modern Europe: A Bavarian Beacon* (Cambridge, 2006).

Leng, T., *Benjamin Worsley (1618–1677): Trade, Interest and the Spirit in Revolutionary England* (Woodbridge, 2008).

Lennon, M., 'Winston Churchill, 1662–1668', *Dublin Historical Record*, 43 (1990), 99–106.

Lindley, K., 'Irish Adventurers and Godly Militants in the 1640s', *Irish Historical Studies*, 29 (1994), 1–12.

Little, P., *Lord Broghill and the Cromwellian Union with Ireland and Scotland* (Woodbridge, 2004).

Lynch, K. M., 'The Incomparable Lady Ranelagh', in J. Butt (ed.), *Of Books and Humankind: Essays and Poems Presented to Bonamy Dobrée* (London, 1964), 25–33.

MacCaffrey, W. T., *Exeter, 1540–1640: The Growth of an English County Town* (Cambridge, MA, and London, 1975).

MacCarthy-Morrogh, M., *The Munster Plantation: English Migration to Southern Ireland 1583–1641* (Oxford, 1986).

MacDonald, M., *Mystical Bedlam: Madness, Anxiety, and Healing in Seventeenth-Century England* (Cambridge, 1981).

—— *Witchcraft and Hysteria in Elizabethan London: Edward Jorden and the Mary Glover Case* (London, 1991).

Madden, R. R., 'Some Notices of the Irish Mesmerists of the Seventeenth Century: Greatrakes, Cooke and Finaghty', *Dublin Quarterly Journal of Medical Science,* 4 (1847), 254–72.

Maddison, R. E. W., 'Robert Boyle and the Irish Bible', *Bulletin of the John Rylands Library*, 41 (1958), 81–101.

—— *The Life of the Honourable Robert Boyle* (London, 1969).

Mandelbrote, S., 'William Petty and Anne Greene: Medical and Political Reform in Commonwealth England', in M. Pelling and S. Mandelbrote (eds), *The Practice of Reform in Health, Medicine and Science, 1500–2000. Essays for Charles Webster* (Aldershot, 2005), 125–49.

—— 'The Uses of Natural Theology in Seventeenth-Century England', *Science in Context*, 20 (2007), 451–80.

Marsh, F. W., *The Godolphins* (1930).

Marshall, A., 'The Westminster Magistrate and the Irish Stroker: Sir Edmund Berry Godfrey and Valentine Greatrakes, Some Unpublished Correspondence', *Historical Journal*, 40 (1997), 499–505.

—— *The Strange Death of Edmund Godfrey: Plots and Politics in Restoration London* (Stroud, 1999).

Marshall, P., *Mother Leakey and the Bishop: A Ghost Story* (Oxford, 2007).

—— 'Ann Jeffries and the Fairies: Folk Belief and the War on Scepticism in Later Stuart England', in A. McShane and G. Walker (eds), *The Extraordinary and the Everyday in Early Modern England: Essays in Celebration of the Work of Bernard Capp* (Basingstoke, 2010), 127–41.

Matar, N., '"Alone in our Eden": A Puritan Utopia in Restoration England', *The Seventeenth Century*, 2 (1987), 189–97.

McAuliffe, M., 'Gender, History and Witchcraft in Early Modern Ireland: A Re-Reading of the Florence Newton Trial', in M. G. Valiulis (ed.), *Gender and Power in Irish History* (Dublin, 2009), 39–59.

McKenny, K., 'Charles II's Irish Cavaliers: the 1649 Officers and the Restoration Land Settlement', *Irish Historical Studies*, 28 (1993), 409–25.

—— 'The Restoration Land Settlement in Ireland: A Statistical Interpretation', in C. A. Dennehy (ed.), *Restoration Ireland: Always Settling and Never Settled* (Aldershot, 2008), 35–52.

McKeon, M., *Politics and Poetry in Restoration England: The Case of Dryden's* Annus Mirabilis (Cambridge, MA, and London, 1975).

Meekings, C. A. F., 'The Chamber of Worcester—1679 to 1689', *Transactions of the Worcestershire Archaeological Society*, 8 (1982), 7–29.

Midelfort, H. C. E., *Exorcism and Enlightenment: Johann Joseph Gassner and the Demons of Eighteenth-Century Germany* (New Haven, 2005).

Miller, J., *Politics and Religion in English Provincial Towns 1660–1722* (Oxford, 2007).

Monod, P. K., *Jacobitism and the English People, 1688–1788* (Cambridge, 1989).

Moote, A. L., and Moote, D. C., *The Great Plague: The Story of London's Most Deadly Year* (Baltimore, 2004).

Morris, H. F., 'The Pynes of Cork', *The Irish Genealogist*, 6 (1985), 696–710.

Newman, W. R., *Gehennical Fire: The Lives of George Starkey, an American Alchemist in the Scientific Revolution* (Cambridge, MA, 1994; 2nd ed., Chicago, 2003).

Nickalls, J. L., 'Albertus Otto Faber, the German Doctor', *Journal of the Friends Historical Society*, 32 (1935), 54–7.

Palfrey, I., 'The Royalist War Effort Revisited: Edward Seymour and the Royalist Garrison at Dartmouth, 1643–44, *Transactions of the Devonshire Association*, 123 (1991), 41–56.

Park, K., 'The Criminal and Saintly Body: Autopsy and Dissection in Renaissance Italy', *Renaissance Quarterly*, 47 (1994), 1–33.

Park, K., and Daston, L. J., 'Unnatural Conceptions: The Study of Monsters in France and England', *Past and Present*, 92 (1981), 20–54.

Pender, S., 'Studies in Waterford History I', *Journal of the Cork Historical and Archaeological Society*, 51 (1946), 10–26.

—— 'Studies in Waterford History V', *Journal of the Cork Historical and Archaeological Society*, 53 (1948), 39–59.

Pink, W. D., 'Alured of the Charterhouse, co.York', *Yorkshire Genealogist*, 1 (1888), 8–9.

Pitt, L., *A Small Moment of Great Illumination: Searching for Valentine Greatrakes, the Master Healer* (Emeryville, CA, 2006).

Power, T., 'Richard Boyle's Ironworks in County Waterford', *Decies*, 6 (1977), 26–30; 7 (1978), 30–5.

Prendergast, J. P., *The Cromwellian Settlement of Ireland* (3rd ed., Dublin, 1922).

Purkiss, D., *The Witch in History: Early Modern and Twentieth-Century Representations* (London, 1996).

Ramsbottom, J. D., 'Presbyterians and "Partial Conformity" in the Restoration Church of England', *Journal of Ecclesiastical History*, 43 (1992), 249–70.

Reay, B., 'The Muggletonians: An Introductory Survey', in J. E. C. Hill, B. Reay and W. Lamont (eds), *The World of the Muggletonians* (London, 1983), 23–63.

Rennison, W. H., *Succession List of the Bishops, Cathedral and Parochial Clergy of the Dioceses of Waterford and Lismore* (Waterford, 1922).

Richards, J., ' "His Nowe Majestie" and the English Monarchy: The Kingship of Charles I before 1640', *Past and Present*, 113 (1986), 70–96.

Robbins, C., 'Absolute Liberty: The Life and Thought of William Popple, 1638–1708', *William and Mary Quarterly*, 24 (1967), 190–223.

Roberts, S.K., *Recovery and Restoration in an English County: Devon Local Administration 1646–1670* (Exeter, 1985).

—— 'Public or Private? Revenge and Recovery at the Restoration of Charles II', *Bulletin of the Institute of Historical Research*, 59 (1986), 172–88.

—— 'War and Society in Devon 1642–1646', *Transactions of the Devonshire Association*, 127 (1995), 81–96.

Roper, L., *Witch Craze: Terror and Fantasy in Baroque Germany* (New Haven, 2004).

Rublack, U., *The Crimes of Women in Early Modern Germany* (Oxford, 1999).

—— 'Fluxes: the Early Modern Body and the Emotions', *History Workshop Journal*, 53 (2002), 1–16.

Sampson, H., 'Dr Faber and His Celebrated Cordial', *Isis*, 34 (1942–3), 472–96.

Scandal on the Corporation: Royalists and Puritans in Mid-Seventeenth-Century Kingston, from the Kingston Borough Archives (Kingston, 1982).

Schaffer, S., 'Piety, Physic and Prodigious Abstinence', in O. P. Grell and A. Cunningham (eds), Religio Medici: *Medicine and Religion in Seventeenth-Century England* (Aldershot, 1996), 171–203.

——'Regeneration: The Body of Natural Philosophers in Restoration England', in C. Lawrence and S. Shapin (eds), *Science Incarnate: Historical Embodiments of Natural Knowledge* (Chicago, 1998), 83–120.

Schoenfeldt, M., 'Reading Bodies', in K. Sharpe and S. N. Zwicker (eds), *Reading, Society and Politics in Early Modern England* (Cambridge, 2003), 215–43.

Scott, J., 'Restoration Process: Or, If This Isn't a Party, We're Not having a Good Time', *Albion*, 25 (1993), 619–37.

Scott-Luckens, C., 'Propaganda or Marks of Grace? The Impact of the Reported Ordeals of Sarah Wight in Revolutionary London, 1647–52', *Women's Writing*, 9 (2002), 215–32.

Seaward, P., *The Cavalier Parliament and the Reconstruction of the Old Regime, 1661–1667* (Cambridge, 1989).

Seymour, St. John D., *The Puritans in Ireland 1647–1661* (Oxford, 1921; reissued 1969).

Shapin, S., *A Social History of Truth: Civility and Science in Seventeenth-Century England* (Chicago, 1994).

Shapiro, B., *John Wilkins, 1614–72: An Intellectual Biography* (Berkeley, CA, 1969).

Sharpe, K., *Politics and Ideas in Early Stuart England* (London, 1989).

Sharpe, K., and Zwicker, S. N. (eds), *Refiguring Revolutions: Aesthetics and Politics from the English Revolution to the Romantic Revolution* (Berkeley, 1998).

Shaw, J., *Miracles in Enlightenment England* (New Haven, 2006).

Shirren, A. J., ' "Colonel Zanchy" and Charles Fleetwood', *Notes and Queries*, 198 (1953), 431–5, 474–7, 519–24.

Smith, N., *Perfection Proclaimed: Language and Literature in English Radical Religion 1640–1660* (Oxford, 1989).

——*Andrew Marvell. The Chameleon* (New Haven, 2010).

Smyth, W. J., 'Making the Documents of Conquest Speak: The Transformation of Property, Society, and Settlement in Seventeenth-Century Counties Tipperary and Kilkenny', in M. Silverman and P. H. Gulliver (eds), *Approaching the Past: Historical Anthropology Through Irish Case Studies* (New York, 1992), 236–90.

Spalding, R., *Contemporaries of Bulstrode Whitelocke 1605–1675* (Oxford, 1990).

Spellman, W. M., *The Latitudinarians and the Church of England, 1660–1700* (Athens, GA, and London, 1993).

Spurr, J., ' "Latitudinarianism" and the Restoration Church', *The Historical Journal*, 31 (1988), 61–82.

—— *The Restoration Church of England 1646–1689* (New Haven, 1991).

—— *England in the 1670s: 'This Masquerading Age'* (Oxford, 2000).

Steneck, N. H., ' "The Ballad of Robert Crosse and Joseph Glanvill" and the Background to *Plus Ultra*', *British Journal for the History of Science*, 14 (1981), 59–74.

——'Greatrakes the Stroker: The Interpretations of Historians', *Isis*, 73 (1982), 161–77.

Stoyle, M., *Loyalty and Locality: Popular Allegiance in Devon During the English Civil War* (Exeter, 1994).

Stubbs, M., 'John Beale, Philosophical Gardener of Herefordshire Part I. Prelude to the Royal Society (1608–1663)', *Annals of Science*, 39 (1982), 463–89.

——'John Beale, Philosophical Gardener of Herefordshire Part II. The Improvement of Agriculture and Trade in the Royal Society (1663–1683)', *Annals of Science*, 46 (1989), 323–63.

Taylor, B. F., 'Conversion, the Bible and the Irish Language: The Correspondence of Lady Ranelagh and Bishop Dopping', in M. Brown, C. I. McGrath and T. P. Power (eds), *Converts and Conversion in Ireland, 1650–1850* (Dublin, 2005), 157–82.

Tenison, C. M., 'Cork MPs', *Journal of the Cork Historical and Archaeological Society*, 1 (1895) and 2 (1896).

Thomas, K. V., *Religion and the Decline of Magic: Studies in Popular Beliefs in Sixteenth- and Seventeenth-Century England* (London, 1971; 2nd ed., 1993).

Todd, M., *The Culture of Protestantism in Early Modern Scotland* (New Haven, 2002).

Twigg, J., *The University of Cambridge and the English Revolution 1625–1688* (Woodbridge, 1990).

Uglow, J., *A Gambling Man: Charles II and the Restoration* (London, 2009).

Walsham, A., *Providence in Early Modern England* (Oxford, 1999).

Walter, J., *Understanding Popular Violence in the English Revolution: The Colchester Plunderers* (Cambridge, 1999).

Walton, J. C., 'The Subsidy Roll of County Waterford, 1662', *Analecta Hibernica*, 30 (1982), 49–96.

Walzer, M., *The Revolution of the Saints: A Study in the Origins of Radical Politics* (London, 1966).

Warmington, A., 'Frogs, Toads and the Restoration in a Gloucestershire Village,' *Midland History*, 14 (1989), 30–42.

Weber, H., *Paper Bullets: Print and Kingship under Charles II* (Lexington, KY, 1996).

Webster, C., *The Great Instauration: Science, Medicine and Reform, 1626–1660* (London, 1975).

—— 'Benjamin Worsley: Engineering for Universal Reform from the Invisible College to the Navigation Act', in M. Greengrass, M. Leslie and T. Raylor (eds), *Samuel Hartlib and Universal Reformation: Studies in Intellectual Communication* (Cambridge, 1994), 213–46.

Weil, R., 'Sometimes a Scepter is only a Scepter: Pornography and Politics in Restoration England', in L. Hunt (ed.), *The Invention of Pornography: Obscenity and the Origins of Modernity 1500–1800* (New York, 1993), 125–56.

Welply, W. H., 'Pedigree of the Tynte Family', *Journal of the Cork Historical and Archaeological Society*, 28 (1922).

—— 'Colonel Robert Phaire, "Regicide", His Ancestry, History, and Descendants', *Notes and Queries*, 12 (1923), 123–5, 143–6, 164–7, 185–7, 376.

—— 'Colonel Robert Phaire "Regicide"', *Journal of the Cork Historical and Archaeological Society*, 29 (1924), 76–80; 30 (1925), 20–6; 31 (1926), 31–6, 78–85; 32 (1927), 24–32.

—— 'More Notes on Edmund Spenser', *Notes and Queries*, 65 (1933), 111–16.

Werrett, S., 'Healing the Nation's Wounds: Royal Ritual and Experimental Philosophy in Restoration England', *History of Science*, 38 (2000), 377–99.

Whitley, W. T., 'Colonel Jerome Sankey, M.P., Ph.D.', *The Baptist Quarterly*, 4 (1928–9), 268–70.

Whitmore, J. B., 'Dr Worsley Being Dead', *Notes and Queries*, 185 (1943), 123–9.

Wiesner, M. E., 'The Midwives of South Germany and the Public/Private Dichotomy', in H. Marland (ed.), *The Art of Midwifery: Early Modern Midwives in Europe* (London, 1993), 77–94.

Wilson, D., 'Valentine Greatrakes—Ophthalmologist', *Transactions of the Ophthalmological Societies of the United Kingdom*, 87 (1967), 893–6.

Woodward, D., 'The Anglo-Irish Livestock Trade of the Seventeenth Century', *Irish Historical Studies*, 18 (1972–3), 489–523.

Worden, B., 'Toleration and the Cromwellian Protectorate', in W. J. Sheils (ed.), *Persecution and Toleration* (Oxford, 1984), 199–233.

Wright, S., *The Early English Baptists 1603–1649* (Woodbridge, 2006).

Young, J. T., *Faith, Medical Alchemy and Natural Philosophy: Johann Moriaen, Reformed Intelligencer and the Hartlib Circle* (Aldershot, 1998).

Zaller, R., 'Breaking the Vessels: The Desacralization of Monarchy in Early Modern England', *Sixteenth Century Journal*, 29 (1998), 757–78.

5. UNPUBLISHED PAPERS AND THESES

Beck, K. M., 'Recusancy and Nonconformity in Devon and Somerset, 1660–1714', MA thesis (Bristol, 1961).

Brod, M., 'Dissent and Dissenters in Early Modern Berkshire', D.Phil. thesis (Oxford, 2002).

Brogan, S., 'The Royal Touch in Early Modern England: Its Changing Rationale and Practice', Ph.D. thesis (London, 2011).

Gentles, I., 'The Debentures Market and Military Purchases of Crown Land, 1649–1660', Ph.D. thesis (London, 1969).

Jackson, P. W., 'Nonconformists and Society in Devon, 1660–1689', Ph.D. thesis (Exeter, 1986).

Kilroy, P., 'Protestant Dissent and Controversy in Ireland, 1660–1711', Ph.D. thesis (Trinity College, Dublin, 1991).

Morrison, J. J., 'John Strype: Historian of the English Reformation', Ph.D. thesis (Syracuse University, 1976).

Parker, C., 'Father Finaghty, Valentine Greatrakes, and Attitudes to the Miraculous in Seventeenth-Century Ireland and England', MA thesis (National University of Ireland, Maynooth, 1997).

Index

Index